CHILD
ART
THERAPY

JUDITH ARON RUBIN

CHILD ART THERAPY

Understanding and
Helping Children Grow
through Art

Second Edition

 VAN NOSTRAND REINHOLD
New York

I(T)P   Van Nostrand Reinhold is an International Thomson Publishing company.
        ITP logo is a trademark under license.

Printed in the United States of America
Designed by Loudan Enterprises

Van Nostrand Reinhold   International Thomson Publishing GmbH
115 Fifth Avenue   Königswinterer Str. 418
New York, NY 10003   53227 Bonn
                                       Germany

International Thomson Publishing   International Thomson Publishing Asia
Berkshire House,168-173   221 Henderson Bldg. #05-10
High Holborn, London WC1V 7AA   Singapore 0315
England

Thomas Nelson Australia   International Thomson Publishing Japan
102 Dodds Street   Kyowa Building, 3F
South Melbourne 3205   2-2-1 Hirakawacho
Victoria, Australia   Chiyoda-Ku, Tokyo 102
                                       Japan

Nelson Canada
1120 Birchmount Road
Scarborough, Ontario
M1K 5G4, Canada

First published in 1978 by Van Nostrand Reinhold

ARCKP   16   15   14   13   12   11   10   9

Library of Congress Cataloging-in-Publication Data
Rubin, Judith Aron.
    Child art therapy.
    Bibliography: p. 301
    Includes index.
    1. Art therapy. 2. Child psychotherapy. 3. Family
psychotherapy. 4. Art—Study and teaching(Primary) I. Title.
RJ505.A7R8   1984   618.92'891656   83-17080
ISBN 0-442-27767-9(pbk.)

Contents

Acknowledgments

Though I alone must take responsibility for what is written here, I wish to thank some of the many individuals whose support and teaching have nourished both me and my work. I begin with my childhood family—my warm grandmother who always understood, my proud father with his high expectations and steady affection, my patient mother with her calming manner, and my companion brother. I thank too my present family—my dependable husband, who was so patient throughout the long gestation period and revision of my first printed offspring; and our three children, whose drawings and words appear within, who helped with proofreading and typing, and who were most understanding at times when I was less available to them than any of us wished.

I thank too those teachers and colleagues, friends and helpers, who have provided good models as well as good ideas, and who over the years have helped me to learn about myself, children, and art. Though there are too many to mention all, I do want to express my gratitude to Margaret McFarland, Ph.D., Naomi Ragins, M.D., Marvin Shapiro, M.D., Judith Schachter, M.D., and Rex Speers, M.D. I especially thank Eleanor C. Irwin, Ph.D., RDT, who has helped me with much of my writing, including this book and its revision. Many others also read it and advised me, among them Susan Aach, M.Ed., ATR, Carole Kunkle-Miller, M.Ed., ATR, Mildred Lachman-Chapin, M.Ed., ATR, Ellen Roth, Ph.D., ATR, and Laurie Wilson, Ph.D., ATR. I am grateful to the University of Pittsburgh, which permitted the work on the first draft of the book to be submitted as a doctoral dissertation, and to my advisor, Nancy Elman, Ph.D. Finally, I want to thank Edith Kramer, HLM, ATR, who gave generously of her time and expertise in suggesting possible revisions, some of which I have been able to implement.

I thank the Pittsburgh Child Guidance Center for support services on the original, and the Western Psychiatric Institute & Clinic for similar services on the revision. I also want to acknowledge the contribution of Norman Rabinovitz and Sheila Ramsey, who were responsible for most of the photographs. Those which are technically poor are photos of slides taken with my inexpensive camera. Additional photographs of art work for the revision were done by the Media Production Services of WPIC, directed by Jim Lenckner. And of course, I want to thank the children and their families, who have been my very best teachers.

Finally, I should like to express my gratitude to the following organizations and publications to reprint fully or in part, material which first appeared in their journals or books. Those chapters in which the material is used, sometimes in modified form, are indicated in parentheses.

American Dance Therapy Association. "Play, Parenting and the Arts: A Therapeutic Approach to Primary Prevention" with Eleanor Irwin, Ph.D. and Penny Bernstein, M.S., DTR, *Proceedings*, (1975), pp. 60-78. (Chapter 18)

American Foundation for the Blind, Inc., "Through Art to Affect: Blind Children Express their Feelings," *New Outlook for the Blind*, (1975), 69: 385-391. (Chapters 9 and 17)

American Journal of Art Therapy, "Mother-Child Art Sessions: I. Treatment in the Clinic; II. Education in the Community," copyright © 1974 by Elinor Ulman, (1974), 13: 165—181, 219—227. (Chapters 12 and 18)

American Society of Psychopathology of Expression, "Special Personality Traits of Child Therapists," *Personality of the Therapist* (Proceedings, International Congress of Psychopathology of Expression), edited by I. Jakab, (1982), pp. 111—116. (Chapter 21)

Arts and Activities, "Art Therapy: What it Is and What it Is Not," (1981), 90 (4): 40—41. (Chapter 21)

Association for the Advancement of Psychotherapy, Inc., *American Journal of Psychotherapy*, "Art and Drama: Partners in Therapy," Senior author, Eleanor Irwin, Ph.D., (1975), 29: 107-116. (Chapter 14)

Association for the Education of the Visually Handicapped, "They Opened our Eyes: An Exploratory Art Program for Visually-Impaired Multiply-Handicapped Children," with Janet Klineman, Ph.D., *Education of the Visually Handicapped*, (1974), 6: 106-113. (Chapter 17)

Beacon House, Inc., "Art-Awareness: A Method for Working with Groups," with Paul Levy, Ph.D., *Group Psychotherapy and Psychodrama*, (1975), 28: 108-117. (Chapter 13)

Doctor Franklin Perkins School, "A Framework for Freedom," *The Arts in Education International Seminar Series*, (1973). (Chapter 1)

High Fidelity/Musical America, "How the Arts Can Help," (May, 1975). (Chapter 16)

Karger, S., "Stuttering: Symptom-System-Symbol—Art Therapy in the Treatment of a Case of Disfluency," with Max Magnussen, Ph.D. and Asher Bar, Ph.D., *Psychiatry and Art*, Vol. 4, edited by I. Jakab, (1975), pp. 201-215. (Chapter 15)

Mental Research Institute and Nathan W. Ackerman Family Institute, Inc., "A Family Art Evaluation," *Family Process*, with Max Magnussen, Ph.D., (1974), 13: 185-200. (Chapter 10)

Museum of Art, Carnegie Institute, Section of Education. "The Arts, the Handicapped, and Therapy," *Prism*, (1981), 1: (4), 4—9. (Chapter 8)

National Art Education Association, "Art Is for All Human Beings, Especially the Handicapped," *Art Education*, (1975), *28*: (8), 5-10. (Chapter 17)

_____, "Art Therapy Today," *Art Education*, (1980), *33*: (4), 6–8. (Preface)

Pergamon Press, "A Diagnostic Art Interview," *Art Psychotherapy*, (1973), *1*: 31-43. (Chapter 4)

Pittsburgh Area Preschool Association, *The Publication: Children in a Contemporary Society* (formerly the *Pittsburgh Area Preschool Association Publication*), "Some Children with Schizophrenia: What They Did in Art," (1972), *6*: 12–13. (Chapter 17)

_____, "A Child's Right to the Expressive Arts," (1972), *6*: 75–78. (Chapter 2)

_____, "Art for Young Children's Growing: Diagnosis and Therapy in the Classroom," (1974), *8*: 40–45. (Chapter 16)

_____, "Understanding Play Interviews: Decoding Symbolic Messages," Senior author, Eleanor Irwin, Ph.D., (1976), *9*: 47–49. (Chapter 5)

_____, Cover drawings and commentaries from various issues. (Scattered throughout the book)

Preface

Roots (Personal and Professional)

Although my personal roots and those of my chosen discipline are not identical or even parallel, I believe it is useful for the reader to know something of the background of the practitioner as well as of the origins of the profession. Both provide the context within which this book was written and can best be understood. I shall begin, therefore, with some thoughts about the sources of my own childhood interest in art, in order not only to introduce myself, but also to suggest some ideas about how and why art is therapeutic for the young.

Like many who have maintained an interest in art throughout life, I cannot remember a time when it was not very important to me. When I was little, I most liked to draw and paint—I still cherish my first oil-painting set, received at ten from a painter uncle. As far back as I can recall, I was always drawing, and it was always a source of good feelings for me. Perhaps I delighted in the organizing of space and shape, enjoying both my ability to do so and the aesthetic pleasure of the complicated designs I drew. Perhaps I relished the symbolic gratification of wishes fulfilled on paper. Perhaps I was motivated by the approval of my proud relatives, who sometimes surprised me by framing my paintings and hanging them on their walls. All were probably determinants of my investment in art, as they can be for other youngsters.

The roots of my interest in art are, as for everyone, deep and old and personal. And even after years of self-exploration, I am not sure of all of the meanings for me of making, facilitating, and looking at art. I know, for example, that sometimes my pleasure was primarily visual and largely extra-aesthetic. I, like others, was curious about what could not be seen—perhaps what was hidden inside the body or behind closed doors. I therefore found it exciting to be able to look with wide-open eyes, to be told that in art looking was permissible when it was elsewhere so often forbidden. I found it both fascinating and thrilling to look at art, which is, after all, private feeling made into public form.

Just as my often intense hunger felt somehow appeased when receiving art supplies, especially brand-new ones, so the looking at art had a nourishing quality as well. It was like a drinking-in with the eyes of a tasty visual treat. To view a whole exhibit of work I liked, was at least as fulfilling for me as to eat an excellent meal.

If looking at art for me was a kind of validated voyeurism, the making of products was a kind of acceptable exhibitionism. So, too, the touching, the delight in sensory pleasures; these were preserved through art in the molding of clay or the blending of pastels. Not only was art a path to permissible regression, it was a way to acceptable aggression as well. The cutting up of paper or carving into clay, the depiction of hostile wishes: these were possible through art, available to me—as to others—in the many symbolic meanings of the creative process.

Sometimes art became a way of coping with trauma too difficult to assimilate. When I was seventeen, a friend died in a crazy, senseless accident. Numbly, I went home to the funeral from the camp at which I was working as an arts and crafts counselor. Numbly, I returned, then succumbed to fever for several days and nights. When I awoke, I felt a strong need to go to the woods and paint. On my first day off I did so, and it felt good. The painting was not of my friend, but of someone playing the piano, making music in dark reds, purples, and blacks. It was a cry, a scream caught and tamed. It was a new object in the world, perhaps a replacement for the person who was gone, as well as a mute, tangible testament. The doing of it afforded tremendous relief. It did not take away the hurt and the ache, but it did help in releasing some of the rage and in giving form to the confused feelings which threatened to overwhelm me.

So, too, with a remembered nightmare, finally drawn and then painted; and in the process of being given form, made less fearful. Years later, I was to discover—much to my surprise—that drawing a dream was to help my little daughter finally to sleep in peace, calming her in a way that verbal reassurance and explanation could not (Fig. 0-1). It now seems to me that this "miracle" of taming fear through forms of feeling is what the medicine men have known for so long: that giving form to the feared object brings it under one's own symbolic control.

Not only the making, but also the perceiving of art was of vital importance to me as I grew up. As a young child, I stared long and hard at a Van Gogh reproduction which hung on our living room wall. The sunflowers were so big and alive, so vivid and powerful, that even in a print they seemed to leap forth from the canvas. And I recall later, as a teenager, feeling the intoxication of a whole exhibit, room after room full of original Van Goghs, wild and glowing. Each picture was more exciting than the last—the intensity and beauty of the images, the luscious texture of the paint seemed to me like the "barbaric yawp" of Thomas Wolfe, another of my adolescent passions.

Many a Saturday afternoon was spent sitting transfixed before one or another of my favorite paintings in the Museum of Modern Art. I think I must have known every line in Picasso's "Guernica," yet still was moved by its power. A large Futurist painting called "The City" was an endlessly fascinating, continually merging sea of images. And another large painting by Tchelitchew, "Hide and Seek," never ceased to magnetize my mind, to both repel and attract me with its heads and veins and fleeing figures. Surely there is much in art which feels "therapeutic" to the viewer, as well as to the artist.

This "magic power of the image" (Kris, 1952) is also one of the ancient roots of the young discipline of art therapy. The use of art for healing and for mastery is at least as old as the drawings on the walls of caves; yet the profession itself is an infant in the family of mental health disciplines. In a similar paradox, while art therapy itself is highly sophisticated, the art process is simple and natural. On a recent walk through the woods, I came across a self-initiated use of art to cope with an overwhelming event, reminding me of my own painting after a similar tragedy. A rural man—a laborer—had carved a powerful totem-like sculpture out of a tree trunk, as part of his mourning of the untimely death of his young wife. His explanation to me was that he "just had to do something," and that the activity of creating the larger-than-life carving had seemed to fit his need, perhaps filling the void left by his loss.

Similarly, people caught in the turmoil of serious mental illness, threatened by loss of contact with reality, have sometimes found themselves compelled to create art as one way of coping with their confusion. Such productions, often found on scraps of paper or walls, intrigued psychiatrists and others at the turn of the century (Prinzhorn, 1972). Fascinated by these outpourings of the troubled mind, they collected and studied such spontaneous expression, hoping to understand better the creators

Fig. 0-1. Nightmare of two dead grandmothers by Nona. Chalk. Age 8.

and their ailments. With the advent of depth psychology, psychiatrists began to find ways to unlock the puzzle of primary process thought, and ventured into decoding the meanings of images in dreams, reverie, and the art of the insane. The growth of projective testing in the young field of clinical psychology stimulated further systematic work with visual stimuli, expressive media, and drawings, primarily for diagnostic purposes.

While these developments were occurring in the area of mental health, educators were discovering the value of a freer kind of art in the schools. Those in the progressive movement were convinced that the creative experience was a vital part of any child's education, essential for healthy development of both cognition and affect. Some art educators were especially sensitive to the value of creative expression in helping children to deal with frustrations and self definition (Cane, 1951; Cole, 1940). Viktor Lowenfeld also developed what he called an "art education therapy" for children with handicaps (1952, 1957). During that same time, art was beginning to be offered as therapy to patients in general hospitals (Hill, 1945, 1951) and in psychiatric treatment settings (Erikson, 1976).

The two women most responsible for defining and founding the field of art therapy began their work with children—in a hospital (Naumburg, 1947) and in a special school (Kramer, 1958)—on the basis of their experiences as educators. Both were Freudian in their orientation, though each used different aspects of psychoanalytic theory to develop her ideas about the best therapeutic use of art. For Margaret Naumburg, art was a form of "symbolic speech" coming from the unconscious, like dreams, to be evoked in a spontaneous way and to be understood through free association, always respecting the artist's own interpretations. Art was thus conceived as a "royal road" to unconscious symbolic contents, a means of both diagnosis and therapy, the latter involving verbalization and insight as well as art expression. For Kramer, on the other hand, art was viewed as a "royal road" to sublimation, a way of integrating conflicting feelings and impulses in an aesthetically satisfying form, helping the ego to control, manage, and synthesize via the creative process itself.

Both approaches are still visible in a field which has grown rapidly over the last 14 years, during which time a national professional organization and many training programs have come into existence. This rapid growth reflects, I think, the power of art as a therapeutic modality. I never cease to be amazed at the potency of art therapy, even in the hands of relatively naive practicum students. Since it is so powerful, it is fortunate that no longer can "anyone with a paint brush and a patient" declare him or herself to be an "art therapist" (Howard, 1964). Indeed, my own experiences in the era before formal education was available in the field bear witness to the need for clinical training for anyone whose background is solely in art and education.

The roots of my interest in art, described earlier, lay deep in the soil of my childhood and adolescence before flowering in a variety of roles: teacher of art to neighborhood children in high school; arts and crafts counselor at summer camps; art major in college; and later, art educator (of children and then of teachers); art researcher; "art lady" (Misterogers' Neighborhood on TV); art consultant;

and—eventually—art therapist. When I first "discovered" the field, I felt like the ugly duckling who found the swans and no longer saw himself as a misfit. As an artist, I had never felt talented enough to make a career of my painting. And as a teacher, although I loved working with children, I had never felt completely comfortable with my pedagogical colleagues. When the Child Development Department at the University of Pittsburgh invited me to work with schizophrenic children in 1963, I was not in any way a clinician. But the work was such a pleasure and such a challenge, and the support from experienced others was so available, that I was readily able to find places to grow and people from whom to learn.

I first sought the guidance of the two pioneers in art therapy mentioned earlier, Margaret Naumburg and Edith Kramer, both of whom gave generously of their time and thought. It was suggested that I learn about myself through personal therapy, and that I learn about being a therapist through supervised work under an experienced clinician. I was fortunate to find both a mentor and a setting where I was able to learn the necessary skills and to practice my trade in all of the ways described in this book. As I began to feel like a "real" art therapist, I also became aware of a need for further didactic learning. This need was met primarily through intensive study of adult and child analysis at a psychoanalytic institute, supplemented by graduate work in counseling at a university.

Although one reason for writing this book was the requirement of a dissertation (justified in my proposal by the paucity of literature at the time by art therapists about art therapy), I was also responding to tensions within myself. Like most creative activities, the book began with the perception of a problem or a felt concern which increasingly demanded a solution. I had reached a point at which I could no longer comfortably pursue any of the many directions I had previously explored, without first finding some order for myself in all that I had learned about children, art, and growing. When I began writing, I felt uncertain about what would emerge on the then-blank paper, just as I had so often felt anxious about what would come from painting on a blank canvas.

One of the best ways for an art therapist to understand therapeutic work is through reflection on his or her own creative endeavors. I shall therefore conclude this sharing of personal and professional roots with a description of an intense painting experience. Because I was so moved by it at the time, I tried to put the event into words, in an effort to clarify and understand it for myself. This is what I wrote, three weeks after it happened:

I would like to try to give words and form to an essentially non-verbal and formless experience, an experience of such power and intensity that it demands clarification, and invites sharing. I wonder to myself, how universal or how personal was this happening? And I wonder, too, what it can tell me about the meaning of art in therapy?

I was painting this past summer, with a strange awareness of functioning on several levels simultaneously. I was the mother who responded to the child who called from his bed for a drink of water. I was also the technician who periodically changed brushes and added colors to my acrylic palette in order to achieve the desired effects. Yet further, I was the artist, deeply and actively involved in the creative process. I felt as if I were locked into an active, tension-producing and rhythmically-resolving process, which simultaneously involved every layer of the psyche.

The painting had begun as a group portrait of my children, full of conscious loving of their exterior and interior selves. I strove intently to draw them as they sat painting around a table, concerned with; reproducing both their features and the warm, proud feelings they evoked. This first stage of the picture seemed to be conscious, careful, with quite deliberate and sincere attempts at naturalistic representation.

Then they went to bed, and I continued with the painting, having temporarily interrupted the process to play my maternal bedtime role. I was aware of my resentment at having to stop work in order to bed them, but even more powerfully conflicted feelings continued to rise to the surface as I continued to apply the paint. An onrush of diffuse and intense destructive impulses impelled me to speed up my work. I found the activity gathering a momentum which seemed not to be under voluntary, but rather unconscious (perhaps preconscious) control.

Before, I had worked slowly, deliberately, and carefully to make them beautiful. Now I worked with a somatic sensation of pressure, as if the intensity and perhaps guilt of the propelling feelings required such speed. With quick, short strokes I modified, and partially obliterated their forms. My husband remarked sadly that I was destroying what had been so recently attractive, but his criticism was acknowledged only intellectually as reasonable. On a deeper level I both resented and resisted the intrusion, and went on at an accelerated tempo doing what at that moment had to be done. The sense of both compulsion and of excitement was almost too great to bear. Yet it was thrilling as well as painful, as the tension quickly mounted. Co-existing were love and hate, creation and destruction, joy and pain.

And yet the figures remained, less clear but perhaps more intense for their ambiguity. I found them more beautiful now, as they reflected the full complexity and ambivalence of my emotions. And I was aware of another kind of tension—that existing between the need to modify and the desire not to destroy, but to enhance. Though executed at a quick pace, each stroke was important and crucial. While working so intensely, I felt simultaneously a high level of ego control, and an equally high level of communication with the unconscious forces which threatened that very control I prized so dearly. At the end of the painting process, my working pace slowed down. With deliberate calm and rather cool control, I found myself standing back looking, modifying, and completing the portrait.

And now, weeks, later, I reflect upon the event. Perhaps it was that very experience of teetering at the brink, of allowing such a powerful upsurge of unconscious and irrational feeling—while maintaining a tight control over it—that is the essence of at least one aspect of the "therapy" in art. For without the experience of near-loss of control, it must always be feared as catastrophic. It is only by "letting go" as fully as possible that one learns that the fantasied fear is a somewhat myth. If one always holds tight the reins of conscious control, there is no danger—yet the danger still exists by implication. The more unknown and unfelt, the more it is feared. Indeed, one might question whether it is ever possible to learn self-control in the deepest, most secure sense, without allowing one's self at times to loosen the bonds of control as well? What is vital to remember is that this was felt as a "peak experience," both frightening and thrilling, both plunging and soaring. It was aesthetic as well as personal, as was the resultant painting.

The implications for the use of art in therapy are manifold—as multileveled as the experience itself. The tension-producing and tension-reducing inherent in an involved creative experience are somatically therapeutic, the interaction of the artist with the work of art in some cases not unlike that with a human partner in a similarly orgastic experience. To experience in any sphere "letting go," yet remaining simultaneously aware and ultimately in charge, is a profound lesson. Whether or not the content of the art work is affectively toned, as in my painting of my children, the dynamics of the creative process itself provide an essential learning experience.

One might also argue that limiting or in any way protecting the client from "letting go" may well serve to reinforce already-crippling fears of loss of control. The art therapist who prematurely limits the client's activity in the name of safety or security, may actually be saying, "Yes, you are right. Loss of control is disastrous in its consequences, so I will set limits and help you to keep a brake on your dangerously strong and destructive feelings and impulses." Yet learning to be in charge of the self may only be possible when one has allowed conscious controls to relax sufficiently to explore the consequences of strong expression of affect, then to find that one may still be master of one's fate.

What is emerging is not a position which suggests no limits at all. Rather, the creation of a work of art (in any modality) has its own built-in limits which provide sufficient safety, along with the opportunity for constructive abreaction and channeling of strong feelings. Indeed, the expressive arts are vital both to healthy personality growth and to therapy precisely because they allow for a channeled, controlled "letting go." The very nature of each art form sets the limits which, when broken, negate the art. Throwing paint on the wall is not the same as making a vibrant picture by slashing with the brush; and random, violent body movements are not the same as strong motions which are "in tune" with the music, the drama, or one's own body rhythm.

Nevertheless, it has been my experience that many disturbed youngsters, whether their superficial behavior is inhibited or hyperactive, need initially to release in a cathartic and often formless fashion, at first unfocussed and heretofore repressed feelings. Only when this has been safely experienced, can the child then give a genuinely artistic form to such feelings. Perhaps it is only then that he feels in control of himself and in charge of the process, not in a compulsively tight, but a relaxedly free way.

Surely my painting process involved regression with control, and while form was given to feeling, feeling was also "given" to form. They intermingled in an inseparable fashion, each one evoking the other, neither one the chronological precursor of the other. My painting was not meant primarily as a communication to others, but rather as a kind of self-communication, a rhythmic dialogue between picture and creator which gradually rose and finally fell in intensity. I think the process was neither primarily cathartic nor primarily integrative, but was both simultaneously, and was meaningful just because of the tension and interplay between destructive and constructive forces. It was both an aesthetic and an intellectual experience, producing art as well as insight.

Introduction to the
First Edition

This book is about children, art, and growing, through a distillation of the reflections and visions of an art therapist. It is about children, how they can grow in and through art experiences, and how to help them to do that in a healthy, therapeutic way. It is a message to those who care for children about some ways in which one may facilitate their becoming through art. Knowing what to do and what not to do, when to do it, and how to do it, are difficult learnings to convey to others. One learns these things over time, through experience and reflection, and they become less and less simple in the process. Nevertheless, this work is an attempt to communicate such understandings as I now possess, in the hope that they may be useful to others.

This book is about children from the time they can use art materials in a meaningful way until they can no longer be called children. It is about all children, including those who simply need to be provided with the most facilitating conditions for growth and development. It is about normal, healthy children and their normal, healthy needs for expression, mastery, self-definition, and ways to cope with stress. It is also about children with special needs and problems—those for whom growing has been painful because of unchangeable handicaps or hurts that are hard to bear, and those who have stopped growing in a healthy way, who have turned back, gotten stuck, and perhaps become distorted and ugly to themselves and to others. This book is about all children, and about their right to an opportunity to become themselves and to deal with their hurts creative way through art. In yet another way, it is about the youngster in f us, our understanding of that inner child, and our use of both little and selves in the service of another person's growth.

ok is about growing in and through art, especially the visual and though other forms are highly-respected siblings and allies. At ut responses to art, to work done by self or others. Mostly it is that children do themselves with creative media, the process and the product of an encounter between a youngster and art materials. And it includes all aspects of that dialogue: the approaching and manipulating, as well as the forming and refining. All are seen as inseparable aspects of art, from sensory exploration to complex intentional configurations, from playful to solemn making. It includes the toddler stacking blocks, the teenager constructing a stabile, the infant molding sand and water, and the ten-year-old modeling clay.

This book is about growing deeper as well as bigger, broader as well as taller, freer as well as older, stronger inside as well as outside. It is mostly about growing affectively, about gaining an awareness, understanding, acceptance, liking, and control of one's feeling-self through art. Growth in art includes perceptual, motor, cognitive, and social development as well. The interest here, however, is in these dimensions mainly as they relate to emotional maturation and integration.

For me growing is growing, wherever it happens; and art is art, whether it occurs in a home, a classroom, or a therapy room. The relative emphases may be different, and indeed the goals are best made explicit. Thus, growth in art education may have to do mostly with the acquisition of skills and concepts about art; while these are seen as a means to a different end in art therapy. There the growth is primarily in the development of the capacity to be a freely creative person with firm, but flexible inner controls. Nevertheless, the emotional components of art may become at times central in the classroom, just as the acquisition of skills may become focal in the clinic. Many things are seen as common to growth in both contexts, like the conditions and attitudes which foster personally meaningful work.

Helping, like growing, can take many forms. Helping a child to grow through art can involve giving, showing, or telling. It may also mean watching, and even, at times, waiting. Many times it means moving in, doing or saying something in an active way. At other times it means being present but silent, respectful of the other's primary absorption in the creative (versus the human) dialogue. Helping means many different things, but always it means being tuned into the other person—behaving in a way which respects his right to his own space, and makes it possible for him to gain control and freedom within it.

My own understanding of "art therapy" is that it refers broadly to understanding and helping a person through art, and that it encompasses a wide variety of dimensions. These include the integrative aspects of the creative process itself, as well as the use of art as a tool in the service of discharge, uncovering, defense, or communication. Art for a child can and does become different things at different times. I find it impossible to characterize the process, even with one human being or in one setting, as being any one thing alone or always. Rather, it seems that for anyone, the art activity over time ranges from being central and integrative to peripheral and adjunctive and back again, serving many different possible functions. What is important is to know what is occurring when it is happening, and to have some sense of its meaning and function for that person at that moment in time. What seems equally vital to me, is that the worker have the flexibility and openness to permit the individual to flow in different directions over time, and the wisdom and creativity to stimulate, unblock, or redirect the flow when necessary.

It is my hope that what I write will have some meaning and some utility for all who care about children. The book is most especially for art therapists and art teachers, but truly for anyone who values the creative process in the child, who wishes to nurture and strengthen it, and in so doing help a child to become the best he can. Such a person might be a clinician who works with children— a counselor, psychiatrist, social worker, or psychologist; an occupational, recreational or speech therapist—or a teacher, nurse, or child care worker. Such a person might even be a parent, and could, most certainly be an artist.

Since it is my hope to communicate experiences and ideas to others from a variety of disciplines and frames of reference, I have tried to avoid terminology which belongs exclusively to one or another professional field and to find a language which will be common enough to make sense, yet rich enough to convey complex meanings. I know that in so doing I may risk oversimplification and lack of depth, yet it seems so important to reach those who work directly with children in art, that it is worth that risk. In this way, I hope to talk meaningfully about the conditions that facilitate creative growth in art, and ways in which one may use art with children in order to better understand (diagnosis), as well as to help (treatment and education). I shall explore understanding and helping in a variety of contexts, including work with individuals, families, and groups; suggest implications and applications of art therapy in educational and recreational, as well as in clinical settings; and attempt some preliminary suggestions of useful theoretical constructs.

The profession of art therapy is young, and is actively working on defining its identity for itself as well as for others. In a sense, it is a technique in search of a theory; and has already found useful many different psychological frames of reference, including Freudian (Naumburg, 1947, 1950, 1953, 1966; Kramer, 1958, 1971, 1979; Robbins and Sibley, 1976), Jungian (Lyddiatt, 1971; Keyes, 1974), Gestalt (Rhyne, 1973), Humanistic (Garai, 1977), and Phenomenological (Betensky, 1977). In the course of my own development, I have read, studied, and worked with different theoretical perspectives, and have usually found in each one or more concepts relevant to the work I do.

Until quite recently, I thought that the solution to my problem would be a kind of patchwork—a mosaic or collage of different ideas from different theories— which together would account for what seems to happen in art therapy. This kind of additive eclecticism may still be the answer, but I currently doubt the value or validity of such a heterogeneous mix. What now seems more probable is that a theory about art therapy will have to emerge from art therapy itself. It will no doubt partake of elements of other perspectives, but it will need to have its own inner integrity in terms of the creative process of which it consists. It may, like some theories, turn out to be a frame into which one must insert different lenses, in order to clearly perceive different aspects of the phenomena observed, analogous to the use of stains to illuminate different aspects of an organism on a microscopic slide.

I do not feel ready to develop and articulate a definitive theoretical statement about art as, in, or for therapy. It is my intention, however, to review what I *know*, what I think I have gleaned from books, from articles, from teachers, from colleagues, from children, and from myself. It is equally my intention to review what I *feel*, what I *believe in* most sincerely and often passionately, the values which have come to guide my seeing, knowing, and doing. My present thoughts and understandings about children, art, and growing will certainly evolve over time, in the future as they have in the past. This statement is for now, for me as well as for others.

November, 1976

Introduction to the
Second Edition

As I sat down to omit, revise, and add material for a second edition, I was struck by the rapid expansion of the field of art therapy during the brief period since the book was first written. In just seven years, the literature by art therapists about art therapy has increased considerably (Hanes, 1982; Moore, 1981), the number of training programs has multiplied, and the national professional organization has grown dramatically. More people, of all ages and in a wide variety of settings, are getting the benefits of art therapy. More children, especially those with handicaps, are being helped by qualified (registered) art therapists (cf. Rubin, 1981b).

Although it would unduly encumber this book to add descriptions of all of the exciting work that has been done in the interim in child art therapy, I have added the names of those publications which seemed most important to me to the list of references at the end of the book (cf. Anderson, 1978; Kramer, 1979; Kwiatkowska, 1978; Landgarten, 1981; McNiff, 1981; Robbins et. al., 1980; Silver, 1978; Ulman and Levy, 1980; Wadeson, 1980; Williams and Wood, 1977).

I have also made some other changes. Specifically, I have included actual photographs of the art work, rather than the traced line drawings sometimes used to illustrate the first edition, since the distortions involved did not compensate for the increased visibility. The chapter on research has been incorporated into the "mainstream" of the book, rather than being tacked on as an appendix. I have added to it some general thoughts about art therapy research, as well as brief descriptions of three studies completed and published in the intervening seven years. I have also added to the text some clarifying paragraphs, minor revisions, and descriptions of recent experiences, such as the work with the deaf in Chapter 17.

New material on the history of art therapy has been included in the Preface, which now deals with both professional and personal roots. A new final chapter has also been added, in which I attempt to clarify the differences between art therapy and two closely-related activities with children: art education and play therapy. I felt this was necessary, since I had stressed commonalities so much in the original that I was concerned about blurring distinctions and confusing readers. In this final chapter, there are also some thoughts about the kind of person who can do effective child art therapy and about some of the complexities of even desirable qualities. The Cautionary Note which now ends the book is a further statement of the fact that doing art therapy with children is a complicated, demanding business. Needless to say, I hope that the changes I have made will add something positive for the reader, and that this new edition will prove even more helpful than the first.

Judith A. Rubin, Ph.D., ATR
Pittsburgh, Pennsylvania
March, 1983

PART I:
THE CONTEXT

CHAPTER 1.

Framework for Freedom

Three years after the profound painting experience and reflections on it described in the Preface, I was invited to participate in a seminar on the arts in education and to think and write on the topic of "order and discipline in art as models for effective human behavior." I did not consciously recall the painting paper, long put aside, but instead thought over my then-notions about order, and found myself continually thinking of freedom as well. Feeling by then more secure about the ideas hinted at earlier, I searched the literature to find what others had concluded about freedom, order, and control in art, especially as they related to conditions for creative growth for children. This later attempt to review and organize ideas around a central topic, was a more precise and academic one than my earlier expression of my vague thoughts. Though different in style, the two stem from the same source and mind, and represent different stages in an ongoing problem solving process. The following represents an attempt to clarify ideas about a still-vital concept.

For me, the notion of order in creative activity is intimately and inextricably intertwined with that of freedom. Man's religious mythology, after all, describes the Almighty as creating a world of order out of a universe of chaos. Neither the extreme of order—rigidity—nor the extreme of freedom—chaos—is conducive to creative function. "The forces of the imagination from which [the artist] draws his strength, have a disruptive and capricious power which he must manage with economy. If he indulges his imagination too freely, it may run wild and destroy him and his work by excess . . . . Yet if he plagues his genius with the wrong kind of drill, and uses too many contrivances and refinements, the imagination may shrivel; it can atrophy." (Wind, 1963, p. 2) Yet in most definitions of the creative process, whether by psychologists, aestheticians, or artists, we encounter seemingly opposed and incompatible states: reverie and alertness,

fantasy and reality, disintegration and integration, unconscious (or preconscious) and conscious thought. Art, so often defined as characterized by order
and discipline, is as frequently related to "chaos" (Peckham, 1965) and "anarchy"
(Wind, 1963).

There is no clear agreement on the precise relationship between these two
sides of the creative coin. They are sometimes described as simultaneous and
coexisting, as in "relaxed attention" (McKim, 1972, p. 33), "contemplative
action" (Milner, 1957, p. 153), or "unconscious scanning" (Ehrenzweig, 1967).
Often they are seen as alternating, as between free association and critical scrutiny. The creative process requires a "flexible alternation of roles [because]
it is impossible to produce free associations, to be freely imaginative, to be freely
creative, if at the same time and in the very moment of 'freedom' one attempts
to maintain a watchful, critical scrutiny of what one is producing." (Kubie, 1958,
p. 54) Barron has described this alternation as an "incessant dialectic and an
essential tension between two seemingly opposed dispositional tendencies:
the tendency towards structuring and integration and the tendency towards
disruption of structure and diffusion of energy and attention." (1966, p. 88)
At times the emphasis is on a more sustained attention or passive receptivity
to spontaneity and freedom, as in the "creative surrender" of Ehrenzweig (1967),
followed sequentially by more ordered activity. "In other words, succeeding
upon the spontaneous is the deliberate; succeeding upon total acceptance comes
criticism; succeeding upon intuition comes rigorous thought; succeeding upon
daring comes caution; succeeding upon fantasy and imagination comes reality
testing . . . . The voluntary regression into our depths is now terminated, the
necessary passivity and receptivity of inspiration or of peak-experience must
now give way to activity, control and hard work." (Maslow, 1959, p. 92) It
is my own feeling that the relationship between these two clusters of experiential
states may be at one time simultaneous, at another alternating, and at yet another
sequential, as true for children as adults.

What seems most critical is the recognition that in creative expression there
can be no true order without some experience of genuine freedom; and that
the provider of art for children must make possible a productive and integrated
relationship between the two. Barron, discussing "the paradox of discipline
and freedom," describes the job well: "The task we face is to avoid sacrificing
one possibility to the other. We must be able to use discipline to gain greater freedom, take on habits in order to increase our flexibility, permit disorder in the
interests of an emerging higher order, tolerate diffusion, and even occasionally
invite it, in order to achieve a more complex integration." (1966, p. 86) If the
control, order, and discipline are to come from within the creator, then that child
or adult must be enabled to confront whatever confusion, vagueness, or inner
reality he needs to understand and organize, if it is at all possible for him to do so.

Without passion, energy, intensity, or absorption, the process of working
with creative media can hardly be called "art." One cannot be "on fire" with

inspiration (Dewey, 1934, p. 65) or "lose oneself" in an aesthetic experience (Neumann, 1971) without free access to joy and spontaneity. "Art is the quality that makes the difference between merely witnessing or performing things and being touched by them, shaken by them, changed by the forces that are inherent in everything we give and receive. Art education [or therapy] then, means making sure that such living awareness results when people paint pictures . . . ." (Arnheim, 1967, p. 342) I do believe from my own painting experience as well as from work with others, that learning how to "let go" is necessary to genuine absorption in a creative process. Even in work with children and adults who have lost confidence in their own creativity, it has been my happy learning that it is not destroyed, but simply dormant, capable of reawakening. While creativity "*may* be weakened . . . its expression *may* also simply become muted, or be altogether behaviorally silent, while the capability remains." (Barron, 1972, p. 162)

Why then, do we so often find in our rearing and teaching of children a "restriction of a natural tendency . . . towards play, music, drawing and painting, and many forms of non-verbal sensory grasping and symbolizations?" (Barron, 1966, p. 87) What has made it so hard for us to provide children with an opportunity to freely "let go" and to express themselves openly in both the form and content of their art? While the puritan value of work vs. play is perhaps partly to blame, it seems to me that a more fundamental problem is our natural human "fear of chaos" (Ehrenzweig, 1967). We are afraid, for ourselves and for those in our care, of the consequences of loss of self, of fusion, of dissociation, of disorganization, and of regression.

While regression may not sound as dangerous as disintegration, we *do* fear the tantrum and other forms of disorderly infantile behavior. We conceive rightly (but rigidly) of regression as associated with conditions of stress, as in the "Q" paintings of the Easel Age Scale which are said to indicate disturbance (Lantz, 1955). But we forget that periods of stress also frequently coincide with increased creative productivity. "Every challenge and every emergency in man's life may lead to new creative behavior. Let us not forget that creativity is often closely linked with periods of biological upheaval." (Meerloo, 1968, p. 11) We forget that, even in the development of graphic skill, there are periodic returns to earlier forms of behavior; and that in art, as in all normal growth, "while the child attains more mature levels of action and cherishes his recent acquisitions, there is also a continual homecoming to earlier gratifications." (Peller, 1955, p. 3) We fear that the learner is "losing ground," forgetting that in work with any new medium at any age level it is natural to begin with a period of free, playful exploration and experimentation.

Regression in the creative process was first described as "regression in the service of the ego" (Kris, 1952), regression, in other words, that is symbolic, controlled, and voluntary. We forget too that in any transitional growth phase, in order to restructure, previous structures must be in some way broken down.

Arnheim illustrates progress toward three-dimensional graphic projection in a child's drawings, noting the many intermediate forms of disorientation. He stresses the necessity, during a time of risk and growth, of some degree of "ugliness." (1969, p. 266)

All who work with children in art, have seen many instances of both temporary and prolonged regressions in the service of growth. For the child who finds security in rigid structure and control, this may be seen in a return to compulsively careful work. More often, it is evident in a return to a less structured and perhaps more playful use of materials. For some very constricted children, forced too early perhaps to be clean and neat, the capacity "to enjoy constructive work with clay or paint is possible only after a veritable orgy of simple messing with the stuff." Similarly, "a very angry child may not be able to settle down to work unless he first gives vent to his anger directly." (Kramer 1971, p. 160).

For many children, both hyperactive and inhibited, experimenting with a freer, more honest form of creating may be essential to convince them that, in this symbolic mode, they can indeed let go, express strong feelings with free movements, and remain in control of impulses which turn out neither to be as destructive nor as disorganizing as anticipated. It is only after such a symbolic "letting loose" that familiarity with the feared experience permits them to freely grow.

Both regression and aggression are difficult for adults to handle. We fear the violence, as well as the vitality of children's fantasy life. Even those trained in clinical work at times have difficulty controlling their inner disgust and horror, in response to the mess and mayhem of a disturbed child's inner life. One helpful beginning is to recognize one's own honest responses, to get in touch with one's own feared feelings and impulses, through introspection if possible, through therapy if necessary. Indeed, it is my sincere belief that the adult who has not yet made some kind of open-eyed peace with his own fantasy life is ill-equipped to help children deal with theirs.

Given an acceptance of one's own violent propensities and most bizarre fantasies, the task is to create those conditions under which freedom can be safely and supportively facilitated. What Milner has said of her own creative efforts applies equally well to the provision of an appropriate environment for children: "the spontaneous urge to pattern in the living organism . . . comes about not by planned action, but only by a planned framework, within which the free play of unplanned expressive movement can come about." (1969, p. 263) The framework is thought of broadly, "in time as well as in space" (1957, p. 157). If indeed there is, as she suggests, "the necessity for a certain quality of protectiveness in the environment," it is because "there are obviously many circumstances in which it is not safe to be absent-minded; it needs a setting, both physical and mental." (1957, pp. 163–164)

The provision of limits and of structure are vital in creating a framework for freedom. "Limits define the boundaries of the relationship and tie it to reality . . . they offer security and at the same time permit the child to move freely and safely in his play." (Moustakas, 1959, p. 11) Overwhelmed and frightened by the sometimes "undisciplined outpourings of the unconscious" (Bettelheim, 1964, p. 44) often caused by lack of appropriate limits, workers in both therapy and education have too often "overstepped their function of providing a secure frame for the free activities and tried to dictate the activities themselves." (Milner, 1957, p. 105) Worse yet, they may prohibit certain activities because of their anticipated disorganizing effect on the child, prematurely restricting and constricting his world. One cannot help but agree with Bettelheim that all too often, "despite loud assertions to the contrary, these adults . . . remain afraid of permitting children to think and act for themselves." (1964, p. 60)

Perhaps, the most critical psychological variable in the freedom/order equation is the adult worker—his attitudes (trust vs. mistrust), expectations (positive vs. negative), and personal qualities (empathy vs. distance). If he hopes to promote individual independent growth, he must learn to trust the child as a human being with an inherent and natural tendency toward growth, order, and integration. He will not be able to provide opportunities for choice, for independent movement, and for self-initiated decision-making without "faith in the inner potential of [his] students so that [he] will trust them when they wish to explore on their own." (Haupt, 1969, p. 43) He must be able to trust each child to make decisions which are best for himself, under optimal conditions for that child.

In my own work with seriously ill schizophrenic children, where they had freedom of media choice, it was striking that those with poor ego boundaries consistently avoided such fluid materials as fingerpaints. They often provided their own kinds of structure, such as one regressed twelve-year-old who always pulled a chair up to sit at the easel, in order to "contain" his usual aggressive hyperactivity. He further controlled his work through repetitive movements, letting his arm go up and down, rhythmically, calming himself with a motion like an infant's rocking.

Another child, blind and retarded, "contained" his experimentation with fingerpaint, previously threatening to him, through the use of a tray. He had chosen fingerpaint and paper at the first group session; but had been both excited and frightened by the texture and by the threat to control posed by the hard-to-find edges of the paper when covered with paint. He had ripped up the product, quite agitated. An observing child psychiatrist had advised against allowing fingerpaint again. Not having heard the doctor, however, the next week Bob requested the paint. When it was refused and alternatives were suggested, he put up a loud fuss. Because of his exasperation, he was again given the gooey substance, this time in a plastic tray hastily borrowed from the school cafeteria. He was surprisingly calm and relaxed throughout, the physical boundaries of the tray apparently allaying his anxiety about edges, thus permitting him to enjoy tremendous sensory pleasure and delight, frequently repeated in subsequent sessions. This boy had once told of accidentally squeezing a soft, gushy worm to death in bed, a memory stimulated while manipulating water-base clay. Perhaps fingerpainting was a way of working through some of the feelings associated with that event, this time under his control and now demonstrably safe and bounded.

Another blind boy contained his exploration of the effects of mixing clay and water within a bowl (Fig. 1-1). In fact, when a group of totally blind children were given the choice of a tray or paper for fingerpaint, all selected the tray with its clearly-defined edges because, as one of them explained, "it helps you to stop."

Clearly-defined limits of time also facilitate creative work. Mary, a blind teenager, once explained to me how she created with plasticine what she called "personality globs," and drew with markers "mind pictures." In both cases, as she proudly demonstrated, she would pause, close her eyes, sit meditatively still, and then with clay or marker do "whatever my brain and hands tell me to do." She made a distinction between drawings done under these conditions, in which she was relaxed and unconcerned about realistic rendering, and those produced with eyes close to paper, a strained attempt at reproduction of the visual world. "I'm more free," she explained, "like I feel more like *myself* when I draw something indirect . . . . I feel good, you know."

Such concrete means of organizing time, space, and the self are often supplemented by symbolic means through art. For art itself offers a kind of protective framework, a boundary between reality and make-believe, which enables the child to more daringly test himself and more openly state his fantasies than is possible without its aesthetic and psychic "distance." "Only in protected situations, characterized by high walls of psychic insulation" can a person afford to let himself "experience disparities, tensions, etc. . . . art offers precisely this kind of experience."

One day, a schizophrenic youngster, a boy of eleven, spent perhaps half an

Fig. 1-1. A blind boy mixing clay and water in a bowl.

Fig. 1-2. Three drawings of a boy by a brain-damaged child. Age 9.

hour in the careful mixing of brown paint (his first attempt at combining colors). Then, rhythmically and somewhat compulsively, he covered the entire surface of a large white paper with the brown mixture, followed by the linear depiction, along with an elaborate verbalization, of his central unresolved (oedipal) conflict. The painting was of a dead king in his coffin underground, who, according to the long and complex story, had been accidentally killed off and then succeeded by his son, the prince. Having succeeded in articulating at least a part of his inner wish-world, he was then free to begin to organize the outer one, creating pictorial diagrams and maps of concepts, places, and ideas.

In art or play the child may do the impossible. He may fulfill symbolically both positive wishes and negative impulses, without fear of real consequences. He can learn to control the real world by experimenting with active mastery of tools, media, and the ideas and feelings expressed in the process. He can gain symbolic access to and relive past traumas, and can rehearse and practice for the future. He can learn to be in charge in a symbolic mode, and thus come to feel competent to master reality.

But it is my conviction that the child cannot learn to control and organize himself, if the structure does not ultimately come from within. It has been argued that prepared outlines are useful to children because they need to learn motor control. Yet a careful look at what children produce spontaneously in the course of their graphic growth demonstrates the normal self-creation of boundaries or outlines within which they color, actualizing an age-appropriate desire for self-set limits on their own strong impulses. One brain-damaged boy might have escaped into abstraction, rather than struggle with his confused body-image. Given a secure, dependable setting and adult, he was able to confront his confusion graphically, to work to clarify his conception, to make sense out of what was formerly chaotic by "figuring it out" on paper (Fig. 1-2).

Because a child is small and dependent, however, he needs an adult to provide him with the physical and psychological setting in which he can freely struggle to order and control. He needs an adult to provide empathic support, accepting understanding, a reflective mirror; to be a "container," a vessel into which he can freely pour his feelings and fantasies; and a reflective, articulate voice which can help him to clarify, explain, and make sense out of them.

So it follows that the adult offering art must provide a framework or structure within which the child can be free to move and to think and to fantasize, not a structure which imposes, controls, and makes a child dependent, for such a framework is a straightjacket and not conducive to growth. Such a restrictive framework may take many forms, from the use of prepared outlines, kits, and step-by-step guides, to generalizations about the best size of paper or brush, or an invariant description of the "right" way to teach art to children. The arrogance of those who have found the one correct way to work with all children in art is equal only to the disrespect on which it is based.

Surely an adult has both the right and the responsibility to set strict limits on destruction of property or dangerous ingestion of art media; but does he also have a right to decide that preschoolers should be restricted from free access to tempera paint because he fears that the child will "drown the graphic patterns of its scribbling in water colour?" (Grözinger, 1955, p. 91) Although the supposedly limited capacities of a retarded child are often used to justify constant supervision, does any human being have the right to decide for another that "creative activity must be held to a reasonable minimum?" (Wiggin, 1962, p. 24)

Fortunately there are many who still believe in the often untapped creative resources of all human beings, who assume the growth potential of others; like the teacher who works with "slow learners" and feels sure that the "children have a rich inner life waiting to be developed in a classroom setting of love and approval." (Site, 1964, p. 19) But "love is not enough" in many cases (Bettelheim, 1950); and what is also needed is a safe and supportive framework for freedom in growing. As Milner discovered in her own struggle to paint: "Fearful subservience to an imposed authority either inside or out, or complete abandonment of all controls, neither of these was the solution." Instead, she found that it was necessary to "provide the framework within which the creative forces could have free play." (1957, p. 101) In therapy as well as in education, in art as in any other form of creative expression, this concept continues to deepen in meaning and validity for me.

CHAPTER 2.

Conditions for Creative Growth

"To create conditions which assist children in releasing that which lies dormant and waiting within them so they may paint their impressions on life's canvas in rich, bright, bold, brave colors is the challenge for all who guide children." (Nixon, 1969, p. 301)

A "framework for freedom" is one way of thinking about appropriate facilitating conditions for growth, something I assume necessary in order to help human beings to actualize their inner creative potential. One must provide a physical and psychological setting which makes it possible for each person to become himself. One must think about materials, space, and time. One may need to provide alternative expressive modalities, like music or drama, for those who cannot find their way comfortably in paint or clay. In order to help individuals discover their own style, one must accept and value whatever they do or say that is genuinely and truly their own; thus, individuality, uniqueness, and originality are prized and rewarded. Similarly, autonomy, independence of thinking and function, and the taking of risks are to be stimulated and reinforced when they occur.

Materials are of many sorts: those to draw with, those to paint with, those to model with, and those with which to construct. Children need to have at least some of each available, as well as surfaces and tools with which to use them successfully. If art materials are cared for lovingly by adults, they will not only remain most usable, but children will then learn respect for the tools of the trade. If they are available in a state of readiness, children may then use them spontaneously without unnecessary frustration or delay in the actualization of a creative impulse. They must be appropriate for the children who are expected to use them— appropriate to their developmental level, degree of coordination, previous experiences, particular interests, and special needs. They are best if primarily unstructured, allowing maximal alternatives for idiosyncratic expression. If materials are of sufficient variety, then children may discover and develop their own unique tastes and preferences, their own favorite forms of expression.

Space involves not only dimension, but also places and surfaces for materials, work, storage, and cleaning up. If basic expressive media and equipment are kept in consistent and predictable places, then children will know where to go to get and to use them. If they are clearly arranged and organized, it will be easier for children to make choices. If they are placed so that children may procure and use them independently, then excessive intervention will not be necessary. A child needs adequate, well-lit, uninterrupted spaces for art, with sufficient definition to provide closure when necessary. A child needs places where it is all right to spill or to mess without fear of adult disapproval. A child does best with options, choices in spaces as in materials, so that there are ways to be close or far, alone or with others (Fig. 2-1).

Fig. 2-1. A girl who is absorbed in her work.
(Photo by Jacob Malezi)

Time in art means often enough and long enough to sustain interest and become involved in a creative process. If the same basic materials are available all or most of the time, they will become familiar. Only then can children truly get to know them, and have sufficient opportunity to practice their use, and only through such practice can they achieve genuine mastery and competence. Children need to know how much time is available, and it helps to have a warning at the point where it is drawing to a close. Ending times are often hard for the young, and one must provide ways for them to adjust to such events.

Order, clarity, and consistency in the organization of materials, working spaces, and time can be helpful; for children with little inner order it is often essential. An alone-with-another time in art can be a powerfully peaceful organizing experience. Even in a group, such an atmosphere is possible. It is most probable where children's bodies, working spaces, materials, and products are protected from disruption by others. Psychological safety is as important as physical protection, for children's feelings need the same kind of respect and concern as their bodies or products.

Safety means that many kinds of expressive activity are accepted: bizarre as well as realistic, regressive as well as progressive, those with negative as well as positive subject matter. Limits help to protect children from their own impulses, so that while it is "safe" to smear chalk or to draw destructive fantasies, it is not safe or permitted to smear people, or to behave destructively toward property. In work with children, it is important to protect them whenever possible from outer as well as inner psychological dangers, such as people and practices which would limit or stunt their creative growth. One thinks especially of the danger presented when others impose outside ideas or standards on the child, invalidating or crippling his own developing images—people who tell him what to do and how to do it, or who supply coloring books and paint-by-number kits.

Respect for the child is shown by allowing him the freedom to choose to become involved or not to participate; to take a superficial and fleeting "taste," or to become deeply engrossed, to select his own medium and topic, to work alone or with others; to explore and experiment at his own pace and in his own way. Respect for each child's uniqueness is also shown by allowing and helping every one to explore and discover his own most congenial ways of expressing himself, his preferred modalities, personal themes, and style. Respect for the child's opinions is expressed through listening and interviewing in a way which encourages him to articulate his own thoughts and associations about both process and product. Respect for the child as artist is expressed through helping him to set his own goals and standards, and to evaluate for himself how well he has achieved them. Respect for the child's tangible productions, extensions of himself, is shown through handling and preserving, and perhaps sharing and displaying them with loving care.

Interest in the child and in his personal explorations and expressions must be sincere if one is to work with children, who are acutely sensitive to phoniness. Such interest may be expressed in sensitive, unintrusive observation, genuine listening, and gentle verbal intervention. Interest is shown by being available to him as a facilitator during the creative process, if he should express or show a need for the adult's help, support, or appreciation.

Pleasure in the child's creative work and growth, is felt often by those who truly value such expressions and experiences. Genuine enthusiasm for a child's involvement or his product is a joy for an adult to express and for a child to hear.

Support for the child's inner creative strivings is expressed through consistent provision of conditions like the above, and is distinct from a passively permissive attitude, which may represent (or at least communicate) a lack of interest or concern on the part of the adult. Support for all children requires awareness of normal stages of development in art, in order to help them to take "next steps." It requires further knowledge of each individual child's developmental and psychological state, his "frame of reference," within which you must meet if you are to lead him forward. Support for a child who is blocked or "stuck," requires especially thoughtful understanding and assistance from the adult. For a timid child, for example, active participation in the art work along with him, may be a helpful concrete expression of adult permission for his own involvement. Support for any child's struggle to grow in and through art requires genuine empathy on the part of the adult, and its communication to the child in a manner best suited to enhance his own expressive development.

I understand the role of a therapist or teacher as facilitator of another person's growth, the shape and form of which vary tremendously from one individual to another. If there are no big blocks to creative development, the provision of facilitating conditions like those noted above may be sufficient to enable the individual to flower. If the blocks are large and severe, some reparative work is probably in order, and will vary in form depending on the capacities and needs of the individual. All such work for me is a challenging, unpredictable, creative endeavor. Each new person is a new puzzle, like but unlike others, with untapped potential for symbolic communication and healthy growth.

PART II:
THE INDIVIDUAL

CHAPTER 3.

Understanding Development through Art

Progression in Normal Artistic Development

The normal sequence of development of art by children has been observed, collected, described, and categorized since the 19th century by specialists in child development, psychology, and art education; but work has focused, probably for practical reasons, on graphic expression (Harris, 1963; Kellogg, 1969; Koppitz, 1968; Lowenfeld, 1957; Goodnow, 1977). Although some beginnings have been made in looking closely at painting (Alschuler & Hattwick, 1947; Lantz, 1955; Smith, 1981) and at clay modeling (Brown, 1975; Golomb, 1974), these efforts have been spotty and unintegrated. Although I have found Lowenfeld's (1957) "stages" to be helpful ways of conceptualizing graphic development, I have not found them to be as useful when applied to painting, modeling or constructing; and I have therefore felt a need for a broader set of developmental categories, which could apply more comfortably to work in all two- and three-dimensional media.

The many different attempts to describe art development make it clear that there is a generally predictable sequence of events for what most children will do in art as they mature. This sequence has a kind of cyclical rhythm—moving forward and backward, expanding and contracting, with a pervasive progressive thrust over time. The different lists of stages developed by different workers reflect not only the regularity of this process, but the fact that the same developmental sequence may be divided in a variety of ways, each with its own logic, and the fact that it may be analyzed in more or less detail from diverse perspectives, each one appropriate to its own frame of reference.

As an art therapist, I find I share with others an interest in both the cognitive and affective aspects of art behaviors, and that I must account for both the process and the product in art development. I also find, since I often work with those whose growth is uneven and delayed, that I have a need for understanding in more detail the beginning phases of art development (cf. Wilson, 1977). Because of my particular perspective, and because I have found no existing set of "stages" comfortably applicable to all modes and to the earliest periods of creating, I have found myself needing to find relevant ways of thinking about art development for my own work. At the risk of oversimplifying what is always a complex and ultimately individual sequence of events, I should therefore like to propose yet another way of describing normal development in art, a way that includes drawing, painting, modeling; and constructing, and which deals in some detail with the earliest period of expression. The stages that make sense to me are as follows: Manipulating, Forming, Naming, Representing, Containing, Experimenting, Consolidating, Naturalizing, and Personalizing.

The "steps" are not so discrete in reality. Indeed, they always overlap, and in a very real sense, live on forever as possible modes of doing. Manipulation, for example, is always present when one uses media, though it does not remain the primary focus of attention and absorption as the child matures. The "stages" refer to what is most central for each period of time, and must be seen as complex, multilayered, and persistent. The separation made here is artificial but, hopefully, helpful in emphasizing descriptively and conceptually those aspects of creating which take successive prominence in normal development.

It is probably not worth debating when "art" begins; but it is important to remember that it is a logical development of the earliest forms of encountering the world through the senses. From the rattle in the mouth, to the stick in the sand, to the crayon on the paper, is not a series of hops but part of a continuous sequence. Different children have different developmental rhythms as they do working rhythms, which may have genetic as well as environmental bases. In any case, "norms" are wide and must remain so, thus calling into question the usefulness of things like drawings for developmental diagnosis, when so many relevant variables are unknown or unspecified.

Manipulating. The first stage of encounter with materials, regardless of their nature, is a manipulative one. At a pre-art phase the manipulation may be inappropriate, e.g., putting clay into the mouth or crayon on the wall. Actually, these behaviors are not wrong from the infant's or toddler's point of view, but are defined as such by the environment, which decrees that you may smear your food in the high chair tray or play with mud and sand in the yard, but may not mark the wall with the crayon or eat up the clay (which indeed looks and smells like food to the very young). In any case, we generally permit infants and toddlers to smear, mark, model, and construct with natural materials as soon as they are able; but restrict them from using art materials until they are able to do so within our societally defined limits.

The sensory qualities of materials are vital during this manipulative phase— the feel of paint or clay, the texture of sand or wood. Equally important are the kinesthetic aspects of the experience—the movement of hands, arms, and often

Fig. 3-1. A toddler can manipulate a paint brush and enjoy the process.

whole body in making marks, molding, or putting things together. When one observes a toddler or preschooler manipulating clay or scribbling with crayon, one becomes aware of how central the motor-kinesthetic aspects of such an experience are for the young child. As the child becomes aware of the fact that it is *he* who has squeezed the clay or marked the paper, he becomes increasingly interested in the visual aspects of his experience, in the shape of the clay or the color of his scribblings. His attention becomes focused not just on the making process but on that which is being made as well, despite the fact that he is not really concerned about a "finished product" at this stage (Fig. 3-1).

Forming. As a child matures intellectually and physiologically, he gains increasing control over his movements and begins to take more deliberate charge of what happens when he uses crayon on paper or plays with clay. He practices and soon demonstrates his control over materials by repeating certain motions or activities, as in longitudinal or circular scribbling, rolling or flattening clay. He starts to consciously vary his manipulations of materials—to make first dots and then lines, or lines and then masses, to pound and then squeeze, to build in a way that is more than just picking up and putting down. He then begins to make "gestalts," separate shapes or objects which have an existence of their own. They are not representational at first, but do represent a forward step of great magnitude in the creation of intentional forms. One such example is beginning and ending a line in the same place in drawing. By so doing, the child creates a separate shape which is perceived as such, and is then related to with other lines, shapes, or extensions.

Naming. Perhaps because people in his environment want so often to know "what" he has made, or perhaps because he has himself reached a point where he begins to think of making a "something," the next step for almost every child is the naming of marks or objects as real things. Adults are puzzled because these masses of paint and configurations of clay or wood in no way resemble the real objects they are said to represent. But they do "stand" for something else in the same way that a block can "stand" for a car or a gun in the hands of a three-year-old. Their identity often shifts, because it is not fixed in any quality of the creation, but in the child's association to the form at a particular moment.

Representing. There does come a time, however, when true representations emerge from the manipulating and forming and naming processes of children with materials. They are often strange to adult eyes, hard to recognize, and frequently mixed on the same picture space or clay board with nonrepresentational items. Yet they are distinct because they do involve qualities of the object being represented. The early human figures, the well-known "cephalopods," for example, do have a shape which stands for head-body, extensions which legitimately stand for limbs, and usually one or more features which resemble that to which they refer (first eyes, then mouth, then others) (Fig. 3-2).

Fig. 3-2. A "head-body" figure done at 3 years, 10 months (left) and a picture of the same person (mommy) done 8 months later (right). Crayon.

There are many strange variations and odd features in early representational art, in drawings, sculptures, paintings, and constructions which refer in some meaningful way to the objects they are said to be. One way of explaining this early work has been to say that the child draws "what he knows, not what he sees." There is some truth in that notion in this sense: that what a child makes represents, as far as he is capable, those things he knows about the object which seem important to him at the moment of his making. But at three or four or five years of age, and for a long time thereafter, he can represent far less than he either knows or sees. Instead, his work is a condensed form of symbolization, showing what he is able to about that which interests him.

Containing.   It is also during this period that designs become not only configurations of line or mass, but that the filling-in of lines and the creation of boundaries become both possible and important. For the child's growth and expansion has to do not only with his increasing capacity to do more things better, but also to control himself and his impulses. The young child often delights in practicing and demonstrating his ability to "stay within the lines" in his own art work, just as he is learning to "stay within bounds" in other areas. He does this quite spontaneously, creating and filling in his own boundaries, a far healthier activity both psychologically and creatively than filling in other peoples' spaces (Fig. 3-3).

Experimenting.   During this early representational phase, the child experiments in a way similar to but different from his earlier manipulative explorations.

Fig. 3-3. A partially sighted boy fills in his own outlines.

Fig. 3-4. Some of Jenny's varied human figure drawings around age 4.

He explores different ways of doing, of making, and of saying things. His human figures are a good index of just how free and flexible is his capacity to experiment, for they are still the most frequent symbol for most children. Lowenfeld (1957) called this period the "pre-schematic" stage, indicating that it precedes chronologically a time of settling on specific symbols for specific objects. But I do not believe that this exploration and expansion of graphic vocabulary is simply a search for a set of symbols. Rather, it is a time of expansion intellectually and in all areas of development. It is a time when children stretch, try their wings, and hopefully are encouraged to explore their environment and their own capacities. In this context, exploration in art in this early representational period is a similar kind of mental and visual thinking, roaming, and discovery.

Part of this experimental phase involves the discovery of many graphic ways to say the same thing, like Jenny's human figures, all done within a six month period in her fourth and fifth years, each one quite unique (Fig. 3-4). At the same time, the child is becoming increasingly adept at manipulating media, his fine-motor control is increasing rapidly, and he is exploring and expanding nonfiguratively as well as figuratively in the area of elaboration. Early two- and three-dimensional designs begin to get more and more complex and, aesthetically speaking, often more "decorative." As the child's representational work expands and becomes increasingly more naturalistic, his nonrepresentational work becomes increasingly controlled, elaborated, and aesthetically interesting.

Consolidating.   At about the time a child enters school, a kind of consolidation takes place in his art work, as in other areas of behavior. He begins to find pre-

Fig. 3-5. "Daddy in front of our house" by Jim. Marker. Age 5.

Fig. 3-6. "X-ray" drawing of a mother with a baby in her tummy. Marker. Age 5.

ferred ways of saying things pictorially, and tends to repeat them rather than to go on, as before, trying out different ways. These "schemata" or symbols are both simple statements, like Jenny's way of representing the human figure, and complex ones, like Jim's way of representing the relationships between objects in space with a "baseline" to indicate the ground on which they stand (Fig. 3-5). Some of these configurations look fairly realistic, while others, like the "x-ray" (Fig. 3-6) or "mixed plane and elevation" conventions (Fig. 3-7), look quite strange. While not naturalistic, even these have a kind of inner logic, and tend to be utilized for a period of time, varying from child to child. The degree of flexibility in the work of any individual child during this stage (which Lowenfeld called "schematic") also varies considerably.

The shift to a different kind of order in schematic symbols or ways of relating them, is paralleled by a shift from a rather egocentric point of view to a more social one. The earliest subject matter for most children is the human figure, most often labelled as self or family members. Gradually, however, as his world and horizons broaden, the child includes other people, trees, plants, houses, vehicles, and eventually people and places both near and far away. While there are cultural variations in popular spontaneous subject matter, there is a general widening, broadening, and expanding of the child's creative horizons over time.

Naturalizing. Throughout the preceding phases, paralleling increasing elaboration and sophistication in nonfigurative work, the child's art becomes more and more naturalistic. Parts of the body are represented in gradually more realistic proportions, spatial relationships become more and more accurate, and relative sizes and colors of objects get closer and closer to the natural world. There comes a time, however, when the discrepancy between what he has represented and the visual facts apparent to his eyes becomes distressing to the child. At this point he experiences anxiety and frustration, attempting to make things as they are, but rarely satisfying himself with his efforts.

This inner dissatisfaction occurs at different ages for different youngsters, and no doubt has multiple cognitive, affective, and social roots. Whatever the cause, it seems to be an inevitable stage in normal development, and one at which many children "give up" in discouragement, turning to other (mostly verbal) forms of expression which are more manageable. During the phase of early attempts at naturalizing his art, the child's products often reflect some awkwardness, associated with the abandonment of the old, comfortable, but no longer acceptable schemata of earlier years. He struggles with proportions, shading, attempts to control the quality of line and color, and feels increasing concern about the realism of both two- and three-dimensional products. Whereas before most children were satisfied, even delighted, with their efforts, now most children are dissatisfied, often discouraged and self-critical.

Fig. 3-7. A family eating dinner around a table. Marker. Age 6.

Personalizing. For most children, the period of naturalizing goes on for a long time, throughout the later elementary school years and into early adolescence. If a child experiences sufficient success in these endeavors, and has enough instruction and practice, he may develop an impressive degree of skill in naturalistic rendering in any of the large variety of media he can now manage physically. Some children, less successful with naturalism but with a strong aesthetic sense, turn to abstract work, and often show a preference for creative activities in nongraphic media, including crafts, where the youngster's increasing fine-motor control can be contained and made productive within a designated skill activity.

Those children who remain active in art in adolescence, often reflect the increasing concern with themselves characteristic of this phase by personalizing their work, self-consciously exploring different styles of working as a way of expressing their own emerging identity. Whether their concern is primarily with how things look, or with how they feel about events; teenagers tend to search for their own particular media and themes, in order to express their personal perceptions of both inner and outer worlds. Their self-criticism and concern with quality increases, and is eventually focused not only on naturalism, but also on other expressive and aesthetic goals. The work may be simple or complex, rich or stark, figurative or nonfigurative. What characterizes all of it, however, is the self-conscious and deliberate quality of the adolescent artist. Whether he works in a free or controlled style, he is more consciously in charge than ever before, in great contrast to the rather unself-conscious spontaneity of the preschool and early school years.

During adolescence, the child's concern with the world often becomes secondary to his preoccupation with himself, and the subject matter of his art reflects this increasing self-centeredness. Whether he represents himself or someone like him, or chooses to "specialize" in a specific medium, subject matter, or type of abstraction, he is basically looking for personally syntonic themes, just as he is searching for a personally congenial style and identity.

General Issues in Development

Some issues span all developmental levels—for example, the source of the imagery in the art of the child. While one might think that it is more likely to be kinesthetic at the earliest manipulative stages (Grözinger, 1955; Kellogg, 1969), other variables may also predispose the child to respond more to the body and less to vision, as with Lowenfeld's "haptic" type, first evident in adolescence. Many stimuli for artistic imagery seem to be largely internal, like instinctual drives, and those body parts, zones, and processes of special significance (Erikson, 1950). Neurobiological sources also seem critical, affecting both responsive and productive image behavior (Berlyne, 1971; Horowitz, 1978). There is provocative evidence for the possibility of innately preferred sensory modalities, and for racially inherited visual propensities (Jung, 1964; Robertson, 1963)—further internal sources of imagery in child art. Significant maturational factors affecting art imagery include cognitive development

(Piaget, 1936), phase-appropriate growth-tasks (Erikson, 1950; A. Freud, 1965), and defense mechanisms (Levick, 1983).

In addition to internal forces, external influences on the child's art imagery are significant at all developmental stages. The influence of others—first mother, then father, then siblings and peers—on what the child produces to please or to compete is probably impossible to quantify, but is important nonetheless. (Cf. Lowenfeld, 1957; Kramer, 1958; Wilson & Wilson, 1979.) Of course, the visual world itself is the source of most art imagery at all ages; but what is most intriguing is how the inner pressures affect the perception and selection of external imagery for art. A child psychologist once scoffed at the notion proposed by some that the children at Bellevue painted boats on the water because it symbolized the separation from their mothers, making the point with some scorn that they drew boats because the hospital was on the East River, and that was all they saw! Despite such persuasive skepticism, one must still account for the *selection* of stimuli, given the fact that there are always many things to choose from, even in a relatively restricted environment. This interaction of internal needs with external stimuli is one of the most fascinating aspects of the study of child art. Some individual youngsters develop preferred art images which seem at the time to carry a special power because of their connection wth experiences of intense meaning/feeling (McFarlend, 1978). While such images are characterized by differing degrees of disguise, they seem to occur at all developmental levels, with multiple cognitive/affective determinants.

There is no question that the meaning of the art activity changes as children mature, as different aspects become more prominent and others less so. Because of these shifts over time, and because of the ongoing maturation of body and mind, issues like mastery, ordering, or finding aesthetic "rightness" are different for a three-year-old than for a thirteen-year-old. The interaction of variables like affect and cognition is a complex one, and yet a separation of the two seems highly artificial when one is dealing with such complex acts as drawing, painting, sculpting, or constructing.

Certainly, how one feels about what one is doing will influence many things, from choice of materials to selection of subject matter to style of work. Whether a three-year-old or a thirteen-year-old works in a calm and deliberate or sloppy and impulsive manner has more to do with affective than with cognitive factors. The interaction of these is complex developmentally, for it is true that most four-year-olds are freer than most ten-year-olds when they paint; yet within each age group there is an equally great range of differences, due as much to personality as to developmental level. Whether a two- or a twelve-year-old uses more or less picture space is probably more a reflection of personality than an index of cognitive or motor development. What is important here from a diagnostic point of view is the need to understand all relevant variables—the cognitive, the affective, and the motoric—and to relate these within a developmental framework which takes into account what is known about most children, as well as what can be discovered about any particular child.

Regression in Children's Art

To understand where someone is functioning in art as well has how he is functioning, it is vital to remember the cyclical and variable nature of normal development. While signs of progress are to be found in the art of most children as they grow, so too are signs of regression. For the growth process is not a simple linear movement forward, but rather a cyclical one, well-characterized in the folk wisdom of "two steps forward, one step backward." There is certainly a degree of variability at any one moment in time in most youngsters' work (Fig. 3-4).

It is particularly essential to know the "norms" alluded to above, and to know them in some detail, in order to be able to discriminate "regression" from some of the strange, illogical, but developmentally "normal" characteristics of early figurative stages—characteristics such as "cephalopods" (head-foot figures) (Fig. 3-2), transparencies or "x-ray" pictures (Fig. 3-6), mixed plane and elevation in the treatment of space (Fig. 3-7), or value rather than reality-based relative sizes (Fig. 3-5). It is only within a framework of normal growth and development in art, and within the narrower framework of a particular child's past and present work, that the concept of "regression" becomes meaningful. Thus, knowing that a young crippled boy of five can draw a detailed clown, we are entitled to label as dramatically regressed his portrait of himself (Fig. 3-8),

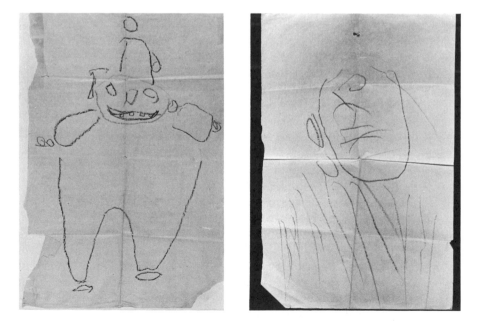

Fig. 3-8. A crippled boy's pictures of a clown (left) and of himself (right). Crayon. Age 5.

Fig. 3-9. Melanie's lonely, hungry eagle.
Scribble drawing, chalk. Age 15.

a poignant expression of his sense of his body as a disorganized entity. Knowing that a child can draw a complex human figure at any age, we may call a later, more primitive one "regressed," in terms of the developmental level he has already achieved.

While not always pure, it may help to think of regression in children's art as being manifest in four major ways: form, content, organization, and the thought processes evident in the work. Regression in form, the return to earlier modes of representation, is perhaps the most common and most easily identified, as in the examples already noted. In content, one may see the representation of symbolic material relating to earlier phases of development. This may be more or less overt, as in fifteen-year-old Melanie's oral-aggressive hungry eagle (Fig. 3-9), may be disguised through a symbol, or may be further hidden in an abstraction.

The other forms of regression may be thought of as more vertical than horizontal, i.e., regression downward from the conscious, rational level of the mind to deeper ones (vs. regression backward in form or in content). It is evident at times in disorganization—in the disintegration of form, in fragmentation, or even chaos, a total absence of order. Another related kind is manifest in the appearance of thought processes characteristic of that part of the mind dominant in dreams as well as in psychosis—the so-called "primary process" of the unconscious. This is seen in the use of such devices as condensation, as when a teenager represented her family as a head with a feature from each member, or displacement, as in Sam's bizarre head with its distorted features (Fig. 14-6). The absence of real time or space in pictures with a dreamlike, surrealistic quality may also be thought of as regression to deeper, more primitive, less logical modes of thought.

a   b

Fig. 3-10. (a) Lisa's usual style of painting and (b) her smeary picture.

It should be noted that not all instances of progressive or regressive behavior in art are evident in the product itself. While one can sometimes guess from a product that aggressive-destructive impulses gained control over progressive-constructive ones, one cannot observe in a picture, the growth in a child's autonomy and independence which may have accompanied its production.

There are a variety of reasons for regression in children's art, and it may be useful to note the more common ones. Some involve external stimuli, such as the medium; chalk, for example, invites smearing and loss of boundaries more easily than crayon, as can be seen in two drawings by a boy done in the same hour (Fig. 4-4). At times the social situation seems to be the primary impetus to regression, through contagion from others. Tim, usually neat and well-organized in his portraits of people, rarely "let go" in his work unless the person next to him in his art therapy group made it permissible to do so. Other causes seem more internal, such as fatigue. The last two pictures in a series of sixteen done by a four-year-old boy were significantly less organized and differentiated than his first two drawings. The most common cause of all seems to be stress. Five-year-old Lisa, for example, reacted by abandoning her normally well-organized decorative painting style for a smudgy smear on the day her mother went to the hospital to have a baby (Fig. 3-10).

Sometimes, however, the major dete
be a kind of naive logic, as in Jenny's
her house are not as detailed since the
is more elaborated (Fig. 3-11). Di Le
a shift in the child's "cognitive-affe
kind of developmentally normal logi
from both a head-on and bird's-eye v
portance, rather than with reality,
more important than the house (Fig

Paradoxically, another major dete
to be progression or growth. A certain a
disorganization, may accompany the struggle involved in giving
and developing a new one. As Rudolf Arnheim has said, in noting this phe
nomenon, "the resulting disorder, though perhaps unappealing in itself, gives
evidence of the searching mind in action." (1969, p. 266)

At times an art therapist may deliberately suggest the loosening of controls
through a regressive, playful approach, in order to allow more personal imagery to

Fig. 3-11. A family doing things inside their house ("x-ray"). Crayon. Age 5.

case with Dorothy, whose rigidly stylized pretty birds were
drawn outlines week after week (Fig. 7-10). Only after giggly
with free painting, which I had suggested, did she articulate her
tions of the symbolic meanings of those birds in her fantasy life (Figs.
The experience of safe but permissible regression may be an essential
or the constricted child. "When it frees the individual from crippling
ons, temporary regression to crudely aggressive art may be an emotional
ry." (Kramer, 1971, p. 161.)

In yet another sense, "temporary regression is a necessary phase in every
creative act," (Kramer, 1971, p. 14) particularly in terms of gaining access to
unconscious and preconscious processes. Perhaps the ability to be playful, to
let go some measure of conscious control "is not regression, [but] courageous
progression." (Barron, 1972, p. 162) While the kind of "regression in the service
of the ego" described by Ernst Kris (1952) is probably less common with small
children than with adult artists, it does sometimes occur that a child with full
awareness deliberately "lets go" of some usual controls, allowing less conscious
processes to dominate. Such was the case with Mary, the partially-sighted girl
of thirteen, who created her "personality globs" and "mind pictures" by pausing,
closing her eyes, sitting meditatively still, and then doing "whatever my brain
and hands tell me to do. . . ."

Whether the regression is experienced as liberating and freeing, or as disorganizing and paralyzing, may best be judged from the child's ensuing behavior and work. "Healthy regression is relaxing and releases energy for further
growth; unhealthy regression stops growth." (Rabin and Haworth, 1960, p. 29)
Often a child will become progressively more and more smeary and disorganized
in the course of a fingerpainting session, but I think that it is often such a
regressive-aggressive interlude which makes possible a kind of freedom and movement in subsequent art work not present in the child's tight earlier creations.

The more one considers progression and regression in children's art, the more
complex they seem. Both can be seen in behavior; sometimes they are reflected
in the products themselves—in their form, content, organization, and the
thought processes evident therein. Regression seems to be caused by a number
of possible determinants, both internal and external, such as the medium, the
social context, the child's state of alertness or fatigue, comfort or stress, and
even growth itself. Regression seems sometimes to be under the child's control—
a logical, useful, healthy phenomenon. At other times, it seems to be out of his
control—a destructive, disorganizing, frightening experience. It can be evaluated only in the context of normal child development in art, the growth of any
particular individual, and the sequence of graphic and behavioral events which
precede and follow its appearance.

CHAPTER 4.

A Diagnostic Art Interview

Many psychologists who have used drawings as a respectable way of finding out where children are developmentally (Harris, 1963; Koppitz, 1968) have also found the drawing of a person and other subjects to be helpful as ways of understanding the child's personality. While large samples of drawings by normal children of different age levels were being collected in order to determine characteristic features at different stages, interest also grew in such questions as what a child's drawings can tell us about his emotional state (Buck, 1948; Machover, 1949; Schildkrout, et al., 1972) and what they can predict about his likelihood of developing a learning problem (Klepsch and Logie, 1982).

Most diagnostic drawing procedures have followed what Hammer calls "psychology's demand for standardization" (1958, p. 54), and control rather stringently the topic and/or the medium. In copying (DiLeo, 1970, 1974) and in completion tasks (Kinget, 1952), a small piece of paper and a pencil are the rule. Assigned topics, such as human figure (Machover), family (Burns, 1982; Burns and Kaufman, 1970, 1972; Hulse, 1952), animal (Levy and Levy, 1958), and house (Kerr, 1936), specify not only what may be drawn, but the medium to be used as well.

Free choice of subject matter is sometimes combined with assigned topics in procedures requiring a series of drawings, such as those reported by Schmidl-Waehner (1946) and Ulman (1965). Free choice is also more common in interviews using media other than pencil or crayon, as in Napoli's work with finger-paint (1951), or Woltmann's with clay (1964b). Rarely, however, are a range of media offered along with a free choice of subject matter, except where the workers have studied art work produced spontaneously in school or treatment settings under naturalistic and therefore noncontrollable conditions (Alschuler and Hattwick, 1947; Elkisch, 1945; Hartley, Frank, and Goldenson, 1952; Schmidl-Waehner, 1942; Bender, 1952). In research or in the clinic, where it seems important to standardize what is offered and to control extraneous influences, only a few reported investigations with art come close to offering a range of media and a free choice of subject matter (Pasto and Runkle, 1955; Schmidl-Waehner, 1946; Dewdney, Dewdney, and Metcalfe, 1967).

Yet in work with children in both educational and clinical settings, I have almost always found it diagnostically useful to allow such an open choice. When I began working at a child guidance center and was asked to develop some kind of diagnostic art interview, I originally planned for a combination of free and assigned topics, feeling that pictures of self or family would indeed be informative. What I found, however, as I began trying out art interviews with different children, was that the youngsters themselves would inevitably structure the hour in such personally syntonic and revealing ways, that any imposition of required media or topics seemed an unnecessary and distorting interference. There are indeed times when it has seemed appropriate to use assigned topics or media, as in a family art evaluation, or in some research projects. For the general purpose of getting to know about a child, however, finding out where he is, what concerns him, and how he is dealing with those concerns internally, the unstructured approach has seemed most useful in a variety of settings.

Perhaps the closest example of an analogous invitation to freely structure time and space, given a variety of materials, would be a play interview for a young child (Axline, 1947; Haworth, 1964; Moustakas, 1953). One major difference between a play session and an art interview is the latter's applicability to a broad range of ages. Just as a child at a prerepresentational level of graphic development could not draw a "person" or a "family," so a teenager is not likely to play freely with dolls or sand. Both, however, can respond appropriately to a range of art materials, each using them at his own developmental level. Perhaps, before going any further, it would be helpful to look briefly at what can happen in such an art interview.

Jamie, a fearful boy of six, came with me to the playroom, having just met me and separated easily from his mother in the lobby. As he entered, he saw an easel and a table, drawing papers in a range of sizes and colors, a sink on which were many kinds of fluid media (fingerpaint, powdered tempera in salt shakers, liquid tempera, water colors) and brushes of all shapes and sizes. On another table he saw both familiar and novel drawing tools: chalk, crayons, markers, "paintsticks," and "tempra markers." He could also see wood scraps and glue, clay, cardboard, clay tools, tape, and scissors. He was told that he could use any materials he wished, work wherever he liked, and could make whatever he wanted.

After carefully inspecting this wide array of materials, Jamie decided to use "paintsticks" (something new); and, standing at the table, he drew with care a triangular shape (in three colors) on the largest size of paper available (18 by 24 inches) (Fig. 4-1a). He then brought some small shakers of powder paint and a bowl of water to the table. Sprinkling and pounding the shakers of color, he talked about his little sister who is "bad—she kicks me!" (Fig. 4-1b). He then used creamy fingerpaint (Fig. 4-1c) and, while rhythmically smearing, told a "make-believe story" about how "the police got me one time. I cut someone's nose off." He then added in a confidential tone that his mother has a rule about cutting noses off—presumably a rule against it.

After washing his hands and joking about things going down the drain, he moved away from me and worked on the floor with wood scraps and glue, quietly and carefully constructing a tall "rocket" (Fig. 4-1d). Again choosing the largest size of white paper, he proceeded to draw with markers a picture of a spaceman who went all the way up to the moon, but who would starve, because the people

a

c

b

Fig. 4-1. (a–g) Jamie's products from his art interview, in order of their completion.

d

e

f

g

on earth had not supplied him with enough fuel to return or food to stay alive (Fig. 4-1e). After meticulously arranging the markers to match the colors on the box, he used thick chalk to draw a picture of "Hansel and Gretel" and "a dirty old witch," working quickly so he would have time to paint (Fig. 4-1f). In his version of the story, the witch first gets attacked (her face literally scribbled over), but then wins, pushing both children into the oven for having been too greedy.

Then, bringing every jar of tempera to the table, he painted a picture on large paper with a flat short brush, excitedly narrating the story as he worked (Fig. 4-1g). First came the house, then the fire, then he yelled, "Help! Help! Fire!" He explained that the "little kid" in the house is yelling for help and wants to get out. But the parents—all the other people in fact—are dead, and the child is the only one left. Jamie then proceeded to try to rescue the boy, by adding to his picture a fire engine with a hose, two firemen, and a policeman, all of whom have come to save the child. He agonized over how the story would end, concluding sadly that the boy would probably perish in the fire despite the rescue attempts. When asked how the fire had gotten started, he said that the boy himself had started it, implying that his death was in part punishment for having acted on that naughty impulse. He was deeply and passionately involved in both the telling of the story and the painting of the picture, the product barely reflecting the intense dynamism of the process.

Indeed, Jamie told a great deal in his hour, through his behavior as well as through the form and content of his products and his associations to them. I got a picture of a little boy who was under pressure (very busy), but coping constructively and productively with this potentially threatening, uncertain, unstructured situation. He demonstrated his capacity to work at an age-appropriate developmental level in his figurative drawings. He showed his ability to tolerate frustration, to sustain his efforts, and to coordinate hand and eye in a complex manner in his construction of the "rocket" out of differently sized wood scraps and glue. He stimulated some hypotheses about why he was having troubles at home and in school: that his major concerns centered around the control of his impulses (his neediness, his curiosity), and the anxiety provoked by his fantasies of the probably disastrous consequences of his anger (injury or abandonment). In the course of the hour he "loosened up" considerably in his art work from his first careful triangle, and not only became quite free, but also increasingly figurative and symbolically communicative, especially in his last three productions.

Jamie did not want to leave, but reluctantly accepted the termination of the one-hour session. What may be one of the most important features of such an art interview is that it is typically perceived as fun and nonthreatening, unlike most testing situations. Though many children spontaneously request another such session, a single one-hour art interview typically provides sufficient wealth of material that significant data is available for diagnostic decision-making.

As an introduction to outpatient treatment in a mental health clinic, there is much to be said for an activity which is a pleasant kind of cathartic (or expressive) projective technique, serving both therapeutic as well as diagnostic purposes.

Jamie had no difficulty getting started, and indeed such a response is the rule rather than the exception. In part this may be due to my confident expectation that the individual will be able to find something to work with and a way to use it, a conviction no doubt conveyed to the child. Although the choice of a topic is sometimes difficult, it has never been necessary to give even the most dependent child a specific suggestion. While most children begin by exploring visually, verbally, or manually the available materials, a few seem almost immobilized by the task of initiating activity. Most often it is possible to help them to begin by simply articulating the kinds of choices available. Fourteen-year-old Donald, for example, stood rigidly and stared at the materials for perhaps three or more tense, silent minutes. When I suggested that he might like to decide whether he preferred to draw, paint, model or, construct, he was able to make a choice and to begin an elaborate wood construction.

Only twice in hundreds of such interviews was it necessary with adolescents (and once with an adult) to suggest that the client begin with a scribble upon which to project and then draw an image. This procedure of creating and then responding to one's own ambiguous stimulus has been used by many (Cane, 1951; Naumburg, 1947, 1966; Elkisch, 1948; Winnicott, 1971b). Like the "doodles" produced on the pad which Hammer (1958, p. 562 ff.) places near his clients for use during therapy, pictorial projections on such self-made Rorschachs may indeed represent a "short-cut" to unconscious material (Elkisch, 1948, p. 254).

Melanie, age fifteen, had been reluctant to draw spontaneously, but was able to project and develop an image of a bird in her scribble (Fig. 3-9). In regarding it, she first decided that it was an eagle, but then shifted saying "I think it's a hawk or something." She continued, saying that she would either like to be the bird or take care of it, finding the latter idea a more comfortable one. She went on to explain that eagles were in danger of becoming extinct through people's neglect, and that she would like to work for the preservation of the species. These comments she then related to her own strong and largely unmet dependency needs—she was living with her brother, but was far from feeling happy or accepted in his home. Less consciously, the eagle/hawk expressed both her hunger and her oral aggression, evident also in the explosive, sullen, angry quality of her speech.

Woltmann commented that "the less structured a nonverbal activity is, the greater are the potentials for projective communication" (1964a, p. 325), and since one must agree with him that "not all children do equally well on all nonverbal projective activities," it would seem appropriate to extend the range of choices offered. Certainly individuals differ in their preferences as well as abilities, perhaps in accord with innate or learned preferred expressive modalities. Perhaps even more significant for diagnostic purposes are the differential responses and associations—tactile, kinesthetic, and visual as well as verbal—stimulated by different art media. Equally important are the inherent capacities and limitations of each medium, and how the individual deals with them. There is no doubt that "materials have behavior-propelling qualities of their own" (Ginott, 1961, p. 55), and one must not forget what Dewey called "the decisive importance of the medium . . . that different media have different potentials and are adapted to different ends." (1934, p. 226)

Getting to know a medium is like making a new acquaintance. Sometimes it starts with a circling around, a looking-at and observing for a long time without direct contact. In a group setting, there might be a close observation of someone else dialoguing with that material, as if by participating vicariously one may have a secondhand trial relationship. Eventually there may be tentative touching, fingering, handling, perhaps followed by a pulling-away, or conversely by a plunging-in. Yet another way of making contact may be impulsive, an initial decision made without hesitation to use something familiar or to try something new. The individual may go about this initial contact in any number of ways—deliberately, cautiously, casually, freely, or impulsively—always telling us through what he chooses and rejects, as well as how he proceeds, important things about himself.

Whatever the child's approach to getting to know a medium, however, that which is encountered has some qualities of its own, intrinsic to it; and central to what it evokes, demands, and stimulates in the child. In that sense, media and processes have inherent "personalities," capacities and limitations, characteristics and idiosyncrasies. For example, one can have many possible responses to the frustration of dripping paints at the easel. How the child handles this kind of problem is one index of his ability to deal with frustration in general, his "flexibility." While creating his "old-fashioned boat," for example, nine-year-old Jim had been rigidly compulsive in his choice of paint colors for successive parallel lines (Fig. 4-2). Having repeatedly but unsuccessfully tried to get me to select the next color for him, he resolved the problem by settling on a magical ritual. He would repeat the rhyme, "Ocka-bocka soda crocka, ocka-bocka-boo, Ocka-bocka soda crocka, I choose you!" each time bouncing his brush in the

Fig. 4-2. Jim's painting of a "design," later called a "boat." Tempera. Age 9.

air over each paint jar in the easel, using the color he landed on at the end of the rhyme. After painting each horizontal stripe, he would carefully remove the color just used from the easel tray. When only one color was left in the tray, he still compulsively repeated the magical rhyme. His potential for more flexible behavior, however, was demonstrated in his handling of the "accidents" occurring in the course of the process. When the purple paint dripped, for example, he said, "Whoo," grinned, paused, and then proceeded, rhythmically pressing the brush against the paper to create more purple spots at patterned intervals.

Both finger paint and clay are regressive and "messy" and have the capacity to be done and undone multiple times, providing the opportunity to smash down or remake a clay sculpture, or to make a series of images in fingerpaint, smearing over between each. One six-year-old girl established a dramatic repetitive rhythm, fingerpainting with two hands at the easel. She would rapidly draw or scratch a picture into the paint, then, just as quickly, cover it over, smearing, scratching, and clawing aggressively at the medium. Her final image was consonant with her gestures, and called "An Angry Cat, with his Big Teeth."

A picture of "Taco, the Horse" was only the last word in a long sentence of images and associations by five-year-old Rose. She had begun by using powder paint and water, angrily banging the paint container, saying "I'll show this bottle who's the boss!" Stating that she hated getting her fingers messy and really hated finger paint, she looked longingly at the moist fingerpaint jars while she mixed the powder paint and water with a large brush. Brushing on the paint, she continued to articulate her concern about cleanliness: "I'll clean up every mess I make, after each little mess, not one big mess. No wonder I never get stuff cleaned up at school. All the kids mess around and piss!"

She then went and got the creamy fingerpaint and glossy paper, vigorously smearing huge gobs of paint on the surface, expressing her ambivalence with grins and verbal ejaculations like "Yuck!" or "Ick!" Her series of done and undone pictures began with a scribble, then a bell, then a heart reworked several times, then squiggle lines called "Snakes Tangling Up," then two squiggles with faces meeting in the center, called "Two Snakes Kissing. Every day they're tangling up!" These were followed by an attempt to draw a boy into the paint, with much reworking and verbal expression of dissatisfaction: "I'm not an expert on this. Ooh! That's a bad boy!" He was quickly erased, followed by her attempt to "just make a Snake," during which she became concerned that "I gotta find the end. He can't got a tail! It looks more like a Horse." This same animal was finally developed into "Taco," who was later described in an interview about the picture as "a boy horse who is goin' to eat grass. His mom is callin' him for supper right now, but he's not comin' to eat. If he's hungry, why doesn't he come to eat? His father is gonna spank him if he doesn't come. His mother will spank him too. He's not allowed to eat any more grass. He didn't hold his temper, 'cause he hit the baby horsie! He told his mom and his mom spanked him. The others are telling his mom too, 'cause he hit his baby!"

Rose's behavior with the materials as well as her series of associations gave a wealth of condensed information in this single process and product. One could note: her attraction to and intense anxiety about the messy, regressive finger-paint, her anger with the materials, her many images of kissing dyads, her difficulty drawing the boy and the snake's tail, and her image of the boy horse (without a tail) who is hungry but doesn't want his mother's food, who is bad for wanting other food as well as for hitting his baby. Together these suggested Rose's concern with being excluded, both oedipally from the parental couple and competitively from the mother-baby dyad. Her rage and intense hunger were both seen as bad, as was her wish to be regressive and messy like the baby. It is not surprising to discover that she was the oldest of two, the younger sibling being a newborn baby boy.

Ben, age twelve, worked long and hard on a clay "statue" of a person to go on the flat slab "pedestal" he had carefully made. He first worked on the body, then added the legs, carefully building in armature-like supports for the limbs. As he added the head and neck, he began to describe the figure as no longer a boy as first indicated, but rather a "girl" of thirty-four whom you could tell was "nice" because "she wouldn't holler much." At this point, he began to discuss grownups who holler, male and female, and squeezed the body, making it taller and thinner. He then began to press it downward, then grinned and smashed it with his fist. He proceeded to secure a bowl of water, and spent the remainder of the hour experimenting with clay and water, saying it reminded him of "mud pies." He shook some powder paint on the clay, rubbed it in, and admired his curved form, saying it reminded him of "somebody being born," explaining that next week he would "make it a man this time." He liked the shape so well, however, that he decided to save it, his final statement in an hour marked by regression (Fig. 4-3).

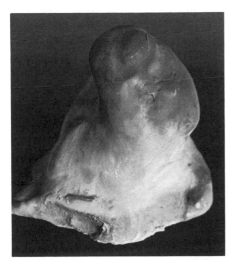

Fig. 4-3. A statue of a person being born by Ben. Clay. Age 12.

Because there are options in addition to media and topic, there are other useful diagnostic indices in such an unstructured interview, such as how the child uses the available space. With a choice of working surfaces and locations, the child may decide to stand or to sit, to be close to or far from the examiner, to look at or work with his back to the adult. Many children try out several options, and often seem more relaxed and more freely verbal when not facing the adult.

One boy sat at the table next to me as he drew his first neat, careful, somewhat stereotyped crayon scene of a farmhouse and pumpkins in a field (Fig. 4-4a). He then moved to the easel, back to me, and began to experiment with thick poster chalk, relaxing and swinging rhythmically as he explored the new, looser medium (Fig. 4-4b). His projected title for his line-swinging multicolored abstraction was "A Colorful Cloud." When asked how the cloud felt, this meek, polite boy said in a soft voice, "Well, the way the eyes are, she's pretty mad . . . at the sun, for drawing all the water out." When he next returned to the table, he animatedly created, wore, and spoke through (in significantly louder tones) an openly angry "Monster" mask (Fig. 4-4c).

a

b

Fig. 4-4. Three products from a one-hour interview, in order (a–c) of their completion. Age 9.

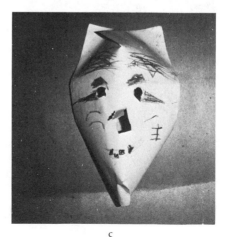

c

While some children remain at the same spot for the duration of the session, most choose different locations for different activities, the sequence varying for individuals. Daniel made his first product, a conical paper "Fire-Starter" containing feces-like balls of clay and wads of paper, standing with his back to me the whole time. He then chose to paint at the table adjacent to me. He became so self-conscious and even paranoid about the observers, whom he knew to be on the other side of the two-way mirror, that he quickly taped his painting on the mirror because, as he explained, "They could spy." When asked who he thought "they" were going to tell, he whispered "Mothers!" Although he was reassured to the contrary, he spent his remaining time covering the entire observation window with paper, drawing "bars" of steel with chalk so that "them little sneakies" couldn't see or hear what was happening in the room.

Just as it is up to him to decide what to use, and how and where to use it, so the child may choose to speak spontaneously or to work in silence. If there is little or no spontaneous verbalization by the middle of the hour, I might actively encourage the child to talk about his ideas and feelings while using the art media. He is given the option of deciding whether to be interviewed about his product directly after it is finished or at the end of the session. While some children verbalize freely and spontaneously while they work, even they can be helped further to associate to the product through an open-ended interview by the worker.

It often helps to encourage the child to gain some aesthetic and psychic "distance" by placing the product in a visually-unencumbered location—as on the easel, table, floor, or wall—where both he and the worker can view it easily and without distraction. Then the subsequent interview is best if it begins in an open-ended fashion, with questions which give maximum freedom of response to the child, such as "Can you tell me about your picture?" or "Does that have a story to go with it?" Sometimes it is helpful to ask clarifying questions about just what might be represented, the age, sex, and character of figures, or the location or activity either shown or implied in the product. Questions which help the child to relate to the representation are useful, such as "If you were in that place, where would you be?" or "If you were in that story, who would you be?" Often children spontaneously speak for their art work, especially when small three-dimensional products make it possible to use them as "puppets." Should this not occur, however, it is not too difficult to stimulate such activity by questions such as, "I wonder what that dog would say if it could talk?" or "Could you speak for your sculpture as if it were a puppet?" The job of the interviewer is to encourage the child to clarify and to extend his associations and ideas, without imposing or intruding one's own projections, a challenging but rewarding task.

Even the most silent child can speak eloquently through art, as in the case of Tommy, a timid boy of eight. He first worked on a wood scrap and glue "Hobby Horse," while sitting on the floor at the opposite end of the room with his back to me. While waiting for part of it to dry, he came back to the table and quietly squeezed and manipulated a small piece of clay, still avoiding eye contact. When asked what it might be, he first called the clay a "Rowboat," then made it into a "Snake" with which he hissed softly in a meek but playful manner. Then he formed it into a "Ball," which he dropped on the table, gradually throwing it down with increasing force, ostensibly to flatten it in order to make a "Pancake." Tommy finally poked features into the pancake, and called his tiny round creation a "Monster Face." When encouraged to use it as a puppet, he was able, with mounting volume and intensity, to express the boy monster's anger at both his mother and his sister who "bother him."

Other youngsters, like sixteen-year-old Marilyn, speak freely from the moment they enter, perhaps aided by the materials. Marilyn worked with clay, commenting frequently about the pleasure of "playing" with the clay, and about the pleasant sensory qualities of the medium, noting that the clay "feels good. It's cool. It's nice and smooth." While she worked, Marilyn spoke in depth and detail about the realities of her current confused state. She described her head of a man (Fig. 4-5) as "a guy . . . very strong, with high cheek bones. And the way I made him, he looks mean, because his eyes are so far in. His eyebrows stick out. He looks like he's looking straight at me . . . because I'm so depressed." In elaborating, she described him as telling her to "straighten up" with a "strong voice," and, when requested, spoke for the man, and answered for herself in a

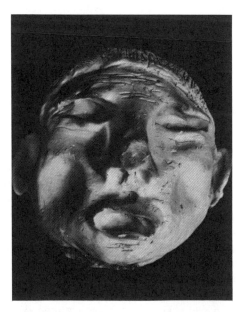

Fig. 4-5. Head of a man by Marilyn. Clay. Age 16.

powerfully moving dialogue. The character was portrayed as an idealized father-lover-saviour figure, upset not out of meanness, but out of deep concern for her welfare. If one looks at the head as a possible self-representation, the gaping eyes, mouth, and ears seem to scream out her own inner panic, anxiety, and emptiness.

Even when a child's product is nonrepresentational, it is still possible to utilize it as a stimulus for projection (as with a Rorschach). Derek's abstract wood scrap sculpture was finally seen by him as a crowd of people, yelling, each going his own separate way. When asked if he knew any group like that, he said it reminded him of his own large family with its busyness and lack of communication. Cathleen, similarly, began by saying that her painting was "just a design"; but upon looking at it longer, said it reminded her of "flowers" or maybe "suns." When asked who the flowers or suns might be if they were people, she quickly identified the smaller one as a girl and the larger one as a woman, stronger than the younger one. Asked if they reminded her of anyone, she said they were like her mother and herself, angrily asserting, "I feel like people are dominating me. I feel like everyone's dominating me."

Similarly, the multicolored fingerpainting which nine-year-old Max produced with powdered tempera paint reminded him of "something you have for lunch." At one point, while engaged in the process of making the picture, he made a mock aggressive gesture toward me with messy hands. At the end of the hour he titled the painting "Something Pretty, like a Rainbow," but went on to modify that image in a more aggressive direction: "Eruptions, Something Erupting, like a Volcano." When asked what might be erupting, he said, "Different colors of gems . . . . Jet is the black one, the blue one is lapis lazuli, the red one is ruby, the white spots are diamonds, the green ones are emeralds, and the yellow is topaz." He elaborated further, explaining that the volcano was spurting out not only beautiful jewels, but also fire and lava. He then shifted in his associations from this anal image to an oral one, saying that the multicolored picture now reminded him of a "Fruit Bowl." Pointing to the colors, he explained, "The purple would be grapes, the green could be grapes, the black could be . . . a rotten bunch of bananas, the red could be apples, and the orange could be oranges." When asked what he might like to eat, Max replied, "Apples," and when asked who was probably going to get the fruit in the bowl, he said that no one would, because his grandmother would throw the bowl in the fireplace unless he stopped her by plugging it up.

For most children there are several products emerging spontaneously from the one-hour session, the average being 2½. In a sample of 50 Subjects (Ss) ages five to seventeen, the mean number of products created by thirteen- to seventeen-year-olds (17 Ss) was 1.76, by nine to twelve-year-olds (14 Ss) 2.71, and by five-to eight-year-olds (19 Ss) 3.42. The availability of more than one item per child is helpful in countering the problems of insufficient evidence and of intra-individual variability (Kellogg, 1969, p. 191); and is in accord with the recommendation of many workers that a sample of several art products is diagnostically more reliable than one or two pieces. Certainly all of Jamie's products (Fig. 4-1) taken together present a richer, truer reflection of him than any one alone.

Sometimes the art interview is a peculiarly sensitive instrument where others are not. Evelyn, a painfully quiet adolescent of sixteen, was thought to be "mildly inhibited," but not "grossly disturbed." Her first production in the art interview, however, was a stark, split, barren purple "Tree" (Fig. 4-6a). Asked where she might like to be if she were in the picture, she said that she would like to be under the tree, next to the tree, and out in the country all alone. She said it was spring, and that the tree never had any leaves, but felt good about it. Her next drawing with fine-tipped markers was a bizarre figure called "Fred," described as "a girl of 18" (Fig. 4-6b). "Fred" was called "crazy" by the other kids, and talked to herself because it was easier than talking to others. "Fred" was "afraid they'll make fun of her if she says things . . . when she cries, they laugh. They laugh too!" Although the referring psychiatrist remarked that the girl's art looked "sicker" than anything else, it was her subsequent suicide attempt which unfortunately validated the disorganization, confusion, and withdrawal evident in her art work and associations.

Harris concluded from his review of the literature that "free drawings are more meaningful psychologically than assigned topics." (1963, p. 53) The assumption implicit in the unstructured art interview is that "we do best for any diagnostic

a   b

Fig. 4-6. (a) A tree and (b) "Fred" by Evelyn. Paint and marker. Age 16.

purpose if we give the patient 'complete freedom' to reveal his own unique reaction." (Harms, 1948, p. 243) The manner in which the child approaches and structures the hour, plus what he produces and how he does it, add up to a rich storehouse of data which may then be fitted together like the pieces of a puzzle to make diagnostic sense. Wolff has articulated the fundamental task facing a clinician following such an interview: "If we have a sequence of [products] and a sequence of associations, our analysis starts in searching for a common denominator to which each element can be related; then, by combining and interrelating all the elements with each other, we may reconstruct the sentence which was spoken by the child's inner personality in the language of pictured associations." (1946, p. 113)

CHAPTER 5.

Decoding Symbolic Messages *

In order to utilize the unstructured art interview effectively, it is important to know how to look, what to look at, what to look for, and how to make sense out of what has been observed. Children respond rapidly, perhaps unconsciously, to the invitation to reveal themselves through a creative modality. They do so in a variety of ways, sending messages at many levels and in many guises. If one wishes to understand these messages, it is necessary to determine what the child is saying by looking at both *what* he says and *how* he communicates.

Any interview provides a wealth of interpersonal behavior within the hour, from the initial meeting to the final leave-taking. Since the session probably represents a novel situation to the child, there are also all of the meanings implicit in the child's response to and ways of coping with this new, unstructured task. There are also symbolic communications inherent in the child's working process, as well as in the form and content of the product(s) which he creates. In all of these areas, there are direct as well as disguised messages being sent both verbally and nonverbally by the child, and responded to by the worker. It is in the evoking, observing, deciphering, and relating of these multiple sources of data that some of the many questions about the child may be answered.

Verbal Behavior. In the course of such an interview, some of the communications are verbal, including especially those associated with the making of a product, as well as in response to questions about it. One looks not only at what a child says, but also at the way in which he says it—the form and quality of his speech: its tempo, pitch, intensity, stress, articulation, vocal quality, and its overall "flavor" (confidential,

*The ideas and much of the wording in this section evolved from collaboration with Eleanor C. Irwin, Ph.D. Portions appear in a jointly-written paper (Irwin and Rubin, 1977).

belligerent, fearful, etc.). Spontaneous verbalizations, made especially when the child is engaged in work with media, often give a "gestalt" of feeling/ideation. For example, the child who pinches the clay and breaks off pieces while talking about how his baby sister gets in his way, may be commenting both verbally and gesturally about his negative feelings and aggressive impulses toward her.

Non-Verbal Behavior. Nonverbally the child speaks just as eloquently. His glance "talks," as he looks at the adult for permission, blame, punishment, or approval. His closeness or distance from the adult "says" something, as does the position and muscle tone of his body, his facial expressions, and his gestures. When Tommy first sat far away with his back facing me, he might have been symbolically saying any of the following: "I am afraid," "I don't want you to see what I'm doing," "I don't trust you," "I wish you weren't here." On the other hand, in moving his chair extremely close to me while he worked on his sculpture (with its many contiguous pairs of wood scraps), Jim may symbolically have been saying: "I want and need to be next to you in order to feel good."

Interaction. How the child approaches and interacts with the adult in general is often an important communication of attitudes and expectations. He may be fairly confident and unafraid to ask for help, or he may be fearful, even paralyzed in silence. Whether shy, friendly, controlling, or helpless, a useful assumption is that the child projects upon this new person the feelings and expectations related to significant others, just as he projects upon the unstructured media his wishes and concerns. One observes to see if he is suspicious or trusting, withdrawn or outgoing, fearful or comfortable, hostile or friendly, dependent or independent, and if these change in the course of the hour.

Task. How the child deals with the essentially unstructured creative task may give some indication of his usual way of coping with a new and somewhat ambiguous situation. Children respond in a variety of ways to the initial request to decide what to use and how to use it. Some respond impulsively, as did Jill, who hastily grabbed many different art materials almost at random, working in a pressured yet disorganized manner. Gary also brought a range of many different media to the working space, but chose them deliberately, then used some of each on his picture as a way of avoiding a selection among them. What is used as well as how it is used are indeed of symbolic significance.

Materials. The materials may be approached enthusiastically or gingerly, at times with a dramatic display of approach-avoidance behavior. Fingerpaint is often looked at, commented on, and verbally rejected early in the hour, only later to be used with (guilty) gusto, as did Rose. Some youngsters are "feelers," touching and sometimes tasting or smelling whatever they can, as though still learning primarily through their senses. They actively explore the materials, and often question what was purchased where and by whom, their behavior reflecting curiosity as well as a kind of sensory hunger. Some children "gobble up" all the materials in sight, grabbing large quantities, suggesting problems with impulse control as well as anxiety about whether there will be "enough."

They may also ask to take them home, as though their needs are insatiable. Once a medium is selected, the way in which it is manipulated gives important clues. Clay may be squeezed or stroked, attacked or caressed, pinched or patted, handled in many possible and always meaningful ways. Aggressive impulses may peek through, as when a child forcibly squeezes off a tiny piece of clay, or presses hard enough to break a crayon or piece of chalk.

Process. Once the child begins to work, the process that follows is as revealing as the decision-making that preceded it. As the child works, the therapist may observe his manner or style of working, the overall form of the working process itself, and the way in which this process changes over time. In the course of the hour, children reveal their individual rhythms, tempos, and energy levels. Some are consistent throughout the session, working at a steady pace. Joanna, for example, carefully executed three slowly-drawn paintings, while Jill was impulsive throughout the hour, not completing any of her carelessly done products. Most children, however, show variations within the session, usually gradually relaxing and "loosening up." As time goes on, the majority become more spontaneous and open physically, verbally, and symbolically. The relaxation seems to be stimulated by the materials themselves, as well as by the implicit permission to express feelings and fantasies freely.

Some children, however, become increasingly threatened and anxious, and seem to either "tighten up" or "let go," exploding or being "flooded" with sudden overwhelming feeling and loss of control, sometimes crossing the boundary between fantasy and reality. A rapid regression and disorganization in behavior and the form of the art products is often associated with the use of fluid and messy tactile media, especially fingerpaint and clay. Their similarity to body products may have exerted a strong regressive pull, stimulating memories and feelings associated with early childhood, as well as impulses. Fifteen-year-old Hannah, for example, playfully hit and kissed the art therapist with the clay "Loving Duck" she had just made, "acting out" the impulse with the figure rather than talking about it or using it symbolically.

Sometimes the emotional "flooding" in an art session is reflected in a noticeable regression in the form of the products, as with Sam's bizarre head (Fig. 14-6), and occasionally in a perceptible impairment of ego functions, manifested in such forms as immature speech, forgetting, or associations to products with a primary process flavor. At his diagnostic interview, Sam had revealed in his painting—a fluid, flowing, amorphous, wet watercolor—the fragility of his ego boundaries. His projections, too, had an illogical quality: "It's like a landscape, a turbulent sea with a cloudy sky. . . . A person, a man or a woman, is running into the sea holding a handbag, like it's running toward the red object, which must be another person . . . playing the violin or some instrument. . . . He's standing there as a lure, like Circe." He then commented that the lady with the handbag had at first resembled a chicken, and that another ambiguous form in the painting might be "a cat or a bird going up out of the water and then flying away."

Conversely, fearful Richard's products became tighter and smaller, as he withdrew verbally in the course of his art interview. Less often, a child's working style may seem to shift alternately between states of clarity and confusion, like Peter, who was disorganized between working periods, but was able to focus as soon as he settled down to work on a product. Whatever the child's process over time—whether more relaxed or more tense, more open or more closed, more organized or disorganized, smooth or disconnected—observing and noting the process is helpful in understanding the dynamic meaning of the emergent expressions and interactions.

Products: Form. Most approaches to understanding children through art focus on the products themselves. While there is indeed much to be learned from these wonderfully permanent records of expression, those process elements noted above seem to me to be equally eloquent clues, especially when observed in the context of what is being created. An art interview provides a unique opportunity for simultaneous multilevel communication. Some children verbalize freely about realistic or imagined concerns while working with the material in either a playful or planful way. I have often observed that using fluid media literally relaxes tension and loosens the tongue, enabling children to say more and to speak more openly than might otherwise be possible.

Indeed, an individual may "play" with a medium in a most meaningful way with no end product, as when Donald systematically trimmed, smoothed, and sliced up clay which he later identified as a "monster." Because of the conscious energy spent on the conversation, a child is often unaware of what his hands are "saying" (perhaps preconsciously), as when Sherry squashed her partly formed clay figures each time a sibling was mentioned (albeit lovingly) in her verbalization; or when Cindy made and unmade breasts and a large (pregnant?) belly on her Buddha-like figure while she talked about various forms of escape from a painful situation at home with her mother.

Formal aspects of art products (line, organization, etc.) may offer important clues to the state of the child's cognitive apparatus; indeed they are the most dependable index of developmental level, far more useful than content. Some widely-held notions about the "meanings" of certain formal qualities, however, such as shading, are questionable. It is my feeling that, like "universal" symbolic meanings, such correlations as that of excessive shading with anxiety may often be valid; that is, perhaps in many cases (maybe even the majority) there is such a correlation. However, to assume when one sees shading that it *always* indicates anxiety, or that small figures invariably indicate constriction, is to make what seems to me to be a grave error. Attempts to validate such indices in the drawings of adults have been less than successful, and are even more doubtful with children who, after all, are in a dynamic process of development (Harris, 1963; Swenson, 1968). What makes more sense to me is to be aware of such common relationships, to have them available as hypotheses, but to remain open to other possibilities. Observing the creation of a product and listening to clues of symbolic meaning (like the kinds of associated comments and nonverbal signals noted above) seems more valid.

Certainly one may look at art products in terms of their degree of organization, clarity, completeness, symmetry, movement, or color. Such qualities are helpful ways to describe and perceive, and at times diagnose. But it is equally important to utilize formal indices with caution, to approach all generalizations about invariant meanings with skepticism, and to rely heavily on what is observed and what makes sense in the context of the actual encounter with a child in art. Many resources relate color to symbolic meanings (cf. Lüscher, 1969), associating black, for example, with depression and yellow with pleasure. Yet black for a black child may signify pride, yellow may relate to fear (Axline, 1964), and color choice must always be seen in the context in which it occurs. One study indicated that preschoolers tend to select easel paint colors on the basis of their position in the easel tray, usually working from left to right (Corcoran, 1954). One of my favorite stories (supposedly true) is of the child who used only brown in her drawings. Her sophisticated mother was concerned about possible problems, and took the girl to a psychologist for testing. At the end of a comprehensive battery, the psychologist, having won the child's confidence and finding nothing wrong, asked her frankly why she always drew in brown. The girl answered quite straightforwardly: "Well, I sit in the back row, and by the time the crayon box gets to me, brown is the only color left." (Kaye, 1968, p.17).

There is no question in my mind that in most cases of deliberate color selection, there is indeed a meaning in the child's color choice. Similarly, varying with developmental level, there is significance in his degree of organization or elaboration. I am equally convinced, however, that to make blanket generalizations about such formal qualities as if they were applicable to all children is folly, and is often responsible for the all-too-common misuse, abuse, and pseudo-psychologizing about children's art on the part of educators, clinicians, and laymen. To divorce the final product from the process which created it is equally foolish. Often it is not so important to know how much space was finally filled as to know the manner in which that filling came about. Certainly this as true of content as it is of form, where the sequence of objects drawn may be at least as significant as the nature of the objects themselves.

Looking at formal aspects of children's art tells us not so much *what* is being said as *how* it is being conveyed. Jane, for example, fills her picture with carefully-executed elaboration telling us clearly, deliberately, and with detail about her concerns. Sally, on the other hand, smears and erases, includes little, and creates an ambiguous form which communicates not only her own confusion, but perhaps also her ambivalence about telling someone else.

Form and Process as Content. Sometimes form may be viewed as content, where vague and inarticulate feelings or ideas are conveyed in the form or process more than in the subject matter. For example, Mickey in all of his paintings, was continually concerned with making and staying inside the lines, suggesting worries about impulse control. Linked with his stories of aggression and punishment told while painting innocuous pictures at the easel, the implicit concern with loss of control becomes an even more probable hypothesis. Max spent a good deal of time while doing his two finger paintings in making and then "covering over" by smearing out what he had drawn into the paint, much as he "covered over" his feelings and impulses with his clever rationalization and intellectualizing. Jim moved his chair closer and closer to me during the joint making of a "city" of wood blocks in which he had insisted I participate. Making sure that his buildings were touching those already glued down by his partner, his wish for closeness and unmet dependency needs were even more apparent in his manner of making than in what he made or the story he told.

Products: Content. The "content" of an art product may be considered in terms of: (1) the verbal and non-verbal behavior occurring during the process of making the object—which may or may not be consciously related to the medium or topic; (2) the manifest or surface topic or subject matter, including abstraction; (3) the associative content in the form of the title or projected images and stories related to the product during or after its completion; and (4) the implied latent content evident in distortions (exaggerations or omissions) or symbol selection, but not necessarily alluded to verbally or in any way conscious to the maker. I find that it makes sense to assume the validity of psychic determinism—that all behavior (including expressive behavior) is not random, but has meaning, though not always easily discovered. Noting the sequence of all events in any encounter between a child and art, and assuming an associative link, can be extremely helpful in trying to decipher the meaning(s) of any particular communication. What precedes and what follows a particular creative act, like the sequence of forms within a product, is assumed to be meaningfully related in a (psycho)logical way (cf. Baruch and Miller, 1952).

In regard to "universal symbols," it is my assumption that such connections must have some degree of validity or they would not have been made in the first place. And indeed, it is striking in one's work over time to discover the frequency with which a sun seems to represent the father or a house the mother. Nevertheless, as with formal "signs," such correlations are considered as hypotheses which may or may not be confirmed by the child's own associations. Thus, extensions may often be "phallic," or containers "feminine," for indeed they do resemble those body parts in their form; but the particular meaning of a specific symbol is only available to the listener/observer with a mind genuinely open to the child's own associations (gestural, physical, verbal).

Common Themes. The "meanings" of symbols in a child's art are not so mysterious if one listens and looks with care, and assiduously avoids allowing one's own projections to obscure what the child is trying to communicate. Common themes are fairly few in number, centering around universal human and developmental concerns. Most relate to aggression or to love and needs for affection. The aggression may have an oral, biting, devouring quality, as when Tommy's clay monster head was said to eat up mothers, sisters, and others who got in its way. Or it may have an anal, explosive quality, as when Mack's fingerpainted "volcano" was said to erupt, spilling fire and lava "all over." Finally, it may have a thrusting or phallic quality, as when Lance's clay knife was to be used to "cut up" enemies. Related are themes concerning autonomy and struggles with authority, as when Evan's female figure in a painting of a man and woman was described as being the boss: "She rules the house, huh? *I'll* rule the house in *my* house!" Often in art such aggressive ideas are "implied" or "potential" rather than being directly shown, as when Mickey's painted cannon was said to be available for use, but not necessarily to be fired.

In the area of sexuality, children often express oral themes relating to nurturance, or to maintenance of physical comfort, as when Cindy's clay figure reminded her of "my mother. She's big and round and warm. . . . That gives me happiness." Conversely, themes relating to lack of protective care, rejection, or abandonment sometimes appear, as when Peggy's clay dog was kicked out and left to die by a mean aunt in her story. Pregenital wishes for a kind of symbiotic union or merger are sometimes expressed, as when Donny's two wood scrap houses came together to hug and to kiss. Sometimes what predominates is curiosity, especially visual, as when Mickey wanted to look into all the windows on Captain Hook's boat in his painting. Closely related are themes of competition, often with an older and stronger adversary (suggesting an oedipal quality), as when John's painted Mustang was to be "the winner" in a big car race. At times the major concern is with some kind of injury to the self, suggesting anxiety about bodily injury as punishment for "bad" aggressive or sexual impulses, as when Ava's deer was missing one leg, or John's painted "super plane" (in a battle with a larger one) exploded because "some guys shot him down." Older as well as younger children sometimes express confusion or ambivalence about their sexual identity, as when Sally's boat rower was alternately identified as a boy and as a girl—the figure, drawn in chalk, was also visually ambiguous. Wishes for genital sexuality in a romantic sense are sometimes expressed, as when Heather's two clay "blobs" got married and quickly produced a clay "baby."

When a particular theme is repeated several times in a child's products, then one can assume its special importance in his inner life. Thus, John created a drawing, a painting, and a scarred clay head, all of which indicated self-injury; and Donny not only glued together his two wood houses, but also projected an image onto his crayon drawing of "two people hugging," underlining the intensity of his symbiotic yearnings. It is not at all uncommon (in fact, it is usual) for a symbol to contain more than one idea; some of its power coming from the peculiar characteristic of condensation, and the possibility of multiple meanings at multiple levels. Thus, Melanie could identify with her oral-aggressive eagle's rage, as well as with its hunger for food and for care (Fig. 3-9). Pete wished both to stay *far away* from the snake he "saw" in his abstract construction, and to *be* the snake, so he could bite those who tease him, both projections referring to aggression but in different ways.

Self-Representations. Sometimes it seems quite clear that the child is representing himself in some way in his product, often creating more than one self-representation in the course of the hour. Thus, Eva, an eight-year-old girl, made a clay "boy bird, Twinkle," who is strong and lives happily with friends in a clay nest, even though the mother and father birds have left home (as did Eva's father in reality). She also created in clay "a plain old deer" with no horns and one leg missing, who said plaintively, "I'm a sloppy little thing, 'cause I don't know how to walk yet. I'm eight, too." This girl, who was indeed "damaged" both physically and psychologically, communicated how she *felt* (the deer) as well as how she *wished* to be (the bird). She then created a drawing of yet another wishful self-image: "a boy angel" who can "fly to meetings," presumably to find his lost father. On rare occasions, spontaneous inclusion of the real self occurs, as when her clay "blob" in dramatic play asked me what I thought of "poor Heather," or when Ava's painted house was said to contain "me and my pets and my friends." It is important to keep in mind that self-representations may reflect the way things realistically are, or may be projections of the child's fantasies—they may convey himself as he wishes or fears himself to be, or may represent different facets of his personality.

Degree of Disguise. More often, however, a child represents himself and his problems in more or less disguised ways, which offer symbolic protection for the expression and communication of unacceptable thoughts. Just as a child may physically "hide" behind an easel or with his back to the worker, so he may hide symbolically, going as far away from direct communication as abstraction. The careful observation of all behaviors related to the product's making, and the sensitive eliciting of associations through creative interviewing, thus become an essential aspect of understanding meanings in children's art.

In considering the nature and degree of distortion or disguise, one may look at whether the child's productions are abstract or representational; and if figurative, whether realistic or fantastic. Even within these categories, it is usually possible to assess the degree of disguise in the kind of representations of self and others employed. One can probably assume that a child who says "me" through an open self-representation or even a child of the same age and sex, is using less disguise than one whose self-representation is of a different age or sex, or seems to be an animal, a fantasy creature, or an inanimate object or abstraction. Even the latter, as noted earlier, may become a stepping-stone for projection.

Attitude toward Product. Whether the child is able, in response to questioning, to make connections between himself and his creations is an index of his capacity for introspection and reflection, of his "observing ego." Especially during the post-creative interviewing phase of the session, the child's ability to step back, look at, and reflect upon both process and product is an index of his readiness to use such an insight-oriented approach in therapeutic work. How the child feels about the product is also useful diagnostically, especially in regard to his self-image and self-esteem.

An art product, the form of which has been "given" to unstructured media by its creator, often feels like a part or extension of the self. Perhaps this is also related to the fact that in an art session, the child is symbolically "fed" with materials, which he then "digests" with his hands or tools, and which finally "emerge" as his own unique creations, analogous to body products. The sense of ownership and identification varies, but is always present, so that the child's feeling about the quality of the product reflects to some extent his feelings about himself, especially his competence. Often children express concern about their skills, as did Evan: "I'm no artist. I goofed up already. I got this picture all screwed up . . . I really goofed it, boy! It ain't too good!" Frequently, a child will speak of others whom he perceives as more skillful: "My art teacher can draw better than me. I'd like to be able to draw that well," or, "I'm a *bad* artist. I'm not as good as my brother. He's a *real* artist!" Some literally destroy what they make as they proceed, identifying it as "no good" or "messed up." Others deal with such feelings of inadequacy by defensively bragging, as did Jim, who behaved in an uncertain manner, but boasted of his efforts at school: "I got five paintings up on the wall. *She* thinks they are masterpieces. I did all five paintings in one period, and she wanted them *all* on the board!" While such expressions of concern or inadequacy are common in the majority of cases, especially with older children, the degree and intensity as well as the modifiability of these self-assessments are clues to the child's feelings of self-esteem. One looks, therefore, at whether the predominant attitude toward the products is one of shame, pride, disgust, pleasure, or ambivalence.

Adult Role.   The role of the adult in both evoking and deciphering a child's symbolic art messages is a complex, shifting, and variable one. Initially, one must set the stage both physically and psychologically, in order to make meaningful work possible. This means providing a range of art materials in a clear and pleasing arrangement which may be easily explored, and providing suitable options in working space and surface for maximal comfort. While one observes the child's way of coping with the task, one must also be ready to intervene at any point in order to facilitate the flow of material.

Such intervention may mean helping a child to get started, as described earlier, which is sometimes a simple matter of restating options or asking questions which aid in decision-making. It may mean helping a child to stop and pause in order to "get himself together," should he seem to become excessively confused or disorganized. It may mean giving explicit permission to touch or to use a medium in a particular way, or it may mean giving technical help in order for the child's apparent creative goals to be actualized. The guiding principle which makes most sense to me is: the least possible intervention for the most tolerable and authentic flow. It is especially important not to interfere or to subtly influence the child's ideas, thus contaminating the data, which is most valid when completely from the individual being assessed. If it is necessary to intervene in any way, the effect of that intervention must be kept in mind, and as soon as possible the adult should return to the role of a neutral observer. The more unobtrusive, acute, and perceptive such observation, the more information one has available for making sense out of the material.

As indicated earlier, it is always helpful to attempt some kind of "formal" interviewing around the product (and perhaps the process), and it seems to help if this is separated in time and space from the making process. Needless to say, there are exceptions to this "rule," especially with children who are so acutely self-conscious that the more casual interviewing possible during the process is the only kind which does not produce acute anxiety, blocking, and defensiveness. As a teenager once said, while we both looked at and discussed her clay "cave," it was easy for her to talk to me "because I'm not looking in your eye. If I was looking in your eye I couldn't say all this." With many, however, it helps to be open about the notion that "we might get some more ideas [about what's bothering you] if together we look some more at what you've made," and either think about what it reminds you of or tell a story about it (or some other ego-syntonic form of association). Finding a way of "tuning in" to the child's vocabulary, mental capacities, interests and concerns is a challenge to the adult attempting to enter and clarify the child's world.

Making Sense. Even when the encounter with the child is over, the diagnostician's job is far from done. One then looks over the material for pervasive themes, for patterns, and for interrelationships among all the behavioral and symbolic sources of data. Sometimes, one primary theme clearly pervades the hour, being repeated over and over, often with increasing intensity and lessening disguise. At other times, several key themes emerge, usually interrelated, one often being the wishful or feared response to the other.

The different sources of data interrelate and function as checks and balances for one another. Whether what is said is synchronous or dissynchronous with what is simultaneously done may provide important clues. A child may be tight with words, with his body, and in his drawings as well. His non-verbal behavior often underlines or confirms what he is saying symbolically and/or verbally The ultimate task for the diagnostician is to integrate and interrelate all of the many data sources into some comprehensible notions about the child.

While many kinds of information can be gleaned from an art interview, it is particularly helpful in assessing the child's major concerns and conflicts, his primary coping patterns and defense mechanisms, and his developmental level. The thematic material conveyed through products and behavior may be most relevant in identifying what he is concerned about; while themes plus disguise and self-awareness regarding his work are all helpful in defining major defenses (Freud, 1936). Certainly, his way of approaching the task and the process are clues to his manner of coping in general. His developmental level, as indicated earlier, is particularly apparent in the formal aspects of his work, for which fairly reliable norms exist (especially in drawing), as well as in the developmental aspects of his core conflicts and major defenses (Erikson, 1950; Freud, 1965).

One area perhaps less apparent in other diagnostic procedures is the child's creativity, a capacity made up of various ego functions, including the ability to regress in the service thereof. One thinks not only of originality, but also of flexibility, fluency, and the ability to create order out of unstructured media, especially to create something which conveys an emotional impact, to "give form to feeling" (Langer, 1953).

Certainly another question which is often explicit in an art interview in a treatment setting is whether or not the child can successfully use this approach in therapy, and if so, how. It is possible that it may be seen as too disorganizing or stimulating, and will therefore be rejected as an option. Or, if it is seen as desirable, it may be suggested primarily for building integrative capacities and self-esteem, rather than as a way of uncovering and establishing insight about unconscious impulses. It is my own conviction that art is flexible and broad enough, that it can be used in different ways by different children, according to their needs. In fact, it has been my experience that such individual use rarely needs to be "prescribed" by others, but will usually emerge quite naturally as the child's own tendencies toward health and integration lead him to use the art media in accord with his own capacities and needs of the moment.

Many art therapists have asked for guidance in how to organize the material from a diagnostic art interview for presentation as a report. I regret not being able to provide a single outline format, but my own experience has been that the material needs to be organized differently in different contexts, and that the only principle which makes sense is to try as best you can to answer the questions of those making the referral. In other words, while all of the aspects noted in this chapter are legitimate sources of data and ought to be taken into account in any subsequent judgment, there is no single "best" way to organize a report.

I have experimented with many structures, each designed to meet the needs of a particular setting and staff. It usually makes sense, for example, to emphasize developmental and cognitive factors in an educational situation, and to highlight psychodynamic ones in a psychiatric setting. In either case, it is important to take into account the level of sophistication of the reader(s) of your report, and to try as much as possible to use language which will have meaning for them. It is also a good idea to specify—as much as is possible—the connections between your conclusions and the data on which they are based. This not only buttresses your contentions, but also serves to educate others about what can be learned from an art interview.

CHAPTER 6.

A Picture of the Therapeutic Process

Inevitably one develops some notions about the problems that children have in growing, the problems that bring them to the attention of the adults who care for them, and sometimes to clinics for help. Almost always, they reflect conflict, some kind of battle which has not been successfully resolved. Sometimes the conflict is primarily between the child and his environment, so that work with parents or teachers may be all that is needed to help him to resume free forward movement. Frequently, however, although the child may have gotten into trouble with his world, the conflict has also become internalized.

I find it useful to think about both developmental and dynamic aspects, in trying to help, as well as to understand. Is the battle between an impulse and a prohibition? If so, is it the sort of issue common to the earliest years of life (such as nurturance or security), or is it characteristic of some later phase (such as competition or identity)? How is the child trying to cope, what kinds of defense mechanisms is he using, and how primitive or sophisticated are they? In this area, I have found the psychoanalytic perspective to be extremely helpful in conceptualizing both the developmental (Freud, 1965; Erikson, 1950) and the dynamic (Freud, 1936) aspects of conflict and the meanings of symptomatology.

I think it matters not so much which frame of reference one uses to understand children's difficulties; but I feel it is essential to have one, preferably one which is fairly consistent, and relevant for a variety of problems. Without a conceptual framework to which to relate the child's symbolic and behavioral messages in either diagnosis or treatment, one's work remains fuzzy and unfocused, without form or aim. Often one must begin in just such a state of confusion, since the signals sent by the child initially may be unclear, inconsistent, disguised, and misleading. But one hopes and works for clarification.

It is helpful in the appreciation of a Renaissance painting to have some understanding of the physical and conceptual structure within, the "underpainting," the perspective, and the iconography of the time. It is equally helpful to have some sense of what is beneath the surface in work with a child. Without such awareness, one is working "in the dark," and may do little good, perhaps even harm. While it is not essential to have a detailed understanding of development and psychodynamics in order to provide good, creative, broadly "therapeutic" art experiences for children, it is my conviction that the more one understands, the more one can help. With the very disturbed child, understanding is essential, since we all know sadly that "love is not enough" (Bettelheim, 1950).

With these notions in mind, I should like to attempt some generalizations about the therapeutic process with individuals in art, with the full awareness that there will always be exceptions to any such statements. Nevertheless, it seems to me as I review work with different children (most of whom came for weekly sessions for one to three years) that some common patterns emerge, although their individual shape and form varies considerably. At the risk of over-simplifying, I should like to hazard the notion that progress in child art therapy consists of a series of steps, most often including: testing, trusting, risking, communicating, facing, understanding, accepting, coping, and separating. These have to do with the child's relationship to the therapist as well as to his own difficulties. Like stages in art development, the separation is an artificial one, since the phases in therapy also involve overlapping, regression, and the persistent presence of all throughout the process.

Testing. Though children vary considerably in how readily they relate to a new adult, there is always some degree of uncertainty and testing in the early stages of the relationship. Even the most needy child, though "hungry" for the adult's attention and approval, is likely, because of past disappointments, to have trouble believing in the dependability of a new adult. During this initial period of uncertainty, some testing often occurs, and takes many forms, including demands for extra-therapeutic supplies or attention and literal testing of the limits of time, space, or behavior in the therapy hour.

What is vital during this phase is that the adult be firm about limits, and yet convey the clear and consistent message that within these, he is totally available to the child. It is tempting to try to build a "good" relationship by giving, by being lenient, by overlooking mild limit-breaking, but such a stance does not build security. While it may be immediately gratifying, it is ultimately threatening to the child, who wants and needs a secure framework in order to feel free to expose and to take risks.

Adults have different reasons for going into service professions, and a not-uncommon motivation is one's own concerns about nurturance. It is not surprising, therefore, that one of the most frequent problems for the inexperienced is setting limits and withholding gratification of the child's urgent demands. It is understandable that one might identify with the hurt and needy child, and in so doing feel compelled to give. It is a hard lesson to learn, but an essential one, that such behavior in the long run does not promote a secure therapeutic alliance, and that one must be firm (albeit friendly) from the start. Understanding the reasons for such a stance helps, and I have no question of its validity.

In the early sessions in which one wants the child to develop trust and a generally positive relationship with the therapist, it is important to be not only consistent but also nonthreatening. The time for interpretations or even confrontations may come later; the early period is a time for making the situation as pleasant as possible for the child. It is a time for helping him to learn what is expected of him in both doing and reflecting upon his art work, for initiating him into the rules of this particular "game." Some people think this means becoming the child's "pal," and though there may be some few cases in which this is the only possible way to achieve a working alliance, it is to be avoided in general. Indeed, one can be friendly without being familiar, warm without being effusive, and interested without being either nosy or chummy.

To be open about one's own life-realities is generally not a good idea. Some think that is what is meant by being "authentic," but I understand authenticity to mean honesty, integrity, genuineness with another human being, not providing him with details about one's own feelings, fantasies, and private life. It is infinitely more fruitful to respond to a child's questions about oneself, by wondering just what he thinks the answers might be. Though this might be frustrating, it should be explained that it will help you to help him more if you know his ideas and fantasies (the stimuli for the questions) than if you answer them directly. Needless to say, one need not be rigid, and sometimes it makes therapeutic sense to convey some information after exploring the child's fantasies. If that is done, however, it must be done with a full awareness of the possible and probable impact on the child, and an alertness to the effects on the child and the treatment of answering any personal inquiry.

Trusting. Developing a feeling of trust and confidence takes different periods of time for different children, and one must be patient. If the therapist can be clear and consistent about all facets of the encounter, from time and rules to materials, space, and mode of interaction, this stability will help to provide a clear and secure "framework" for further work. Thus, it matters that one meets with the child at a consistent place and time, that one has the same supplies available in the same locations, and that one handles routine transactions (greeting, cleaning up, leaving) in a predictable manner. There is enough uncertainty and anxiety in a troubled child; nothing can be gained by increasing these through inconsistent behavior on the part of the adult.

Protecting the child from unnecessary intrusions and betrayals is also essential. Clearly, this means making sure that the space and time to be used are kept free from disruption. It also means being clear and open about the purpose of note-taking if that occurs, while also exploring the child's fears and fantasies concerning who might see the notes. Obviously, it is both unprofessional and unethical to discuss the child's confidences with anyone not legitimately involved in the treatment, and one must never disclose "private" information to parents, schools, or others related to the child, without involving him openly in such an act. While it may not be easy for a child to believe that the therapist will really treat his communications as private, it is essential to convey this protective framework to the youngster, at the same time exploring whatever distrust and concern he may feel. If one wishes to have an interview observed for any reason, such as training of students, it is only ethical to obtain the child's consent, in spite of the fact that it might be possible here as elsewhere to do so without his awareness. It is difficult enough for a child to risk openness about his innermost fears and fantasies under the most ideal conditions; it is unfair and dishonest to expect him to do so, if the therapist is not behaving with him according to the highest standards of personal and professional integrity.

The development of trust is a gradual process, and like any other kind of growth can regress under stress. It may become apparent in the child's behavior and interaction with the adult in general, and is especially obvious as the verbal communications become more confidential. It is also apparent in the child's symbolic communications, as these move from more disguised and defensive ones to more open and expressive ones.

Carla, a youngster frightened by vivid nightmares, required a long time and some active help from the therapist before she was able to risk drawing the monsters of her scary dreams (Fig. 6-1). Once she began, however, she drew them over and over again, in different forms and in different media. At one point, she would cut out her monster-drawings and place them inside of cut-paper "cages" she had carefully constructed. And for two weeks, the monsters in their cages were placed in my desk drawers, which I was told should be locked so that they couldn't escape. As she became more familiar and comfortable with these images, it became possible for her to extend the fantasy in dramatic play.

One week, she spontaneously used soap crayons and painted my face as the monster, asking me to pretend to attack her in a make-believe drama. The following week, she reversed roles and became herself the feared monster, attacking me as the frightened child. It was during this period of work that the nightmares ceased, never to reappear in the course of her therapy. She went on to repeat and work through in her drawings and dramas, and was thereby able to risk confrontation of the images, and then to risk confronting the aggression as her own, as well as belonging to others.

Risking.   The process of risking disclosure of previously buried thoughts and feelings, hidden even from the child himself, is inevitably a slow one, even when it at first seems otherwise. Laura relaxed rapidly at first, despite years of having been "closed up" according to parents and teachers. Her creation in the first session was an elaborate but rigid wooden robot (probably a self-representation), and the story was told with much hesitation and discomfort. In the second session, however, she relaxed after using some fingerpaint, and produced a "flood" of fantasy material based on two of her pictures. The stories poured out of her, as if a dam had been forced open, suggesting intense pressure for release. Following this open meeting, she withdrew dramatically, coming in and working with materials silently, resisting interviewing about the products, and even finding the art creation itself difficult for several weeks. It was many months, with forward and backward movement over time, before she could even hesitantly convey the confused fantasy world which had "burst forth" so prematurely in that early hour.

Communicating.   To establish trust and enable a child to risk facing the fears within, it is necessary to find ways of communicating which are meaningful for both parties. It may take time, and even some trial and error, to discover the words and images and frames of reference which "make sense" to a particular child. While this is especially difficult with nonverbal, retarded, or psychotic youngsters, it is an essential condition for effective work with all children. Generally one finds a combination of verbal and nonverbal ways of relating and communicating. They may change over time with any one youngster, requiring constant alertness. Finding an appropriate and workable "wavelength" on which to communicate is a challenge, and may require a good bit of risk-taking and creativity on the part of the therapist, but it is clear that even with a high level of trust, little work can get done without effective communication.

Fig. 6-1. Carla's nightmare monster. Scribble drawing, marker. Age 8.

Communicating with one who cannot or will not speak is an especially arduous task, and one where the articulation of themes in art becomes an obvious asset. Jeremy, age seven, was an elective mute—a child who was capable of speech but chose not to speak to all adults and most children. His early drawings were clearly meant as communications with little disguise of his pressing concerns. Jeremy's pictures are a marvelous example of the articulation-power inherent in art when a child wants badly to send symbolic messages. A typical one shows family members involved in mutual battles (Fig. 6-2). First he drew the two roads on either side, with a chasm filled with blue water in between. A car, identified as his mommy's, was drawn over the water, then a triangular rock which has caused the car to "trip." He was uncertain whether it would drown or make it over to the other side of the water (reflecting his ambivalence and anxiety regarding aggressive feelings toward mother). He then drew a car on the edge of the other cliff, then a helicopter shooting at it, then an airplane shooting at it (upper left), and finally a rescue car at the left shooting back at the helicopter. His younger sister was said to be in the car on the edge, his father in the helicopter, and his older brother in the rescue car on the left. He, Jeremy, was in the plane not involved in the battle (middle left). This information was conveyed by pointing at himself and nodding his head yes or no in response to my questions. Sometimes I was unable to understand him, and he

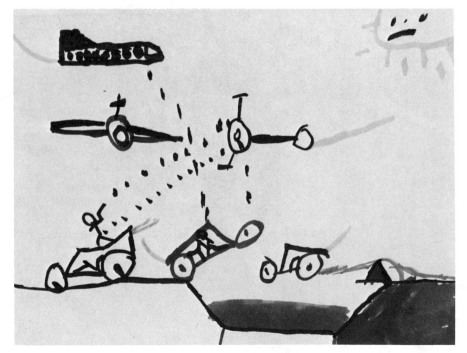

Fig. 6-2. Jeremy's drawing of battles and action. Marker. Age 7.

would write words in order to communicate. It is clear that, despite his unwillingness to talk, Jeremy was quite eager to convey messages, and was able to do so very
dramatically through his action-filled story pictures and accompanying gestures.

Facing. Probably the hardest part of all therapeutic work with children is the
time when the child has not only communicated something risky, but is then ready
(albeit ambivalently) to face that information. It was one thing for Tommy to tell
a story about a snake whose eyes were going bad because he was too greedy; it was
quite another for him to relate that story to himself and his progressive blindness.

It is not always necessary to insist on a confrontation of such issues. For some,
especially the very young and not too disturbed, it seems possible at times to "play
it out," for most communications to remain at a symbolic level. Lori was able to
work through her anger at her mother and father, as well as her guilt and fears
about their divorce, in her art, with only rare spontaneous references to herself
and her own feelings. In one session, for example, this four-and-a-half-year-old
girl identified her fingerpainted creature first as "a Monster," then as "a four-and-a-
half-year-old boy playing outside by himself." She explained that his older brother
had gone in to eat, but he didn't go in because "he doesn't like his mother's food."
When asked why that was so, she replied, "He hates her." I noted that he must
be awful mad about something, so mad that he wouldn't let her feed him. She
grinned and then asked if it was okay to be angry. I said it certainly was okay to be
mad, but wondered if the boy would be getting hungry soon, to which she jauntily
replied, "Then he'll go in and eat!"

Barry, on the other hand, could have gone on playing out dramas of injury,
abandonment, and wishful fantasies forever, it seemed, with little change in his
disruptive behavior at home and in school. For him it was necessary to go beyond
a reflective or nondirective approach to a more interpretive one, in order to help
his ego gain cognitive as well as affective understanding of his feelings and their
consequences. It was long, hard work, six years in fact, and encountered many
periods of quiet as well as stormy resistance, but I think that without such connections, he would have continued to deny his blindness in private fantasy play, to
act out his aggression volcanically in his environment, and to miss out substan-
tially on the learning and growing opportunities available to him.

It is not easy to decide in advance when a child may need to do more than to gain
integration through a sublimated expression in order to get well. When art therapy
is adjunctive to other forms of psychotherapy, this is certainly a sufficient goal.
But art therapists are often asked to work independently, especially with children
who can relate in no other way. When art is the sole mode of treatment, then art
alone may not be enough, and it becomes essential to expand the therapy both in
depth and breadth—sometimes into other forms of communication, like drama,
movement, music, and poetry. This has occurred spontaneously so often in my own
work that I am convinced it is a natural thing for children to search for congenial
forms of expression, and unnatural to restrict them to any one creative modality.
Had Carla stopped at the representation and locking up of her nightmare monsters,

I think she would not have been so well able to feel and then understand how much of the aggression she feared was her own (projected). By taking the role of the monster in a spontaneous drama, she was able to experience her own angry feelings, and later to see how those angry monsters in the dreams and drawings might not only be scary grownups, but might also be scary angry wishes in herself. Such experiences suggest that even though an art therapist's primary tool is art, it is important to be able to comfortably utilize other expressive modalities, including words.

Facing fearful fantasies or feelings may be easier in some forms than in others. All of the arts offer some distance and disguise, which may be left undisturbed, if a reflective approach seems to enable the child to move along both in and out of therapy. Where it is necessary to intervene more actively, to help the child see connections between his expressions and himself, then the facing process may be a painful one, often taking much time, with many attempts to avoid or resist on the part of the child. Understanding and accepting these defensive maneuvers and respecting the child's need to protect himself are just as important as accepting the bizarre and "bad" fantasies against which they defend. My general feeling is that defenses should be left alone unless it seems necessary to undo them, usually to free the child because they are crippling, in order to help him achieve awareness and (ultimately) mastery of some disabling conflict.

The facing of previously unconscious—and therefore unacceptable—wishes and thoughts is difficult for anyone, child or adult. It is not too difficult to get at them symbolically. It is much harder, but sometimes necessary, to get at them directly. If done with caution, with the general cooperation (trust) of the child (despite many inevitable moments of anger and anxiety), it can be hard work well done, and a sense of accomplishment can be felt jointly, even with a young child. The degree of understanding of which the child is capable, will of course vary according to his age and intellectual endowment. What is needed is enough to help him to integrate this newfound awareness, and to move on to more adaptive ways of thinking, feeling, and behaving, through changes inside himself.

Understanding. It takes a long time, from the first glimmer of hard-to-handle conflicted aspects of the self, to reach the point at which the child can accept, without undue anxiety, these previously-hidden "secrets." Carla was in therapy for a full year following her first drawing of her nightmare-monster (Fig. 6-1). Toward the end of our work, the focus of her concerns had shifted to issues of nurturance, identity, and separation, the latter intensified when termination was decided upon. It was not easy for this little girl, the oldest of four children with an immature, emotionally needy mother and an unavailable father, to give up her special relationship with her therapist. Given six months and the opportunity to set the final date herself, she managed to work through the rage and hurt she felt. In the course of feeling anger at me for abandoning her (kicking her out), she was frequently reminded of her early angry monster dreams, drawings, and dramas.

For her last project she decided that she would make a film about "How Monsters Are Really Make-Believe," so that I could show it to other children who had fears such as hers. Using a super 8 mm. camera, tripod, light, and simple animation techniques (cf. Fig. 6-3), Carla cut out monster heads which were moved around the walls (magically), finally scaring a little girl (Carla) who was at the sink. After this, the girl comes to see me, we return to look at the heads together, and find they have disappeared. It was a creative and effective way for Carla to "review" the main problem for which she had come, to remind herself of what she had learned, and to deal with her envy of future patients through transforming her rage into a wish to provide understanding for them (the film). While she no longer had the nightmares, and had not for over a year, it had taken her some time to integrate her slowly dawning awareness, understanding, and acceptance of her own aggressive impulses. This "working through" process is often accomplished through

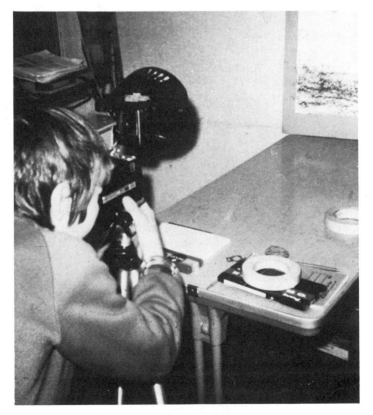

Fig. 6-3. Donny filming a drawing-in-progress for animation.

repetitive confrontations with the feared idea, through drawing or playing out a loaded theme, often with a limited amount of modification. While this process may seem like a "stuck" one to the therapist, it is a necessary one for the child, who may be going through something analogous to a "desensitization" process, gradually becoming more and more comfortable with previously-unacceptable ideas and feelings.

Accepting.   Barry, a totally blind boy, came to the clinic on a weekly basis for almost a full six years. He was a complex boy with long-standing and complicated problems. For one period lasting almost a year, he played and replayed scenes of doctor and patient, dentist and patient, nurse and patient, in settings labelled first "the clinic," then "doctor's office," and finally "hospital." He took both roles, and eventually involved me as mother, doctor, even child. He played himself at his then-age of ten and at earlier ages, sometimes saying the patient was someone else. He created a series of doctors, some good and kind, some harsh and insensitive, some permissive, some demanding.

While there was variation in the play (which was usually stimulated and facilitated by water, cotton, or clay tools), there was much repetition. Yet it is not surprising that Barry, who had been hospitalized over fifty times before he was seven, should have needed to master these traumatic experiences by replaying them (Erikson, 1950). Nor is it surprising that he not only needed to relive the events, but also to relieve the rage by taking the active role, when in reality he had been passive and helpless. A baby sister of whom he had been jealous had died of cystic fibrosis shortly before the final removal of his eyes at age five. It seemed as if his repeated dramatizations around doctors and, finally, operations, were related not only to the trauma itself, but also to his unconscious guilt for the death of his sister, presumably punished by the removal of his eyes. He needed to accept both his "badness" (anger) and his blindness.

Coping.   Pete began to see himself as possibly able to function independently of me, then of his mother, after two years in weekly individual treatment. But it took him another two to consolidate this gain in his self-image and self-esteem. Only gradually was he able to try out at school and with peers a more assertive self, and then to do so at home with his parents with much hesitancy. For him, separating from the clinic after four years was as anxiety-ridden as the development of a self independent from that of his mother. He vacillated for months, ambivalent about both coming and leaving. Following a summer in which he "took a break" during school vacation time (three months) with just a few phone calls to "touch base," he returned to "wrap up" his work in a most unusual way. He spent the next four months writing a story, dictating it to me each week (finding his own typing too slow for his ideas), rereading before beginning the following week.

The story entitled "What Will We Do?" concerned two boys who ran away from home, each representing a facet of Pete himself. One was bold and daring, the other cautious and fearful; in a sense they represented what had been dominant in the old Pete, and what was wished for and nascent in the new adolescent Pete. The story with many ups and downs. could be seen as a symbolic review of his own treatment, including a long and involved trip into a well (his unconscious?) and the meeting of strange, messy creatures therein.

At the end of the "book," he announced that he was ready to end, and was able to follow through successfully on that decision. He provided himself with some "transitional objects" (Winnicott, 1971a) by taking some photographs of his art work, of the office, and of me, and carrying the prints proudly home with him when he left. Although moderately retarded and minimally brain-damaged, he had improved significantly in his school work, peer relationships, and previous symptomatology (nightmares and suicide attempts). Perhaps because of his retardation, perhaps because his ego was less strong and had real deficits (his mother was herself a seriously disturbed woman), it took him a long time after achieving the ability to risk and to face things, to accept them enough to be able to cope effectively. His understanding was never deep or full, but was sufficient. This was evident in the story, which reflected some comprehension on his part of relationships between feelings, ideas, and actions, as well as between fantasy and reality.

Separating. Pete, in coping with the termination of a four-year art therapy process, was for much of that time, working on and working through issues related to separation. At the end of any process of therapy—whether mutually arranged or unilaterally imposed, after six weeks, six months, or six years—the child inevitably has mixed feelings about ending a relationship which has become important to him. As with many earlier separations, the step out of the clinic represents growth and progress, but it also entails loss and accompanying feelings. While there is often decreasing dependency on the therapist and increasing competition of other interests ("Why do I have to come on such a nice day? I'd rather play ball!"), there is still usually some anger at the adult who is realistically "in charge," whatever attempts may have been made to involve the child in the process of setting the termination date.

Lori, age five, reminded me that it was her last day, and announced at the beginning of her session that she intended to use some of everything in the room. Accidentally spilling some paint, she played at being a bossy mother while we both sponged it up, saying "Do what I say! Don't step in this while it's wet!" But she stopped abruptly, said she didn't want to make believe that day, and then wondered if I had hidden the ice pick used to open clogged paint shaker holes. When she found it in its usual place, she pantomimed stabbing me with it, saying that she wasn't really going to kill me, but was only making believe. She put on her soap crayon "makeup," looking in the observation mirror as in the past, and commanded me imperiously not to watch: "If you look, I'm going out the door!" When I suggested that perhaps she would rather go out the door by herself then have me tell her it was time to leave on the last day, she nodded and said, "I know this is the last day, and I'll cry, and I said I'll miss you and Dr. L." (whom she also saw weekly).

Going on with her fantasy of walking out on me, she said "I'm gonna leave here, and I'm gonna drive my own car, and leave my mommy. But I might *lost* myself.

Then I might walk at your place cryin, 'I lost myself!' " She then wondered if I might buy her play clothes for her birthday, and if we could exchange telephone numbers. She created a huge, rather sloppy painting, and then said her farewell message on the tape recorder: "Goodbye. I'm not gonna see you no more, but I'm gonna cry if I don't see you no more." I told her that I would miss seeing her too, and she went on "Well, see, if I don't see you no more, I might cry. I wanna hear myself talk." After listening to her speech on the tape recorder, a faint smile occasionally brightening her sad face, she said we should kiss goodbye, which we did. She was thus able in her last session not only to express her anger, sadness, and sense of abandonment, but also her affection and her growing autonomy.

Chip was twice Lori's age when it came time to say goodbye, and had come to the clinic for perhaps three times as many sessions over a two-year period. Arranging for alternate weeks during the last two months seemed to help in his "weaning" process, but the same ambivalent mixture of anger, sadness, and pride was apparent. A month and a half before the last session, he drew with chalk a violently scribbled mass which he called "The Tornado." He said that a mighty tornado had whipped everyone, including powerful King Kong, and that only Godzilla remained in the world. "Then something landed on his head, and he said,'I'm goin' down.' " His second agitated chalk scribble was called "Fire." In the middle of the fire he said there was a devil, a woman. With a grin, he said, "I was her boyfriend once." He had indeed seen me at one point as his girlfriend-mother, and it is likely that the tornado and the fire represented not only what I was doing to him by sending him away, but also how he was feeling towards me.

The following week he asked to look at the animated films he had made and then wanted to invite his mother in for the remaining half hour. They worked at either end of a table, each with clay. He made an open container similar to a closed "secret message box" he had made in his first session, while she modelled "a woman about to have a baby," lying flat on her back with her arms wide open. Each seemed more open to the other than in previous joint sessions, and perhaps his mother was symbolically expressing her wish that Chip be "reborn" through his therapy.

In his final session, he literally reviewed his treatment pictorially, by drawing a "time line." On the left he put the number six, the age he was when his troubles began, then a picture of his parents with a little figure in between (himself) and the word "Marryed" above. To the right he drew a judge in a courtroom, saying it represented him going to have his name changed, which happened when his stepfather adopted him. Describing it, he made a transparent oedipal slip: "We were married—I mean mom and dad, and then I went into court for my name change. Then there is mean Dr. S. with his knife and fork doing that operation on me." (He had undergone an operation for an undescended testicle, which seemed to have intensified his castration anxiety.) The final image was of a building: "And then I went to school—first, second, third, and fourth grade. Now I'm going into fifth. Here's a picture of my school with its smoke stack. This is white." At this point in his narration, he added a door to the school building, implying that he could now comfortably leave. He entitled the picture "The Impossible Dream," suggesting perhaps that the clinic was a place to have wishful dreams, but maybe also to confront fearful ones. He went on to review his therapy more explicitly: "At the beginning, I was really worried about my mother and father. Sometimes I got furious at her, like I am today, but now I can love her too. I really was worried that they didn't care about me, but now I know they do." His mother, interestingly, had said that she perceived their therapy as having enabled each family member to like himself and the others more.

Indeed, one might think of the entire process of therapy through art as involving separating—separating fact from fancy, reality from fantasy, and in a deeper sense, separating a child from the conflicts that have caused him unhappiness. In the course of such work, a strong attachment to the therapist is formed, in which the child can trust and then "open up," and through which, symbolically, some of the conflicted issues can be made apparent and resolved ("transference"). In the same way that unconscious material is "projected" onto unstructured media, so past expectations and unresolved interpersonal issues are "projected" onto the neutral therapist. By accepting and trying to understand distorted transference reactions, just as one tries to understand symbolic representations, one gets a sense of the child's inner world. The "separating" from the parent-therapist in the transference, toward whom the child has experienced strong emotional reactions, takes place along with separating from the real person-therapist, who has accepted the child and helped him to create a more contented self through art.

CHAPTER 7.

Some Case Studies

While the process of therapy in and through art generally follows the steps outlined in the preceding chapter, the precise shape and form is always peculiar, idiosyncratic, and one of the great fascinations of such work. While general goals and hypotheses about the troubles of a child can be thought out in advance, one can only guess at the particular way in which any youngster will use the opportunity for help. As with growth in general, the rhythm of growth and change in treatment varies considerably and cannot usually be rushed. One must expect not only forward, but backward movement as well; not only openness, but also retreat and withdrawal. Sometimes things go smoothly overall, and sometimes they are rocky from the very beginning; generally, there is some of each. When things get so rocky or murky that the therapist feels at an impasse, it is extremely helpful to seek consultation, no matter how many years of experience one may have under one's professional belt. Indeed, it may be an index of maturity that one is able to perceive difficulties, acknowledge them, and even to transfer the case if that seems the best solution after exploring the roots of the problem.

The degree of success or failure with any particular child is hard, if not impossible, to quantify. When treatment terminates through mutual agreement, one hopes that the child will then be able to go on growing and coping on his own, not that all problems will be gone forever. I was once invited to participate on a panel about "learning from failures in art therapy." I was grateful, for it gave me an opportunity to review for myself as well as for others, a case which had felt most painful to me at its closure and during most of the work. In reviewing I not only relived the experience, but was able to see, for the first time, that perhaps the failure had not been a total one after all. Since we tend to hear and read mostly about successes, I think it would be helpful to look at "failures" as well, as in the case of Ellen.

Ellen

What was perhaps most poignant about this failed encounter of two human beings was that it began with a promise of progress, and only gradually became increasingly and consistently painful. We started out, this almost-thirteen elective mute and I, on what seemed like a hopeful note. I knew from the record that in her two initial contacts at the clinic, she had not only refused to come into the building, but had turned her silent back on the psychiatrist who tried to interview her in a parked car. I knew that at the Children's Hospital where she had been sent for observation for the next month, she had talked to no one, had refused to return home upon discharge, and had finally been placed with her grandmother, one of the few people with whom she was still speaking.

I knew that her hurt, anger, and withdrawal were longstanding, that she had not spoken to those closest to her for almost two years—first her deaf older sister, then her intelligent but alcoholic mother, then her father, and most recently her best friends. Though this brilliant girl was still communicating verbally with a few friends, her four younger siblings, and her grandmother, the door to her world had been closed on her parents and sister for a very long time.

Knowing her history of rejecting therapists, I was pleasantly surprised when she willingly separated from her grandmother and accompanied me to the office. I was further delighted when she picked up some clay, manipulated it while standing with her back to me, then sat down at the end of the table facing me. She proceeded to draw a series of carefully elaborated, tight, complex designs. Between the second and third drawings, she moved her chair a little closer to mine, although she remained tense and silent throughout.

Our first crisis came unexpectedly, when it was time to end. As she picked up her drawings, I asked if she would leave them at the clinic—indicating that she, like the other individuals I see, could have a shelf on which to safely store her creations. (I find it useful to save the work for the duration of the therapy, and most children acquiesce when assured that they can have back anything they want once therapy is finished. When a child is determined to take something home, I ask if I can keep it for a week, in order to make a slide, or—if the urgency is too great—if we can xerox a copy.) In response to my request, Ellen angrily blurted out her first and only words: "You didn't *tell* me!" Then, still visibly upset, she refused the idea of a photocopy and departed, clutching her drawings tightly to her.

So I was relieved when, the following week and thereafter, she not only did not indicate any desire to take her art work home, but willingly came, and moved within the next hour from a tight checkerboard design, to a shield, to more figurative work—first a lighthouse on a cliff over water, then a pitcher with a cocktail glass, and finally, a looser, more colorful tree with a warming sun above (Fig. 7-1). Softly, but clearly, she responded with short phrases or single words to my questions about the pictures, indicating that she would be swimming in the water near the lighthouse far from her home, but if given the choice, she'd prefer to be near the sun-drenched tree. The pitcher and glass were said to contain tea she would have made, but would not drink. A guitar drawn last on the other side of the paper, was said to remind her of a friend who plays one. There was a stylistic movement from tightness to somewhat greater freedom, and a symbolic sequence from isolation to implied possibilities for warmth as well as relationship. These, along with her willingness to answer my questions, albeit minimally, filled me with hope for the future of our work together.

And so it went the following week, when, although turning her back to me as she worked, she produced first a painting of a girl playing ball near the street, then a headless figure on the other side to which a head was quickly added by taping a torn corner of the paper above the neck. Despite the continued rigidity and tension of her posture and drawing movements, she was indeed using more fluid and more messy media (tempera paint and chalk) than the thin markers she had chosen previously. She was even willing, upon my suggestion, to engage in a dyadic drawing, in which I, with a red marker (to differentiate our lines), attempted to mirror her rhythm and movements and to echo her swirly blue shapes. Though she shook her head negatively about discussing the joint process, she had been intensely involved throughout, and there was a strong feeling of communion.

Fig. 7-1. Ellen's drawing from the second session. Marker. Age 13.

The following week I drew a picture of her at work, in an attempt to continue the nonverbal pictorial dialogue of the preceding session. Meanwhile, she drew with markers a girl in brightly-colored clothes, then a fat balding man on a stage, with a road in the distance (Fig. 7-2). Still responding softly to questions, she identified the girl as young, going shopping, and not wanting to get married. The man was said to be about forty, carrying an oil can because his car was stalled on the road behind him. She said he was sad, and that he would speak loudly if he were to talk. On the other side of the paper, she drew in the corner a drag race with three differently-shaped cars (Fig. 7-3). She would be driving the middle one, but did not know if she would win.

Fig. 7-2. A girl and a man on the stage with a stalled car by Ellen.

Fig. 7-3. A drag race by Ellen.

The following session was the last prior to an interruption for my vacation, which was to last for three weeks. Although she was still quiet, and sat with her back at an angle to me, Ellen for the first time filled up a picture space with a single and colorful representation, a stylized female bird (Fig. 7-4). The bird was later identified as mean, with not too many girlfriends, married to a nice kid who's ugly but rich, and who has gone to the store to buy provisions. This was followed by a scene of two swans swimming in the sea by a cliff (Fig. 7-5), freer and warmer than her first one. And finally, a cartoonish pirate with eyepatch, whom she later described as weak now, having formerly been strong, but injured in a sword fight because of his big head (Fig. 7-6).

Fig. 7-4. A mean female bird by Ellen.

Fig. 7-5. Two swans by Ellen.

Fig. 7-6. Ellen's drawing of a pirate.

Fig. 7-7. Ellen's first drawing after a six-week break.

The interruption became a very long six weeks, due to scheduling problems in the Fall. It seems to me, in retrospect, that the break may have been more damaging than at first it seemed. Nevertheless, the first session in the Fall did not seem to be any cause for alarm. Beginning with several tight, geometric, linear designs, she continued on the same paper with a fishbowl, a horse's head, then a tree, then a geometric flower pot, and finally the three creatures in the center, the last with an angry tongue sticking out of a twisted mouth (Fig. 7-7). I noted with relief that her posture while drawing these latter images seemed more relaxed. She later told me that all three were female, the one on the left older, the one in the middle younger, and the one on the right very angry. Asked who she might be in the drawing, she pointed to the fish in the bowl, and then to the horse.

Triumphant at the emergence of aggressive affect and provocative symbolism, I looked forward confidently to progress in the approaching months. Only gradually did I realize that we were grinding to a halt. At her next session Ellen drew, carefully and with absorption, an enlargement of the strange cephalopod of the preceding week (Fig. 7-8). I used watercolors, in an attempt to echo the expression of feelings

Fig. 7-8. Ellen's first enlargement of her "creature" one week later.

as well as to stimulate the use of other media, to draw an ambiguously sad-angry girl with long nose and prominent eyes, similar to but different from Ellen's creature. She called hers a girl who was both happy and sad and said, about the one I had drawn, that the girl was "sick because she's going to the doctor [who will make her] worse and sicker." She was clearly afraid of this process she had begun, but how frightened I did not yet realize.

Despite my most cautious and conscientious efforts to empathize with her anxieties, to accept whatever she was capable of doing, the process from then on was like a needle stuck. Once in a while, more often in the early months, there would be variations on her single theme—the face divided, the use of different colors, a different treatment of the hair or a shell around the multiply-determined body-face. But Ellen's back turned more and more to me, and though I occasionally drew, to contain my own anxiety and frustration as much as anything else, she had tightly shut the door on me. The soft verbalizations to questions disappeared, head-nodding followed for a while, and then questions, which felt too much like tooth-pulling to me, were discontinued in favor of silence and my wondering, thinking aloud about what was going on (along with an unspoken hope that she would initiate contact if not pressed).

As the same figure continued to be drawn week after week, and Ellen seemed more and more frozen, I felt more and more helpless—fully a failure where once I had hoped to be a savior. Week after week—through October, November and the succeeding winter months—the same tight, silent girl came in, worked for a full hour on her generally-same drawing with only minor variations, and left when I indicated that the time was up (Fig. 7-9).

I sought consultation from everyone and anyone. They were full of ideas, as was I, about the possible symbolic meanings of her repetitive pictorial statement and were equally full of ideas about how to help her to give up her defensive withdrawal. Some suggested being totally quiet, some suggested playing music. Both were tried, for about a month each, with little observable effect. Frequently I felt like reaching out and touching this frozen girl, yet always stopped short. In response to suggestions that I interpret directly and openly, all else having failed, I stepped up my comments about mid-February, and it did seem that she was listening, though she did not respond overtly.

In mid-March, though her therapy-hour behavior and drawing had not changed, her grandmother brought in a book Ellen had made, called "From Isolation to Involvement." This volume, with photographs and poetic text, seemed a statement of an intention on her part to move back toward relating to others. Many phrases in the text sounded familiar, like things I had said to her in the recent sessions, and I brightened at the thought that perhaps after all there was some positive effect. Ellen continued, however, to draw the same rigid creature, to face me with her back, to avoid eye contact, and to shut me out as much as possible in our remaining sessions, which turned out to be five in number.

The last session in late April began like all the others with the making of the same strange figure. But at one point in her drawing Ellen stopped, as if immobilized, appearing more openly fearful than usual. Welling up with anguish for her aloneness, I first spoke of, then acted on an impulse to put my hand on her shoulder. It was close to the end of the hour. She did not respond in any observable way, remained tense and frozen, then went on with the picture and left at the end, walking out more rapidly than usual. She went back to her grandmother's and, for the first time in almost a year, telephoned her mother. The purpose of the call was to tell her that she did not want to come to the clinic any more, "Because I don't like Mrs. Rubin." A note I sent her the following week remained unopened, though apparently kept, and she returned no more. But, she proceeded then to gradually return to her parental home, first for weekends, then in a few months, for good. According to her mother, contacted two and one-half years later, she returned home warmer and more open than ever in the past, and became a truly solid member of the family, as well as an academic success and a cheerleader in high school.

Fig. 7-9. One of Ellen's many drawings of the creature, six months later.

Despite the family's pleasure at the eventual outcome, I felt extremely discouraged, and more like a failure as a therapist than ever before. Because I was so deeply distressed, I was forced to cope, to deal actively with the experience. Fortunately, I was in psychoanalysis during the time I worked with Ellen, and was able to spend many hours on the couch exploring the feelings and fantasies stimulated in me by this difficult, rejecting youngster. I probably learned the most from probing my countertransference reactions, my exaggerated and distorted responses to her which stemmed primarily from my own unresolved conflicts. Not only was she thus helpful to me in my personal analytic work, but the awareness of how my reactions affected my behavior as her therapist ultimately led to more appropriate interventions with others, as well as with Ellen.

This painful sense of bewilderment as a therapist led to yet another significant kind of learning. What I discovered was that my attempts to find answers from *outside* (as from consultants), were less fruitful in some ways than my efforts to find answers from *inside* (the analytic work on how and why I was responding as I did). I therefore learned that in a situation of puzzlement as a clinician, to look externally for help is only part of the task; to look internally for understanding is equally essential.

Dorothy

Some years ago I worked with Dorothy, a seriously disturbed brain-damaged girl suffering from some loss of vision and hearing, and from childhood schizophrenia. Adjunctive art therapy sessions were made available to Dorothy, as they were to all ten children on her residential treatment unit. She came every week from November through March, and usually stayed for about one hour. At first, her teacher having introduced me as an "art teacher," Dorothy wanted and expected some instruction in art. Rather quickly, however, she accepted the open-ended nature of the sessions, soon overcame her quiet reserve and initial disappointment, and began to relate in a warm and trusting way. Although she could speak, she did so rarely, since her speech was so distorted that it was very hard to understand. She was a fairly articulate draughtsman, however, and from the first, was able to express her fantasies and ideas quite clearly through pencil and paintbrush.

During her first three sessions, Dorothy concentrated on the drawing and painting of birds, an animal she often pretended to be by making birdlike noises and flapping movements with her arms (Fig. 7-10). She seemed "stuck" on a rather compulsive and careful way of doing this repetitive subject; so during the fourth session, after her attempt to paint a large bird with tempera and some frustration due to the lack of small brushes, I suggested she try just using the paints without planning in advance. She did so, and became quite excited and delighted at her new freedom, literally dancing and yelping with glee as she let loose, slopping on one bright color after another. When finished with her first such effort, she asked for the largest size of paper (18 by 24 inches) and announced, with some excitement,

"I'll make a monster!" She did a rather fanciful and colorful painting of a multi-limbed creature, and followed this by saying "I want to make another monster," this time first drawing a birdlike creature saying "Growl!"

The following week, she began with one of her old careful birds, an eagle, first drawn and then painted. She then drew at the right what she later called a "dummy," a crayon figure of a boy with strings like a marionette standing on a ladder, with his arm in the eagle's mouth (Fig. 7-11). "I want to do another one!" she said, after naming the first "The Dummy and the Eagle." Her second drawing, in pencil, is an even more graphic picture of the destructive effects of the eagle's rage. The figure (called both man and dummy) with a chewed-off arm, eyes bandaged, violently hurt, has an explanatory narrator at the upper left saying: "Egles. Egles are mad. They want to kill man and eat them." (Fig. 7-12).

Fig. 7-10. One of Dorothy's many bird drawings. Pencil. Age 10.

Fig. 7-11. "The Eagle and the Dummy" by Dorothy. Crayon and tempera.

Fig. 7-12. Dorothy's pencil drawing of a destructive eagle and its victim.

Perhaps for the first time, the aggressive aspects of Dorothy's bird fantasy were clarified for those who worked with her, maybe for Dorothy too. The following week, emphasizing the flight aspects, she drew a saucy bird, then covered it over with dark paint, saying frequently "Go home," a commonly verbalized wish of hers. A girl was then drawn in a cage (the hospital ward as she experienced it?), saying "Boo hoo!" with a large monster-like creature at the right saying "Ha ha!" This was followed by the drawing and painting of a large and a small bird, along with arm-flapping and repeated rhythmic chanting of the words, "Go home! Go home! Go home!" Her final product in this emotion-filled session was a rather lovely, carefully painted, large and majestic bird.

At her ninth session Dorothy shifted gears in her imagery, and began a long period of representing the children on the ward, first in rows, later involved in typical activities. Her perception of them was so accurate that it was possible for anyone who knew them to identify the figures. These drawings were done mostly in marker, along with much verbalization about the children and her relationship to them. This subject matter occupied her for the next six weeks, with increasing action and drama in the pictures. While she was always careful to include each of the others, she never drew herself. In the last one, I asked where Dorothy was, and with a grin she pointed to the bird flying overhead.

At her fifteenth session, Dorothy again shifted symbols, drawing carefully a pictorial "list" of clothes, later identifying them as all belonging to the youngest child on the unit, a boy of five of whom she was jealous. She said she wished she had clothes as pretty as his, and that hers were so ugly. The following week the clothes were drawn first, then a picture of an older boy and the younger one, in which the older one has thrown away the little one's doll and he is crying (perhaps her jealous wish as well as empathic fear). In the next session, she began her "cat phase," and for seven weeks made pictorial "catalogs" of cats, pictures of cat families (Fig. 7-13) and of her fantasy-wish of being dressed in a cat costume—a bit more realistic than actually becoming a bird. At her twenty-fourth session, the next to the last we were to have, she drew a picture of the young boy and many articles of his clothing, afterward circling those which she also possessed. She was talking much more by then, having improved considerably in intelligibility through intensive speech therapy, and had many questions about "endings."

At the last session, we reviewed the art work in her folder, a useful way to help a child to get closure. She was very interested, studying the pictures quietly and closely, with little verbalization. The most potent pictures, those dealing openly with hostility, were passed over rapidly, and the greatest time was spent looking at those of the children on the ward. She looked longingly at her portrait of the "Tortoise Shell Family" (Fig. 7-13), remarking that the mommy and daddy weren't there (though previously she had identified the larger ones as parents), and that the cats want to cuddle up to people. No doubt the perceived loss of parents was related to the impending loss of her art times and art therapist, to whom she had grown attached. She did one more drawing of clothing, an item or two belonging to each boy on the ward, then put her arms around me, saying "I like you," and said a rather

Fig. 7-13 The "tortoise shell family" of cats by Dorothy. Marker.

clingy goodbye. Though she was not able to express her anger at me then for leaving her, when I visited the craft class on the ward one month later, she showed me a drawing of "Mrs. Rubin being Attacked by Soldiers for being Bad."

The experience with Dorothy, as with all the children on that unit, was a powerful one. At the time I had no previous experience in a clinical setting, and was just beginning to read about art and child therapy. I was fearful, cautious, and generally nondirective except for setting and maintaining reasonable limits. I read the literature on art work by children who were psychotic, and discovered that Dorothy's use of animal symbols and perseveration of themes were not uncommon (Despert, 1938), and that her high level of productivity, including the speed and fluidity of her work, had also been noted (Montague, 1951). Perhaps, as some suggest, Dorothy's art was a device used to maintain contact with reality, and her pictures of the children a way of drawing a map of the world in order to find her place in it. Certainly, even in my naiveté, I could see that there was considerable value in this experience for this child. The opportunity to draw her fantasies and to explore the world in pictures seemed to afford her relief from some inner pressures. Perhaps it was a way of orienting herself and structuring reality, as well as a way of externalizing her fearsome fantasies. While some people worried that she was using art as an escape, I felt that art became a place for her to feel good because of her competence, to experience some sensory and playful pleasure, and to find her way back to reality through her fantasies, by airing rather than burying them.

Randy

A different sequence was found in the art work of Randy, a twelve-year-old encopretic from the same ward. Very bright, also schizophrenic, Randy was much more verbal and articulate than Dorothy, superficially more in touch with reality, but inwardly unsure of the distinction between real and pretend. In the course of twenty-three weekly art sessions, Randy began with a variety of fairly realistic topics, using a range of drawing media, working in a casual, rather sloppy way. He drew and painted zebras, rockets, school, fireworks, an explosive Civil War scene, food, rainbows, a series of underwater and cave scenes, and a series of concentric designs. At his seventh session he announced that he didn't want to paint that day, although it was usually his first choice. Instead he drew a picture of outer space, with a red planet (Mars) and yellow pieces—bits of stars which have exploded. Some he called "constellations," specifically "the King" and "the Queen."

This drawing led to his decision to create a book, "Our Trip Through Outer Space" on which he worked steadily for the next five sessions, producing a series of pictures about a Martian and me in outer space. During the next six sessions, he painted a variety of other topics, generally more realistic, including a castle, a zebra, an ocean scene, a jungle picture, "Darkness in a Mysterious Cave," a painting of his school on fire, his "enemies" at school (those who tease him), and a volcano. At the seventeenth session he returned to the space series, and made a cover including the "new earth," myself with "one of the newest space hairdos," my "old pal, the Martian," and Randy wearing "the newest style in space suits." At his next session he painted an imaginative landscape of the Sierra Nevadas with "an ice-capped mountain." And the following week he initiated another long stretch on the book project, devoting his last four sessions to an "earth series," similar to his space series, but literally more "down to earth." His oedipal wishes for some kind of romantic relationship with me became clearer in this less-distant and less-disguised sequence. In his drawing of our visit to Egypt (the Martian having dropped out of the story early in the "earth series"), he drew me in fancy clothes, wearing a see-through dress and a fancy hairdo, while he, having dug in the earth for buried treasure, gives me a a gift of gems (Fig. 7-14). In his picture of Scotland, his amorous wishes were even more apparent: he drew himself as an adult-looking Scotsman holding onto my belt so that I "won't trip," and looking very much as though he has me in tow, under his firm control (Fig. 7-15).

Randy, like Dorothy, spent his last session reviewing his art work in sequence, often expressing surprise at things he'd forgotten (repressed) since doing them. Best-recalled and most-liked were the two series, in which the work had generally been his most careful and best organized. As he reviewed the drawings, his most frequent remarks were to admire the clothes or hairdos he had designed for me. His final picture was of me on the edge of a cliff in the Philippines, for which he made up the following (oedipal) story in the review session: "A sailor from the *Bounty* was trying to kiss one of the island girls, and she backed off and fell down the mountainside, and then there was a war. The island girls fought the men and the men fought the sailors and the sailors fought the island girls. Everyone fought everyone!" I wondered why the island girl had backed away from the sailor, and he replied, "She backed off because she already had a boy friend." His very last drawing, done in the ten remaining minutes of the session, was, rather appropriately, a battle scene: "The Revolutionary War."

Fig. 7-14. Randy giving the art therapist a gift. Marker. Age 10.

Fig. 7-15. Randy holding onto the art therapist with a belt. Marker.

Randy and Dorothy were both schizophrenic, which means that they were very sick children who lived in a confused world where reality and fantasy were often hard to disentangle. Most children learn to tell the difference between real and make-believe in the course of their early "pretend" play, gradually developing the ability to discriminate. Nevertheless, many children have problems in the course of their growing up, sometimes caused by worries and fantasies, wishes and fears, which live within and are kept alive, in part through staying buried (another way of thinking of repression—keeping things out of consciousness). These hidden feelings may also have hidden consequences, so that the child becomes inhibited in his learning or his play through a generalized kind of restriction motivated by a vague sort of anxiety, the causes of which are often not known to him or to others. One of the tasks of treatment is helping a child to express and to articulate those hidden wishes and fears, so that they may then be faced, dealt with, and seen as different from reality.

In the course of art therapy, vague, unfocused, and fuzzy images and ideas often become more articulate and clear. When Alschuler and Hattwick compared normal preschoolers' use of easel painting and dramatic play, they concluded that the themes were more explicit in drama, and "that easel painting may be of particular value for expressing generalized emotions, conflicts, and difficulties which are at a non-verbal, non-overt level, i.e., for expressing felt tensions rather than problems and conflicts that have crystallized at the conscious level." (1969, pp. 140–141) Looking at children's use of both easel painting and the similarly unstructured medium of clay, these investigators found that "both media seem to stimulate children to symbolical expression of feelings which they are either not ready or not able to express in more articulate fashion." (1969, p. 137) Even when an idea is beginning to get close to consciousness, it frequently is expressed in art long before it is talked about. "Children, particularly, nibble at communicating ideas graphically and symbolically before entering into the more open verbal arena." (Hammer, 1958, p. 582) Children (and adults) find some things difficult if not impossible to put into words, even when there is complete awareness.

I once had the opportunity to work with a young child and her mother, in tandem with a child psychiatric resident. The doctor would see the mother while I saw the child for forty-five minutes; we would then exchange clients for the same period of time. At our weekly collaborative meetings about the two, my colleague soon dubbed the art work a "preview of coming attractions," since what was expressed symbolically to me in art was likely to be verbalized to him within the next few weeks. In long-term work with children and parents, individually as well as in families and groups, this phenomenon has been repeated over and over. Even when verbal expressive modalities, like drama, are part of the treatment, concerns are most often expressed first in art.

Randy's two series, on space and on earth travel, gave him an acceptable and organized framework within which he could explore and symbolically gratify his curiosity and his sexual fantasies regarding his female therapist (who probably symbolized his mother). While it was necessary for Dorothy to "loosen up" with a free painting experience in order to look at her feared fantasies, it seemed important for Randy to "get himself together" in order to depict his wishful thoughts. His early work was sloppy, often diffuse, while his work on the series was both thematically and aesthetically more organized. Different children clearly have different needs in order to get to a point at which they have a safe "framework for freedom." Given support and acceptance, they often provide for such needs on their own, as did Randy. My suggestion to Dorothy, however, that she try painting without drawing first, was a deliberate intervention. There are many such ways in which a therapist can facilitate the child's struggle to grow, a challenge to one's own ingenuity and creativity. Active intervention is a tricky business, to be done only with acute awareness of internal and external motivations, and of the possible effects on the child and his treatment. At the risk of stimulating misguided maneuvering on the part of others, I shall try to describe some possible therapeutic moves in the following chapter.

CHAPTER 8.

Ways to Facilitate Expression

There are many resources with which to help a child in the context of individual art therapy, some environmental and some personal. The former are a bit easier to see and to describe, and include the manipulation of space, time, furniture, lighting, and materials, as well as the introduction of possible themes or formats for work. The adult may choose to be a quiet observer, an active questioner, a parallel participant, or a joint creator with materials. Possibilities for expression in other modalities may be enhanced by the availability of tools such as a typewriter, a tape recorder, musical instruments, puppets, miniature life toys, and props. One can facilitate dramatization by "interviewing" in an official sort of way, using a fake or real microphone, as well as by engaging in a drama by taking a role. Most often, such variations in technique arise out of a feeling that the child is stuck— unable to proceed easily without some help—though sometimes they emerge out of a feeling that they will further enhance an already comfortable flow of creative material. Much of my awareness of such possibilities has been given me by the children themselves—a continuous ongoing process.

Though it is impossible to choose typical sessions, since each child and each moment are in a very real sense unique, it might help to look at a selection from different stages in treatment, and from work with children of different age levels and with different problems.

A Scribble. The scribble drawing is often used by art therapists as a way of helping patients to overcome their inhibitions about drawing ("anyone can scribble"), and is especially helpful for children who are stuck on some particular schema, or blocked in their imagery in a more global way. It enables patients to find and draw images they would probably not have created "from scratch," and often assists in the emergence of imagery that is "waiting in the wings."

Carla, a child who had been referred for treatment by her mother because of frightening nightmares and disobedience, hid her worries behind colorful abstract paintings during the early weeks of art therapy. Many of these were striped, and were soon described as "bars," behind which the feared monsters of her dreams were waiting. When asked, after several weeks of talking about them, if she could draw the nightmares, Carla said it would be much too risky to do so. In a rare directive intervention, I suggested the next week that she might like to try a "game," the "scribble drawing," in the hope that some of these images would emerge. The timing must have been appropriate, for the first picture to be found in a scribble and then developed was of a nightmare monster, grabbing and about to devour the little girls in its clutches (Fig. 6-1). Carla worked on the drawing as she described the drama therein, adding blotches of red paint with vigorous pounding of a splattering red tempera marker. These blotches were called "soldiers," an army coming to rescue the children from the monster's clutches. Finally, the soldiers won out, though it was not easy for Carla to decide how the story would end.

A Theme. While the most significant themes usually emerge spontaneously in art therapy, there may be times when it helps to suggest a specific topic to the child. Eleanor, a depressed deaf teenager, dealt with an unstructured art evaluation by first using colored pencils to draw two flowers on a 12-by-18-inch piece of manilla paper. She was very careful, outlining first, then filling in, often looking at me as if to make sure that what she was doing was acceptable. She indicated that the flowers would be hers, titled the picture "Rose," and then pointed to the words she had written when finished drawing: "I don't have more idea." In response to her distress at having to make yet another selection, I wondered if she could draw a feeling, probably suggesting that topic because I sensed that she was feeling a great deal, but not showing it in her art or associations.

Since Eleanor still seemed quite tense and unable to move spontaneously, I said she might want to find a color of paper that was like the feeling she had in mind. She grinned, selected a 12-by-18-inch piece of red construction paper, asked in writing how much more time we had, and then expressed her concern more directly by writing "I think something's hard." Despite her anxiety, however, she proceeded to draw a picture of a girl with an angry mouth and eyes, adding the ears at the end (Fig. 8-1). On the side she wrote: "A girl was mad." When I asked why the girl was mad, she wrote: "Because she fight with her friend." When asked what the fight was about, she responded "She stole your girlfriend's purse. Your friend was very mad with her." When I asked what sort of things made her mad, she wrote "with school," and "bad swear." When asked if there was any person who made her mad, she wrote the name of a person in authority at the school; but when I asked if this woman was mean, she quickly responded that she was a "nice lady and explained to people." She looked uncomfortable about having identified this woman as the target of her anger, but quickly indicated, in response to my query, that she would like to come again for art.

Fig. 8-1. "A girl was mad" by Eleanor. Marker. Age 15.

A Medium. While it is usually best to allow a free choice of materials, there may be times when a suggestion is helpful. Sometimes it is a technical matter—letting the person know that a thin brush is available and will work better for the picture he has sketched out, or that plasticine might be more appropriate than water-base clay for the sculpture he has in mind. Such technical assistance requires familiarity with art media and their properties, and is a vital tool in the armamentarium of an art therapist. In a different way, one might suggest the use of a medium or process for more psychodynamic reasons. It is my firm belief that to "prescribe" is in error—that to "tell" a constricted child to use fingerpaint so it can "loosen him up" is not only to promote an authoritarian relationship, but also potentially to cause anxiety in the child. There are times, however, after a fairly stable alliance between patient and therapist has been formed, when one might offer some specific suggestions, being as explicit as possible about the reasons.

Jerry, a partially-sighted boy suffering from encopresis, one day made a clay head using plasticine. Since he had chosen to use clay of a single color, his limited vision made it very hard to see where to put the facial features. Indeed, he was quite upset with his finished product, saying that the head looked "all messed up" (Fig. 8-2). I suggested that it might be easier if he made the features with clay which was of different colors than the face. He proceeded to make a large head of a man, with a mustache and beard like his father's, and finally said that it was his dad. He was much more satisfied with this product than the first (Fig. 8-3).

He also went on to use the difference between the two heads in a most creative way. He played out a story, calling the second head "a big man with a big face" and the first "a little squished-up man with a little squished-up face." In addition to his blindness, Jerry had a growth hormone deficiency which made him look "squished-up." In the story, the little guy ends up killing the big one, who has been very critical. Jerry had finally found a way to play out, using the two heads, his angry death-wishes toward his father, whom he held responsible for his mother's desertion of the family (following violent fights between the couple). It was likely that his anal "messing" was an unconscious expression of this hostility, directed partly toward the caretaking parent who actually had to clean up the mess.

At the end of the session, Jerry said that the little guy in the story was wishing for something that was hard to say. After much encouragement, he whispered, "blind," and then said there was another word he was also finding hard to say, which turned out to be "handicapped." I wondered if the little boy in the story was wishing to get rid of those, and he nodded vigorously in the affirmative. I asked if he had any idea why the little boy had that problem, and he whispered, " 'cause he's bad!" I asked if he was bad for wanting to kill the big guy, and he nodded yes. This suggested that the little "squished-up" person was in such a bad physical state *because* he was so angry, and that his blindness was seen as a punishment for his badness (see Chapter 9). In this instance, the suggested use of the medium facilitated not only the making of a more articulated art product, but also enabled the child, through subsequent

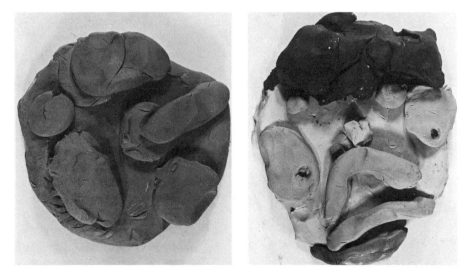

Fig. 8-2. A clay head, all one color, by Jerry. Age 11.   Fig. 8-3. A multicolored clay head by Jerry.

dramatic play, to articulate further the unconscious fantasies underlying his conflicts and his symptoms.

A Dream. Sometimes it is helpful to suggest to the child that something being discussed could be represented, especially if the topic happens to be one with potentially high therapeutic yield, like a dream. It is a reversal of the more common situation in art therapy of asking the individual to "tell about" what has been created; here, one asks the person to create what is being talked about. In the middle of a year of weekly art therapy sessions, eight-year-old Chip began an hour by mentioning that he had been having scary dreams. I wondered if he could draw one, and he agreed with the notion that he could "tell me" better that way than with words. He proceeded to use markers on a large (18-by-24-inch) piece of paper to create a rather elaborate, detailed drawing of what he called a "Nightmare" (Fig. 8-4).

He said, "This monster is known as Godzilla. He's a monster on television." He then asked if I had to take notes, to which he was by then accustomed, worrying that I "might show it to like, say, Dr. H." (his parents' therapist). Reassured that the notes would not be shown to anyone—doctor, parents, or teachers—he went

Fig. 8-4. Chip's drawing of a dream about Godzilla. Marker. Age 8.

back to describing the characters and the story. Godzilla, with his outstretched arm and pointing finger is saying "Kill!" while a plane and a tank try to attack him. He then described how the bullets would "ricochet and hit the tank, then ricochet and hit the plane. I'm gonna make another plane that's being blown up. . . . I'm making a smaller plane, like an F-11, the yellow one on the right." As he drew, he dramatized, making noises like "bang-bang," as the bombs crashed into the ground. The black airplane on the upper left was said to be a B-52, and was also attempting unsuccessfully to shoot at the monster, its bullets boomeranging too. The last item drawn was the little figure held in the monster's hand yelling "Help!", a boy whom Chip thought would not be rescued. Indeed, his conclusion about the nightmare dream-drawing, was that Godzilla would probably kill everyone including Chip and his buddies. Then, as if to defend against those helpless feelings, he reminded me, "I'm a better artist than you, so watch out!"

This statement was followed by a seductive invitation "Wanna make a castle with me?" I commented that I would enjoy watching him make a castle, and he replied, "I'd rather you help." I then noted that he often wanted help with things, and wondered what it had to do with needing to get help from his mother in order to be sure of her love. He nodded in a way that signified some real understanding, and proceeded to build a castle with blocks, describing it as "a little shelter in case of Indians." He got inside it, then went behind it and yelled "Crunch!" followed by "He killed himself!" He then asked me to push him in the "cart" (a large wagon he could sit in), and then turned and yelled with mock fury, "Get out of my castle, you!" He agreed with my notion that perhaps he was feeling angry because I did not agree to build with him, and left in a bouncy mood.

The suggestion to draw the dream not only helped Chip to clarify his scary experience, but also led to some play which helped both of us to understand better the relationship of the angry impulses symbolized in the dream to his wishes for protection and for a more exclusive relationship with his mother. Though at one point he turned the aggression inward ("He killed himself!") as he often did in reality (being accident-prone and voicing suicidal ideas), he was able finally to direct it to the adult where it belonged. The shift from art to drama in his session often occurs in just such a spontaneous way, and can sometimes be facilitated through simple suggestions, as in the following session (the eighth of twenty-five sessions) with Lori, a four-and-a-half-year-old girl.

A Mask. Lori went immediately to the sink, mixed powder paints from shakers in their dry form, and said it looked like salt and pepper. "My mom uses pepper on her eggs," she said, adding that she herself hates pepper. About the paint, she instructed me rather imperiously: "You better get more. . . . Whatever I ask for, you'll get!" While mixing orange paint with water to make "orange juice," she said, "My mom's with Dr. L." Asked how that made her feel, she said, "It makes me feel *real bad*—and I don't like it. It feels like my mom leaves and she forgets me." A few minutes later she said, "Oh, that was just a *dream* about my mom leaving me. . . . Would you take me home with you if my mom went out and left me here?"

Seeming quite anxious with these thoughts of abandonment, she recalled a "hide-and-seek" game she had initiated in past sessions. When it was suggested that there were other hiding games she could play, such as behind a mask, she responded eagerly with the idea that she and I should each make a "Scary Monster Mask," which she proceeded to do on a piece of cardboard (Fig. 8-5). On the back, she drew "a Happy Monster," and explained the plot of the game: "I hurt you and you get dead—not for real, just for pretend."

She then used her mask and pretended to be an angry monster who was very scary, saying repeatedly in a growly voice, "I'm going to kill you!" She also period-ically turned the mask around and played the role of a happy, conciliatory monster. She drew several more "Happy Monsters," and directed me to draw "a Scary Monster Lady Mask." In the middle of this intense dramatic play, she said, "I get scared a lot. I get scared, like monsters." She was very much involved in trying out both angry (scary) and conciliatory (happy) roles with the masks, growling and gesturing aggressively at me in true monster fashion. At the end of her dramatic play, she said, "I ain't mad no more," explaining that she was mad "sometimes, but not all the time."

In the few remaining minutes, she got some clay and began by pounding it very hard. She drew a "happy" face into the clay with a tool, and then used another tool to poke holes all over the clay, attacking the face vigorously and aggressively. She left the session in a very bouncy mood, in contrast to the rather subdued state she had been in when she first entered.

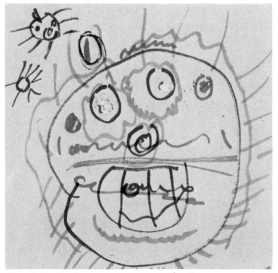

Fig. 8-5. Lori's scary monster mask. Crayon on cardboard. Age 5.

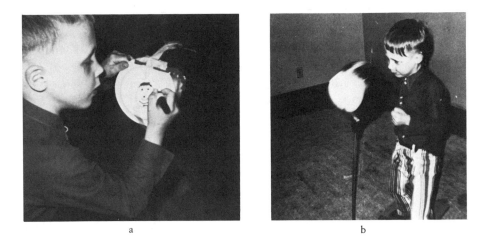

Fig. 8-6. (a) Drawing an enemy and then (b) punching him on a bag. Boy, age 6.

A Target. Lori had been quite anxious about the possible potency of her anger, that it might lead to being abandoned by her mother as she felt she had been by her father since the separation of her parents. Her worries about loss were evident in the beginning of the session, while the anger only emerged in the course of the drama, facilitated by the monster mask.

Chip, the eight-year-old described earlier, one day came to the clinic full of unfocused anger, and expressed a wish to punch the punching bag in the large room where he had once been part of a group. I suggested that it might help to imagine a more specific target, to pretend that the bag represented different people, a suggestion to which he responded with enthusiasm.

First he said the bag was his mother, and he hugged and kissed it passionately, saying over and over again, "I love you, I love you." He then decided it would represent his stepfather, whom he kissed and hugged, and then punched and yelled at, speaking of this man's "yelling anger." Then he said the bag was "Mamorelli, the worst kid in town. He's older. He beats me up." Slugging as hard as he could, it was clearly more comfortable for him to pound Mamorelli than either parent. However, he returned to the idea of the bag as mother, again saying "I love you," then shifted to his stepfather, alternately loving and hitting with vehemence. At the end he said to the bag-father, "I want to be your friend. You've been mean and nasty and cruel, but I really want to be your friend." Then he turned, and told about how his parents fought violently, got angry and hit each other, and how scary that was for him (cf. Fig. 8-6).

I reminded him that once before he had drawn a picture of the target of his anger (a peer) and had thrown clay "bullets" at it. He decided to paint a picture of a boy which he then taped onto the punching bag, and hit again with vigor. He commented, "Love and violence can't go together." I wondered if indeed one couldn't have very strong violent angry feelings and loving ones toward the same person at different times, or even at the same time? He seemed intrigued with this notion, but wasn't ready to accept it, asserting again that they couldn't possibly go together. His next activity was a spatter painting on huge paper with tempera paints, which was described as a picture of a friend with "black and blue marks all over." When I wondered how the person had gotten them, he said "He must have been punched by somebody else." While he then swung on the tire swing in the same group room, he wondered aloud, "Don't you get scared with all this violence?" and "How can you stand all that violence?" and we talked together about how scary it was to him.

Such explicit dramatizations of children's hostility allow for release of affect and for a temporary discharge of surplus energy. In addition, they provide the child with an experience of expressing intense aggression without harm to anyone. But it is vital that the therapist make it continually clear to the child that all of this aggression, while very *real* as an impulse, is *pretend* as an action, against a *make-believe* adversary. Moreover, it is the therapist's responsibility not only to permit such experiences as ways of discharging and focusing overwhelming affect, but also to help the child see that the task in growing up is to find more constructive ways of expressing such energies, while learning how to put his angry feelings into words rather than actions. In fact, if one can learn to integrate loving and aggressive impulses, as Chip was struggling to do, then one can use the energy in a healthy, constructive fashion.

A Tape Recorder. Some children have great difficulty talking freely about their products, but often can be helped through the use of "props," such as a tape recorder (real or mock). Glen, an eleven-year-old boy who had recently attempted suicide, was almost done with ten months of bi-weekly sessions in art (alternating with meetings with a child psychiatrist). He had by then learned how to describe his art work, but was still not too comfortable doing so, usually restricting his remarks to brief comments. He loved the microphone and the tape recorder, however, and responded to my introduction of these with a much more elaborate description of his picture than usual. The drawing, done in sketching pencil on a large (18-by-24-inch) piece of white paper, was of a ship, about which he had expressed some uncertainty regarding the addition of a sail (Fig. 8-7). When I handed him the microphone, he performed as if he were truly on the air, and his first nonstop statements were as follows:

This is Glen Smith talking about his latest art piece. Now in this drawing I have a sketch of the USS frigate, Constitution, being fired upon by an unknown British ship in the background. Now this scene— many scenes like this have happened during the Revolution, with Bonhomme Richard and John Paul Jones and many other ships, especially the privateers, who guarded along the coast and attacked on small British ships. This I chose to have the sails down, with the anchor in the water, and the ship is not moving, as you can see. Now, I have crows' nests, but I didn't sketch any people. Now, this British ship is firing upon the Constitution and soon, when the Constitution is alerted, it will turn, pull in its anchor, pull up sails, turn around, and prepare for battle. Of course, in the background, I drew a smaller ship. It looks better, I think. On the forward masts, you will see banners, flags, and on the real ship, these banners never were. Only on Spanish ships were these banners placed; and when I drew the United States flag. I drew it pretty large, because I have been on a ship, and I saw Admiral Perry's ship, and the flag was very large. Now, over in the forward part, the bow, I have riggings shown where there were ropes with crossings going up to the forward mast. And on my model ship there were many riggings, but of course I cannot place all of the riggings on the ship I have here.

Now as you can see, on the British ship I have smoke around one of these cannons, a symbol that it has been fired, and the splashing in the water near the ship, the USS Constitution. If you would look toward the forward part of the ship, you would see the front forward pole where lines and masts and ropes from the mast come down, and seamen use these ropes to lower the sails down and leave them up, so that the ship will run under full speed. In the back you'll notice I have a rudder, which is controlled from the back of the ship, and it moves the ship back and forth whichever way it is turned. On this ship I have placed many cannons, but really, the Constitution has two decks of cannons, which I only drew one. But of course in this small drawing, I couldn't possibly fit two. So, settle for the best I guess. On the mast I have the sails lowered, on really the opposite sides of the mast—the poles, see. Really, the sails are rested on the top, and they slide down so that they'll be easier for the seamen to lower the sails. But in this fashion of drawing, I put the sails on the bottom, for they were really on the bottom of the ship, and it would take too long to get the sails up. And, if you'll notice, toward the middle of the Constitution, you'll see a lifeboat here. Now, really on the Constitution there were about six lifeboats, but see, on this kind of drawing, you can't put that much detail in. This is Glen Smith, just talking about his latest art piece. Bye.

After that rather obsessive but rich description, poured into the microphone, I decided to ask Glen some questions, in order to clarify for him and for myself, the nature of the conflict suggested in the drawing. Our interchange went as follows:

JR: Mr. Smith, I just have a few questions to ask you about that battle that's going to be waged. Is that cannonball going to hit the Constitution, or just what's going to happen to it?

Glen: Well, uh, his, on this particular ship, the cannonballs weren't explosive. They would hit the ship, making a very big hole, or hitting the mast, knocking it down, and if it hit the right place, it would sink the ship. But his cannonball isn't hitting the ship.

JR: I see. Well, now, you said that the Constitution is going to realize that this other ship is attacking it, and is going to kind of turn around and gird itself up for battle. What do you think the outcome will be of that battle? In other words, who's going to win?

Fig. 8-7. Glen's drawing of the U.S.S. Constitution. Pencil. Age 11.

Glen: Well, the Constitution, really. Because the Constitution, throughout all its history, has won all the battles it's ever fought. And now it is in Boston harbor, and it's a tourist attraction, attracting many tourists. . . .

JR: Glen, if you were going to be in this scene, where would you want to be, and what would you want your role to be? In other words, which ship would you want to be on, and what would you want to be doing?

Glen: Really, I'm not sure of the Captain on the Constitution, but I wouldn't like to be him, 'cause during all the battles of the Constitution, this captain has had many troubles and many hard battles. But, uh, this question is sort of hard for me to answer. Supposedly, I'd like to be, uh, really, I'd like to be the crewman on the Constitution. I'm not sure of the position I'd like to be on the ship, at the time.

After clarifying aloud in some detail what different crewmen do, Glen decided, I think I'd like to be—I guess, a gunner. I'm not sure which gunner I'd like to be, but it really doesn't matter. And the gunner is—being gunner is a very dangerous job too. Like the battle of the Bonhomme Richard and the Serapis, these two ships were actually locked together, and the gunners were in very serious trouble. The Constitution won, because while the battle was going on, men climbed up the riggings, got onto the crow's nest, and threw hand grenades and shot rifles down on the other ship. That's mainly what won the battle. See, smart maneuverings by John Paul Jones swirled the ship away from the other, giving the Serapis straight shots from the rear. But luckily, they missed the ship altogether. The Bonhomme Richard turned, and gave it a broadside of all her guns, and eventually sank the Serapis.

I then commented on how much history I was learning from Glen, and asked "If you had been in that battle, what do you wish you would have done?" to which he replied:

Well, really, I don't know Well, let's look at the facts. These two ships were locked together. The captain of the British ship was mortally wounded while leaning over the railing, leading his men. He was in a sword fight with John Paul Jones on the main deck of the ship. While they were fighting, another crew member—a crew member aboard the British ship—accidentally shot their captain. Now, in this battle, I would have preferred to be John Paul Jones, showing courage and strength in this battle.

At this point, having not only talked enough, but having just brushed perilously close to his core conflict by "accidentally" killing off the captain (father), Glen abruptly said, "Let's play it back now," indicating a wish to stop as well as to review, his long, exhibitionistic recording.

Poetry. The tape recorder was an asset to Glen, as to others in satisfying and channeling his wishes to show off, to hold the phallic microphone, and to be a "big shot" as if on television. It enabled him to say much more about his picture than had previously been the case when I asked him to talk to me about drawings. For some, writing words down is easier than saying them aloud. Evelyn, the creator of the bizarre drawing of "Fred" (Fig. 4-6b) and the lonely tree (Fig. 4-6a), while hospitalized after her suicide attempt spontaneously began writing poetry as well as making art. Sometimes her poems were as simple and stark as her tree:

"I wanna cry
Cry until there is no water left in my body
BECAUSE
GOD DAMN IT
I AM AFRAID!"

Sometimes they were a bit more complex, and conveyed ideas that were perhaps best put in verbal form:

> Your mind is a safe place to stay
> Because no one can hurt you there . . .
> Not even your *friends*
> You do not have to plead, beg, cry!!!
> For someone to believe you
> When you tell the truth.
> Oh hell man!

Prose. Evelyn was a very bright girl, for whom poetry was, as for many adolescents, a highly appealing expressive modality. Pete, a pre-adolescent boy, was a slow learner with a learning disability and suspected mild cerebral dysfunction. He had always had difficulty in school, and was generally fearful, confused, and frightened by the angry feelings toward his dad which were becoming apparent in his art therapy. One week he said he wanted to type a story, then dictated it to me as his secretary (at my suggestion, since the typing was becoming too frustrating for him). This is the story he told (it is relevant to note that his father was practically blind in one eye):

> THE LUCKY SOLDIER
> Just as the soldier entered the battlefield, he saw only two things: dead bodies all over the field, and people dropping from every direction. He was so scared that he ran to an old shack. After two hours of hiding, a German force raided the shack. A captain saw him hiding. He said to the captain, "Please don't shoot me." The captain said, "I'll give you a 50/50 chance. If you can tell me which eye is artificial, I will let you go. If not, I shall have to kill you." The soldier stuttered for a moment. At last he whispered, "The left." The captain replied, "You are free! But don't ever come back again!

In the scary but wishful story, the soldier-boy's deficit helps him to escape the dangerous captain-father, while Pete was still struggling with wishes to act autonomously in defiance of his stern, punitive father, whose rage he had good reason to fear. The telling, as well as the subsequent illustration, rereading, and photocopying of the story, helped Pete to review and rethink it, something that was usually difficult for him. The simple fact that, by rereading the story, he could get in touch with the feelings and wishes involved, enabled him to stay with them and to talk about them in relation to himself.

A Picture-Taking Machine. Just as the tape recorder or the typewriter preserves the sound or the words, so those magic machines which preserve images (including still and moving picture cameras) can be helpful in art therapy. Making instant photocopies of drawings to which the child is deeply attached, or which he may wish to give as gifts to other significant people in his life, is a way of facilitating his work, recognizing its importance, and keeping a record for therapist and patient.

Thirteen-year-old James,   hy, constricted boy, was keen on keeping his book on his newly created character   The Pencil Snatcher." The book itself had been the result of a deliberate ploy, for when this very tight, inhibited child who drew compulsive and impersonal pictures commented in a mumble that he wished he had a sketchbook, I had impulsively given him a plain pad I had just gotten for scratch paper. He had come in the following week with a series of rather aggressive humorous cartoon drawings of kids and teachers he disliked. He had then revealed his secret fantasy character, probably a self-representation—"The Pencil-Snatcher"(Fig. 8-8). While pictures of the pencil-snatcher and his bird friend were brought in week after week as the story emerged, James could not part with any pages from the pad. Thus, it was helpful to make copies on the machine, both preserving the images for my file, and giving them additional importance in our therapeutic "detective" work.

Fig. 8-8. The pencil-snatcher sneaking away by James. Pencil. Age 13.

For Tommy, who was going blind, the fact of a machine which made images through light took on additional meaning. He often wanted to make copies of his black line drawings, ostensibly to give them to family and friends, and because he took tremendous delight in making the "magic eye" of the photocopying machine work with the push of a button. Often the pictures related to the feelings he was experiencing as his sight worsened (Figs. 9-2, 9-3).

Flashlights and Candles. A child who was afraid of the dark wanted to turn off the lights and use flashlights or candles. From this experience I discovered that both art and drama sometimes come more easily in a dimly lit room than in a bright one, especially when the fears or fantasies center on what happens in the dark. Carla, who suffered from nightmares, used candles, flashlights, and even spotlights for several months to create changing atmospheres for changing productions. Her pictures and stories were of scary sounds heard while people slept at night. I was cast in the role of punitive mother who finally abandoned a frightened little boy (Carla). Later *she* became a mother—first a mean one, and later a kind one—who stayed and comforted and even fed the hungry child (me), despite my "naughty" curiosity.

Extending the Range. Tommy was distressed by his progressive loss of vision, but found it hard to put his anger into words. Some of this feeling was first expressed through banging hard on a drum and later on a xylophone. In the process, we both discovered a marvelous rhythmic and melodic gift in this little fellow, and recorded his compositions and concerts on tape. Musical instruments, puppets, miniature life toys (toys that can be moved around in clay "worlds" or on sand tables), and the willingness of the therapist to move in other creative directions can help a child to find the most appropriate and comfortable means of expression—just as, within art, the therapist can help the child to find the best medium for his particular message (cf. Fig. 9-5).

Conclusion

Although it may seem strange to be describing so many dramatic interventions in a book on art therapy, I find all expressive modalities to be intimately related, especially in work with children. To restrict a child rigidly to work in any one art form would be to inhibit artificially a natural, organic flow of expression. In some of the instances described in this chaper, expanding the range of expression was made possible simply by having other modes available and being receptive to their use. In others, it involved making a specific suggestion, which seemed likely to facilitate the child's ability to say —creatively —what was on his mind. It is probably in this area, and especially when interviewing about products, that the child art therapist's own creativity can be most useful—indeed, the more imaginative the idea the better, as long as the inventiveness is used to serve the child's needs for expression and understanding, and not one's own.

In a broad sense, the challenge and the task are always to use whatever resources seem best at the moment, and to be open and creative about the many possibilities inherent in space, materials, and oneself. Whether one attempts to uncover or to support defenses depends on many complex issues involving the dynamics of the child's psyche and of change over time—issues best learned in close clinical supervision. With most children, it is possible to trust the youngster's own ability to defend himself when necessary, to stop or to change gears if things become too threatening. As time goes on in work with individuals, one gets a pretty good sense of how much anxiety and frustration they can handle, and when it is necessary to intervene. One learns to trust not only the child's self-protective system, but also one's own "sixth sense" or "third ear." Such sensitivity and empathy is especially difficult, but even more essential, when one is working with a handicapped child.

CHAPTER 9.

Art Therapy with the Handicapped Child

Therapy with the handicapped child is generally similar to work with those who look and act "normal," but who have emotional problems. It is true that the child with a physical or sensory handicap has a problem that "shows," and even one with an invisible deficit like retardation is usually discernibly different from other children. The handicapped, however, are much like other children in their interest in media, desire to be independent, concern with mastery, and feelings of fear, jealousy, and anger. Yet they are different, too, mainly because their handicaps seriously affect their perception of and relationship to their world. Because they are in many real ways "deprived," even with the best of care they tend to be very "hungry," more ready—starved in a way—for sensory and creative, as well as affective and interpersonal experiences.

Because their handicaps are a reality for them, unlike the imaginings of the child whose bodily integrity has never actually been threatened, they often gaps where they are deficient, and to build the kind of safe, comfortable situation necessary for effective therapy. Thus, a blind child needs to be spoken to more often than a sighted child, needs to be told what is available and where it is located, and needs to be reassured vocally of the adult's continuing presence.

Because their handicaps are a reality for them, unlike the castration fantasies of the child whose bodily integrity has never been genuinely threatened, they often have particular problems in dealing with feelings and fantasies about their disability—especially how and why it happened to them, and how they can cope with it now and in the future. Since I have had the privilege of learning a great deal from some blind children who have come to our clinic, I should like to use the work with them to exemplify some of what occurs when one deals with a troubled child with a deficit that is a reality.

Julie

The provision of materials ·that the blind can appropriately use is important and helping them to get started may involve more instruction and demonstration than for a sighted child with more previous creative experience. Once begun, however, a diagnostic art interview with a blind child is not very different from one with a sighted child. Julie, age nine, first said that she was surprised at the playroom with its media and sink: "I thought it was going to be like an office." She selected fingerpaint first, noting, "I used to have fingerpaint at home. Something happened to it. My sister always loses it." After this reference to things that get lost because of someone else's intrusion, she went on to tell me of her art classes in school, and that the arts and crafts room was "a busy room," in contrast perhaps to the quiet of the clinic. While she was tentative at first with the fingerpaint, Julie soon relaxed and moved more freely, beginning with one fingertip and finally using both hands. As she rocked and swayed rhythmically, smearing the paint, she began to talk about things she disliked, saying, "I *hate* shots and time tests and TB tests. . . . I had to have an operation. I got scared. I don't remember it too well." She quickly switched from this rather uncomfortable topic to a somewhat more manageable one, problems at home with her two younger sisters. She finished her fingerpainting, washed her hands at the sink, and asked to use markers, then crayons, making tight little squiggles in a line, saying it reminded her of "writing braille."

While she spoke in her first two sessions about angry feelings toward sisters, by the third she was drawing on sandpaper ("so you could feel it"), and talking about the "old and crabby" woman escort who walked her over from school. She then made brief references to anger at her parents, especially for sending her away to school on a scary bus. This was clearly difficult, however, so that much of the anger toward parents, especially mother, was displaced onto siblings and adult women at the school. Pounding the clay with vigor at the end of the third session, Julie said of her housemother, "Some kids say I don't like her. She's so rotten and so nervous and contrary, so mean and contrary."

During her fourth session, Julie scribbled with markers more freely than before and discussed other children's handicaps and fears and then some of her own wishes and feelings. She wondered if by coming to the clinic she might get her eyes magically fixed: "I thought Child Guidance gave you glasses, that they would check your eyes." She said she liked coming to the clinic, but wished I could stop being a consultant to her school: "I don't want you to go to school." When I commented that she might feel jealous that I would come and be with other children, she nodded her head vigorously, all the time scribbling intensely. She tried to identify crayon colors, was unsuccessful, and seemed sad but relieved, saying she has to "pretend" some of the time that her limited light and color perception is greater than it really is.

During her fifth session, Julie announced that she wanted to make a movie, and then proceeded to arrange building blocks and clay figures she had made on the floor in a living-room setting, using them to enact a "scary story." In the drama, two children, a girl of seven and a boy of nine, are sitting near a stage built of blocks, when they hear a knock on the door. One asks "Who is it?" to which a deep, scary voice responds "Dracula!" The children then say "Come in," and afterwards, "What do you want?" Dracula, still menacing, growls "I want to kill you. I want to kill you!" The girl defiantly replies, "Kill me? Go ahead!" to which the monster responds by trying to do so, and in the process knocks off the upper level of the block stage. The girl says angrily, "See what you did? *You ruined my stage!*" to which Dracula replies, "What did I do? I didn't ruin anything. *We've got the lower stage still.*" The boy then asks, "What would you like?" Dracula replies, "To eat you and to kill you," to which the boy compliantly answers, "Go right ahead." Dracula then proceeds to kill both children and weakly moans, "Ooooooo, I died. I killed one lady, and now I must suck her blood." Another Dracula monster arrives and proceeds to join the first in sucking blood, Julie (as Dracula) sucking water out of a baby bottle she had previously rejected.

When asked about the motive for the killing, Julie explained "He's mad at them-at-um-that lady because she gave him some bad food." It appeared that aspects of Julie herself had been present in all of the roles, from the fearful-brave children to the angry monster. The stage whose upper portion had been knocked off, might also have symbolized the girl, whose upper receptors (eyes) had been damaged ("ruined"), despite the fact that the lower-stage body parts were still intact.

The following week Julie began by using clay, and recalling aloud times when she still liked to suck out of a bottle, even in kindergarten, but feared her mother might object. She then worried that I might disclose (presumably to her mother) what went on in the sessions, saying "You never told anybody what we do, did you?" I commented that it must be very hard for children to believe that adults would keep secrets, and she said solemnly, "It's very hard for children, and the thing is, they see movies and they get very frightened. . . . You know what I'm scared of? In the car by myself, if the car would move. If somebody's in the car with me and it moves, it's okay—my sister or somebody. What's the best thing to do?" She asked this with some urgency, and then went on to explain that this was a worry she had had for a long time, and that she even has "bad dreams" that a car starts and is moving, and she is alone and can't stop it. I wondered why she was thinking about this sort of problem, since she had also told me that it had never happened in reality. She responded, with evident anxiety, "Because they say that people have been getting killed!"

She then went on, "You know how I started that? I dreamed that I was in a car and I heard the car go out of gear, and the wheels too, and it started to move, and I jumped out of the car, and I cried." She remembered having such a dream several times, most recently after she had returned to school following Easter vacation. She went on, by then sucking water with anxious intensity out of the baby bottle: "I dreamed that several girls came, opened up the door, and the car stopped. You see, if there's somebody with you they do something. Three girls all opened the door. . . . I think I dreamed about one where my Aunt Ruth left me in the car, and the car rocked back and forth and I just stopped. I've even told my sisters not to mess with the gears. Every time my sister talks in the car I get nervous. . . . I have the dream at home and at school." When I asked what she thought the danger was, she replied, "You'll be mashed." Continuing to suck the water, she spoke of other scary things, like thunderstorms and electricity. She recalled a time when she had almost gotten hurt by touching an electrified fence, saying "I wanted to see what it was like. I guess it was just my curiosity. I had to touch it with just my finger. It shakes you up really good." She went on to worry more about cars rolling and people getting hurt, by this time working with sandpaper on some soft wood. She liked the sounds made with the sandpaper, and experimented with various rhythms, saying "Did you ever hear of a song called the 'Sandpaper Ballet?' Well, that's it!"

The next week's appointment was cancelled by her dad because of his anger over the clinic bill, ironically due to a misunderstanding of the amount owed. Julie came in a week later, but was aware of her father's threat to pull her out of therapy abruptly. As she modelled some clay, I asked her how all this fuss made her feel. She said, "Kind of terrible. It made me think that they were poor . . . I want to be a grownup." When I asked how coming to the clinic made her feel, she expressed her ambivalence, noting that she had to miss a club meeting at school, and that "Last week I felt very sad not coming; no, I guess I had mixed feelings." She said she was feeling bossed about coming or not, and also about taking part in a school play. "I really don't like people bossing you around." When I asked what she does when that happens, she replied sadly, "Nothing. I just get mad. I go in my room and I put my head down, and I might be punished. When people tell me I don't speak up, I get mad too. I *do* speak up! Whenever I have a headache I tell the nurse. I was worried about it—about not getting to come here. I was afraid you'd get angry!"

I wondered why she thought I'd be angry and she said, "Does it scare you? Does it scare you in the lobby?" I said that perhaps it scared her to feel angry and led her to worry that I might not approve. She explored aloud the idea of getting angry at me, but dismissed it, saying, "Go ahead and talk back, and you'll get in trouble." I wondered how she thought I would react, and she said, "I'm a little worried about you. If it's a he that comes before me, then I'll really be angry. Sometimes I wish I could see, but even though your parents can see, they could still learn a little bit of braille." I noted that she seemed to wish people understood more about what it was like to be blind; and she explained how hard it is at the seashore, saying "Because pebbles hurt your feet. There's real big waves and I'm still scared. I'm gonna tell people it's not true."

She then said there were some other things she would like to tell people, including: "I wish I could see," and "Nothing—what I really *can* see," and "I can read braille," "I can wash dishes," and "I can sweep the floor—with your hands, with your hands!" She went on, "Some blind children can be cured. They could be—but they were probably born that way." I wondered why she thought children became blind who were not born that way, and she said quite clearly, "Their parents prob'ly beat them. And this guy beat this little boy. So I just feel like shooting the parents. Did you ever read in the paper about some children? They put them against the wall and then stamp on their stomach. That's the way to murder them!" I said she seemed concerned about parents being angry at children or maybe vice versa, and she said that she sometimes got mad when her mother did things for her that she wished she could do herself. "Maybe it's hard things, like tying your shoes or something. She does it. Well, I *try* to do it. If we're going somewhere, I don't do it 'cause she's in a hurry."

She was making a container out of clay, and called it "a bowl, a cup, a dish, or a basket," asking "Could you paint this kind of clay if you wanted?" I said she could do that if she came back next week, and she said with fervor: "I do want to come. Could I pretend about being in a car next week?" I said we had a big cart that she could sit in, and she went on, "Our car shakes and vibrates. I get scared it is really moving. Our garage door scares you to death." When I wondered about the basket, she grinned and said, "The basket is yours. We'll paint it next week." I had the feeling at that point that I was indeed being used as a "container," one into which she could risk pouring previously unspoken fears and fantasies. Probably the threatened termination led her to want to dramatize the scary dream quickly, in the hope that I might help her with it.

When she arrived the following week, she immediately began the drama announcing: "For this week there is a long car accident, and people committing suicide. The story takes place in a shopping center. The characters are: the police-man, nurse, housemother, doctor, and a school teacher, and Julie—me." Before she started the story, she commented with irritation on how it makes her angry that people rush her in the morning, and recalled how mad she had gotten at her house-mother: "Some people really boss you. I got really angry yesterday. She made me pick up those books—from playing school. And everybody else played, but I had to do the cleaning up. That also makes me angry. It makes me mad. I'm sick and tired of it!" Following this direct ventilation of angry feelings, she began what Susan Aach has called a "genesis" drama, an attempt at explaining in a fantasy the origin of her blindness.

"It is about a car accident. I'm waiting in the lobby for a nurse. The mother left the child at home. My mother went shopping without me in another car and she locked me in. And then the car started moving, and it went out of gear by itself, and. . . . " She hesitated to play it out, saying she'd just *tell* it, so I wondered if I could interview the characters, and she agreed. As the mother, she said: "My daughter was in the car. I do *not* like my daughter. She shall be beaten and killed, because I *hate* her, because she never does anything but lay around, because there is nothing to do. She will not go outside, and it was a nice day. . . . It makes me think she's sick. She is *pretending* to be sick. She is *pretending* to be sick! Because

she does not want to do any chores!" I asked the mother if she had any other
children and she named Julie's real younger sisters. "But it is only the *oldest* who
will not do her chores." She then yelled viciously, "Get over here, young lady!
Get over here! You're gonna be beaten!" As the interviewer, I wondered if maybe
her oldest child had trouble with chores because she was blind, and wondered too
if the mother had any idea of how that happened. She replied, "I think I socked
her in the eye with a stone!" She then turned to her daughter and went on, "Young
lady! I want you to get out of that chair. We're gonna go home and lock you in
the car. The trip is over." I then asked Julie if it would be all right if I were the
policeman, I said I would not let a mother do such a terrible thing to her child,
at which point Julie got some clay, made a round, big bomb, and pretended to
kill the bad mother.

We discussed the story at the end of the session, and the following week Julie
wanted to replay it, first dictating the following distorted review into the tape
recorder:

"The Accident. Once upon a time I was in this car, and I pretended that I was
going to the Monroeville Mall. And then some old lady locked me in the car. And
I had a car accident and broke my leg. And then I went to the hospital. And then
I called the police, and the police was going to bring in this old woman that locked
me in the car. So I had a session with the judge, a trial. I was the witness. At the
trial I had a clay time bomb, and I blew the witch up, and the witch died. And then
there was this nurse who pretended to be a housemother. I mean, there was this
housemother pretending to be a nurse, and she-she-she-blew up too. And then
there was another one who was a very nice nurse. She took the bandage off and
let me out of the hospital, and that was the end of the story." She then went on to
tell what the story for this week was to be, though it was played out with much
more violence and gore than in the preview. "This week there was a long car
accident and people committing suicide. It takes place in a shopping center. The
characters are: a policeman, nurse, housemother, doctor, and school teacher—and
there's me, and I'm the one that has the car accident. I'm supposed to go a long
way down a great big hill and bump into something—crash!"

In both stories a girl gets injured in a car accident caused by her mother, who has
left the child in the car alone and "forgotten" to put on the brakes. The implication
is that the mother had deliberately caused the blindness; and in both stories the
girl's rage is expressed through bombing and killing the mother, with support
from the policeman, the judge, and the nurse. When asked what the moral of the
stories would be, Julie said: "Mothers shouldn't hit kids hard." Of course, it is
essential in work with such children not only to help them get in touch with their
rage, but also to help them to protect their loved ones from that anger by finding
more appropriate ways of expressing their frustrations.

Julie's father continued to be upset about the clinic bill, and abruptly decided
that she could come only one more time. In this goodbye session, we talked about
how hard it was that a child could not be the boss of her own therapy, and how angry

she felt at all the grownups, including me, for not preventing the premature termination. Fortunately, enough work had been done that significant changes in her symptoms had taken place: she was less inhibited in self-assertion, and in the use of her hands for learning braille. While she had not resolved all of the underlying conflicts, she had come to know her anger and her helplessness, and was finding that she could speak up without hurting anyone she loved.

Candy

The problem of coping with the fact of a missing or malfunctioning body part is a big one, and one which every blind child must confront. The fantasy that it is mother who has either not given the child the proper equipment, or has taken it away because of some "badness" is a common one, as in Julie's stories. Candy, a cerebral palsied blind child, in her first art interview made a clay "doggy" (labelling a mass of clay as a dog), and went on to spontaneously create a drama in which a mother dog is taken away. One of the inhibitions for a blind child in expressing anger toward a parent is the child's very realistic dependency on that parent, his feelings of helplessness and vulnerability at the thought of separation.

Candy first put her clay dog "down in the cellar," and the dog yelled "She dropped me!" Having let out a bit of aggression, she went on: "Let's pretend the dog is a mother. They're cuddling up with each other, and they're sleeping" (putting a smaller piece of clay next to a larger one). "This is the mother doggy, and this is the baby doggy. . . . The baby doggy goes right behind the mother. Then they give the mother doggy away!" When asked who would do that, she said, "The little boy. He took her to the dog pound." Smacking another piece of clay vigorously, she shouted angrily, "Bad boy! You know better than to give those doggies away! I'll let you have it! You bring those doggies back!" She then stabbed a hole in the boy, saying "Boy! You're gonna die! There! You're dead! Pretend this [a wooden clay tool] is like a knife. I killed him for good." In a later story during the same session she told of a father who "died of old age. . . . Nobody killed him. I didn't kill him."

And in yet another drama built around clay work at the end of the same hour, she expressed anxiety about being hurt: "Don't kill me! Oh! The bad guys are gonna kill me! I didn't do anything wrong! Oh, help! I didn't do anything wrong! I didn't do anything wrong!" At this point I asked who she was in the story, and she said she had been the mother. She then pretended that I was her little girl and she was my new mother: "You need a new mother. You can get one right this minute. . . . I'll make the pancakes. I'll take her place, and she's dead. . . . My children punched me and they pulled my hair." Having thus worried aloud about being a mother and getting that aggression herself, she decided to undo the fantasied mother-killing and replacement. With surprise she announced: "Your mother's back! You can tell her how well she was in the heaven." Then, as if the impulse was still too strong, she went on, "Maybe your mother—maybe she got sick. I guess she'll come back tomorrow."

In addition to the mother-killing wishes, blind children often have fantasies, and sometimes symptoms, which involve stealing. In part, this seems to reflect a feeling that something has been stolen from them (their sight), that they are missing something that is rightfully theirs, and that they are entitled to retrieve it. In Candy's second diagnostic art interview, she pretended to be both a robber and a policeman, saying "I'm gonna steal your money . . . because I like it." As a very strict policeman (conscience), she then arrested the robber and put him in jail. The persistent robber returned, however, and the policeman said, "You're back again! What is the *matter* with you?" That question, however, may have been too close to home, as it was followed by an abrupt shift in her play.

In the subsequent drama, holding a piece of wood and one of foam, she began to move both objects toward and away from each other, enacting an approach-avoidance conflict, saying "And the wood came along and asked if it could go out and play. And they play, and then they hit each other. You're bad! No, you're bad!" "Finally the stick says, I don't wanna play anymore! then both say 'I'm leavin'! No, *I'm* leavin'!' and the wood stick shouts and hits the scratchy thing, and it's all killed. . . . 'Oh no! I'm killed! Why did you kill me? You've done something wrong! No *you!* No *you!*'" The pressing dilemma seemed to be whether the mother had done something wrong, or whether the child was bad and had caused the handicap herself as a punishment.

Using fingerpaint next, enjoying the feel of the creamy substance, Candy imagined someone not being pleased with the fingerpaint which says, "I'm too *mushy* for you!" As she continued to use the paint, she went on to talk about funny and then scary stories about ghosts, potions, and especially "magic potions that make you sick, which means you have a hard time breathing. . . . A witch is also scary. She could give you loads of bad stuff. . . . She gives you a potion, and you attack her, and she goes away." The fantasy that maybe a witch-mother's bad food (potion) caused the handicap is also a rather common one.

In an equally common attempt to master the anxiety caused by this fantasy, Candy then pretended to put her fingerpainted hands into and onto lots of things, saying *she* was "polluting." She said to me, "Pretend you walk funny, and you—Who's gonna wipe the pollution out? Pretend you felt sick. I'm gonna put pollution inside your smile. I'm gonna put—I'm gonna put pollution inside your *eye*. . . . Pretend I put pollution in your sock. Pretend you hurt your arm with pollution. . . . I'm gonna put pollution on your dish. Now you eat it, and you die." Having pretended to blind me as well as to kill me off, she became anxious, and there was an abrupt shift in the play, as Candy attempted to undo the effects of her angry retaliatory impulses: "There's never gonna be pollution again. The pollution will all go away. I'll never be a pollutor!" She then stuck a piece of clay on her finger, and enjoyed having it there, resisting removing it as the hour ended.

Coping with Blindness

The use of art materials like clay as fantasied replacements, additions, or perhaps protectors, is also common with the blind. As with the clay on Candy's finger, both Barry (with his artificial eyes) and Tommy (with his progressive vision loss) at different times made "casts" or "extra fingers" with clay or Paris-craft. In each case, it seemed to be a way of compensating in fantasy for the missing body part or function, and may also have served as protection against the ever-present threat of further injury. A similar compensatory mechanism seems evident in Tommy's super-powerful, indestructible sculpture, the "Bionic Susquash" (Fig. 9-1), who can see, hear, and perform perfectly.

The feeling of having been irreparably damaged and totally vulnerable, was poignantly conveyed by Tommy in his two drawings done at the clinic of "Tommy Martian." In the first (Fig. 9-2), he is shown with "tentacles [and] a beam-arm" along with "the ship he was in." Though the figure looks intact, Tommy explained, "He *crashed*. He bumped into a *bomb* flying saucer." As if he had done something wrong, though unspecified, he went on: "They were after him." Then he went on to describe what was happening, talking while he drew the second picture (Fig. 9-3):

Fig. 9-1. A "Bionic Susquash" who can magically grow new parts. Clay.

Fig. 9-2. Tommy Martian with tentacles and his spaceship. Marker.

Fig. 9-3. A second drawing of Tommy Martian "all messed up."

"He wasn't dead when he crashed into that ship. They're trying to kill him. A blade-type ship cut him right in half. They're trying to kill him. He was flying *his* ship. Then this one came over, got beside him, drew its blade, smashed into him, and now he's dead. . . . There's his body laying down on the ground: his head flew over here, his neck is here, one leg is over here, and one leg is over there. He's all messed up."

All blind children, whether or not they end up at mental health centers, go through a process of trying to come to terms with their handicap, a process which usually involves denying, wondering, wishing, raging, mourning, and then attempting to accept it. At first, it is most common to try to deny the reality, to say like Candy did in her first session, "I know color. I can tell colors, like green, red, pink, yellow, blue, white, orange. I like purple. Purple's my favorite." Knowing that she did not have either color or light perception, I wondered if she meant that she knew color names, but she insisted that she could see the different hues. Barry, with his two artificial eyes, at first asserted that he was the only child at the school who wasn't "really blind." These of course represented attempts to deny the reality of the handicap which, as Tommy said symbolically, can feel like being "all messed up."

The awareness that one is different and more vulnerable is not always verbalized, but may be powerfully conveyed through art. Janice, in her first art interview, spoke symbolically of her greater vulnerability and anger at feeling so helpless. She drew a Snowman Family of three, and when asked who they were, wrote the names of herself and her parents below the figures. She said that the parents don't fight, but "I get angry the most." When asked the cause of her anger, she said with vehemence, "I just never want the sun to come out!" I wondered if that was because her snowman would melt, and she said "Yes." I then said, "Doesn't the sun melt the parents too?" to which she bitterly replied, "No, 'cause *they're* unmeltable!"

During a session held several months later, Janice went on to express her resentment and retaliatory rage at the sighted, especially those on whom she felt dependent. She painted "a building which is a hospital, and in this hospital—there's just one patient in this hospital. . . . The one patient is Mrs. Rubin. . . . She had an accident. She bumped into another lady's car and . . . she punctured her eye." When asked what would happen she said with a grin, "It's gonna blind her," going on to explain how Mrs. Rubin would then be unable to work with children in art. When asked how she herself felt about it, she asserted with a sly smile, "I don't feel anything. My sight's coming back!" Having verbalized this wish, she went on to deny her handicap completely, saying "I can see just like a regular person!"

Barry

Working with blind and otherwise handicapped children in therapy is not an easy thing to do, but is always a challenge as well as a powerful learning experience. Sometimes progress can be painfully slow. It required six years of work for Barry to move from his statement that he was the only child at school who was "not really blind," through his fantasies, wonderings, wishes, rages, and mournings, until he could rather calmly talk about "the real Barry, you know, the one at the School for the Blind." It took six years for him to be able to talk about his impulses, rather than act on them—to not break a window, but to tell a story about "Barry, and how he would *like* to break a window when his sister calls him a blind cripple."

Barry had begun in his work with many indications of his feelings of vulnerability. In his first art interview, he had carefully poked rows of holes into clay with a tool, and had spoken of falling down a deep hole, "where maybe you couldn't get out!" Like many, he had attempted to achieve freedom from the constrictions imposed by his handicap, creating numerous clay rockets (Fig. 9-4) and stories about being an astronaut in outer space. These wishful denials of reality included such thoughts as: "It would be fun to go, because you could *see* things, and you could walk on the moon." As if he could not, even in fantasy, escape from danger, however, he added: "If I walk on the moon myself, I'm afraid I'd fall through." Nevertheless, like other handicapped youngsters, he was full of compensatory omnipotent fantasies, imagining himself as the "King of Space" or the "President" of the country.

Because his world was so constricted, his therapy became for him, as for other such children, a central event in his life. He not only developed a strong, and initially positive transference, but fantasized that it was returned, as when he asked in the second month of therapy, "When you go home, do you always think about me?" While such occurrences are common for many physically normal, troubled youngsters, they are intensified for a child whose existence is really restricted, for whom the expression of strong feelings may seem more risky. Because of his particular handicap, he like others relied not only on art media, but also on sounds, music (Fig. 9-5), and dramatic play, with a special function for the tape recorder which he would use to review what had occurred, much as a sighted child could look back at his art work.

On his last day, with his usual dramatic flair, he announced that he was going to give a "speech" announcing his "resignation" from the Child Guidance Center, a fairly realistic reflection of how far he had come:

I've asked for this time to speak directly to you all about my resignation at the Pittsburgh Child Guidance Center. During the past several weeks I've been thinking about this plan to resign, and two weeks ago, I told my therapist I was done. But as I resign, let me resign in good spirits. For the past few years we worked on problems, how I've handled things, and tempers I've lost.

I'm through all that. There are a lot more things to accomplish. . . . It's hard to do, but I have to, because I believe that the time has come that I should resign here. I hope all will be well. After this I'll go back home and work with problems and do heavy work. . . . I leave with no bitterness. I leave with this conclusion to the years of work. Sometimes we will have fights, we will be angry, sometimes we will be all right.

Hopefully, I might report and come back and visit the people here. . . . I trust you all will remember the past and think of the future. I want to say goodbye to everybody over here—Mrs. Rubin and Miss Driben [a blind social worker] and the ladies in the waiting room. I came here in 1969 and ended in 1975.

My conclusion is this—I told a few school friends that I was resigning Child Guidance Center after I made the decision. They said good. My girlfriend is just as proud as I am. . . .

I hope I'll get through this blind school. I may be an elevator operator. I can't be an airplane pilot. . . . I'd like to be a radio reporter. . . . I've been working hard in class, in school—in social studies and math. As I leave, I conclude with one final word: I hope nothing goes wrong here. I hope everybody remains the same shape, and all the people I know—I'll be talkin' about you, and I hope in the future things become better off for you. So farewell, goodbye. For the past number of years, we worked hard on courageous problems at home and at school. Farewell.

As Barry listened to a replay of the tape of his speech, he was solemn, but seemed sure of his decision, which was indeed difficult after such a long time. He did call every few months "to see how things are over there," and six months later asked to come in for "just one visit" in order to tell me his latest New Year's Resolutions.

In the years while Barry was still at the school for the blind, he kept in touch with me through occasional phone calls. He still liked to create rockets—his symbol of unrestricted freedom, his fantasied escape from the constrictions of his blindness. He no longer believed, however, that he could be an astronaut or an airplane pilot. Instead, he worked hard as a student and became an active citizen in high school, then went on to secure and keep a job at the local guild for the blind, traveling to and from work on a bus. He continued to develop his dramatic gifts, too, performing at a local cabaret on amateur night as a comedian, calling me proudly to let me know, in case I could attend. In his periodic telephone contacts during the eight years since he terminated therapy, I have had the impression that Barry has found a way, not only to succeed as a blind person coping in a sighted world, but to be reasonably happy as well.

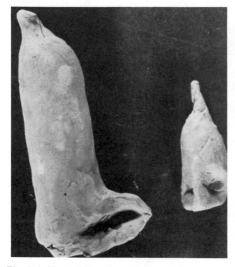

Fig. 9-4. Two of Barry's many clay rockets used for space fantasies.

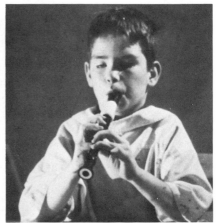

Fig. 9-5. Barry playing on a recorder during a therapy session.

PART III:
THE FAMILY AND THE GROUP

CHAPTER 10.

A Family Art Evaluation

Young children are realistically dependent on the adults who care for them. They are still "becoming" as human beings in interaction with those adults. It is, therefore, especially important in working with children to know about, and sometimes to work with, their families. Even if the primary mode of treatment is individual, it is often helpful at the beginning or in the middle of the process to meet with the entire family. In getting to know other members, and in understanding how they relate to one another, a family art evaluation has proved extremely useful, and has been a diagnostic option at the Western Psychiatric Institute & Clinic, and before that at the Pittsburgh Child Guidance Center, since 1970.

I was inspired by the pioneering work of others with families (Kwiatkowska, 1962, 1967, 1971, 1978; Kraft and Austin, 1968; Zierer, Sternberg, and Finn, 1966), but found it necessary to develop a session appropriate to the needs and capacities of our relatively young clinic population and their families. I was also fortunate to have the interest and support of the Chief of Clinical Child Psychology, (Max Magnussen, Ph.D.) who collaborated in the design, development, and implementation of the technique (as well as on the paper on which this chapter is based).

We tried various formats, including an open-ended one like the individual art interview described earlier. We found, however, that such an approach is more threatening to families, especially for the older members, perhaps because people were exposing themselves to one another as well as to a therapist. Lack of structure also seemed less fruitful in getting the kind of data wanted, e.g., how individuals in a family perceive and relate to one another. After experimentation with many possible tasks and sequences, we arrived at a series of three, best done in a two-hour time span, which seem most productive under most circumstances.

The session is usually conducted in a large group room, though the setting can be any space big enough to contain working surfaces for all family members.

Ideally, there would be space for a large round table, some smaller tables, some easels, and a supply table. The whole family may be seen at any point in the diagnostic evaluation or during treatment, and the referring clinician(s) either co-lead the session with me or conduct it after consultation. Although shorter time periods have been tried and are possible, two hours is a comfortable span of time for most families. It seems best to invite all members of the family living at home to attend if that is possible, with the exception of infants and toddlers who could not realistically participate. Three- and four-year-olds who are able to sit still and use art media, however, have often been involved. The only exception to the format for a child at a prefigurative level is that the projection of an image onto a scribble is not possible (see Task 1). It is no problem, however, for a youngster to "scribble" a free drawing. I prefer to have minimal information about the family prior to the evaluation, and feel that this enables me to be more free and objective in my observations. I find the same to be true with the individual art interview described earlier, though in both cases reading the record after the session can help to put one's initial diagnostic hunches in perspective.

Format

Through experimentation with possible modifications, Dr. Magnussen and I arrived at the following sequence of tasks:

1. *Individual Picture from a Scribble.*   Seated around the circular table, each member chooses from the drawing tools in the center (pencils, crayons, chalk, markers, pens) and on the small (9-by-12-inch) white drawing paper in front of him, draws a continuous line scribble with his eyes open or closed, whichever he prefers. When finished, each is encouraged to examine his scribble from all possible points of view, in order to "see" pictures in it. Each is then encouraged to select one or more images, elaborating them into a picture to which he then gives a title. When all are done, they take turns placing their developed scribble drawings on the easel, the creator of the picture first describing his work, the others then responding to it (Figs. 10-1, 10-2, and 10-3).

2. *Family Portraits.*   Each individual is asked to create an abstract or realistic portrait of the family in two or three dimensions. All are shown the range of media available on the supply tables and sink (drawing materials as in Task 1, watercolors, tempera paints, finger paints, clay, wood scraps, glue, assorted sizes and colors of construction paper). The possible work spaces in the room are pointed out (easels, tables, floor), and each person is encouraged to work wherever he wishes. When everyone has completed a representation of the family, the works are taped on the wall or placed on the table so that all portraits are simultaneously visible. Members first react spontaneously to the array of renditions, each person eventually being asked to describe his work, the others commenting and questioning as they wish (Figs. 10-4, 10-5, 10-6, and 10-7).

3. *Joint Mural.*   The family is asked to create something together on the large 3-by-6-foot paper taped on the wall, using thick poster chalks. It is suggested that

they first decide together what they will do, and then work on the paper. When the mural is finished, all look at it and are encouraged to discuss the group experience as well as the product which emerged (Figs. 10-8 and 10-9).

4. *Free Products.* If an individual completes either of the first two tasks before all members are done, he is encouraged to create art products using any medium and topic he desires (Figs. 10-10 and 10-11).

In spite of prior preparation by the referring clinician, most family members, especially adolescents and adults, are apt to be self-conscious about their lack of ability in art. As they first enter and are seated around the table, therefore, an attempt is made to explain the purpose and nature of the interview, and to elicit any questions or concerns they may have before beginning. Exploring aloud such worries, anxieties, and confusions as may exist is often essential, and always helpful in overcoming normal resistances to exposure. It is emphasized that artistic skill is not expected and is indeed irrelevant, that individuals are encouraged themselves to explain and explore the meanings of what they produce, and that the evaluation is conceived of as a learning experience for both family and clinicians. People are naturally fearful of being "seen through," of exposing something to others of which they themselves may not be aware. While there is some justification for this anxiety, it is my sincere belief that the meaning of anyone's symbol must ultimately depend on his own associations to it, and that the "expert" in the interpretation of anyone's art work must be the person who did it, at least as much as the analytic observer. Ideally, understanding of meanings emerges out of a joint consideration of the work and associations thereto. It is, therefore, possible to present the session to the family as a collaborative undertaking.

Prior to the termination of the interview, the family is encouraged to explore any concerns, questions, or issues about themselves that may have arisen in the course of the session. Questions such as "What happened that you did not expect?" or "How typical or atypical was your family today?" are helpful ones in engaging the family in the learning process. Most families, in fact, do find a way to use the session itself as a means of self-analysis.

Although colleagues sometimes express concern about the threatening possibilities of a family art evaluation, experience at our Center has been that most families can handle the session quite comfortably. The atmosphere typically becomes increasingly informal and relaxed during the session, especially when two hours are available. My impression is that this is due in part to the opportunity for selection of an ego-syntonic medium, style, and location during the second task. In addition, the presence of younger children in many families is an asset to their more self-conscious parents and older siblings, for they tend to enjoy the procedure, often request more such sessions, and clearly help the others by their natural, spontaneous behavior.

Scribble Drawings. The sequence of tasks is designed to provide a maximum of information about individual and family characteristics with minimal stress. Thus, the making of a *scribble* as the first task puts the non-artist at ease, despite the

Fig. 10-1. Scribble drawing by Mrs. I.: "Barbed wire fence." Marker.

fact that it is a powerful diagnostic tool. Sitting together around a table is conducive to informal communication among family members, and since the paper is provided at each seat, the only choice required is the drawing medium. The scribble technique is drawn from previous work in education (Cane, 1951), therapy (Naumburg, 1966), and diagnosis with both individuals (Ulman, 1965) and families (Kwiatkowska, 1967).

The request to develop a picture from an image or images perceived in a scribble presents each family member with the task of structuring his own self-created, ambiguous stimulus. Like the Rorschach, the projective content and associations are idiosyncratically valid, as are the formal aspects of how the person performs the task. Further projective and interactional data on each individual is available as he responds to other members' drawings during the discussion. (Such as a six year old's response to his mother's picture of "A Smiling Doggie": "Maybe they chopped his tail off!") Who sits next to whom, who interacts with whom, and the nature of the interaction all provide further useful data.

Mrs. I., for example, was at first unable to see anything in her line, but when encouraged to look again, finally said it reminded her of "a barbed wire fence, like in a concentration camp" (Fig. 10-1). She thus let us know how she felt about being cooped up with five active children and no husband, and perhaps about the art evaluation itself, during which her youngsters were getting quite rambunctious as she sat passive, helpless to control them. Mr. F. at first said that his scribble drawing "might as well be a Bum as a Clown," but finally entitled it "Clown," emphasizing the lighthearted elements (Fig. 10-2). He thus suggested some ambivalence in his self-image, and reinforced our impression that he used humor as a defense against strong feelings, especially of depression.

Carl and Carol I., eight-year-old twins, each saw monsters in their scribbles (Fig. 10-3). Carl, the initial referral, said his monster was a boy of six who was

Fig. 10-2. Scribble drawing by Mr. F.: "A bum or a clown." Crayon.

Fig. 10-3. Scribble drawings of monsters (a) by Carl and (b) by Carol. Crayon.

"stupid, eating everything, eating people. People call him names like bighead or stupid." Carol described hers as a girl monster who "likes to go and eat people's guts and eat people when they bother her sometimes." The disorganization of her drawing, its oral aggression, and her critical attacks on others' pictures, led to her being seen as a patient at the clinic as well as her brother.

Family Portraits. The second task requires not only the production of a family portrait, a very common procedure, but also provides a free choice of materials and working location. The "abstract family portrait" described by Kwiatkowska (1967) is suggested as an alternative possibility, and no specific instructions are given beyond the initial request to create the family using any medium. Thus, the products range from static to active, from heads to full, realistic drawings, paintings, reliefs, or sculptures in both clay and wood scraps. It is not unusual for diagnostically significant omissions, condensations, and elaborations to occur; nor is it infrequent that an individual will create a second representation of the family in another medium, often revealing even more than the first.

In addition to the possible projective significance of such factors as sequence of figures drawn, relative size, position, etc., there are additional data concerning family relationships from the way in which the members position themselves in the room and interact spontaneously in the course of this second task. For example, Mr. and Mrs. F. and their sixteen-year-old natural daughter stayed together, verbally interacting, at the round table at which they had developed their scribbles. The two adopted youngsters, Jack and Jody (the eleven-year-old identified patient), each isolated themselves at separate tables away from the trio and worked silently at the task. As with the scribble drawings, much is also learned from responses to others' productions, as well as from each individual's projected image of the family.

Fig. 10-4. F. family at work on Task 2

Fig. 10-5. Family drawing by Mr. F. Line drawing of a crayon original.

Mr. F. said he was "trying to get a feeling of closeness" (Fig. 10-5). Actually, he drew himself, his wife, and his two natural children in a tight group, then subtly isolated his two adopted children (Jack and Jody). They are slightly apart from the others and were drawn last, although he had stated that he drew the family "in the order of the ages of the children." Jack, Mr. F.'s eight-year-old adopted son, chose for his family picture to represent only his baby brother in their shared bedroom, describing himself as "outside trying to get in" (Fig. 10-6). Further evidence of sibling rivalry was found in his response to his mother's family drawing (Fig. 10-7). He said with irritation that her picture of the baby, not physically but psychologically present during the evaluation, was "too big!"

Fig. 10-6. Family drawing by Jack F. Marker.

Fig. 10-7. Family drawing by Mrs. F. Line drawing of a crayon original.

Mrs. F. said she drew the family "holding hands—a happy, close family." Her picture helped to confirm our feeling that Jody and Jack were being subtly excluded from the family circle, or at least put on the periphery. A similar impression was gained from Mr. F.'s family drawing, Jack's family portrait, and the way in which the members positioned themselves during the second task. Though both parents denied conflicts within the family, these diagnostic signs suggested that the task of emotionally including the two adopted children had not been fully accomplished.

During the second task, the range of possible media available makes it possible to observe closely individual styles and modes of decision-making and working. Flexibility or rigidity of response to such possible variables as the running together of watercolor paints may also be observed. Not only may the individual's selection and handling of the medium be significant, but equally revealing are the responses of other family members, as when a mother becomes upset at a child's "messing" with fingerpaint or clay.

Family Mural.   The last procedure requires the family to make (sometimes to abdicate) a joint decision, and to implement it in regard to a commonly assigned task. In format it is not unlike other group mural techniques, and as a group task it is related to the joint projects used by others in family art interviews. In the open-ended, free-choice decision-making around content, with not even a beginning like a scribble or a topic to focus upon, individually significant themes quickly emerge, as does the family's habitual problem-solving strategy. It seems that the degree and kind of organization in the final product reflect the family's ability to function in a unified fashion, though they may not necessarily experience the process as comfortable. The manner in which members participate in both the decision-making and the execution phases of this task, gives further evidence of family characteristics and interaction patterns. In the open-ended discussion following the group task, further information is gathered, such as who the members felt to be in charge, how typical the interaction seemed, etc.

The F. family considered several options and was able, with little friction, to come to a joint decision to draw a dinosaur (Fig. 10-8). Although eight-year-old

Fig. 10-8. F. family working on their dinosaur mural.

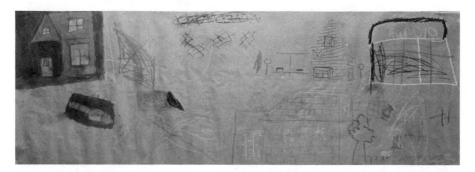

Fig. 10-9. House mural by the I. family. Chalk.

Jack did not participate initially, annoyed that his idea had not been chosen, he finally joined the others who were working together smoothly, efficiently, and with evident pleasure in the joint endeavor. The bright, playful fantasy and overall organization of the mural reflect the imaginative strengths and cohesive potential of the family group that created it (Fig. 10-8). The I. family, however, unable to engage in any group discussion prior to drawing, impulsively began to work independently and somewhat competitively, as reflected in the scribbled attacks on several portions. A shared sense of family identity and wishes may be reflected in the common theme (houses), while the disorganization and confusion apparent throughout the hectic, two-hour session are mirrored in the disjointed, isolated, patchwork quality of the family's joint effort (Fig. 10-9).

Free Products. Free products, though not assigned, usually occur for at least one or more individuals for the simple reason that people work at different speeds. A crayon drawing by Glen, done while the others were finishing family portraits, was a graphic appeal for "help"—the word shouted by the boy in the parachute who is being shot at from below by an older boy in a dragster (Fig. 10-10). Glen, age six, attempted to both emulate and challenge his older brother throughout

Fig. 10-10. Glen's free product. Crayon. Age 6.

the session, while his mother effectively withdrew from any kind of interaction with either boy. He seemed to feel unprotected and vulnerable, and the story about his drawing was that the two therapists would rescue the parachuting boy, clearly a projection of himself.

Mrs. Y. was tense, constricted, and withdrawn throughout the art session; her pictures were tight, compulsive, and unelaborated, her verbalization sparse. Her drawing of a teepee, made while waiting for the others to finish family portraits, was somewhat looser than her other products (Fig. 10-11). Her association was that the Indian inside was sending smoke signals, asking for help for an unspecified problem, much as she herself, hiding behind an anxious silence, was mutely asking for assistance at the clinic.

Like any assessment approach involving the whole family, a family art session provides an opportunity for direct observation of their interaction. Like any activity approach to family diagnosis, a family art evaluation provides an event in the present that can be observed as it occurs, and can be a focus for discussion in the group. Because more than one person is active at one time, multiple observational opportunities are also available.

And in common with any diagnostic approach using art and nonverbal communication, defenses are frequently bypassed. As in group art therapy, communication through shared focus on products is often easier for family members in regard to each other, as well as to the clinicians. Those who have systematically compared

Fig. 10-11. Mrs. Y.'s free product. Marker.

family art evaluations with family verbal diagnostic interviews, have consistently noted the additional significant understandings obtained through art (Kwiatkowska, 1967). A recently developed Family Puppet Diagnostic Interview is perhaps the most similar of other activity assessments with families (Irwin and Malloy, 1975).

There seems to be no question that "the family art evaluation session gives an unusually rich amount of information with a minimal expenditure of the family's and the therapist's time." (Kwiatkowska, 1967, p. 54). Since this interview has been adjunctive to more traditional diagnostic procedures at our clinic, it has been possible to informally compare and contrast the findings from it with those of other assessment approaches. On a small sample of cases Dr. Magnussen and I tried to arrive at diagnostic formulations, independent of other approaches to the same family within the Center. In general, it was possible to demonstrate that remarkably similar findings occurred.

A family art evaluation session elicits a number of different kinds of diagnostic data, which provide a built-in system of checks and balances for assessment. In the course of the three tasks and discussions, one observes a great deal of behavior—verbal and nonverbal, independent and interactional—on the part of each individual family member. There is much symbolic data in the products produced—in their form, content, process, and style of execution—and in the associations to them from each individual, to his own works and to those of others. By systematically varying the specificity and degree of choice (in topic, medium, location, etc.) inherent in each task, as well as the degree of closeness or interaction necessary for its completion, it is possible to gather extensive data on individual as well as family dynamics. Because there is so much activity to be observed, it is helpful (though not essential) to have two clinicians involved, just as it is helpful to make videotape recordings of these sessions when possible.

One advantage of the combination of multiple sources of data is the possibility of finding degrees of commonality. For example, if symbolic art content parallels observed behavior, the diagnostic impression is reinforced. To verify or refute such an impression, the interviewer(s) might point out to the family the consistency or inconsistency of the findings, to get further reactions from them. In this way, the family is involved directly and openly in determining the significance of their productions, interactions, and verbalizations. The family can in many cases actively assist in analyzing the data, interpreting it, and rejecting or accepting the therapists' impressions.

To illustrate the procedure of putting together the various sources of data, it may help to look again at the F. family (Figs. 10-2, and 10-4 through 10-8). Both parents thought they had successfully handled their own feelings regarding their two adopted youngsters, and had integrated them well into the family unit. However, there was ample evidence of the two children's subtle exclusion: their vocal concern that their art work would not be acceptable to their parents, their sitting apart from the others during the second task, Jack's drawing the "family" as consisting only of the baby, shown as displacing him from his bedroom, father's unconscious sequencing and placement of figures in his family drawing, and mother's placement of the two adoptees on the edges of the group in her family portrait. Although the referral had been made because of Jody's underachievement in school and possible learning disability, it was clear that her position in the family could well be one source of her problem, and that intervention efforts needed to involve the whole F. family.

When Dr. Magnussen and I first developed our family art evaluation, we were surprised at the amount of resistance among our colleagues. Despite our assurances that Kwiatkowska's pioneering work at NIMH had resulted in routine use of a similar tool there, many expressed concern and uneasiness, though usually interest as well. It naturally takes time for clinicians to become familiar with and to utilize a new technique. With an increasing emphasis on family approaches to diagnosis and therapy, the popularity of art-centered family tasks has continued to grow in the years since they were first introduced at our Center. It is my feeling that the clinician's own comfort in presenting and conducting such an interview is the primary factor in the patients' ability to handle the stress. As noted earlier, most families tend to accept the procedures quite readily, and even to enjoy the session to some extent. Here, as in any use of art in a clinical setting, a vital variable in the comfort equation for the client is the clinician's own feelings about introducing the activity.

Thus, when workers are comfortable, things tend to go well, even under conditions which might conceivably produce more stress than the usual circumstances. A good example of clinicians' positive expectancy effects was the experience of a child psychiatrist and a social worker, co-therapists for a parents' group. After one month of weekly meetings, the couples were told that each entire family was to come in for an art session, that would be videotaped and later reviewed in the group. All five families were seen for a family art evaluation within the next few weeks, each session lasting for an hour and involving several tasks. The cotherapists then proceeded to review the tapes and art work with the couples' group, taking two weeks for each family. The group discussed them in detail, attempting in the process to learn more themselves and to promote constructive change. The group leaders were so pleased with the results of their innovative approach that they later wrote and presented a paper describing it (Henderson and Lowe, 1972).

My experience with them and with others has confirmed Kwiatkowska's observations that such procedures are eminently teachable, requiring minimal background in art (1967, 1971). The work of these two colleagues with the couples' group also exemplified the possibility of modifications of the interview for different purposes. Because of their plan to review the entire procedure in the group, one hour was considered the maximal time. A more limited space was utilized, so that the videotape would include all members at all moments. A rug on the floor necessitated some limitation of media (e.g., no paints or wet clay), though the principle of choice of materials and location was retained. Because of less time, it was decided to use only the second and third tasks, to omit the largest size paper for

Task 2, and to present a more limited and quickly usable selection of two-dimensional media. What was learned was not only that the whole conception was feasible, but the fact that the necessary limitations and modifications did not seem to inhibit the emergence of useful and relevant data.

Modifying the evaluation is frequently useful, and at times it can be extremely helpful. In no way do I think of the family art evaluation described here as a fixed, invariant, rigid procedure from which no deviation is possible. Instead, it represents the three tasks and sequence which so far have proved most comfortable and productive with families in our clinic if enough time is available. With less time, one must choose, as did a former psychology intern at the Center, who in her first job at a California clinic used a five-minute group mural (a time-limited version of Task 3) as part of a brief family evaluation procedure (Goldstein, Barasch and Deeton, 1975).

Once, when working with a family which included a blind child, I found myself modifying the session in relation to her particular needs. A totally verbal task was added as the first activity, one in the expressive modality most comfortable for her. This was followed by a request to represent the family in any medium, with clay and wood scraps provided for the girl. She selected five flat wood scraps varying in shape and size, and glued them on a piece of cardboard in a way that clearly reflected some wishes and perceptions about her family. After selecting a shape for each person, she placed her mother at the left, then her father (noticeably bigger than the others) on the right, then her older brother in the center "by himself," then herself (the smallest and thinnest piece of wood) right next to her Daddy, and finally her younger sister "near Mommy." Her deliberate selection of sizes, shapes, and thicknesses, along with her conscious placement of people, gave us a good understanding of her perception of intrafamilial relationships, despite the fact that she could not "draw a family."

Her fourteen-year-old brother, who had been sulking quietly saying he couldn't create a family, was stimulated, perhaps through rivalry, perhaps because it was less threatening, to use the same medium himself. He placed his self-symbol alone in the center, showing it shooting missiles at the other four family members, each in a corner—a fairly accurate image of how things were at that time. Thus the materials proved to be useful not only for the child with the sensory handicap, but also to overcome the inhibition and resistance of her brother.

In the course of developing the evaluation, Dr. Magnussen and I experimented with a variety of times, sequences, tasks, and settings. There are clearly pros and cons to all possibilities, and a carefully controlled research study would be necessary in order to truly define which portions or aspects of the procedure are most significant diagnostically. Often, if much time is spent on the first two tasks (or if the family comes late), I have found it necessary to suggest a time limit for the third, which seems if anything to help people get started, although it may obscure the conflicts which might become apparent if more time were available.

A family, of course, is a particular kind of natural and interdependent group. As a group, it has characteristics common to all groups, so that it is not surprising that procedures utilized to assess families can also be used productively with different kinds of groups. Asking group members, perhaps at varying points in time, to "represent the group" for example (Denny, 1972; Hare and Hare, 1956; Rubin and Levy, 1975), may be extremely helpful in getting a sense of individual perceptions of the unit. Similarly, it may happen spontaneously, or one may request that group members work together on a joint project, like a mural, which is as likely to reflect their decision-making and interaction processes as with a family. Understanding such group communications at a deeper symbolic level is as possible as with individual products, and is well-described in a book about ongoing mural work with adults (Harris and Joseph, 1973).

It should be noted that caution is as important in "reading" meanings from pictures by or about families or groups, as in work by individuals. While there are many suggestions about the meaning of such things as omission, size distortions, or placement in family or group drawings, these have never been experimentally validated and probably ought to be regarded as hunches to be confirmed or refuted by additional data. Two studies currently under way at our Center are examining the assumptions implicit in much clinical decision-making about families and groups from art. Preliminary results from both indicate that the situation is indeed a complex one, that murals by a group may or may not be judged in a way similar to how the group perceived the process. Despite a large body of literature which confidently generalizes about the meanings to be "read" in drawings of or by families or groups, one must be aware that these are no more than logical assumptions, perhaps true in many or most cases, but not necessarily in all (Rubin and Rosenblum, 1977).

CHAPTER 11.

Family Art Therapy

While family art therapy can and usually does involve the entire nuclear family as in the family art evaluation, one often finds it helpful to work with smaller components of the larger unit.

Family-Member Dyads

Unquestionably, the most important and influential dyad in a child's life is himself and his mother, and it is useful to have occasional mother-child sessions both early and late in treatment, for a variety of purposes. The following examples illustrate just what can occur and how it can be used to facilitate the work of child art therapy.

Mrs. D., a recently divorced mother, and Lori, her four-and-a-half-year-old daughter, were seen weekly by myself and a psychiatrist, each client spending forty-five minutes with each worker. Following the first five weeks of such sessions, the psychiatrist was to be away for a week. We agreed in our collaboration session that a joint art session for mother and child might serve useful diagnostic and treatment purposes. Both clients agreed to the procedure, though each expressed some ambivalence about sharing their hitherto private time, place, and helping person.

In the course of five art sessions, Lori had moved from careful, compulsive drawing and painting, to the mixing, then tentative use, and finally free smearing of fingerpaint. While she was mixing she had verbalized concern about her mother's probable negative reaction: "My mom will be real mad. . . . I ain't gonna paint 'cause I'm not allowed. . . . My mom says so. I ain't gonna fingerpaint." In the session preceding the joint one, she had involved me in fingerpainting alongside her, perhaps to provide concrete adult approval for such messy activity, taking a bossy "teacher" role: "You start here. . . . You *have* to put your fingers in it." In anticipation of the joint session, she had announced, "I can show my mom how I mix the paint, how I do all the things. We can stay a long time and have fun together. We need lots of water to mix and mix and mix and mix!"

Mrs. D., during her first five art sessions, had expressed much concern about her poor artistic ability, and guilt over limits she had placed on the children (like fencing them in the backyard). While she knew it was "good for kids to get messy," she said she was "a real bug on neatness," and that "once you give them an inch, they do everything." She had expressed symbolically her own fears of loss of control, as well as her covert rejection of the children and wish to escape from them. Once she had pictured Lori and herself as scribbles of strikingly similar shape, with a line around both because it was "so important that we be together." She saw her child as "a carbon copy of me," while projecting her own depression onto the girl and over-identifying with her: "She and I are the same."

Although Lori had said at the end of her first tentative fingertip exploration of a paint mixture during her third session, "It's fun to fingerpaint," during the joint session she stated, "I hate it . . . because it is sloppy." She nevertheless mixed and used fingerpaint, working on the table surface next to her mother, who refused Lori's request to join her in the activity and did a neat drawing instead. The child next invited her mother to join her in using clay. Reluctantly, Mrs. D. agreed, and proceeded to imitate her daughter, who made a snowman figure quite like one she had modelled the previous week. At that time, she had made two "little girl snowmen," who had engaged in a dialogue like puppets, Lori crouched under the table manipulating them. Although she asked her mom to join her for such a dialogue in the joint session, Mrs. D. refused with evident discomfort. Lori then manipulated both her snowman and her mother's. Speaking for both, she directed the drama more to me than to her mom. She identified her snowman as "a little girl, almost five," and the larger one as "the mother," who gradually became more and more punitive towards the "messy," "bad" little girl.

Although painful for Mrs. D., the joint session illuminated for her the intensity of the pressure experienced by Lori over messiness and helped her to recognize her own fears of loss of control. And, in her attempt to duplicate Lori's snowman, she realized in our later discussions that she was perceiving a false identity between herself and Lori. She commented many times throughout the joint session and in later ones about what she saw as Lori's greater ease and freedom in the same art room where both had been for five previous sessions: "*She* really knows her way around here. . . . *She* really makes herself at home."

Billy was a thirteen-year-old boy whose mother was concerned about his rebelliousness. He was seen for a series of assessment sessions, which included not only individual art sessions for Bill, but some family sessions with his mother (his father was dead and an older sister no longer lived at home). In the first joint session, because both mother and son had talked about problems between them, I asked them to draw a picture together in order to observe them interact. Although they discussed it and tried to create a joint picture, they ended up dividing the paper in half, working on opposite sides, each drawing his own version of their jointly-selected theme: "Our House." They were astounded at the end to discover how different were their representations. Billy's house had "dark clouds over it," while his mother's looked quite cheerful. They decided that they often perceived the same thing quite differently, and agreed that this was one of their main problems in both communicating and getting along. Billy became openly tearful about how he felt his mom not only misunderstood, but also rejected him. His mother had as much difficulty hearing what he was saying, as she had had in noticing his drawing while working on her own during the joint picture.

At the second session, I used one of Wadeson's task ideas (1973, 1980), asking each to draw a portrait of the other on opposite sides of a table easel (Fig. 11-1). Each then "corrected" the other's art work, modifying it as he or she wished. Billy felt that his mother had portrayed him as bigger than he really was, sensing her covert wish to have him replace his recently dead father, to be "the man of the house" while at the same time she complained about his assuming that role. Mother saw Billy's drawing of her as having both mouth and eyes that were too large. She modified these features, and then added to it what she felt was a "more attractive" hairstyle and earrings. In fact, she made the portrait much more seductive, while at the same time speaking of it in a critical, distancing fashion. This ambivalent message was confusing to Billy, because it echoed his own adolescent revival of oedipal wishes and his need to separate. Mother described Billy as "putting up a wall" between them, while Billy felt that his mom was "holding me on a leash." The intense ambivalence on both sides of this mother-son relationship was apparent in their drawings and responses to them, as well as in their behavior, and it became clearer to the participants in part through their graphic representations.

Fig. 11-1. Billy and Mrs. K. drawing each other at the easel.

While mother and child are the most common and perhaps most frequently conflicted dyad within the family, there may be reasons for inviting other family members to an occasional joint session with a child client. Laura's mom and dad had recently been divorced, and it was very important to Laura to have her dad come to the clinic and have a session with her (especially since he had not participated in her therapy except financially since the evaluation). The joint session was dramatic— the father came a half hour late, and was then quite demanding and critical throughout Laura's productions. She worked hard to please him, but it was clear that gaining his unequivocal favor was a difficult, if not impossible, task. She was glad that he had come at all, though deeply hurt and angered at his lateness. This single brief experience with her dad was helpful to both of us throughout her four years of treatment, because it was possible not only to look at what had happened, but also to use it as a reference point for subsequent events and feelings about her father.

Donny was eager to have his older brother join him, and Ross finally agreed (unlike many siblings who are quite jealous, and themselves request such a privilege). During the first joint session, Donny, usually quite inventive, spent all of his energies either trying to get Ross to do what he wished, or imitating Ross's efforts. He attempted to get his brother to do a joint drawing, but Ross, quite independent, refused. Donny finally tried to copy Ross's picture, though he felt discouraged about the outcome. A year later, he again wanted Ross to come, and I thought it would be of interest to see if things were different. Indeed they were: Donny went about his own business quite autonomously, only occasionally asking for Ross's attention to show his brother what he was making. Much to my surprise, and Donny's evident delight, Ross ended up imitating Don, using the same materials and process (pounded soldering wire) to create abstract metal sculptures and candle-holders.

Aside from learning more about specific intrafamilial interactions, such dyadic sessions may also be useful in helping the child to feel and see things, like competitive strivings. Lynn, for example, thought she wanted her younger brother to join her toward the end of her therapy, perhaps to dilute the intensity of feelings she was having toward me around termination. But after about ten minutes in the playroom, she decided that Tommy had been there long enough, and told him that his time was up for the day. After taking him back down to the waiting room, she returned and informed me that it was making her "too jealous," and it was making her mad like it did at home, when she had to share her mother with Tommy. The experience was helpful to both of us in looking at her envy not only of her siblings at home, but also of the other children who came to see me at the clinic.

As in other contexts, joint work in the course of individual, group, or family sessions can be approached in an open-ended fashion or with some direction by the therapist. Deciding how to proceed here, as elsewhere, is primarily a function of the goals of the session. After almost a year of separate individual work with eight-year-old David and his mother, both her therapist and I were discouraged, feeling that we had progressed little in loosening their close ties to one another. We decided on a joint half hour, to be followed by separate half hours with each. During their "together time," David and his mom were asked to work together, which they did with hardly a word. Using watercolors, they created a picture of Lake Erie, where they had been on vacation, a peaceful image of water and land with a common linear boundary.

While there are certain elements in the picture itself suggestive of wishes for a kind of symbiotic "fusion" on the part of each person, this was even more evident in their almost mystical nonverbal communication during the process of painting it. At the end each said they had known what the other one was thinking, revealing a joint belief in their ability to read each other's mind. As mother put it, "I always know what he's thinkin', sometimes before he does," while David nodded his head in agreement. After doing and discussing the peaceful symbiotic scene, David's mother took advantage of the remaining joint minutes to complain angrily about his messiness, and his strange and bothersome interest in collecting junk. When alone, David created a series of "Beautiful Mess" paintings using a swirling technique with bright enamel paint, and talked about how hard it was to feel mad at a mother with whom he also felt so close, interdependent, and identified.

While this book is not primarily about work with adults, there are times when art therapy is used with individual parents whose children are also in therapy and sometimes with couples. Mr. and Mrs. C. came weekly for child-centered counselling. Art was used during an early family evaluation session, and minimally during the diagnostic interviews. While it was not the primary medium of communication for this verbal and concerned couple, it became especially useful in dealing with the most loaded and difficult areas of their marital relationship when these emerged as significant factors in the child's problems.

During one session, after much veiled and indirect expression of resentment from each parent concerning unmet needs and disappointment in the partner, I wondered if each could draw the other, since their perceptions of one another seemed to be an area of difficulty. After working on opposite sides of an easel, they looked at and discussed their drawings, both of which became reference points for the remainder of the treatment. Mr. C. had represented his wife as "The Rock of Gibralter" (11-2), a tower of strength and stability in the shifting currents of life. At first he said that was how she was. Later, he responded to her hurt and anger at such unrealistic expectations, with the admission that he had wished that she would never show vulnerability or weakness, but that he had been disappointed. Mrs. C., on the other hand, was finally in tears about how impossible it was to please him, how hard it was to get his sympathy and concern when she herself was needy, conveying her own sense of deprivation. She represented him as all wrapped up in his hobbies and his work, with no time left for his family (Fig.11-3). Her drawing showed him playing his guitar and daydreaming about his various interests, none of which included her or the children. While at first defensive about what he felt was an unfair portrayal, Mr. C. finally agreed that perhaps there was some truth in it after all. In fact, it was he who then recalled how he had placed himself away from the others in his family drawing a year earlier.

Perhaps six months after this incident, a good deal of work was done for three weeks with nonverbal dyadic drawings, in which issues around communication could be experienced and then discussed in an affectively charged manner. Since both parents tended to intellectualize frequently and successfully, art was often useful to help them get in touch with their feelings. In fact, it seems that the two kinds of families which benefit most from art therapy are those who either talk little and distrust words, or those for whom talk has become a way to escape and to hide.

Fig. 11-2. Mr. C.'s picture of his wife: "The Rock of Gibralter." Marker.

Fig. 11-3. Mrs. C.'s picture of her husband and his many interests. Marker.

Conjoint Family Art Therapy

The W. family was recommended for conjoint family art therapy, in part because of the parents' poor history of relating to helping agencies. Three of the four adopted children (ranging in age from five to twelve) had already been referred for help at various points in time, and the two boys who were sent to our clinic had received some short-term intervention at different places in the community. The parents had typically been seen as resistant, had not come in for their own interviews, and were by the time we met them openly distrustful of mental health facilities. An older uneducated couple, who had taken in foster children and then adopted them, they were vulnerable, and frightened of being exposed as poor parents and of having their already shaky defenses further undermined. Yet it was clear that without some change in the family structure, neither potential patient had much of a chance for healthy growth himself.

Much to our surprise, they enjoyed the family art evaluation to which they had come with all the children. During the session and in subsequent contacts they spoke of how much fun it was, how much nicer than what usually went on in such places. They were not such confident artists, but they were less confident articulators (of words). So they were offered weekly conjoint family art therapy (in addition to individual psychotherapy for each boy), in the hope that this time they might find treatment more tolerable and not run, as in the past.

The family did come regularly for six months, working in art as a group for an hour (following the two boys' individual therapy hours) with myself and a child psychiatrist, Juergen Homann, M.D., M.P.H. Although they still terminated treatment before we thought they were ready, they did come for longer than they ever had before, and participated intensely while they were engaged.

Most of the time, the simple provision of materials and an open invitation to use them as they wished was enough to allow important themes and issues to emerge. The only structure Dr. Homann and I usually provided, therefore, was to suggest that we spend some time at the end talking together about what people had made that day, and organizing the five- to twenty-minute discussion time so as to make sure each person had a chance to talk. Occasionally, we would find ourselves suggesting working in a particular way (e.g., dyads) or on a theme (e.g., wishes), but that was very rare. With this family, as with most, the open-ended approach seemed to be most fruitful over time, with some variations as we therapists sensed a particular need for focus.

In the beginning, each parent tended to work with one of the children, usually seeming more comfortable, perhaps less exposed, than if he or she had worked alone. We were able thereby to focus their attention on some of the child-parent issues causing stress in the family, especially those around limits and authority. When Bill and his Dad, for example, worked together on their "Smoking Picture," they talked about who was boss on the picture as well as on issues like whether or not to smoke, to disobey, etc. When Josh and his mom, on the other hand, made a three-dimensional farm together, Josh remarked with a surprised smile that he didn't know that she liked him well enough to work with him for so many weeks, since she openly favored his brother most of the time (Fig. 11-4).

Much to our surprise, the parents actually requested couple sessions (for one hour prior to the family meetings) for the last two months, in order to deal with some marital problems of which they had become aware during family therapy.

Although it was our feeling that they terminated prematurely, there had indeed been some important learning and changes during their treatment. While they came and worked, conjoint family art therapy did seem to be the "treatment of choice" for this generally resistant group.

While family art therapy seems to work well with those who are inarticulate or do not trust words, it seems to be equally appropriate for those at the other end of the verbal continuum. The E. family was intellectual, and all members were highly articulate. The son, Tim, was brought for therapy because he stuttered. Tim had been involved in a children's art group prior to family therapy. The latter was initiated in part because of the sporadic persistance of his symptom, and was based upon the family's response to a family art evaluation. (A detailed description of work with this family will be found in Chapter 15.)

Most of the sessions were conducted in a free-choice fashion, with a variety of materials and working surfaces available. Occasionally, however, we would find ourselves suggesting working in a particular way or on a theme. While such structured approaches were rare, they were usually stimulated by our feeling that the E. family was just "on the edge" of some awareness which we could help to illuminate through a creative intervention. The same principle applies to work with individuals and all kinds of groups, including families; that is, most patients of any age will express through their art the concerns that are troubling them, given a facilitating environment and therapist (a "framework for freedom"). Once in a while, however, it seems that the issues "just beneath the surface" can be externalized more rapidly and more comfortably if the therapist provides an avenue for their expression. (See Chapter 8.)

It should be clear from the above examples that there are many possible ways of working on intrafamilial problems through art therapy. The possible groupings

Fig. 11-4. Josh and Mrs. W. working together on a clay sculpture.

and ways of structuring the transaction are many. Work with all or part of the family unit may be the primary treatment method, or may be introduced periodically as seems indicated. Just as occasional joint parent-child art sessions seem useful, so it also happens frequently that an occasional session with all family members serves to provide information or facilitate communication in the course of other forms of treatment. Laura was seen primarily in individual art therapy; while her mother was seen mostly individually, and for a sixth-month period in a single parents' group. Several sessions, however, involved the entire family, in addition to some mother-child meetings. In one family session, I decided it was important to help mother see how she had insulated herself, withdrawing from her four young children and their needs which she felt as incessant demands. I therefore suggested a "game" which all could play, which I thought might clarify this situation.

Each family member was first asked to make a small plasticine self-representation. Then, without talking, they were asked to move around on a shared "territory" (a large piece of posterboard), until each found a place he wanted to settle on. When that was done, each was asked to further define his space, using felt-tip markers, still without talking to each other. While mother placed herself in the center, her territory seemed closed in, with only minimal indications that her space was "reachable" by the others. Each child isolated himself in a corner, providing protection through a large house, a big fence, or a powerful pet animal. The children were then able to talk about how each felt he had to fend for himself, and of how uncertain they were about support from each other, as well as from mother. She, responding empathically, revised her original verbal description of her space, saying that the paths she had drawn were meant to lead into it, and that, although it was hard, she really wanted to be available to her children. While the session did not solve the problem, the experience served to get it out in the open, where it could be dealt with more easily by all family members.

CHAPTER 12.

Mother-Child Art Therapy Group

There are many possible ways to group people in art therapy. One is to work with the nuclear family or with portions of it, as described in the preceding chapter. Another is to work with more homogeneous sets of people, like single mothers, or same-age children, or patients with a common problem. I have found a particular hybrid approach to be quite useful in a variety of settings, one which involves groups of mothers and their children meeting together all or part of the time. This approach is in a sense midway between more orthodox family and group art therapy, with elements of both involved.

The first mother-child art therapy group in our clinic was proposed after noting the many interactional problems between mothers and their young disturbed children, the difficulty of getting from many an undistorted picture of the parent-child relationship, and the problems for both in trying out new ways of relating. In a memo to the staff, the criteria for referral to the group were: a primary problem in the mother-child relationship, the absence of serious pathology contraindicating either peer or joint group treatment, and the ability of each to profit from the proposed format of weekly group art therapy for the child and a discussion group for the mother, with occasional joint sessions.

Prior to final selection for the group, the clinic social worker, who was about to lead the parent group, screened the mothers in individual interviews, and I saw each child for an art interview. All had previously been seen, in most cases by other clinic personnel, in a routine intake procedure, culminating in a diagnostic conference. Two of the mothers and their children had been receiving individual therapy prior to entry into group; four began treatment with the group. All six children (four boys and two girls, ages five and six) received no other form of treatment during their involvement in the group. Four of the six had no father in the home (two through death, two through divorce); of the other two, one had a father whose work kept him away from home except on weekends, and the other's mother was on the verge of separating from her alcoholic husband. The autistic five-year-old son of a seventh mother was judged unable to participate in the children's art group, but was able to attend the second joint art session.

The mothers first met with their leader for three weeks; I observed their third session. The fourth week, the mothers came to the room where both child and joint groups were to be held, and had an art therapy session in which the assigned topics were family drawings and pictures of each one's "life space." The instructions for the latter task were to choose paper of a size and color that seemed "right," and to make a picture of one's life space at the present time, including the most important elements, both positive and negative. Each activity was followed by discussion, centered around the sharing of each mother's product with the group. Both projects were selected as ways of assessing where and how the child client stood in the mother's current perception of her family and herself. As might be expected, these drawings revealed many aspects of each woman's self-perception as well.

Mrs. T. first drew her husband, then herself, then her psychotic five-year-old son, then her two teenage sons from a previous marriage (Fig. 12-1). Another woman asked if her husband was shorter than she in reality, as she had pictured him. She replied hesitantly and with agitation, "I don't know *why* I made him that way. He *is* taller, but when I'm with him, I feel in this respect that I'm—I feel *bigger* than he does. Now I don't know *why*, but I *do*. I mean, I always—my father and my brothers and the other two boys are exceptionally tall, and I know, and I feel—well, he's thin, too, thin built, and I feel like, I—like if I *fell* on him, I'd *crush* him! I don't know why, but I do. . . . Yeah, there's somethin' about, uh—I guess I feel like a *massive* person. I don't know, I feel like a man or somethin'. My husband is more strong, but I get the feelin' that—uh—I always *have*." The discrepancy between fact and feeling, so clear in this drawing, helped the others to read their own productions more symbolically.

The same woman told more about herself in her life-space picture, which, unlike others, was mostly significant people. She put herself in the center, explaining: "I'm middle-aged, and in the center or middle of life. I've lived half as long as I'm gonna. I'm red." Her husband, also red, is above her, with lines pointing to him. Lines also lead from her figure left to her brother ("in and out of my life"), left to her sixteen-year-old son ("green, the color of hope"), and right to her nineteen-year-old boy ("blue, he's okay"). From her head a line leads right to a small black figure, her autistic child, the color representing "my worries about him." A dotted line leads to her sister-in-law in pink ("she's like a sister to me. She lives in California, but I feel very close to her"). Below are three "boxes" of activities: the left one depicts housework, which she "hates," the center and right boxes show "talking to my boss" and "talking to my friends," both of which she enjoys. She elaborated verbally on her worries about her youngest child, and on her feeling of having few sources of emotional support.

Many of the women felt equally alone emotionally, including one who had represented herself and her children as flowers (Fig. 12-2). She incorporated the

Fig. 12-1. Mrs. T.'s family drawing. Marker.

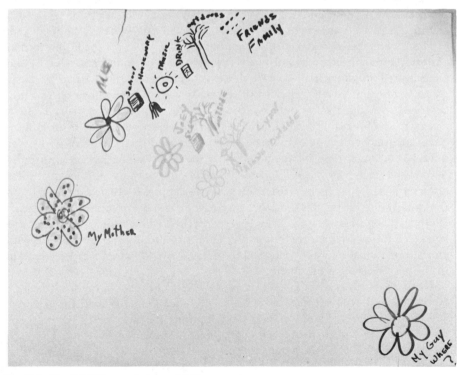

Fig. 12-2. Mrs. B.'s "life space" picture. Marker.

children's colors into her self-flower, saying "My children are just a part of me." One of the largest items in her picture was a flower representing, she said, "My mother. This ugly little daisy. It's big and it's ugly. I love her, but I don't *like* her too much. She'd love to have my children. She's overbearing. She keeps the kids, and there's a conflict between my mom and me about raising the children. I intend to go to California and find a guy, and get away from her." Another woman also expressed ambivalent feelings about her mother, while regarding her drawing: "I love my mom, but there's things she does that I dislike." While it took all of them many months to acknowledge as freely their mixed feelings toward their children, this sharing of such thoughts about their own mothers made that later step easier.

The children's art group began the following week, meeting for the same one-and-one-half-hour period as the mothers' group. Joint sessions were held at varying intervals, the specific dates mutually decided upon by myself and the mothers' group leader during our weekly collaborations. My cotherapist was a male clinical child psychologist, who joined the children's group during the fourth session, and who also participated in these decisions.

The first joint art session took place after the children had met as a group for four weeks, and was conducted in an open-ended fashion. A wide range of art materials was available, as well as a variety of possible working surfaces in the large group room. As the mothers and children entered, they were told they could work with anything they liked, anywhere they wished, and could make whatever they desired.

There were, therefore, many opportunities for observation of dyadic interaction patterns. From the moment of entry through each decision demanded by the unstructured activity period, we were able to get a rich picture of each pair in a busy, pleasant, only mildly self-conscious situation. As with the naturalistic observation described in a therapeutic nursery school, "there is little doubt that . . . direct observations of the child and of his interaction with his mother add considerably to the overall understanding of his personality and specific pathology." With further joint sessions over time, we too found that "the observational advantage extends beyond the diagnostic stage," and could verify "the obvious usefulness of these observations for the therapist in enabling him at all times to obtain a total picture of the child and to pinpoint the mother's changing areas of strength and weakness." (Furman, 1969, pp. 98–99). These were particularly helpful in planning and managing the treatment program, and videotape records of some provided us with an additional chance to study those subtle behaviors which often escaped attention in the busy working atmosphere.

We tried to observe as closely as possible, and to tune in to all of the rich behavioral and symbolic data available in the situation. One pair, for example, isolated themselves at an easel, backs to the group, the girl sharing her mother's discomfort in being exposed to so many people. These two stayed close to each other and worked jointly throughout the session. Each member of another pair, in contrast, behaved as if the other was not present, each "doing his own thing" in separate parts of the room. This behavior was followed by the mother's laughing ridicule of her son's chosen product during the later sharing time, as well as by a competitive, peerlike interaction during the snack. When their separate-but-equal behavior was noted by another mother during the following week's adult group discussion; this woman spoke of her intense discomfort, feelings of inadequacy, and jealousy of her son's greater ease in the art room setting.

With another dyad, there was considerable evidence of covert maternal rejection of which we had not been aware. The woman watched in what appeared to be a kind of icy horror, while her child thoroughly enjoyed smearing with powder paint, water, and brush on an extra-large piece of paper. Her cold, disapproving glance was probably harder for the boy to cope with, than if she had expressed her anger more directly. Although she sat next to him throughout the session, there was hardly any verbal interaction. When she spoke of her feelings in the mothers' group the following week, she stated angrily: "I had no interaction with my son. He was very wound up. He ran like a *wild* man. . . . It's not typical of him. He's very neat at home." Another mother, whose son had engaged in a similar kind of exploration with paint prior to more structured products, was able to share with the first her own joy and pleasure in her son's unexpected freedom. Since other mothers also let the first woman know how they admired her child's control of his potentially explosive medium, she began to see some of the irrational aspects of her anger. Having expressed that anger openly with the group for the first time, she was then able to perceive and discuss her own fears of loss of control.

The mothers were able to help each other, not only in the discussion the following week, but during the joint art session itself. One woman had effectively isolated herself and her daughter from the rest of the group by choosing to work at the smallest table in the room. She sat stiffly, looking tensely and anxiously around, while the child proceeded to draw. When the girl sought her mother's attention, there was at first no response, eventually stimulating a whiney pleading, which succeeded in producing an irritated glance at the child. The one lone mother, whose autistic child was not present, sat down at the table with this pair, effectively intruding upon their self-imposed isolation. The child, who had been asking vainly for a warm maternal response, immediately began a "pictorial dialogue" with the other mother, drawing a "baby kitten" next to that woman's larger animal, which the girl had already labelled "a mother cat" (Fig. 12-3(a)). Thus reinforced in her attempts to relate positively to an adult, she proceeded to draw a mother cat of her own (Fig. 12-3(b)), and then another identified as her own beloved pet (Fig. 12-3(c)).

Having been unable to involve her own mother in art work, the child experienced through her interactions with another mother, the satisfactions of a shared creative experience. Her own mother, meanwhile, was able to observe the other woman's pleasure as well as the girl's happy responses. When the other mother left the pair to engage in a lengthy period of fingerpainting, the girl and her mother began what became a truly interactive effort, in which each made parts of a bird nest scene with clay. They even tried their own joint fingerpainting at an easel, with surprising mutual pleasure. While this mother's involvement with her child

Fig. 12-3. (a) Cats drawn by another mother and (b and c) by a little girl. Chalk.

was stimulated in part by the feelings of rivalry aroused by the other woman, she eventually allowed herself to learn to relax and even to enjoy the fingerpainting, her earlier tension lessening noticeably.

The second joint art session, held six weeks after the first, was more structured. Based on suggestions from the mothers and our collaborative considerations, each pair was asked as they entered to engage in at least one joint project. All media and working surfaces were the same as in the first session, but this time there was the explicit task of deciding together what to use, where to work, and what to make. As in the first session, the working period was followed by a snack, and the sharing with the group of one jointly-chosen collaborative product from each mother-child pair, with mother (not therapist as in the first) as interviewer.

Since seven weeks had elapsed between the first and second joint art sessions, we were also able to observe any changes in individual and interactional behavior. One mother and her child, who had shyly isolated themselves during all of the first joint session, now sat at a table with others, worked independently most of the time, and actively joined into the conversation among the three pairs at the table. Both partners, previously locked into an overly interdependent relationship, seemed to be readjusting in response to the girl's newfound self-assertion and drive for autonomy, along with the mother's growing self-confidence. This was particularly apparent during the post-product interview of the child by the mother, as well as in the subsequent spontaneous interview of mother by child, who was teasingly provocative about her mother's clay "ice cream cone."

Another pair, who had worked at opposite ends of the room with little awareness of each other during the first session, now not only worked together as required, but did so in a comfortable, cooperative manner (Fig. 12-4). Although their three joint drawings reflected the dominance of the mother in style and conception, as opposed

Fig. 12-4. A mother and son working together on a drawing.

to others in which a child had clearly been in charge, they were deeply and happily involved in the working process. Most impressive was the mother's unanticipated sensitivity and understanding in her role as interviewer.

Of course, the persistence of maladaptive behaviors or attitudes was equally visible, as with the mother who had been so angry at her child for being sloppy and wild during the first session. Though slightly less tense during the second joint group, she seemed to have little pleasure in the process. A therapist sitting nearby observed that nearly all of her spontaneous conversation with the boy was critical, although they created three joint felt pen drawings. Her sparse verbalization was restricted to telling him what *not* to do, or what he had done *wrong*, an attitude also reflected in the brusque, irritated tone of her later interviewing about their chosen product.

While the diagnostic value of joint art sessions for the treatment team is obvious, what is less apparent, but perhaps more important for therapy, is the educational potential of such sessions for both mother and child. Each is able to observe other modes of response to the same situation, to know and to see alternatives. Certainly both the child who made the cats and her mother, were able to learn from the other mother who drew along with the child. Perhaps some of the greater freedom and lesser self-consciousness of the previously isolated and interdependent mother-daughter pair was, at least in part, due to their interaction with two other "teams" around a shared table during the second joint session. It is also possible that the mother-son pair who stayed far apart during the first session, were able to collaborate so well during the second, because each had observed other mother-child pairs doing so with pleasure.

A mother might also perceive her child in a new light from his behavior in a joint art session. Such a new perception usually involved a comparison of the child's behavior in the session with his behavior in the past, with that of his peers in the group, or with the mother's own anticipation. The powerful effect of an adult's expectations on a child's behavior, has been forcefully demonstrated in a study concerned with "interpersonal self-fulfilling prophecies" (Rosenthal and Jacobson, 1968).

One mother, for example, stated in the mothers' group meeting the week after the first joint session that she had been "pleasantly surprised" by her son's behavior during the art activities. She had expected him to be what he had been when he first came to the clinic, a tense, anxious, compulsive little boy. Instead, she discovered an unanticipated degree of freedom in his work and his interaction with her.

The mother of the autistic child brought him nervously to the second joint art experience, and was relieved and pleased by her son's ability to handle himself appropriately in this very stimulating environment. They completed two joint paintings with tempra markers, the process thoroughly enjoyed by both. Even more valuable for her were the comments of the other mothers, for when they met for a half hour of discussion following the joint session, the group told her she had been drawing for them a grossly distorted picture of her boy. Since their assertions were based on a full hour of observing his behavior, and since they had by then been meeting together as a group for fifteen weeks, she was able to trust and to accept their feedback.

The mothers seemed gradually to be learning to sense, if not to translate accurately, the symbolic meanings of their children's creative expression, and in the interviews as well as their discussions, gained new insights into the children's inner lives. They were learning in effect that "your child makes sense" (Buxbaum, 1949, p. 51). For example, while I was interviewing one little girl in the first session about her two clay turtles, her mother was able to see the relationship between the story of the five-year-old girl turtle's victory over her baby brother turtle, and the child's wish to win out over her own younger sibling. This same mother, interviewing her child during the second joint session, smiled knowingly when the girl identified the larger of two clay baskets as hers, and the smaller one as her younger brother's. Later in the interview, a "little boy mask" made by the child "opened his mouth up" and was "screamin' because he can't find his basket;" and again, the mother nodded with understanding when told that the sister had stolen it. Over the succeeding months, this woman often brought in art work created by her daughter at home or in school, along with useful and perceptive ideas about the possible meanings to the child.

Another mother, who was becoming aware of her son's wish to replace her divorced husband, seemed to understand the meaning of the following interchange about their picture:

Boy: The tree is tryin' to reach over to kiss the airplane.
Mother: Is he gonna reach the airplane?
Boy: If he tries harder, he's gonna bust!
Mother: Do you think the airplane *wants* him to reach her?
Boy: Yeah! He does!
Mother: He does?
Boy: They wanna get *married*.

The mother raised this story in the discussion following the shared experience, and wondered aloud what her own role and wishes might be in stimulating and seductively reinforcing his fantasy. Her ambivalent (seductive/rejecting) behavior had been observed by the therapists, but for the first time she became aware of her role in inhibiting her son's resolution of the oedipal conflict.

The joint art sessions were also found to be particularly useful reference points for a series of parent conferences on each child's progress in treatment, held five months after the groups had started. For example, one mother, unable to see the extent of her own role in her daughter's problems, began to discuss her own difficulty in identifying and expressing angry feelings. She could perceive her child's surface compliance, but was helped to see the girl's need to deny her hostile impulses by recalling the following excerpt from her interview of her daughter about the child's picture entitled "That's Me with Some Dots."

Mother: What do the big dots mean?

Girl: Happiness.
Mother: What makes you happy?
Girl: That you're near me.
Mother: They mean happiness too? You told me before they meant anger.
Girl: They mean happiness now.
Mother: You changed your mind.
Therapist: Can you feel angry sometimes at somebody, and then sometimes feel happy with them?
Girl: No!

When the mother connected the meaning of this interchange with her own hunch about why the girl had profusely praised everyone else's picture, she could see the relationship of the child's problem to her own. This interview with her marked the beginning of her own real commitment to the group.

Later joint sessions made possible the assessment of change over time in dyadic interactions, as well as any differences between individuals' behavior in the joint group vs. the homogeneous groups. Over time, the differential between the two situations decreased, with the children tending to make more blatant their pictured conflicts. In a later joint art group, for example, a child with severe castration anxiety drew at the easel, in front of his mother, a picture of "A Lady with a Weiner," and a missing, injured eye (Fig. 12-5(a)). He openly stated his assumption that girls have penises, and his fear that they once had them but lost them. Although his mother was acutely uncomfortable during this display of his concern, his picture and comments became the focal point for a mothers' group discussion following the joint art time, about the reality of fears for bodily integrity among young children. This same boy followed his initial drawing of the "Lady" accompanied by much anal humor (in response to which his mother alternately laughed and scolded severely), with an undisguised portrayal of feces emerging from rectums (Fig. 12-5(b)). His mother wondered aloud why he had been so "vulgar," and was helped by the other mothers to see how often her laughter and attention had reinforced this behavior.

Any number of possible formats could be employed for such joint sessions, depending on the goals of the team for group members at the time they occur. One structure we used was to suggest that perhaps the children would like to tell the mothers what to draw. Of the three pairs present at that session, two boys thoroughly enjoyed being in charge, though neither was completely satisfied with his mother's performance. In the children's subsequent discussion of the experience, one boy who had vigorously complained of his mother's "mistakes" right after she left the room, within ten minutes was denying any disappointment in her. He was helped by listening to another boy's irritation that his mom did not draw the building he had in mind: "I wonder if *you're* thinkin' about one thing, could the *other* person think about yours, that you're thinkin' about? . . . I was thinkin' about if the building isn't *exactly* the same as you thought—as you're thinkin' about." A productive discussion ensued, about the difficulty of communicating to grownups, especially when you have an image that must be translated into words.

The third boy, who felt quite weak and incompetent to direct his strong, critical mother, refused to be in charge, requesting that she tell him what to do. Interestingly, one of her chief complaints about her son had been his inability to do anything well or to follow directions. She gave him enough instructions to fill up several papers, but he carefully persisted in attempting to draw, in the eventually crowded picture space, everything she suggested. When there was not an inch left on the paper, the mother stopped, and the child's pride in his mastery of the difficult task she had set him was clear to all. In the later discussion, she was helped to see how much pressure she had put on him, yet how well he had handled her demands. He, on the other hand, stimulated a discussion among the children about mothers and teachers always telling kids what to do, never seeming satisfied, demanding more and more. The boy who had drawn the feces excitedly joined in, helping us to better understand some of the meanings in that picture: "You know what my mom says? She always says, 'Go to the bathroom! Unless I *make* you go to the bathroom! And fast, too! I'll *make* you go! It'll probably *hurt!*' "

a   b

Fig. 12-5. Two blatant images by a boy of six during a joint session: (a) "A Lady with a Weiner" and (b) Feces. Chalk.

We had anticipated that while the mothers would feel somewhat uneasy and self-conscious during joint art sessions, the children might resent the adults' intrusion in their room, and might be less than willing to share space, materials, or their group leaders with their parents. They surprised us, however, by looking forward to and clearly enjoying the joint sessions. As one boy put it after the mothers had left, and all had agreed that they liked it better "with the mommies," "It was fun. . . . A good, fine time." When asked the week before Christmas what they would like to have for a party, most responded with "candy canes" and the like; but one boy answered, "the mothers," to which the others enthusiastically agreed. They worked hard decorating the group room before the mothers' arrival, complete with a sign saying "Love to all the Kids and the People . . . Welcome to the Mothers."

The use of joint mother-child group art sessions at intermittent intervals seems to provide useful diagnostic and therapeutic opportunities for all involved. Like any other treatment format, this one is potentially as flexible as any other. Thus, I recently led an ongoing mother-child group with preschoolers which met jointly for forty-five minutes every week, followed by separate group activities (forty-five minute discussion time for mothers and snack for children). Since art activities are among the few in which adults and children can participate simultaneously, each at his own level, yet can work together on joint projects, they are particularly appropriate for activity therapy or educational approaches involving parents and children. For a mother and her child, such a shared experience, weekly or periodically, may indeed help them to develop "a new code of communication." (Ginott, 1965, p. 25)

CHAPTER 13.

Group Art Therapy

Throughout history, from the cave to the cathedral, people have worked together on creative products. Since the Renaissance, however, art has been thought of more as an individual activity than as a social one. Nevertheless, a prominent art educator has recently noted the resurgence of "group art" in and out of the classroom (Hurwitz, 1975), and art therapists increasingly find themselves working as frequently with groups as with individuals. The early years of group art therapy featured an emphasis on work by individuals done in a group context, usually followed by some discussion of each person's production by the individual and/or the group (Bach, 1954; Baruch and Miller, 1951; Dunn and Semple, 1956; Potts, 1956). While there was in some accounts an explicit awareness of the communicative function served by the art work among group members (Sinrod, 1964), the emphasis was still on each individual, rather than on the group as an entity.

With the growth and prominence of group psychotherapy, and the concomitant emphasis on the understanding and utilization of group process as a tool for change, group art therapy has increasingly looked at group issues, especially through the medium of joint projects. Such group art activities are particularly useful as ways of helping individuals to experience, externalize, and examine their interrelationships, as exemplified in the joint mural of the family art evaluation. While these usually involve discussion as part of the interactive process, some workers have also described working together without verbalization, as in a "pictorial dialogue" (Boenheim and Stone, 1969) or "interaction painting" with a psychotic patient (Horowitz, 1973), with a neurotic (Finley, 1975), between couples (Wadeson, 1971, 1973), or in a group (Rhyne, 1971, 1973). Work with groups in art has been described within a variety of theoretical frameworks, including Gestalt (Rhyne, 1973; Keyes, 1974), Jungian (Dougherty, 1974), Humanistic (Denny, 1972), and Freudian (Harris and Joseph, 1973). As with representations of the family, pictures of the group have been utilized as a way of looking at members' perceptions of that unit (Hare and Hare, 1956).

Sometimes representations of the group are either created spontaneously or emerge in projected associations. In the sixth month of an ongoing weekly adolescent group, for example, Hannah first labelled her vibrant-colored abstract acrylic painting "Hate, Hate, Hate!" Looking at it during the snack-discussion time at the end of group, she pointed to the areas of color, identifying each one as a member of the group, with herself next to the leaders in the center. Pointing to a strip of gray at the left-hand corner of her painting, she said, "There's Matt, trying to squeeze in, and this is Lanny next to him" (a strip of dark gray). It is significant that both boys were the only black members of the group and that Hannah's projective comments had been preceded by a discussion about discrimination, in which she had made a "slip": "I don't think people should show discrimination for the colored people. . . ." Lanny had reacted angrily, and had corrected her: "You shouldn't say discrimination *for* black people. You should say discrimination *against* black people." It was indeed true that the two black boys had not been accepted or trusted readily by the others, so that Hannah's image of their exclusion was close to the reality at that time. Her perception of herself as close to the leaders, however, reflected a wished-for intimacy and favoritism, clear from her demanding behavior, but more of a fantasy than a reality.

While most publications on group art therapy have dealt with work with adults, some have described work with children and adolescents in a variety of settings (Bender, 1952; Davis, 1969; Dunn and Semple, 1956; Kramer, 1958, 1971, 1979; Landgarten, 1981; Namer and Martinez, 1967; Sinrod, 1964). An extensive literature on play therapy groups (Axline, 1947; Ginott, 1961; Lowenfeld, 1971; Schiffer, 1969) and on activity and activity-interview groups (Konopka, 1963; Slavson and Schiffer, 1975) is also closely related to work with children in group art therapy. (See Hanes, 1982, for excellent literature review and abstracts.)

In a sense, when approaching therapy through art in a group context, one is taking advantage of the potency of both art and the group. Describing a self-awareness group with adults, Vich and Rhyne explain how their previous work had made them: "aware of the power of the small group process to expand the usual range of human awareness. [They] believed that adding visual, tactile, and kinesthetic means of expression and communication to verbal methods could further extend this range for individuals and the group." (1967, p. 1) From a similar but different point of view, having a therapeutic art experience within a group adds another dimension which, though it may be inhibiting for some, may be facilitating for others. Some children, for example, are painfully self-conscious when alone with an adult; often they have lost faith in grownups, but are still optimistic about trusting peers. For such youngsters, the group is a much safer, more dependable, and more comfortable context within which to explore themselves.

By far the most frequent and, I believe, most useful way to approach group art therapy is in an open-ended fashion. As with individuals, a "framework for freedom" allows unique and common concerns to emerge organically in a natural and comfortable way. Because an art therapy group, when unstructured, allows for individual freedom of movement and activity, a member can either choose to observe or to participate, to talk or to remain silent, to be alone or to be with others, to work independently or to work jointly, to relate actively or to distance himself from others. As individuals begin to relate to one another, they are stimulated, get ideas, gain courage, help one another, and sometimes decide spontaneously to work together on joint projects. There are times, however, when some structure or direction from the leader seems appropriate.

It is possible to provide varying degrees and kinds of structure, depending on the goals for any particular group at any particular moment in time. Thus, in early meetings, it is important to set the stage for later work by clarifying the nature of the "contract" between members and leader(s), and enabling people to feel secure and comfortable in the environment as well as with each other. For preschoolers, the most comfortable beginning format is probably an open one, where a free choice of media and activities is provided, and individuals are encouraged to explore, select, and get to work.

For older children, however, some initial warmup activities or a specific task may ease adjustment to the unfamiliar space and people. Thus, a group of five- and six-year-olds began around a table, exploring in turn a "Feely-Meely Box," a game in which one feels what is inside the box without seeing it and describes and guesses what it is, mirroring in the game some of the mystery of the new group. After telling each other their names and grades, they were ready to explore the art media, to choose and to work on one or more projects for an hour, returning to the table for a snack and sharing time at the end.

Finding ways of overcoming learned inhibitions about work in art is especially essential with adolescents and adults, for whom one must often "unblock the natural impulse to draw." (McKim, 1972, p. 49) Warmup techniques all have in common the dual goals of reducing self-consciousness and freeing personal creativity. Some involve an explicit de-emphasis on representation, like making an abstract color picture of feelings (Culbert and Fisher, 1969). A short time limit for exercises facilitates spontaneity, and reduces anxiety about the finished product. Sometimes it helps to suggest closed eyes, enabling individuals to work freely without judging the product. It also helps at times to use visual starters, like beginning a picture with a scribble, a line, a piece of paper, a photograph, or a blob of paint on wet paper. Such exercises not only help individuals overcome blocks, but enable them to get in touch with more personal imagery.

A playful approach to the activities can also reduce self-consciousness, and can be accomplished by starting with an introduction "game," by suggesting the possibility of working in a comfortable place, such as the floor, or by asking participants to "fool around," especially with a "contact" medium like plasticine, in order to get to know it better. Sometimes a group is helped to reduce concern about the finished product, and to get to know each other by working together and sharing responsibility. In some groups, a simultaneous nonverbal mural, done with poster chalks on a large sheet of paper on floor or table or wall, can be a powerful experience of "letting go." As with "round robin" activities (taking turns molding a chunk of clay or drawing on a sheet of paper passed around the group), such shared involvements carry both risks and opportunities. If managed insensitively, they can unleash potentially threatening hostility; if handled carefully, they can enable group members to feel an almost instantaneous sense of community.

In addition to warming up in a way that enhances comfort, an early need of group members is to get to know one another. While this will occur in time, and may indeed be best left undirected, there are times where it may facilitate the process to give specific tasks related to this need. Thus, a group of mothers of preschoolers was asked to begin by introducing themselves pictorially, which helped them to start work as well as to learn about each other. A group of adolescents was asked to describe with any medium what they wanted to gain from the group; and their pictures and sculptures had astounding communicative as well as expressive power.

Just as the range of productive tasks is infinite, there are also endless possibilities for beginning with responses to artistic stimuli. For, example, a group of mothers of handicapped children was asked to select from among a series of photographs the one that most reminded them of their disabled youngster. A group of elementary-age children was asked in an early session to choose the picture they liked best and the one they liked least from among a selection of reproductions of paintings. As with productive activities, the subsequent discussion may focus on process, product, or both. The group members can be led to examine how they made their choice, why they chose a particular item, as well as to look at and further associate to the product selected, perhaps by telling a story about a picture or imagining why a person in it is feeling the way he looks.

Some kinds of groups, focused around a particular topic or problem, perhaps short-term and limited in scope, may do best to proceed in a "theme-centered" manner (Cohn, 1969–70). In a series of art-awareness groups for adolescents in various settings, it proved productive to focus on a particular theme or task at each session, with only occasional free-choice meetings (Rubin and Levy, 1975). Since the explicit purpose of the groups was to help teenagers to express, define, understand, and accept themselves, topics tended to center on identity issues. These included thinking of their real selves in terms of time, as in a life-space drawing, a picture of their future goals, or a life-line pictorially representing their past. They were also asked to think of their inner selves, in terms of fantasies, wishes, dreams, or fears, perhaps with such explicit topics as "My Worst Fear" or "Myself as I Wish to Be."

In these art-awareness groups, and in others where intragroup issues needed to be externalized, another aspect of self-definition was an awareness of one's place in a social milieu. For example, in order to enhance sensitivity to others, an "active watching" exercise was developed, similar to "mirroring" activities in movement and drama. One person is the doer and another is the watcher who, with or without the medium in hand, attempts to "get into" and reproduce simultaneously the other's rhythm and way of working. A third person may be asked to observe the dyad, later giving feedback to the other two. If roles are rotated, each individual becomes sensitized to the idiosyncratic way in which each person works, learning through a kind of "body empathy" about another's art-movement style.

Interpersonal issues of territoriality, authority, and control are always present whenever two or more people work together. In a nonverbal pictorial exercise, in which two people work together silently on a shared picture space without prior discussion, such issues come to the fore, and can be discussed following the activity (Fig. 13-1). Transactional themes can also be the explicit subject matter of an assignment, as in a boss-slave game. Here, one member of a dyad tells the other what art materials to use and how to use them, with or without an observer. They then switch roles and do it again. Later they discuss their experiences together. Not only can dyads or triads discuss such events, but later can join with others who have done the same activity, and can then learn about other small-group perceptions of the issues involved.

In order to clarify and to enact in time and space "finding one's place in a group," it is useful for each person in a small group to make his own three-dimensional self-image (of clay, plasticine, or wood scraps); and then to move it silently, along with others, on a large paper or board representing a shared "world space." A nonverbal movement-drama ensues, at times going on for many minutes with great intensity,

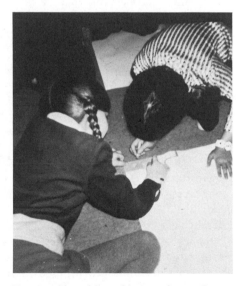

Fig. 13-1. Two girls working together on the same space without talking.

until each person has finally found his "spot." When all are settled into their places on the shared territory, it is suggested that they further define the space through line drawings on the surface. They are then asked to discuss the entire transaction, sometimes assuming the relative positions of their self-symbols for the discussion, whether "huddled" together in a bunch or separated in some way. Such an exercise is extremely helpful in enabling individuals to clarify the roles they assume in a group, such as intruder, compromiser, outsider, facilitator, disruptor, etc.

The specific technique or format of an exercise—media, theme, instructions, number of people involved, spatial relationship, time available, focus of the discussion, leader involvement, etc.—should relate to the goals of that particular exercise, in the context of the comfort level of that particular group. There are always variations among group members in openness to risk-taking. For some, the risks are primarily interpersonal—revealing too much about oneself through transparent symbolism, being judged and evaluated, excessively dominating a workgroup, etc. For others, the risks are more often of an intrapsychic nature—fear of loss of control or disorganization, worry that unacceptable aggressive or sexual impulses will emerge, etc.

One way to enable individuals to protect themselves against undue risk-taking is to provide options. Thus, whether a group is structured or open-ended, the decision about whether to participate is always left up to each member. Similarly, some degree of choice, even within a structured task, should always be present (paper size, medium, role, position in space, etc.). In a group, an explicit limit on negative judgmental evaluation of others' productions may be necessary, to reduce the degree of threat involved in "opening up" both symbolically and verbally. It is made clear that each individual is his own expert, the sole recognized authority on the meaning for him of his own art. If he chooses to respond to another's work, he is seen as using it as a projective stimulus for himself, but not as being able to validly interpret another's creative expression.

Within a framework of constant respect for and protection of individuals, one may use all of the tools at one's disposal: leader(s), space, time, materials, degree of structure, nature of the task, etc. Given these tools, one may creatively design activities which best meet the needs of any particular group at any moment in time. The role of the leader may vary in the course of a session from instructor to passive observer or active participant, to discussion-leader. In activities like the "active watching" or "boss-slave" exercises the critical tool is the dramatic structure of the task—the specific roles individuals take in regard to one another.

In choosing materials to achieve an experience of regression, clay and fingerpaint should be considered. Similarly, a three-dimensional self-symbol (of plasticene or wood) seems most appropriate for an exercise which requires its movement on a flat surface. And, while other materials can be used, colored cellophane has particular values in the task of representing a small group. In a threesome or foursome which has worked together, for example, each person may be asked to choose his own color of cellophane, creating a color coding for each group member, who then represents individually his own pictorial sense of the group during the previous interaction. The nature of the material permits not only color coding and variation in size, shape, and placement; but also, because of its transparency, makes possible literal overlapping. Thus, group members can represent fusion or intimacy, at times even showing one member as covering the others, perhaps experienced as (s)mothering the group. Clearly separated forms, conversely, are felt as isolation or interpersonal distancing. An infinite number of subtle variations in group representation become possible, far more than could be conveyed verbally or with other media.

The activities described above are examples of ways of manipulating the many variables at one's disposal in order to achieve a particular goal. Nevertheless, even in a group with a central theme like "art for self-awareness," it seems vital that some time be spent in a free-choice situation, in which each person follows his own creative self-defining bent. It is my feeling that the question is never one of either-or, of structure vs. no structure, but rather an ongoing task with every group of planning, or picking up on, ways of enhancing therapeutic movement at any moment. In most cases, some combination over time of open and more structured activities seems to be appropriate, and indeed, seems quite compatible, enabling participants to experience a greater variety of media and roles than they might otherwise explore.

Groups and How They Grow

Each new group is a new adventure and may require more or less structure depending on many variables, including the length of time it is to meet, the membership, the context, the mutually acceptable "contract," etc. Just as the ultimate goal in enhancing self-awareness and acceptance through art is unique to each individual; so the uniqueness of each group and of each leader or team, demands a high degree of openness and flexibility in thinking about how to achieve such a goal for each member as well as for the group, which has a strange but very real life of its own.

A group is both a collection of individuals, and a becoming entity somehow made up of those individuals, yet qualitatively different from a quantitative summation of its members. It is not unlike a collage or construction, where the final product includes each component part in its original form. And, like a collage, a group represents the creation of a new gestalt, wherein each component appears differently from when it is seen in isolation from the total work. Unlike a collage or construction, a group changes its shape and form over time in an organic fashion, as the members deal with each other and the leader(s) around the critical issues of each phase. Some of the key issues in groups are intimacy, trust, rivalry, peer pressure, and authority. While these are all present to some degree in individual therapy, those related to the power and danger of alliances between members are unique to the group, and are part of what give it therapeutic potency.

There appears to be a fairly uniform pattern of growth in groups which, like graphic development, varies in tempo, but is quite predictable in sequence, whatever the age of the members. Groups usually begin as collections of individuals, each relating separately to the leader, often with rapidly increasing rivalry for the leader's attention and approval. Over time, usually after some testing of each other and the leader, members begin to form alliances among themselves. These tend to be primarily dyadic, though occasionally include more than two members, and might reflect subgroups related to sex, age, psychopathology, etc. The dynamics of small groups have been fairly well studied, and seem to be quite ubiquitous (Bion, 1959; Cartwright and Zander, 1981; Freud, 1922; Yalom, 1975), including what goes on in art therapy groups of any age level.

An art therapy group, like any kind of activity group, makes possible a kind of natural simultaneous interaction of individuals, in a way that is both informal and relatively unthreatening. One can talk about one's product while working, not "on display" to the others, or can choose to tell everybody about it in a sharing time, usually provided at the end of group sessions. One can learn by watching others, gaining confidence and participating vicariously, and by working with others, thereby learning about sharing and cooperation, as well as mutual respect for individual differences. For the therapist, being able to observe a youngster in live interaction with peers as well as with oneself, affords a much richer understanding of the reality as well as the distortions of his social behavior. While the presence of peers may make it harder for some to talk about their art, for others the desire to be accepted, or even natural competition, may enable them to overcome inhibitions in telling stories or associating to their products.

Not only can individuals in a group explore their own ideas in relation to their work, they can also utilize the work of others as a stimulus for projection and imagination. Sherry, age seventeen, had spent most of one session working hard on a life-size Pariscraft sculpture of her father, explaining that then she could tell him off without having to hear his reactions. Sam, looking at her unfinished figure, commented that he looked "like a person fighting in order to bring out his emotions," and that he had an "expression of frustration," representing how Sam himself was feeling at the time.

A year later, when Sam was getting close to an awareness of his repressed anger, he projected a destructive wish as he (calling himself "Dr. Fraud") analyzed my ambiguous, abstract watercolor painting: "The picture shows that she's afraid she's going to die. There's going to be a great storm that comes up, and it's going to cast her over a big cliff. . . . She will break her neck when she falls face down on a carving bush, and no one will ever remember her. They won't even find her after she's eaten. Everyone will forget about her, and no one will remember her. Nothing will be left behind, and there will be nothing good that would have been done in her lifetime. Her good spirit will drown in the sea." Sherry, looking at the same picture, expressed her own anxiety, as she described what it said about the artist: "She likes adventure, but she's afraid of it. She gets lost easily, and she's afraid to be by herself. She has a deep fear of being in the woods, 'cause some lion is going to attack her."

Sam, unable to stop, had more to say about what the picture showed would happen to me: "There's going to be a stoneless plot for her, so no one will ever know where she is. Every once in a while we will throw a worm on her and hope that her body gets eaten up. When she lands in the bush, she will get buried, and everyone else will throw up on her. Cow dung will be thrown on her grave, and then everyone else will live happily ever after. No one will ever notice that she's missing, but everyone will be cheerful." Sam told the story with great relish, and denied vehemently the suggestion that it might have something to do with his anger that I was about to be away from the group for almost a month for vacation. Nevertheless, he had an especially hard time leaving the group room that day, as if to confirm the interpretation through his behavior.

As time goes on, children with common or complementary problems tend to form subgroups, sometimes sharing such concerns openly as well as symbolically. In the ninth session of a group of five- and six-year-olds, for the first time, instead of working independently and relating primarily to me, the four members present formed two pairs. Jenny and Lisa worked side by side at a table with clay, while the boys mutually created and painted a large city of wood scraps, after some competitive but cooperative block building. When I asked Jenny to tell me about her "Skyscraper Building" she said, "You live there and so does Lisa. You used to have a father, but he died." (Both girls' fathers were dead, Jenny's through suicide.) When I asked how the father had died, Jenny replied, "He took too much medicine . . . 'cause he was sick, and then he thought that would make him better." She then added with excitement, "You can have another father. . . . You get one at the store. You have to try to catch one. . . . When you see a pretty man, then you catch him. . . . A handsome man."

Lisa had listened to this interchange silently, and when I asked her what she thought of Jenny's idea said, "I don't want to." She went on to explain that she liked the idea of living with me in a skyscraper building, but not of catching a father. I tried to clarify for Jenny: "Lisa says she'd just as soon not. She'd rather just stay there with me, and you're saying you'd rather find a father. Do you think sometimes when you had a father, and then he's gone. . . . "At this point Jenny interrupted me, saying, "He died!" Lisa also quickly stating, "He died." "Yes," I said, "That happened to both of you, didn't it? You both had fathers and they died, and Lisa's not so sure she wants another one, and Jenny, you're saying that you think you *do* want another one. So you feel differently." Lisa, who was feeling quite angry at her father for dying, spent most of the time making "little monster faces" out of clay, who had nothing to say, except that they were "mad."

The Use of Structure in Unstructured Groups

There are times in an ongoing group where most sessions are open-ended, when a suggested structure may help members to deal with particular emerging concerns. During the sixth month of weekly group meetings with five- and six-year-olds, I decided one day to introduce the idea of a spotlight and shadows, stimulated by their increasingly vocal worries about what they "saw" in the dark. A filmstrip projector in a darkened room threw a large spot of bright light on the wall. I suggested first that the children move freely in the light and look at their shadows. Next, they took turns if they wished, finding a pose, freezing in that pose, and standing in front of the large sheet of white paper taped on the wall, while one of the leaders traced their shadow on the paper. Those waiting their turn sat at the table and worked with clay, using the light from the back of the projector, enjoying the excitement of the "scary" atmosphere. Some chose to finish the shadow-tracings by filling in with paint or other media, others left the outlines untouched. What seemed most important was the experience of being in the dark with shadows that you could look at, know about, and even capture on paper, further defining them if you wished.

With a group of inpatient psychotic children ages nine to twelve, a predominant theme of their art work and discussion had been their unhappiness about being hospitalized, and their often mixed feelings about returning home after what they knew to be time-limited treatment. Following several open-ended sessions, therefore, I suggested that perhaps they might like to think about a theme, specifically "Where I Would Like to Be Right Now." Essie wishfully painted a peaceful house by a lake and mountain out in the country, with only animals inside. Ben, whose mother had abandoned him, was even more fantastically wishful, as he painted a huge castle, a tree whose limbs reach toward it, and a vibrant sun, in bright colors. Rob constructed out of wood scraps a complex of houses and buildings, first naming it as the hospital (where indeed he did feel safe), then saying it was a graveyard (perhaps the more fearful aspect of interment). Glen drew an elaborate picture on oversize paper of a wishfully intact family, house, and yard with swings; radically different from the chaotic broken home to which he could not return, instead being housed at a state institution for the retarded. The children were able to share, in both the doing and the discussion, their intense wishes for a better place to go than reality held in store for any of them.

Individuals can easily use a common task or theme to deal with their own idiosyncratic concerns, as long as it is sufficiently flexible. Thus, each child in the group of five- and six-year-olds made a bendable doll with elasticlay, and a wood scrap house for it to live in; yet each doll and house and associated story was as individual as the child who created them. Lisa's doll, for example, was "a little girl" who has "a bad boy and a bad sister. The bad boy hits me and the bad sister hits me too," Lisa said, talking for the doll and paralleling her own sibling rivalry situation. Steve's "boy" doll lived in "a new house, and we're gonna move into it. . . . It's very beautiful in the new house," just as Steve's mom was constantly promising a new life style which never happened. Jamie's doll was called "my man, Smokey the Bear," and as he was then developing intense affectionate (oedipal) feelings toward his female therapist, Jamie explained that "Mrs. Rubin lives with Smokey the Bear." Jenny's house was small and, like Jenny, a bit disorganized. In it, Jenny said, lived a dog doll who needed to have his temperature taken repeatedly, a subject of intense interest to all of the children.

Group Themes and Concerns

This same group of children often shared other concerns as well, and became especially involved over time in the playing out and reworking of dramas involving the male therapist as a monster who scares, captures, threatens, and is eventually robbed or killed off by the children. It was introduced quite spontaneously, when one of the children during the snack, made a "monster" with the gumdrops and toothpicks provided, and the others suggested they "play monster" afterward. The two girls went with the monster (father) as assistants, while the four boys chose to go with me (mother), suggesting we hide under a large workbench, which they dubbed "the safe place." They gave the monster a bag of clay which they called gold, then told him to "be asleep" so they could steal his treasure. The excitement and challenge of venturing forth against the powerful father-monster was great for the boys, while the "private" assistantship was satisfying to the equally oedipal girls.

As an index of the intensity and seriousness for the children of this make-believe, Tim arrived the following week wearing an outfit with many pockets, in each a paper knife with which he planned to kill the monster. Over time, they demanded repetitions of the drama after snack time, often putting on paint make-up in order to scare the monster or to be a better monster assistant, depending on which role each wanted to take that day. They introduced variations and modifications, and eventually were able to find a way to reform the monster and make friends, neither killing him off nor punishing themselves by being jailed or killed off in retaliation. While the theme may have touched on separate issues for each child, it carried enough meaning for all of them that it was a highly popular activity, requested almost weekly for about six months. One might hypothesize that it enabled them to deal with numerous issues around oedipal wishes and conflicts over aggression, with which each one was coping in his own way.

Creative Play with Food

Using gumdrops and toothpicks as a snack with dramatic potential is only one of many ways to extend the possibilities for creative fantasy. In a group of nine- to eleven-year-old boys, for example, small multicolored marshmallows were made into objects or figures with toothpick connectors. Matt created an airplane, happily suggesting that he, as the "bombardier," would hit all the schools, so there would be no more school. Tommy's marshmallow man was described as "big and mean," then was toasted and eaten. Similarly, using icing dispensers, the boys created faces on large round cookies, then used them as puppets who talked with each other, before eating them up.

In the group of five- and six-year-olds described earlier, the children one day made creatures of marshmallows and toothpicks, and were able to use them dramatically. Jack, whose brother had died of a cerebral hemorrhage, for the first time was able to express almost openly some of his mixed feelings about the event, about which he had only giggled nervously in the past. He said that both of his figures were boys, then put one down and said sadly, "His brother died." When I asked what "he" did, Jack replied, "Then his father cried. And he felt sad, and he laughed." I wondered how it happened, and Jack said, "An accident. His mother was in the accident too, but she didn't die. . . . His father said 'Don't die.'" I asked if the brother died anyway, to which he replied, "Yeah, he died." Then I asked how the little boy felt, to which Jack replied seriously and with feeling, "Sad, sad, sad. . . . Yeah! I was sad when *my* brother died." "I bet you were," I commented, after which Jack went on with material he had until then been unable to verbalize: "Yeah. My brother died, and the veins in his head broke, and all the blood came out from his veins. But my brother didn't have an accident when he died. His veins broke."

Role-Taking in Interviews

In the above illustration, it seemed easier for Jack to gain psychic distance by talking about, rather than for, his creature. Sometimes it may be more comfortable for a child to express himself by taking a role, either as what he has created, or in relation to it. Twelve-year-old Fred, for example, was being asked lots of questions by others in his group about his drawing of "Joe Frazier," also called "The Stupid Man," a boxer who had challenged Cassius Clay to a duel and gotten badly beaten (Fig. 13-2). At one point he responded to a question with "Ask Cassius Clay," and I suggested that he might speak for Cassius Clay himself. With a deep voice, he went on and described quite vividly his worries about the dangers of aggression: "Well, he tried to get smart with me in the first round. He punched me on my nose, so I just had to yoke him up. He got me mad. . . . I just kicked a few teeth out. He was so scared that his teeth turned orange, and all the rest of his body turned all colors. Boy, the hospital says they can't even put him in critical condition!" I asked, "Are you worried that you might have hurt him in a way that they can't fix him up, Cassius?" to which Fred replied, "You better believe it!" I reminded him that there were rules in boxing, and that a referee could stop a fight so a man couldn't get too badly hurt, but Fred shook his head, saying sadly "The referee was his mother-in-law." It was my feeling that Fred was telling us of his own worries, that his mother would not be able to prevent him from carrying out his aggressive wishes toward his father, indeed that his impulses were murderously dangerous.

Interviewing Each Other

In a group, children can and do interview one another regarding their art work, learning further to develop an "observing ego," by helping someone else to do so. In the following excerpt from a taped interview with a group of ten-year-old boys, Victor helped Jerry to define his product, as well as expressing some of his own curiosity:

Jerry: I made a sculpture of this mountain with a pond on it, and with a stream running down. It's made out of clay, and it's on a piece of cardboard. At the top, in the pond, I have glue around it . . . and I have water in it, real water. Are there any questions?

Victor: Does anybody live on it?

Jerry: It's a deserted island.

Victor: Can the water run away?

Jerry: Not right now, but it's supposed to. I have to put a drainage system in it. Actually, it's sort of like a circulating system.

Victor: Do you have any living animals there?

Jerry: No, there aren't any, but there's mice thrown into it, by sea or else by land. It's a lake with a stream running down.

Victor: Does the lake run into a river or an ocean?

Jerry: It runs into the ocean. It's an underground spring. Any other questions? Thank you very much.

Until this session, Victor had been inhibited during the discussion time, despite his interest in holding and using the tape recorder microphone. Indeed, he was able to ask questions of others for some weeks, before he could elaborate easily on his own creations.

Fig. 13-2. "Joe Frazier" or "The Stupid Man," a boxer who got beaten up. Marker.

Re-Viewing in a Group

Reviewing what has gone on over time in a group, as with a family or individuals, is often possible through looking back over art productions. In addition, slides of products or activities and films or videotapes of sessions can enable the group to relive and review what has gone before. With the five- and six-year-olds described earlier, one discussion session was organized around viewing slides of wood scrap houses they had made; eliciting a whole new set of projections about these constructions. Another focused on slides from a recent joint session with their mothers, enabling them to talk about some of the feelings they had experienced which could not be easily shared during the joint discussion time. Over a year after an adolescent group had been meeting, an hour was spent reviewing all of the super eight millimeter film shot, most of it taken by the group members. While no one was able to talk about changes in himself, many were able to see positive changes in each other, pointing them out with delight. Most dramatic were their changed perceptions of the leaders, seen as having been nicer in the past, related to their present disillusionment with formerly idealized parent figures.

Individual Growth in a Group: Don

Change in a group can be seen as members develop trust and the group takes on shape and definition as an entity in its own right, becoming more cohesive. In this context, the individuals in group treatment also change, as they utilize the resources in art and each other to work on and solve their conflicts. Don, for example, began by working alone, making compulsive abstract designs (Fig. 13-3(a)), but gradually moved toward more communication with the other boys and in his art. At first, he sat closer to others, still silent, and became somewhat freer in his abstractions, needing fewer boundaries and allowing himself more range within them. He then turned to work with more tactile media, such as clay, perhaps stimulated by the others, and first made tame animals (dogs and cats), then larger, more aggressive ones (lions and dinosaurs). Eventually, he was able to model and paint a boy who had been violently wounded, with red blood streaming out of his maimed body (Fig. 13-3(b)).

While he declined to say who it might be the week he made it, the following week he whispered to me that he knew who it was, but was afraid to tell the others. I asked if he could tell me, and he whispered, "My brother." I then suggested that it might help the other boys in the group, many of whom had similar angry feelings and wishes toward siblings, to know that they were not alone. During group discussion time at the end of the session, he tentatively whispered that it was "somebody younger," then "somebody I'd like to throw something at," and finally, "my brother." The others responded with relief, and an outpouring of their own hostile impulses to hurt younger siblings along with fears of their strength and destructiveness. Don was delighted, and responded the following week by becoming very messy, smearing and mixing lots of tempera paint colors with another boy, for the first time allowing himself to regress and to interact freely with other group members. His products for the next two weeks were not much to look at, but the process he engaged in was vital to his own eventual recovery. He followed this aggressive/regressive phase with a freer kind of order in his work, selecting a tempera painting with movement, color mixing, and clear but not rigid boundaries, as a gift for his individual therapist when he terminated treatment months later (Fig. 13-3(c)).

Group Growth: New Members and Endings

While the most effective ongoing therapy groups in my experience are those with a fairly stable membership, it is often necessary to admit new members when others leave the group. The introduction of a new member is like the coming of a new baby, for in many ways a group comes to represent for its members a symbolic family, the leaders seen as parent figures and the members as siblings. Not only do the members need preparation for such an event, but their ways of dealing with it may be indicative of how they feel about other family members at home. Jamie, for

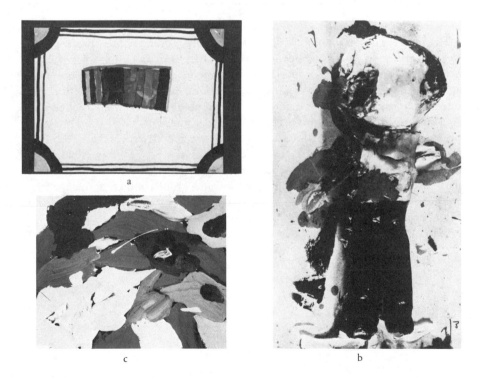

Fig. 13-3. (a) A tight drawing; (b) a bloody sculpture; and (c) a free painting by Don. Age 10.

example, was very upset on the day that Sally entered his group for the first time, making many silly aggressive remarks, even "attacking" the paper on which she was drawing by writing his own first initial. Jenny, on the other hand, was delighted to have another girl in the group, and quickly latched on to Sally, asking her to draw next to her on mural paper, eventually trying to copy Sally's picture.

Endings with groups are much like terminations with individuals—no matter how long or short the time span of meeting, there are feelings about ending related to separation issues for all members. These can be stormy as well as sad, and often require much time, if a group can be open about a termination date, for adequate working-through. In most long-term groups, the introduction of the idea of termination is followed by both regression and aggression. In two groups, dramas of capturing and killing off the leaders expressed the intensity of the members' rage at being "abandoned." These were followed, as in most termination processes, by expressions of sadness —of "mourning" —for ending a therapeutic relationship is a real as well as a symbolic loss. If there is sufficient time and all goes well, the loss is accepted along with all of the feelings involved in saying goodbye.

Conclusion

Art in a group is in some ways different from other group approaches, especially in comparison to discussion formats with adolescents and adults. Like play or activity approaches, it makes possible simultaneous communication between and among group members, throughout the working period, and allows for more informal nonspotlighted communications as preparation for those inhibited about speaking openly to the whole group. Unlike games or crafts, the art activity provides not only for mastery of skills, but also for symbolic expression of conflicted inner feelings, fantasies, and fears. Because of the range of possible media, individuals can discover their own preferred materials and processes, and thus work on individual identity and mutual respect within a group context. Both expression and reflection are possible, as in individual art therapy, and each may sometimes be enhanced, stimulated, and facilitated in a group setting.

CHAPTER 14.

Multi-Modality Group Therapy

For a long time, as an art teacher and later as an art therapist, I never realized that what I did with visual and plastic media was related in any but a semantic way to work in other art forms. I had always loved various kinds of literature, film, music, dance, and drama, but had thought of them as essentially different and unique creative modalities. I have since discovered that, while in many ways they are indeed distinct, in other ways they are not. This paradox derives from what I have come to perceive as their organic interrelatedness—as forms of thinking, and as ways of sending and receiving messages.

This first was apparent to me when I became a mother, and watched my infants explore the world with all of their senses. It was even more evident as they grew older, and began to express themselves in rapidly shifting, but closely related ways. They cooed, they rocked, they touched, and they moved, all in ways that conveyed meaning. These expressions were often combined—the coo and the gesture, or the manipulation and the body rhythm. As I related to them, I too used various forms of communication in my maternal efforts at contact. I would touch, I would rock, I would make sounds and gestures, I would use words, and sometimes I would direct their attention to visual phenomena. Thus, very early, we were each using all of the precursors of those forms of expression which, in their later development, we call the arts.

By the time they were preschoolers, my children would play in a similarly multi-modal fashion—often swaying while they made pictures in the sand, growling as they pretended to be giants, or singing while they built with blocks. In nursery school, this fluid interrelationship of expressive modalities is still possible during the time set aside for "free play." Anyone who has observed youngsters in such a context knows that spontaneous drama will emerge almost as frequently during their play with blocks, sand, or clay as it will when they are engaged with dolls, puppets, or dress-ups. Similarly, music is not confined to the time spent using rhythm instruments, but erupts spontaneously in hums and tunes, often self-created, while they are also engaged with paint or clay. One of my favorite schizophrenic children used to dance whenever she would paint, so that to be with her was to witness a genuine multi-media "happening." Another would rock and hum while he moved his paint-filled brush up and down on the easel paper, as gracefully as if he were in a meditative trance.

Although I started out using only art materials in my clinical work, I soon began to perceive certain aspects of what was happening in dramatic terms. Sometimes it was unfocused—the gestural drama of the sweep of a brush or the caress of clay. At other times, it was the narrative quality of the story told while smearing fingerpaint, or the explicit drama of the pictured or sculpted scene. On a more formal level, there were moments when a child would pick up his sculpture and transform it into a puppet, speaking *for* it in a way that was qualitatively distinct from speaking *about* it. Or he would make sound effects for the explosions he was drawing, nonverbally enlivening the action represented. Perhaps his face would become a mask from soap crayons or fingerpaint, or he would spontaneously make a mask or a puppet and utilize it dramatically. The chopping up of clay while describing it as the destruction of some animal or person, or the literal wiping out of a creature drawn into fingerpaint, was clearly as much a dramatic as an artistic event; and the familiar telling of a story about an art product could only be perceived as containing powerful dramatic elements.

I learned, therefore, from my own children and my young patients, that at their source in the human being, expressive modalities are not separated by hard and fast lines, but may instead be seen as points on a continuum: from the body to the sound to the image to the word—dance, music, art, and drama. My patients also taught me to be flexible, to be ready to follow a person into another creative modality, if that is where his spirit leads him.

Carla, for example, went from drawing her nightmare monsters to cutting them out, putting them in "cages," and "locking" them up. The next step in her working through process required an even greater use of dramatization, as the two of us enacted the roles of scary monster and frightened child (cf. Chapter 6).

On the basis of such child-initiated experiences, I became convinced that art alone may not always be enough, and that it is often essential to expand the therapy in other directions. This has occurred spontaneously so often in my own work that I am sure it is a natural thing for children to search for congenial forms of expression, and is unnatural to restrict them to any one creative modality. Had Carla stopped at the representation and even the locking up of her nightmare monsters, I think she would not have been so well able to recognize that much of the aggression she feared was her own (projected). By taking the role of the monster in a spontaneous drama, she was able to experience her own angry feelings. She was, therefore, ready to see, later on, how those angry monsters in dreams and drawings were not just scary grownups, but also scary, angry wishes in herself. Such experiences suggest that, even though an art therapist's primary tool is art, it is essential to be able to permit the use of other expressive modalities, especially when they spring spontaneously from the child himself.

The spontaneous emergence of drama in the course of art therapy has occurred many times in work with individuals of all ages and with all kinds of handicaps, in all kinds of settings. Sometimes it is stimulated by the media themselves, as when Barry, who was blind, felt wet watercolors on a brush, swabbed them on his arm, turned the brush over, and "jabbed" himself with the pointed end—reenacting the experience of an injection. At other times, the flow from art to drama is stimulated by the identity given the medium, as when a little girl pounded and yelled at her clay blobs, like a punitive mother scolding and spanking her naughty children. In such instances, it seemed that what the child needed to communicate required the action that only drama could provide.

Such an evolution from art to drama has happened as many times with groups as with individuals. One day I came to work with an art therapy group, having gotten a cut, stitches, and a bandage on my leg the night before. Thinking my accident might stimulate concern about bodily injury in the children, I had brought along a new sculpture material—Pariscraft (gauze impregnated with plaster of paris). Almost all of the boys in the group of twelve-year-olds not only modelled forms with the Pariscraft, but they also experimented with "casts" on fingers, wrists, etc. One boy had wrapped some around both an arm and a leg, and came to the discussion time limping and saying that he had had a serious accident. I interviewed this "victim," who explained: "I got all broken up with blood." At this point, another group member announced that he was the doctor, saying: "This is my patient. Well see, he got hit by a car, and broke his leg and arm. Up here, he got a hole in his arm, and through it you can see his veins and stuff. His leg—I gotta fix his leg up some more. You see, it's bad." After the doctor assured all of us that he would be repairing the patient, the victim dramatically unrolled his bandages and triumphantly announced, "I'm cured!"

At times the sequence is reversed and a story emerges first, to be followed by its enactment, using art media to help in the telling. Chip, a boy concerned about castration after an operation for an undescended testicle, joined a group of six-year-old boys and girls and told a story about a baby with a broken leg whose mother is very upset. In order to play out the story, Chip made a life-size baby of brown clay with one leg missing. Asking that I play the mother, Chip as the doctor explained that "All babies are born without another leg! You dummy!" As I and my "husband" (another group member) spoke of how sad we were, Doctor Chip tried to magically restore what was missing, adding another leg to the clay baby. My "husband," who had his own castration anxieties, playfully knocked off the new clay leg each time it was attached, to which Chip responded as if immobilized, saying there was nothing he could do to help. Finally, the male cotherapist entered the drama as another physician. He helped Doctor Chip to repair the baby and prevent the father's aggressive attacks, so that the mother was able to take a whole baby home. While the clay infant was powerfully formed, by itself it could not carry the affective impact of the drama built around its missing or damaged part.

Experiences like those described above led a decade ago to a proposal for an art-drama therapy group with my colleague, a drama therapist (Irwin, Rubin, and Shapiro, 1971). As we considered working together, we worried about Suzanne Langer's comments "that there can be no hybrid works belonging as much to one art as to another" (1957, p. 82); and that "there are no happy marriages in art—only successful rape." (p. 86) Neither of us wished to lose our still-fragile professional identity, much less to rape or be raped. We were each committed to our particular art form, and had some trepidation about the proposed union. We also feared the potential competition in working together, as well as the loss of integrity possible in each modality.

We began our work with six boys, ages nine to eleven, previously referred for art or drama therapy. Prior to beginning the group, we each met the six boys in an individual art or drama diagnostic interview. (Irwin and Shapiro, 1975) The art sessions were unstructured. The drama interviews were similarly open, with puppets provided as primary projective materials along with costume pieces and props. The child was invited to make up and play out a story. Analysis of the data from these helped us to make up a behaviorally balanced group of boys, who could tolerate regression and could use creative modalities as media for change. In these initial sessions we got to know the boys, and they got to know each of us and to try out in private the "tools of the trade," which they were later to put into practice in the group.

Initially we thought we would have alternate sessions, with art activities one week and drama the next. However, it quickly became apparent that the boys would not adhere to such artificial boundaries, and each meeting verified the children's need and willingness to express themselves freely in both modalities. This was clearly demonstrated in the very first session, and proved to be a recurring pattern in the life of the group.

In the first meeting, the boys soon verbalized their anxiety over the newness of the situation. As they fingerpainted around a table, they shared stories of witches and vampires who really suck blood, of boats that capsize when one is unprepared, and of bombs that suddenly appear and explode without warning. At that point, one boy angrily left the group, and went off in a corner to paint an "ugly picture" of me. Unable to finish, he returned a few minutes later, held out his forefinger which was covered with red paint, and said, "I need a doctor. I'm cut." As the drama therapist entered the fantasy as the doctor, he elaborated, "I was cutting open my cat and got blood all over my hands." This stimulated the others, and soon the air was filled with dramatized fantasies of hurts and injuries. One boy, who had previously drawn himself in a grave with a scary monster standing over him, immediately imitated the first, and covered his hand with red paint, too. That, he said, was "my brother's blood, because I just killed him, and he's lying in a coffin."

Perhaps meeting each of us earlier in an intense diagnostic session facilitated this rapid involvement in dramatic and pictorial fantasy, and the high degree of trust which made it possible to share and verbalize anxieties. Perhaps, too, the alternation of picturing and wiping out, possible in the regressive medium of fingerpaint, and the mutual discussion of fantasies, induced a state of readiness for the castration-murder-doctor drama. So intertwined were the two modalities that it became impossible to state that a session was pure art or pure drama. From that point on, therefore, materials for expression in both modalities were available every week to extend the range of possibilities for symbolic expression. For art, there were various drawing, painting, modelling, and construction materials; for drama, there were puppets, plain gauze masks, simple costume pieces, props, cloths of various sizes and textures, stage lights, etc.

A further expectation related to the need for planned vs. spontaneous activities. We had planned, and introduced quite consciously, a number of combined art-and-drama techniques into the early sessions, in order to help the children learn to use both modalities. Most simply, we would often suggest the telling of a story about a picture. During the first session Tommy had made with yellow fingerpaint a peace symbol, representing the same conflict he was to play out a week later with his two puppets labelled "War" and "Peace." In associating to the picture, Tommy began to talk about the problem of aggression, and his concern about war and killing. When asked what peace meant to him, he answered: "Peace means a lot to me . . . . I think peace means people talking together and children playing together instead of fighting . . . fighting with their fists."

Conversely, we would sometimes suggest that someone dramatize his art work, as when Matt was encouraged to act out the story he had told about his tempera painting of "A French Soldier Going to an American Fort." He said that the soldier had gone to George Washington to ask for reinforcements in a battle with the Indians; but he puzzled over the outcome, explaining that General Washington "sometimes says yes, and sometimes says no." In part in order to solve the dilemma, Matt took the role of George Washington, and acted out the story with Dick who, as the French soldier, came to see the general. Matt, as Washington, finally agreed to the Frenchman's request for two hundred soldiers who, he explained, would win the war using cannons against the Indians' arrows, but would, of course, be badly wounded in the process.

Yet another combined approach was to suggest doing art work based upon a drama. In a later session, for example, following the spontaneous dramatization of a spy story, we suggested that the boys picture some of their feelings about the events they had just played out. Matt quickly produced a drawing of a man attempting to shoot a woman (Fig. 14-1), thus describing pictorially his impulse to attack the therapist. This latter notion was confirmed when he grinned and commented to me, "That lady in the picture looks like you!"

In predictable fashion, art materials were often used to make puppets, masks, costumes, and props, which the boys were then encouraged to use in dramatizations, or more simply, to be interviewed as the character they had created. Jerry, for example, was quite proud of his vampire mask, to which he later added a self-made costume and, as Dracula intoned: "I suck ze blood. Some blood eez better zan others." When he needed a stake to complete his vampire attire, he carefully made it himself, from cardboard.

In retrospect, it may have been useful to introduce these combined art-and-drama techniques to the boys in the early sessions. But it was soon apparent that they were capable of creating their own imaginative combinations, quite independently of the leaders. In fact, in time it became clear that the boys' creative and ingenious uses of unstructured art materials, often led spontaneously into drama, promoting a natural and dynamic flow. Thus, a cardboard carton was not only used for the suggested "box sculpture," but also became a boat for Ben, a house for Matt, and a puppet stage for Dick. Similarly, soap crayons became makeup, as the boys painted their faces, externalizing their specific inner fantasies (Fig. 14-2). Jack, for example, streaked his face and hands to become Frankenstein acting out the role of a monster who wanted to chase me in order, he said, to devour me. Cotton and yarn provided for collage, also became beards, moustaches, and wigs.

A natural merging of art and drama often occurred, as associations to the boys' creations were spontaneously dramatized. Thus, using styrofoam, papers, and colorful pipe cleaners, several boys one day made magnificent king and queen boats. It was only natural to sail the boats (in an empty portable sandbox), relating action-filled stories of races, battles, attacks, wins, and losses. To extend and clarify each child's fantasy, one of us interviewed each boy "at the scene" of the event, as though for a radio or television program. The same playful interviewing procedure was often used after a drama, to help the child achieve ego distance from the play, and to help build bridges and strengthen boundaries between reality and fantasy.

Fig. 14-1. Matt's drawing of a man trying to shoot a woman. Marker.

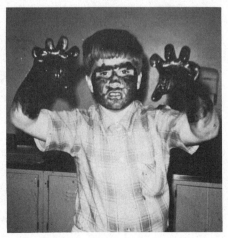

Fig. 14-2. Soap crayon "makeup" turns Jack into Frankenstein. Age 9.

We had originally expected the children to show individual preferences for either art or drama. Although initially this was so for some children, by the end of several months it became much more difficult, if not impossible, to select a preferred art form for each child. Most often, a child began with the modality which was most comfortable for him, but, as his confidence and curiosity increased, he would usually explore and try out new ways of expressing himself, especially if a respected peer was involved in an activity.

Frequently issues were first explored symbolically in art, and later expressed in dramatic form. Although two of the boys seemed to utilize solitary or dyadic play with puppets as a way of expressing feelings before they could comfortably make and keep artistic productions, most of the group members began with art and moved to drama. In general, a dynamic interaction took place, with individuals using both modalities to express and to work through conflicts.

Matt, for example, at first, went off to work alone at the easel, painting pictures of George Washington, "the father of our country," an idealized parent symbol. His other favored symbol was a pirate—Black Hook or Bluebeard—who represented evil, aggressive impulses toward authority figures, always shown as damaged in an eye and/or leg. Two of Matt's paintings in his art diagnostic session, were of Washington's house, Valley Forge, shown with a quiet cannon outside, and Black Hook's Boat. Matt had told a story in which Black Hook "almost" had his leg bitten off by a shark. In the third month of group, Matt painted a burning church, in which the steeple is destroyed. Soon after, he painted his first picture of two airplanes, a big and a little one, locked in a fierce battle. In these products and stories, one could see Matt's anger at his all-powerful parents, his ambivalent wish to attack and to identify with his policeman-father, and his fear of his father's retaliatory super-powers and of being punished (damaged).

In time, however, this conflict moved from solitary art at the easel to more direct avenues of expression, as Matt repeatedly symbolically attacked and destroyed the powerful parent forces. He would tease both therapists, calling us witches, verbalizing his wish to make us his "slaves," and taking an imperious and authoritarian role. Gradually, he gained the courage to argue with the other boys, and one day a verbal fight actually escalated into a physical battle. When it was suggested that perhaps the combatants could fight it out on paper, the two made a large mural, intently drawing and painting Japanese, German, and American planes in an air war (Fig. 14-3). As they worked side by side, the air was filled with accompanying shouts and sounds of battle. After the mural was finished, all of the boys prepared plasticine "bullets" and, yelling out their fantasied stories of the war being fought, they let loose with a hail of bullets, directed at the mural in barrage after barrage.

When the battle was over, they returned to the refreshment table to replenish their bodies with food. Still excited by the drama, the boys were interviewed as the "sole survivors" of the terrible battle. Matt, of course, identified himself as George Washington, and related his version of the conflict. Suddenly, in response to an unrelated noise outside the room, the boys spontaneously dived under the table for cover, yelling "Duck! There's one plane left, and it's bombing us!" In a fantasy of retaliation for their aggression, one boy lost his leg, another his head, and another (Matt) his arm. The drama therapist quickly became a medic, who magically restored damaged body parts. The boys then returned to the battle, and putting up the last few pieces of the mural, they bombed the enemy again, saying that they had to "get that last enemy plane." After the "war," we "decorated" the boys with quickly made medals for their bravery in battle, as they talked and shared their feelings about what had just transpired.

Such an interweaving of art and drama occurred many times. In a sense, the above drama and its variations were preparation for a later hospital scene, in which castration and other themes were more clearly played out by the group. Just as each child can use the same medium in his own way, so each boy used the dramatic structure of the hospital to enact his own conflicts. One, for example, was "dying of thirst," afraid of abandonment; while another played a wild, "crazy" patient "falling apart inside" from his inner confusion. Matt, who by this time had started to work through some of the anger at both parents, lessening both his rage and his castration fears, was able to be a kind and helpful doctor in this hospital drama, repairing injuries and replacing missing parts. For him, as for others, the group experience provided multiple opportunities to express, understand, and work through both intrapsychic and interpersonal conflicts.

It was indeed possible within the group structure, for individual members to work on their particular areas of difficulty, as well as for the group to work together on shared concerns. Because of the unstructured nature of the one-and-a-half hour sessions, it was possible for a child to work alone on a particular problem area, or, if he chose, to join in dyadic or group interaction. The flexible setting encouraged the exploration of multiple alternatives in time, space, and support, as the children worked toward clarification and resolution of their conflicts.

Because of the essentially individual nature of art and the group nature of drama, we had expected that the boys would generally work independently in art and together in drama. Much to our surprise, and perhaps because of the simultaneous availability of materials and space for work in both modalities, it soon became apparent that individual, dyadic, and group involvement were possible in each area. There were often times when children worked alone in art, thoroughly engrossed in their activity; but there were also times when individuals engaged in solitary dramatic play, particularly with puppets. Children would frequently work in parallel or cooperative dyads in art, or in dramatic play; and at times all members of the group ended up working together on some cooperative productive task, like making a mural or decorating each other (Fig. 14-4). Spontaneous dramas also evolved in which every group member took part in a way that truly reflected individual as well as group needs and concerns.

A similar range of interactions occurred with the boys' use of other human beings in the group. Just as they seemed able to use each other as companions, helpers, observers, or protagonists, so they were able to use the adults in multiple ways. We were surprised and intrigued by the range of roles in which the boys put us, including observer, teacher, co-worker, role-player, limit-setter, and commenter. The nature of the group served to stimulate various projections on the two therapists, and the enacting of "dramatized" transference behaviors. As the children relived and explored feelings and impulses, they were often inclined to dramatize the transference relationship, prolonging and further exploring the fantasy through enactment.

Thus, for example, when Matt had begun to taste the sweetness of power in dramatic play as a general, he pretended to be omnipotent, and ordered me about, saying peremptorily: "Slave, get me the tape!" or "Come here, missy!" Later, playing Santa Claus in a spontaneous drama, he told me I was his doll, under his power, and must act in whatever way he commanded. Once the children learned to take roles and to pretend, they often elected to relate to us in this dramatic way, because it served their needs so well. It made possible, of course, a greater flexibility for us too, since one could play out the assigned role and discuss it later, or could respond therapeutically in character, e.g., "You like to boss me around don't you?" or as one's real self, e.g., "If you could really be such a powerful boss, what else would you order me to do?" This dramatized way of working enriched the experience for the child, and offered multiple opportunities to explore emotional conflicts, as the child turned from one art form to another, from one adult to another, "working through" using all available resources.

The therapeutic utility of the activity was enhanced by the post-play discussion. These end-of-group round-table talks over refreshments were essential in helping the children to integrate the preceding activity. While a great deal of sharing of feelings usually went on during the "doing time," the last half hour of each session was used to help the boys focus on the meaning of what had occurred, and verbalize feelings and understandings. The arts are powerful tools which stimulate regression (the rate of which sometimes has to be controlled by the therapist) and aid in the uncovering and expressing of conflict. The post-activity discussions were

Fig. 14-3. Part of the mural of an airplane war made by the group.

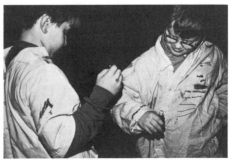

Fig. 14-4. Two boys help each other use paint to become "generals."

an integral part of the therapeutic process; during these, the children were helped to use what they had made (art) or done (drama) as a vehicle for verbal expression, insight, and change.

Thus, the making and doing which served to complement each other as expressive tools, were themselves enhanced by talking. The suspension of the reality principle which occurred during the time of artistic or dramatic creativity was replaced by a consideration of that activity in the light of the child's past, current, or future realities. Not only did such sharing of anxieties, wishes, and fears help to dispel each boy's "delusion of uniqueness," but the differentiation of real and fantasied actions enabled the children to gain mastery over their impulses, just as they gained increasing mastery over the media and tools of the two art forms.

Dr. Irwin and I worked with the boys in this group in the way described for a little more than a year, at which time termination seemed appropriate. Later, we worked for two years with a male child psychiatrist, Dr. Guillermo Borrero, and a group of adolescent boys and girls, ages fifteen to eighteen.* They came for two hours a week, each with a different diagnostic label, each in some kind of psychological pain. A wide range of flexible, unstructured materials that could be used in a variety of ways—for art, drama, poetry, music, movement, and photography—were made available to them. As in the earlier group, many things could happen simultaneously and the members were able to use all of these different modalities as ways of communicating to us and to each other.

Paula one day sat at the table with the others, yet quiet and apart. She was obviously depressed, but could not talk about it. She wrote slowly on a piece of paper, and later showed it to the group: "I sit here wondering why there is so much sadness in this lonely room. Although it is filled with people, I feel like the world is falling in on me, which I really don't understand—this feeling of sadness is hurting me in a way no one understands. It's like the world is against me, like I'm in a world of my own. . . . It is a lonely feeling, which hurts. O God help me." Her anguished cry on paper was read and heard by the others, who then responded warmly to her distress with support and affection.

On another day, Paula, then working actively on her black identity, proudly wrote and read aloud her poem, "Who Am I?"

> I'm the child of the man.
> The child of the man
> Who no longer wants to live.
> The child of the man
> Who wonders why he is the man
> And I'm the child.
> I'm the child of the man's Pride.
> I'm the child of the Black man's Pride.

*Some of what follows was written in collaboration with Dr. Borrero and Dr. Irwin.

I'm the child who fights for freedom.
I'm the child who lives for freedom.
I'm the child who does not have any freedom.
I'm the child who lives in a world of Poverty.
I'm the child who lives under the (white) man's laws.
I'm the child who has gone out to see what life is all about,
    and has gotten her mind together. . . ."

Another girl, also not very comfortable with speech, wrote a poem following an assault, reflecting both her anger and her wishes about being a woman:

Woman was created from the rib of man.
She was not created from his head to be above him.
Nor from his feet to be trampled upon—
She was created from his side to be equal to him,
And close to his heart to be loved by him.

Matthew, even less verbal, often found music and movement to be his most congenial modalities for expression and communication. Sam, although quite articulate, was most comfortable with art. Thus, on a day when Lanny was depressed and uncommunicative, Sam was able to let him know he cared by drawing a portrait of him, rather than by saying anything in words.

In one session, unusual because the other two leaders were out of town, I sat with three boys and one girl around a table. Matthew focused on playing a record he had brought in, asking me to write down, and all of us to listen to, the lyrics which he felt related to him: "I need to belong to someone. . . . I feel like a motherless child." (His mother had indeed abandoned him.) Another song, which he played and replayed, ended "I guess it goes all the way back to my mom and dad—two people I never chanced to know. I wonder why I miss them so. I never had a mother's touch or a father's hand." Sam, sitting next to Matt, first wrote "private" messages to me in German and Russian, then worked with clay, first manipulating it and finally making a figure he called "Need," a sad, large-headed, abstract-looking man (Fig. 14-5b). Lanny was relatively quiet, doodled for a while, and finally drew a man with a strong head and overelaborated neck, during a discussion of getting high on drugs. Sherry drew a childlike scene of "a place with kids," explaining that it showed how she pictured the Child Welfare Shelter where her younger brother had been placed when he had run away from home the previous week. She related her idyllic image of the shelter to her own wishes to "get away," a move she was able to make several months later.

At one point all four became quite demanding of attention and of supplies, as if to highlight the absence of the other two leaders. I, therefore, pretended to be a waitress, taking orders, before going to my office to get the art supplies. Their orders were for extravagant quantities of money and food, and reflected the hunger and competitiveness which was intensified with only one leader. They were also mutually supportive and helpful in many ways during this session, as if they were banding together in the absence of two of the parent figures.

Most often, members would not remain clustered at any one place throughout the two hours, but would move around as their needs and wishes dictated. Spontaneous musical and dramatic "happenings" thus occurred quite often, making the situation unpredictable and exciting for all of us. The dramas often began with one member, but were flexible and spontaneous enough for others to participate in both the planning of the story and the expression of different roles. In one round-robin story which grew out of Sherry's telling of a dream, the plot was fluid enough for each one to add his own uniquely meaningful touches, as in this excerpt from their discussion:

Sherry: This could make a good movie, maybe a cartoon . . . . I'm goin' on a boat across the ocean. Someone pushes me off, and I find myself in the cellar of a mysterious friend. . . .

Sam: And your friend was this penguin, this really huge thing—a glandular case—and then the penguin says, "Come and help me. We must fight together. . . .

Cindy: And then the penguin grew wings, and flew away. Then it made do-do's all over everything. . . .

Lanny: And then I grab one of those birds, and carry him home, and use it as a flap-jack!"

Thus they were able to work together, not only sequentially and side by side, but often in mutually supportive interaction. Many times one person would teach another a skill, and often two or more members would work together on a sculpture, a painting, or a construction. Dramas with puppets, masks, and themselves evolved fairly often, with different members taking different roles, usually around a mutually meaningful theme.

Sam, oversized (six feet nine inches tall), overweight, and extremely bright, had dropped out of school, and had literally locked himself in his room before coming to the clinic. He had been in individual and family therapy for several months, and was referred to the group, partly because he was talented in art, but particularly because he had withdrawn completely from peers. In the group, he began by isolating himself behind an easel in a corner and working on a series of brightly colored, organic, curvy, voluptuous paintings. During those early months, his work in clay was equally soft, undulating, and fluid (Fig. 14-5a). But in the fourth month, for the first time he played a role in a drama, that of a defense attorney, where his debating experience enabled him to be verbally aggressive and competitive. His art work around this time started to gradually change, extensions emerging from the clay, projections thrusting out from the flowing masses. In his paintings too, there were more often clearly separated parts, shapes, and colors becoming more varied and differentiated. Gradually he began to try other media, like wood, which gave his creations even more form, stability, and power.

As though a structure was forming internally as well, Sam began in minute, playful ways to display some of the anger he had always repressed. After about a year of group therapy, he spontaneously created a vivid, powerful drama which seemed to represent the psychic awakening he was experiencing. Saying he was playing a crazy person, he cowered fearfully, retreated inside a womblike enclosure (a large wooden box), and pulled it out the door. Opening the door brusquely, he walked back in, appearing to be a totally different person, stamping and speaking loudly, angrily, and strongly: "Where is that fellow? That other fellow who is so scared all the time? If you see him again, tell him to get out of here!"

He repeated the drama the following week, after proudly reporting the sale of one of his paintings for $25 to a local bank. This time he involved the other two leaders in the drama but had some difficulty being assertive with them. He dressed Dr. Irwin as a witch and Dr. Borrero as a king and then struggled in pantomime with these powerful parent figures. He was able to win out with the witch-mother, but often weakened with the king-father. Unable to use words to express his anger at the male leader, we suggested he try numbers, and he then carried on an intense, angry dialogue using numbers, with dramatic intonation and affect. The outcome was a compromise, in which a third Sam finally emerged, not the violently angry one or the fearful cowering one, but a strong, reasonable (integrated) self.

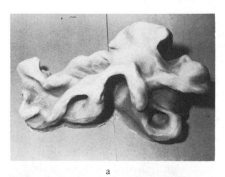

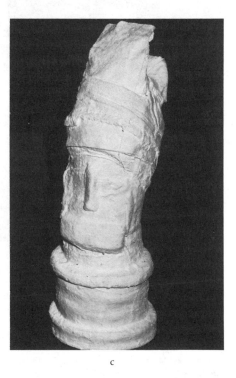

Fig. 14-5. Three sculptures by Sam: (a) An early undulating mass, (b) "Need," and (c) a late head of a King.

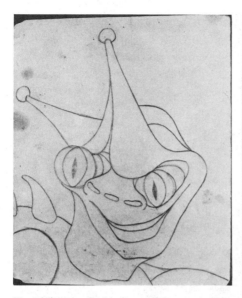

Fig. 14-6. A head with distorted features by Sam. Pencil. Age 16.

Fig. 14-7. Sam's drawing of the view from his college window. Pencil.

Simultaneously, his art work began to change significantly. He began to move from abstraction to representation, sometimes even making people—faces that were often distorted and grotesque, perhaps representing some of those long-repressed inner feelings (Fig. 14-6). The same damaged self was in a story he had told several months earlier, after hospitalization and some regression. He described a Martian invasion and an Earthling, clearly self-projection, about whom he then felt almost hopeless:

About this time, one of the most primitive of the Earthling creatures wanders to the far side of the ship, and is immediately stranded, and can't get back. The Martian scanner analyzer at this time determines that the earth creature doesn't have enough life support system. The Earthling creature will die. The Martians will have to intervene to save his life. . . . The elevator hydraulic on the lift is raised, and three Martians go out to rescue the primitive Earthling, who is now dying. This is a great victory for the Martians, as they can now examine an Earthling, and now they can condition it, and can observe very closely its behavior patterns. The only disadvantage for the Earthling is that he'll find out. . . . The disadvantage for the Earthling is that there is intense physical pain in the cranial brain area. . . . The Earthlings are very weak creatures. The Earthlings must realize that the Martians are omnipotent. They are not only superior but omnipotent. However, the Martians respect the Earthlings for their ability to grasp *some* information, and find that the Earthlings could no doubt be developed into an intelligent-like life form. The end.

Dr. Irwin, to whom he told the story, asked: "You mean there's some hope for the Earthlings?" Sam replied slowly, "Well, some hope . . . rather remote. At times it seems nonexistent, but there is *some* hope." His characterizations of himself and the leaders reflected both his fears and his hopes for change through therapy.

Change for Sam, as for all, was often slow, with regression as well as progression over time. Becoming aware of all of his feelings, happy as well as sad ones, he struggled to integrate this newfound awareness of his inner life. As he became stronger, he related more and more to the others, developing genuine friendships like those he later formed in college. One of his favorite creations was a powerful phallic head of a king, symbolizing perhaps the strength he was beginning to realize without fear in himself (14-5c). Later, his letters from college were full of humor, and sometimes included drawings, like a view from his window (Fig. 14-7), that were far more realistic and healthy than those he had done in the past.

Lanny, often depressed, had a hard time expressing himself in the group. His first drawings were of heroes, but they were usually incomplete (Fig. 14-8a). Almost all of the powerful athletes were missing parts of their bodies—sometimes an arm, sometimes a leg—and were often subtly cut off by the edge of the paper. For many sessions, he worked on an elaborate picture of superheroes, like the Green Lantern

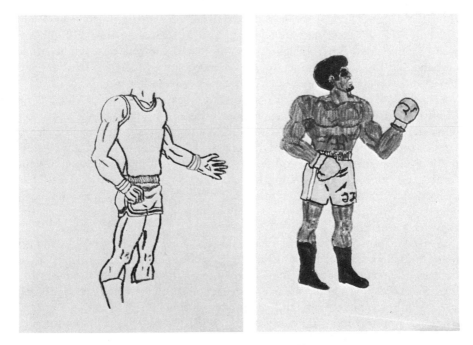

Fig. 14-8. An early (left) and later (right) athlete drawn by Lanny.

and the Green Arrow, perhaps triggered by his feelings of vulnerability in the group. This same sense of helplessness seemed evident in his spontaneous dramatizations; no matter how his role began, he almost always ended up as a victim, hurt and injured.

As a dental patient, for example, he was so passive and wobbly that he kept tumbling to the floor, as though—like a baby—he could not sit up without support. He had actually begun as the dentist in the drama, but was unable to maintain the assertive role and soon switched to the weak patient, who finally had to be tied in the chair to keep him from falling on the floor. In the same way, he volunteered to be a tough cop, driving his police car, when all of a sudden, he changed the script, and was hurt and injured in an accident. Rescued by a doctor, he seemed to enjoy the idea of being a passive patient, even when put on the table for an operation. Without a whimper, he masochistically submitted to the doctor's primitive brand of anesthesia—a hit on the head with a wooden spoon.

In a later drama, he played a boss who was able to give orders and be a big shot with his secretary but could not confront the angry male employee who he was supposed to fire, cowering and able to gesture assertively only after the man left the room. As he was taking these first tentative steps to express anger in dramas, however, his drawings began to change. More often, the sports figures were more complete, with few, if any body parts missing (Fig. 14-8b). Trying other media, he made a tall (phallic) three-dimensional plastic construction, and later a huge sword and a clay dagger. One day he playfully pretended to be superpowerful and slowly lifted up a "heavy" chair, said to weigh "at least fifty thousand pounds." Becoming more comfortable with this aggression, he played the role of a domineering husband, bossing his wife around. He demanded special food, insisted that she slavishly follow his commands, and indeed was quite authoritarian.

Having learned to express his aggression outward instead of inward, he experimented with many roles, sometimes using a toy gun to attack or protect himself from his enemies. Full of courage, he one day challenged the male leader to a mock pantomime battle. When Dr. Borrero showed him how to fight in slow motion, he was able to exert the necessary control, yet still win the contest. He kept coming back for more, repeating his slow-motion in-the-air knockouts, thus mastering the anxiety about the once-feared effects of his own aggression. And, equally important, he was able to sit down and talk with the leader about the experience when it was over.

As is clear from these examples, leaders in such groups must be prepared to play many different kinds of roles. Most of the time, this means setting the stage, then observing, listening, and responding empathically. There are times, however, that it may mean helping a group member to make something, teaching an art process, playing an instrument or moving alongside someone, taking a role in a drama, narrating a drama, and making organizing interventions—like thinking through and planning the drama by listing the scenes. It may also mean suggesting particular techniques like "role reversal" or "doubling," or using a psychodrama tool, like talking to an empty chair as if a person were in it.

Often it means having one's flexible antennae out, and quickly responding to an emerging theme or activity, facilitating it as best one can. In one improvisation, Lanny started to frantically gobble up bunches of french fries, saying that they were thermometers and would make him strong. Drs. Irwin and Borrero became M.D.'s who tried to figure out the best course of treatment for such a fantasy, drawing X rays which showed the thermometers, measuring him with a yardstick to confirm that he was growing stronger, etc. It was probably helpful to Lanny that the leaders were able to join into the spirit of his zany drama, and to use their own creative resourcefulness to help him deal with his wild fantasies. In this group, as in the earlier one, there developed a pervasive feeling of excitement, fun, playfulness, and shared community, in which each member helped each other to become himself.

Experience with these and other multimodality groups suggests that a successful "union" between two or more expressive art forms is possible, and in fact results in extension and enrichment for workers and youngsters. I know I learned a great deal from working so closely with a drama therapist, and value that as much as any other outcome. Enlarging the range of possibilities for the group members made possible "different strokes for different folks," as well as different modalities for different expressive purposes. It now seems artificial to make distinctions, to create boundaries, and to limit a therapeutic experience to any one expressive modality. Rather, it seems natural and right, with groups as with individuals, to allow people to move freely in accord with their inner dictates.

Experience with these older youngsters in a free creative approach contradicts the notion that "the expressive methods are most rewarding with very young children." (Rabin and Haworth, 1960, p. 10) It further corroborates what others have said, that "the inner life of fantasy never loses its meaning." (Davidson and Fay, 1964, p. 506) "When we help children see, hear, taste, and smell a variety of things, their feelings can lead them from art into poetry, drama, music, song, movement, and back into art again. Many relationships occur in the child himself as he moves among these experiences. Joyous, active participation in all of the arts, develops both the skill to create within the discipline of each art form, and the insight which selects the right form to express the need of the moment." (Snow, 1968, p. 20)

As Dr. Marvin Shapiro, a child psychiatrist, once wrote: "In many ways the full experience has an analogy to the growing child. The baby, in learning about the world, mouths the object, smells it, feels it, presses it against himself, and uses as many sense modalities as he possibly can to integrate his concept of what the object is. In this way, the child learns and expresses an interest and curiosity in the world around him. In the same sense, we too must use more than one sense modality in grasping the full impact of an activity, an experience, or an object, out of the swirling confusing life around us. By taking such a multi-medium approach of varied sensory participation, the therapeutic potential is greatly enhanced, and increases the possibilities for change in the children." (Irwin, Rubin, and Shapiro, 1971, p. 16)

I am not advocating that we should all be "generalists" in the creative art therapies. Although the relationships among different expressive modes within humans seem evident, it also seems clear to me that to be proficient in the discipline of any one art form requires years of patient learning and integration, especially in order to use it effectively with others. What I *am* suggesting is that we be more open-minded in our approach and in what we make available. Although the creative materials in my office are still mainly art media, I also have some puppets and miniature life toys for dramatic use. More important, I try to be open and receptive to expression in any modality—which may take the form of art, drama, movement, music, or creative writing.

Dr. Marvin Shapiro, a child psychiatrist/psychoanalyst, wrote the following words, which constitute an excellent rationale for a multi-modality approach to treatment: "In many ways the full experience has an analogy to the growing child. The baby, in learning about the world, mouths the object, feels it, presses it against himself, and uses as many sense modalities as he possibly can to integrate his concept of what the object is. In this way, the child learns and expresses an interest and curiosity in the world around him. In the same sense, we too must use more than one sense modality in grasping the full impact of an activity, an experience, or an object, out of the swirling, confusing life around us. By taking such a multi-medium approach of varied sensory participation, the therapeutic potential is greatly enhanced, and increases the possibilities for change in the children." (Irwin, Rubin & Shapiro, 1971, p. 16)

CHAPTER 15.

Case Illustration: Understanding and Helping

While many clinical illustrations have been used in preceeing chapters, it may help to take a relatively long look at one child, and how he and his family were understood and helped through art. The child's name was Tim; his family was educated (both parents had been to college), and was financially comfortable. Tim's primary problem, and the one for which his family had initially sought help, was stuttering.

Tim had been taken to a university speech clinic when he was five and a half by his mother, who stated that he had "had trouble with the beginning syllables of some words and stuttered . . . since he first started speaking." She labelled his problem as "average to moderately severe." Tim was seen at the speech clinic for six sessions and two re-evaluations. His parents were seen for several counselling meetings. Later, he and his mother were referred to the child guidance center for a mother-child art therapy group which was then about to begin. In making the referral, the speech pathologist described Tim's problem: "one of disfluency which is effortless, and inconsistent over time with . . . no immediate need . . . to receive direct speech therapy." The clinician stated that Tim was being referred primarily because he was "an anxious youngster, highly dependent upon adult approbation, and reluctant to make decisions on his own." It was inferred that the art therapy group would enable Tim to, become freer and more independent. It was also suggested in the referral that the proposed occasional mother-child art sessions would be helpful: "It would be to their mutual advantage to engage together in some enjoyable activity without the interference of Tim's intrusive and highly verbal four-year-old sister."

Tim was ultimately seen at the child guidance center over a span of two-and-one-half years, first in the art therapy group with periodic mother-child sessions, and later in conjoint family art therapy. Critical to our understanding of his problems were an initial individual art evaluation, joint mother-child sessions in a group, and a later family art evaluation involving his parents and sister.

Diagnostic Art Interview

During his initial one-hour art evaluation, Tim gave a glimpse of some of his major concerns and ways of dealing with them. He was at first hesitant in choosing materials and finally solved the dilemma by eagerly collecting as many different types of drawing media as he could fit on the table. He was careful to use some of each, making sure that marker tops were put back on immediately, and frequently running to the sink to wash off his hands.

He had a hard time deciding what to draw, and made a persistent effort to get me to give him a topic. Assured that I understood how hard it was, but that I was certain he could think of something if we could be patient, he finally said he would like to draw a dinosaur. Unable to settle on a theme any more comfortably than on a medium, he soon switched to a monster or Frankenstein. All of these must have been a bit too threatening, however, for he finally chose to make a crane (Fig. 15-1). It is interesting that the form of his crane resembles the shape of a dinosaur—his first idea—and even has "teeth" at the end of a long, thin, extension. The crane was said, while he drew, to have dug a U-shaped hole in the ground; a symbol (hole) which was to appear again in Tim's work, in this case quickly filled in (as if to leave it open might entail some risk).

In one of the windows of the houselike crane is the face of a three-year-old girl, close to the age of his sister. Since the girl is said to be operating or running the crane, with its possibly phallic extension, one wonders if Tim has represented here his feeling that his sister was "running" him? It became quite clear, even in that first hour, that Tim perceived his younger sister as more powerful than himself.

He next chose to paint at the easel, selecting the longest-handled (most phallic)

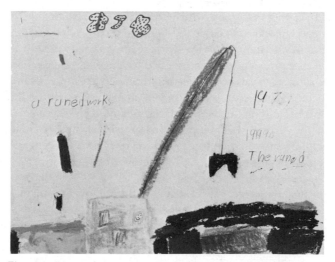

Fig. 15-1. "A runed work," (a crane) by Tim. Mixed media. Age 5.

brush. Again, he was unable to select from among the array of choices, and took all of the available colors to the easel tray. He began by outlining a square house with a flesh tone, then drawing two triangular (breast-shaped) roofs symmetrically placed on either side of the top. He was, as he had been when drawing, quite deliberate and careful, and painted over the outline of the house several times. He referred to the tempera paint as "temper" paint, and each of the many times he went to the sink to wash, jokingly called the paint on his hands "my temper problem."

Indeed, his unconscious equation of uncontrolled aggression (temper) and regression with fluid media (tempera), became even clearer as he went on with the painting. Though he began by filling in the outlines of the house carefully, he soon started to mix colors within the thick walls, eventually holding his long brush with both hands, and twirling it rhythmically. While he had been mildly disfluent and rather tense initially, he seemed to relax both physically and verbally during this regressive mixing and twirling. He covered what he called his "mess" of colors with white paint at the end, saying firmly, "White solves the problem." He finished his hour by manipulating a piece of clay, labelling his painting "The Dinosaur Picture," and telling the following story: "It started at the beginning of time, and there was a big hurricane came, and it blowed down the dinosaur house, and that was the end of the dinosaur."

Thus, considering both the process of his work and the form and content of his products, Tim in his initial interview not only showed how he could relax and become almost fully fluent using an expressive medium, but also outlined some of his primary concerns and ways of coping. He indicated that his sister represented a powerful threat to his autonomy and potency. He showed that he felt not only weak, but dependent and vulnerable, demonstrating a need for help in getting started, and for protection in the form of thick walls (the house), compulsive care (his use of every color and frequent hand-washing), and perhaps phallic weapons (choosing the longest, thickest brush). He hinted at oral-dependent needs and wishes in his "hunger" for materials and advice, as well as oral-aggressive impulses in the dangerous "teeth" of the crane. The hole dug by the teeth had to be quickly filled in, just as the regressive mess in the dinosaur house had to be painted over with white, as if some form of defensive "whitewashing" could solve "the temper problem." He seemed to be expressing behaviorally and symbolically his anxiety that, if he could not contain his messy, angry impulses (especially toward females), he might, like the dinosaur house, get "blown up."

Group Art Therapy

On the basis of this first interview, group art therapy did seem to be an appropriate form of treatment for this constricted child, who needed to move in the direction of greater independence and freedom at his own pace, with peer role models and neutral adults to assist him. When anxious in the group, Tim's symbolic defenses were similar to those hinted at in the diagnostic session. He made numerous thickly-bounded, well-defended fortress-like sculptures of clay, of wood scraps (Fig. 15-2), and some paintings of similar quality. Often what was inside (the hole or opening) would be prominent, as in his many clay "caves." He would sometimes compulsively cover over a whole sheet of paper with chalk or paint, as if his fear of loss of control, especially in anger, had been translated into a fear of emptiness or of open spaces and holes. Similarly, he would, when unhappy, sit alone and draw repetitive abstract designs, numbers, or checkerboards, or would compulsively cut out small squares of paper.

Fig. 15-2. A house by Tim done in group. Wood scraps and glue. Age 5.

Such occasions, however, were as rare in the group as the times when he actually stuttered. By and large, he was able to move from a timid, watching position to an active one in a short period of time. He soon became fluently expressive of ideas, feelings, and speech. He utilized the opportunities in the group to try out regression, aggression, and progression in both interactional and symbolic behavior, using both the two leaders (parent figures) and the other children (surrogate siblings) as well as the art media. He gained support from the other children, especially those who were more free. With them he safely regressed, mixing "gooshy" fingerpaint and playing at being a baby. He risked aggression, with ugly paintings of me as a witch, and attacked the male therapist with vigor in several dramas. He risked initially frightening activities, like being pushed high on a tire swing, and worked on cooperative and competitive products with the other children. Most often, Tim's self-portraits done in the group were strong and adequate, just as he was trying out his potency in behavioral and symbolic ways.

Parenthetically, it seems clear that the group provided not only materials, but safety, permission, support, stimulation, and protection. A child like Tim might have taken much longer to "loosen up" in individual art therapy, though this is not an easy thing to predict. There is no question, however, that the group helped him, especially one other boy who was as loose as Tim was tight. It was a lovely "therapeutic alliance" in that both derived mutual benefit from the friendship, each learning from the other the freedom or control he needed.

Joint Mother-Child Art Sessions

The first joint art session of the children's and mothers' groups was held following six weeks of separate group sessions, and was designed for diagnostic purposes as open-ended, in which we would just watch and see how each pair would behave in order to learn more about each dyad and how to help them. Tim began by proudly making and then showing his mother a smeary painting on an oversized piece of paper. His mother then did her own huge abstract painting. Tim began to follow her, slavishly imitating her next drawing in terms of medium, color, and style, and became noticeably more subdued than at the beginning of the session. He then drew a second picture of a three-year-old girl operating an immense crane. The girl was immediately identified by his mother as his sister, who was said to be more assertive than Tim. He selected his large smeary painting as the one to share at the end with the group, and called it "The Sun Blowing Up." He explained that the sun blew up "because the moon was in the way of the sun, and the moon touched the sun." When asked what sex they might be, he stated firmly that the sun would be a boy and the moon a girl, and that the story would be the same. This competitive theme was repeated in a puppet drama several weeks later, in which a younger sister kills her older brother, and is so powerful that even lions can't contain her.

During the second joint session attended by Tim and his mother, our goals were still primarily diagnostic in terms of each mother-child dyad, but the approach was structured around authority and control. It was suggested that one member of each dyad direct (or "boss") the other in doing a work of art. Tim directed his mother in a rather structured drawing of a road with cars and houses on either side. She often added items he was not specifying, such as lines on the sidewalk, apparently not submitting to his control. Although their second effort also began with Tim "bossing" her, he became frustrated by his mother's unwillingness to follow his directions accurately, and "took over" the drawing himself. She then assumed the "boss" role, and instructed him for the remainder of the drawing.

The last joint session of the art therapy group was open-ended. Tim and his mother chose to work jointly on a drawing with some sense of uncertainty about who was in charge. They then created a wood scrap construction on a common base. Tim made a garage with diagonal walls, much like his fortresses, while his mother created a tall structure alongside his diagonal barriers.

Tim was a member of the children's art therapy group, which met weekly for one-and-one-half hours for fourteen months. He attended quite regularly and participated intensively. Despite clear positive gains evident in group, at home, and at school in personality, self-concept, and social skills, the disfluency continued to be of concern to Tim's parents, though it was highly variable, practically nonexistent in group, and was not heard at home for long periods of time. Because of his parents' continuing emphasis on and anxiety about his "symptom," and based upon evidence in Tim's art work, dramatic play, and the joint sessions with his mother, a family art evaluation was conducted involving both parents, Tim, and his younger sister.

Family Art Evaluation

During this two-hour session, which was conducted according to the format described earlier, some hypotheses about the family dynamics and interaction were confirmed. Mother emerged as dissatisfied, describing her dull life situation in her scribble drawing entitled "Baskets for Boredom Blues." Father revealed his possible identity conflicts in a scribble drawing of a "Kabuki Actor" (Fig. 15-3).

During the second task, the family literally spread out all over the room, each one working independently. Tim's sister's picture of the family consisted of one member: "Mother Going to a Party all Dressed Up." Tim had difficulty with this task, made several false starts, was quite self-critical, and finally drew "Me and Daddy Playing Ball." Both parents also represented the family only in dyads. Mother drew herself with Tim and her husband with her daughter as partners in a square dance, while Father drew two sets of parent pairs and child pairs. No one showed the whole group interacting as a unit.

While deciding on the topic for their third task, the joint mural, Tim made suggestions which were verbally agreed to, but not actually followed. In the execution of the mural, it was not clear which parent was in charge, though there was a sense that the control had shifted from father to mother. The family members stood side by side as they worked on the wall, occasionally working in parent-child

Fig. 15-3. Scribble drawing by Tim's father, "Kabuki Actor." Chalk.

pairs but most often independently. While the joint mural represented the seashore where they had shared an enjoyable family vacation, the sense of togetherness about which they reminisced was absent from the interaction in the room during the two-hour session. When interactions occurred, they were primarily dyadic and generally competitive, no matter who was involved.

It seemed to Dr. Magnussen and me, who jointly conducted the session, that Tim's father, with his own insecurity was not consistently able to provide an effective role model for his son. Both females were the dominant family members and the males interacted with them in a conflicted manner. Tim also seemed to bear the brunt of the negative attention of the family by being critically teased by both sister and parents, thus effectively absorbing and neutralizing areas of conflict between the adults. Both parents were bright and articulate, able to rationalize most effectively, yet both reacted strongly and perceptively to some things they felt they "discovered" about themselves and the family through the art session.

Combining impressions from this session with additional data from a history-taking interview by a psychiatrist with Tim's mother, the assessment team became further convinced that the persistence of his symptom was rooted in its function within the family system. It was felt on the basis of our contacts, that it was necessary to induce change which would permit both the family and the child to "give up" the stuttering. Conjoint family art therapy was recommended for additional reasons. First, it was necessary to work with the entire family unit in order to shift the focus of concern from the boy's speech to the intrafamilial disfunction. Second, it was decided to utilize a modality which had a chance of "cutting through" the very adequate verbal defenses of all members, especially the parents. It was because of the evidence gathered during the family session, as well as the fact that the family liked it and found it both fun and thought-provoking, that conjoint family art therapy was the treatment modality finally recommended. It seemed both appealing and appropriate for this group.

Family Art Therapy

The family came for weekly conjoint art therapy for a total of thirty-two sessions, half lasting one hour, half one-and-a-half hours. In the course of this work, through the use of art work and discussion, the family's definition of "the problem," as well as their attention, shifted from the boy's speech to his personality, to his sister's personality, to marital difficulties, and then to individual problems of both parents.

Tim's art work during the year of family art therapy was sometimes an indicator of the internal changes that were slowly taking place. His formal pictorial defenses, such as covering-over or compulsively numbering and organizing, continued to come into play when he was anxious, particularly about competition and aggression. At first his sister, even in her abstract work, was more intense in color and tone than he. As time wore on, however, he became the leader and she the follower. He drew birthday cakes for her at her request, for example, showing her the "right" way to do it, and she was grateful.

Tim continued to mess and regress, both when anxious and when angry, though less often in the family than he had in his group. His interest in holes and in openings continued, but he was increasingly able to leave them open and to explore beginnings and endings, as in a maze. At the end of the year, he proudly made of clay a completely open, undefended "Fort" and a "Pool Table" (Fig. 15-4), discussing with pleasure how the balls fall into the holes. His houses also had more windows, suggesting that his feelings and curiosity had been freed to function in a more normal way.

Although his projected images of himself in the group had usually been strong, he was sometimes criticized and pressed to achieve more in the family context, and was frequently dominated by one of the other family members. It is thus not surprising that he often drew himself, at least in the first six months, as vulnerable to rejection or injury in pictures showing: a boy alone in the rain looking sad, a faceless boy about to crash on a sled, a snowman who might melt in the sun, a creature yelling "Help!" or perhaps most poignant, a boy with no mouth, holding on to a pet snake, whose tail he decided needed to be further extended after the drawing was finished (Fig. 15-5).

Fig. 15-4. Tim's clay "pool table," done during family art therapy.

Fig. 15-6. A paper plate/tongue depressor puppet: "The Beautiful Gisela" by Mrs. E. during family art therapy.

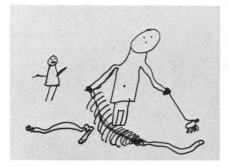

Fig. 15-5. A boy holding onto a pet snake by Tim. Marker.

Conversely, both his sister and his mother usually pictured themselves as central figures, usually pretty and desirable, often rich and brilliant. In a spontaneous family puppet drama, which "happened" during one session, mother was the star, "The Beautiful Gisela" (Fig. 15-6), over whom there was a struggle between two men, "Handsome Harry" (handsome but poor) and "Dopey" (dumb but rich). Mother often pictured her own dilemma in the family sessions as lack of fulfillment, with occasional pictorial implications that there was "no way out."

Although Tim had gradually expressed anger more and more freely in the group, aggression was slow to be expressed directly in the family context. Tim's picture of his sister's "tummy" with an aggressive line pointing at it was done in the family art evaluation, her drawing of him punching her in the stomach six months later, and his own representation of a dyadic aggressive interchange three months after that. Two months later, he drew a series of fifteen "Meanies," most of them representing his own rage and a few seeming to be symbolic attacks aimed at other family members (Fig. 15-7). He drew "Meanies" furiously, then drew a pair of dinosaurs (Fig. 15-8), and finally proceeded to loudly verbalize his anger, for the first time shouting assertively in the family as he had done in the group: "You don't care! You just don't respect me like I respect you!"

His frequent representations of himself and his father in dyadic relationships, while at times competitive, most often seemed mutually supportive. Indeed, it was as if the two males needed to stop competing and start supporting one another, in order to gain equal status with the females in the family. Tim's picture of "Me and

Fig. 15-7. One of Tim's many "Meanies" done in haste. Crayon.

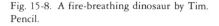

Fig. 15-8. A fire-breathing dinosaur by Tim. Pencil.

Dad Playing Tennis" on one side of the paper, with "Mom Divin' Down" on the other, was a graphic statement of such a wish. His drawing of two serpent-like phallic creatures about to destroy a house drawn by his mother suggested a similar impulse to achieve dominance.

As with individuals, it often seems that families develop a preferred symbolic idiom, which may communicate complex ideas within the group in a condensed and emotionally loaded manner. Some family themes and symbols became evident with the E. family, both in free drawings and in those suggested on occasion by me and Dr. Magnussen, who worked with them as cotherapists. One such symbol was the house or "home." In the second month of family sessions, Tim drew four careful houses, similar to a configuration done previously in a joint session with his mother. One month later, his house drawing had many windows, and he drew another with two pointed towers and even more openings. His mother drew a detailed picture of the family outside the new house they were hoping to buy. There was a shared fantasy that this house would be the antidote to family tensions; and an idealized memory treasured by both parents was of a "perfect family" they had once met whose home was "a haven from the world's pressures."

All of the pictures drawn in response to two themes suggested in the early weeks of treatment took place inside the home. The first topic was "the main problem in the family that you would like to work on." Father drew mother abandoning him with the two screaming kids at the supper table, complaining that "She never joins us" (Fig. 15-9). Mother, meanwhile, drew him reading while the kids argue and she wearily does the dishes, begging him to intervene in the fight between the children (Fig. 15-10). Not seeing the other's drawing until completed, each was astounded at how similar were their feelings of abandonment and resentment; they were then able to be more understanding of each other, rather than so defensive.

Another shared, wished-for romantic solution was to be "somewhere else." Father's solution to family problems was a drawing of the group walking in a line in an idyllic autumn forest setting. In addition to the mural of the seashore done in the family evaluation session, Tim had done a free construction of "Me and Dad on the Boat Vacation," and there was much talk by all of how good things had been when they had all gone away together.

In response to a suggestion several months later to "draw things the way you wish they were," mother made a picture in which a maid is cooking a meal in the kitchen, while she and her husband have a drink on the sofa, romantically planning a trip to Africa as she thanks him for the beautiful flowers he has sent her. The children are notably absent (Fig. 15-11). Father, however, had a very different wishful image. In his picture, his wife is happily cooking the meal, both children at her side; on the other side of his drawing she is sending him to work with a kiss, while the angelic youngsters (complete with halos) wave goodbye from their windows (Fig. 15-12). Their conflicting images of perfection and their mutual dissatisfaction were poignantly evident in these drawings, and became an increasingly open topic of discussion.

Before Mr. E. left on a trip, he drew himself writing a letter home, and then complained that no one ever answered his letters, and that they had even argued on the telephone the last time he had called from far away. A month later, mother drew about her loneliness while he was gone; but when father returned two weeks later, he drew himself on a lounge chair on a beach with two unidentified companions, ruefully labelled "two ladies" by mother. Three months later, the adults' mutual feelings of hurt became such an intense focus for their discussion that the children, no longer involved in or playing out the parental battle, worked quietly and cooperatively, producing some impressive joint constructions.

Two other interesting family symbols in their art were the roller coaster and the seesaw, each appearing on some group and some individual drawings (Fig. 15-13). The roller coaster was a symbol for the excitement and thrill of activity, and of a scary sense of helplessness, with an attempt at mastery. The family life style was

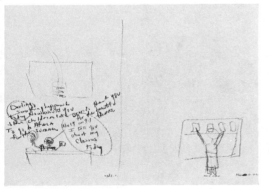

Fig. 15-9. Mr. E.'s picture of "the main problem in the family." Marker.

Fig. 15-10. Mrs. E.'s picture of "the main problem in the family." Line drawing of a marker original.

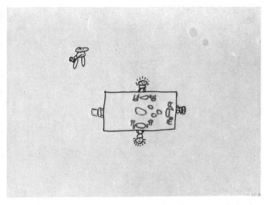

Fig. 15-11. Mrs. E.'s wishful picture of how she wanted things to be. Crayon.

Fig. 15-12. Mr. E.'s image of how he wanted things to be. Crayon.

indeed rushed and hectic, and anxiety-provoking to Tim in particular. His style was slow and deliberate, quite out of phase with that of the other members, in some ways resembling his speech pattern.

The seesaw symbol was most useful to us in dealing with the theme of competition. As with a roller coaster, it is possible to be up or down, but not both simultaneously. As with so many images of the family by all members, the functional human unit is a competitive dyad—one wins while the other loses, one must be down in order for the other to be up. Somehow, the notion of the "balance" position had rarely occurred to them, as both mother and father needed so badly to achieve, to get what they deserved, and not to be in a submissive, helpless position. Tim's sister could be quite aggressive, identifying alternately with her mother and father. Tim, on the other hand, with his slow, deliberate style, was left out of the family rush, and usually lost the family competitive game. They all needed a loser, someone who was "down" on the seesaw, and that was Tim.

Tim's defense in the family group was often to move away from the circle, to work alone quietly and self-sufficiently, in contrast to the dependency seen in his diagnostic interview. One day, frustrated by how cleverly and effectively the other family members could intellectualize with words, I suggested that they try to work together on the same sheet of paper without talking. They drew silently for a surprising forty-five minutes, each using different amounts of space, mother moving around and eventually drawing on everyone's area. Tim began by drawing a house in the center, but was soon surrounded tightly on both sides, and left to work alone with clay at another table. He tried to get his father to join him, and his father did so for a while, but then rejoined the females, still at work on the nonverbal drawing. When all were seated discussing the picture, which was most useful in helping mother to acknowledge her intrusiveness, Tim felt safe enough to go up to the drawing and add some more details to his house. While working with the clay he had dug a very large hole for what he called a "bank," something strong in which he could safely store and protect what was valuable to him.

Fig. 15-13. The roller coaster by Tim and Mr. E. Crayon.

During one of the last few family sessions, Tim created a clay pool table with open holes (Fig. 15-4) and his first open fort, after many closed-in structures. While his parents had refocused on the boy's speech at a point of tension in their marital relationship, and had suggested another speech evaluation, they had finally decided not to do that. When the adults began to deal seriously with their interpersonal difficulties, Tim's speech noticeably improved, as did his mood, and particularly his ability to relate productively and appropriately to other family members.

The last two sessions were devoted to evaluation, in which parents and children reviewed the art and the therapy; the consensus was that there had been positive changes within the family. Our final meeting was with the parents alone, in which they first spoke with pride of the improvement in their children, particularly Tim. They then turned to each other, and plunged into the most open and intense interpersonal confrontation they had yet experienced in the clinic. Each identified the other angrily as "needing psychiatric help." In spite of such anxiety-provoking attacks, it was clear that they were ready to deal with marital issues, as well as with individual ones. Each was more open to the idea of therapy for themselves, and it was our recommendation that they seek help as individuals and/or as a couple. Most important, the spotlight was no longer on Tim's almost-absent symptom, but rather now on the family system, resulting largely from work through the symbol-art.

Tim's speech behavior in the course of his work at the clinic, in the group and with his family, had changed from stuttering to fluency. A follow-up contact one year after termination of therapy revealed that Tim had not stuttered for the past six months. Stuttering for Tim may have been an indirect means of expressing anger, of fighting back, "talking back" to his parents. Although his parents wished to eliminate his annoying symptom, this was not possible without changes both in Tim and in the family system. Family art therapy made it possible to focus on the conflicts within and between all members, and allowed Tim space and support to compete openly and to be verbally aggressive, without fear of losing or of punishment. Such work would not be possible without the involvement, investment, and sincere hard work of everyone in the pleasurable/painful task of family art therapy.

PART IV:
THE COMMUNITY

CHAPTER 16.

Helping the "Normal" Child through Art

From the cave man through the Sunday painter, normal people in ordinary settings have been using art for personally helpful purposes. Sometimes the contact with art is a simple matter of unwinding, like going to a gallery, leafing through a photographic essay, or perhaps doing some embroidery. At other times, it may be a way of dealing with experiences which are difficult to assimilate. Whether creative or responsive, the therapeutic value of art is not limited to the clinic or the hospital, nor to deviant populations, but is known by everyone who has derived release of tension, sensory pleasure, or a feeling of integration from an aesthetic experience.

Art educators recognized the broadly therapeutic and growth-enhancing potential of their subject soon after it became an accepted part of the school curriculum. Especially during the middle decades of the century, when the progressive movement emphasized the virtues of art as a vehicle for self-expression, its function as a way of dealing with feelings was applauded by many. As can happen with good ideas, however, some of the mental health significance and value of art for children were misunderstood and misused in the schools, distorting the original intent. Oversimplified and potentially harmful applications became common, and the reaction away from such values in art education, most prominent in the sixties, was an understandable response to the abuses of what were (and still are) basically sound concepts.

Therapy was seen as "not in itself a terrible thing, but at the expense of art." And it was sadly true that "too often the experience . . . focused on psychological catharsis rather than on any aesthetic shaping." (Kaufman, 1969) Misunderstandings of permissiveness had resulted at times in aimless, formless regression. Regrettably, "the misuse of the psychological approach had taken its most serious toll in the application of pseudo-therapy and the homespun analyst." (McVickar,

1959, p. 13) Although Viktor Lowenfeld's advocacy of an "art education therapy" may have contributed to the confusion, he himself told art teachers in his lectures: "We must not engage in any diagnosis of children's drawings, which is drawn from inferences." (1982, p. 13) He felt that art contributed to psychological integration because of the synthesis involved in the creative process itself. "Because whenever we move from chaos to a better organization in our thinking, feeling and perceiving, we have become a better organized individual. And this, indeed, is the common goal of any therapy. Therefore, aesthetic experiences are greatly related to this harmonious feeling within our own selves." (1982, p. 30) It should be clear from these statements that art education and therapy share a common goal of promoting maturation and order. In fact, despite the common mythology of the art therapist who promotes "letting it all hang out," for some practitioners the quality of the therapy is related to the quality of the product (Kramer, 1963). Like the art educator who wrote the following words, many art therapists who value sublimation as a primary healing element in the creative process believe that "the more emotion, the more of himself is poured into a painting or a lump of clay, the greater both the therapeutic value of the work and its artistic merit." (Gezari, 1967, p. 5)

The educational pendulum seemed for a time to be swinging back from a concern with "behavioral objectives" to one of "humanizing the school," and the notion of "affective education" (teaching about feelings and interpersonal issues) was then seen as relevant (Bessell and Palomares, 1969). Here is a statement by an art educator regarding aesthetic education: "Art education, that is the education of feeling, is the only kind of art education that can help people become more human." (Flannery, 1973, p. 14). It is important to note that this educator was not talking about therapy, but about a kind of education in art which values feelings as much as facts.

Just a decade ago, when staff members of a prestigious art education project were asked to rate goal-statments, one of those at the bottom of the list was "the maintenance of sound mental health as a goal of art education." (Walker, 1970, p. 9) At about that time, it was my feeling that to advocate such a goal in art education was to swim against a powerful tide; yet it does seem of late that if the tide has not turned, the undercurrents and cross-currents of differing values are becoming stronger. Hopefully, the current climate of questioning will allow for further debate, discussion, and definition of both boundaries and areas of shared territory in art education and therapy (see Chapter 21).

The similarities, while not in any way implying identity, are indeed provocative, for "there is much in the professional work of a good therapist that can also be made part of the work of a good teacher." (Jersild, 1955) I would support Ruth Shaw's assertion that "probing lies outside the province of the teacher," and that teachers must "beware of developing a morbid curiosity," (1935, p. 84); but would submit that a teacher or parent can be a vital force in a child's mental health, through the provision of the conditions outlined in Chapters 1 and 2, and the facilitation and acceptance of the child's authentic creative work. While it may sometimes be helpful to reflect feelings back to the child (Axline, 1947, p. 144), it is often enough to simply be present in a supportive and accepting way.

The quality of the relationship may be the key element, as implied in this description of effective child therapists: "To discuss this natural facility for therapy a bit more, we see it as being very similar to that possessed by those we call natural teachers. . . . We see them as therapeutic personalities, whether or not they are therapists by profession. Something nice happens to us when we are with them." (Hammer and Kaplan, 1967, pp. 35-36) An artist/teacher says much the same thing, from another point of view: "But not only writers and artists are practicing psychologists without that title; any parent, nurse, teacher, doctor and employer daily employs psychological knowledge acquired by experience and has always done so." (Petrie, 1946, p. 55) If the teacher, therapist, or parent behaves sensitively, providing appropriate conditions for human expansion, "this kind of experience provides the child with the climate conducive to change and growth." (Hammer and Kaplan, 1967, p. 36)

There seems little disagreement on the importance of a healthy human relationship between teacher and pupil, parent and child, or therapist and patient. There are legitimate questions, however, regarding the appropriate province of home and school, and about the relative importance of different goals in art education. Mattil, an art educator, in a monograph entitled *The Self in Art Education,* speaks for the same values: "We have tried and we are trying through good art experiences to develop self-confidence, self-awareness, self-esteem, and self-growth." (1972, p. 13)

A good art program, after all, helps children to learn to look with open eyes at the world around them, and to do so in a refined way, noting descriptive as well as evaluative differences. It helps them to encounter the environment without fear, and with a perceptual vocabulary that enables them to organize their experiences. It helps children to articulate and expand their aesthetic awareness of the physical world and the world of art, enabling them to appreciate and work for beauty, which enriches and enhances their life-space. A good art program helps children to understand concepts related to things like change (as in color mixing) or stability (as in construction), concepts which relate not only to the arts but to dealing with the physical world in general. It helps children to think creatively, divergently, to explore alternative solutions to problems, to expand the ability to take risks, to fail, and to cope in a flexible way.

A good art program, after all, helps children to become successful in managing the tools and media they need to master in order to make personal statements, helping them to feel better (because they have mastered something), and to be able to speak more clearly through art (to express themselves). It helps children to define themselves and their experiences, through forming unformed media, developing their own themes and styles, discovering and delineating their identities. It helps children learn how to share, to respect each other's work, and to live together in a social environment. And a good art program helps children to learn how to give form to their feelings, especially those which are difficult or impossible to put into words. One aesthetician, Suzanne Langer, believes that "there is an important part of reality that is quite inaccessible to the formative influence of language: that is, the realm of so called 'inner experience,' the life of feeling and emotion. . . . The primary function of art is to objectify feeling so that we can contemplate and understand it." (1958, pp. 4, 5)

This value may be the one most often related to therapy, but it seems to me that in a broader sense, all of the values inherent in art can be thought of as therapeutic, in helping a child to feel better about himself as a competent person who can meet the challenges of living, including the painful ones that are part of everyone's childhood. Certainly there is much evidence that troubled or disadvantaged children can be helped to develop more positive attitudes toward learning, toward others, and toward themselves, as a result of a good creative art program. Whether the children are on a psychiatric ward (Sanders, 1938), pre-delinquent boys in a summer studio (Lettis and Summers, 1968), in a special class in a public school (Orzehowski, 1959), youngsters with learning problems in an arts workshop (Diamond, 1966), or nonwhite children in the inner city (Barclay, 1970; Scott, 1971), much evidence exists that art in and of itself can be therapeutic.

Achieving competence for one who has never known success can indeed be an important and significant event. Jackson and Radcliffe report that "one boy was a problem child to all of his teachers until he discovered art through stitchery, which was instrumental in changing his whole viewpoint and personality." (1969, p. 20) Pluckrose tells a similar story about Peter, slow and apathetic about learning, who discovered an interest and ability in block printing: "From that moment onward his whole attitude to school changed. Coming early to work on his linoblocks, staying late to complete his printing, Peter became the class expert. From a failure whom everyone despised and ignored, he became a child with something to offer his classmates. In addition to this, he also began to take greater care with his other school work." (1967, p. 7) A third grade teacher makes the same observation: "Time and again, I have noted the catalytic effect of art in a student's life. The shy one becomes confident—the slow-learner shows a new eagerness. For it is by creating something unusual that he discovers his worth." (Lehman, 1969, p. 46)

While there is a time and a place for an art therapist in a school (Cohen, 1975), working individually with preschoolers undergoing transient stress (Salant, 1975), or elementary school children with learning disabilities (Gonick-Barris, 1976) or emotional problems (Wolf, 1973), there is also a therapeutic role for the classroom or art teacher, who can help to prevent emotional difficulties from mushrooming and causing significant problems that require therapy.

Dealing with Stress through Art

No one is in a better position to understand and to help children deal with stress through art than a teacher or parent. Unlike the therapist in a clinic, he knows the child over time, both extensively and intensively. He is in a position to recognize signs of situational stress, by noting variations in a child's usual working style. When Lisa's mother went to the hospital to have a baby, for example, Lisa's painting that day was a smeary regressive mass, done with agitation (Fig. 3-10(b)), radically different from her usual well-controlled decorative designs (Fig. 3-10(a))—a clear signal to her teacher that she was upset.

Joan, usually quite sociable, was uncharacteristically quiet when she entered the after-school workshop room one day. She said a perfunctory hello to her best friend, threw her coat on the chair, and went straight to the easel. Taking a brush out of the black paint, with vigorous, slashy strokes, she quickly sketched a picture of a boy in tears, a bicycle in the background (Fig. 16-1). When she was finished, she sighed and stepped back to look at her painting. As the workshop leader, I asked if she felt like talking about the picture, and she said "Oh, it's just a boy." After a pause, however, she went on: "He's crying, beause he lost his bike, and he's afraid to tell his mom, 'cause she might be mad at him." I wondered if she knew anybody to whom that had really happened, and, with tears in her eyes, she blurted out: "Me. Just this afternoon. I couldn't find it. And I'm really scared!" The picture-making helped her to deal with what had happened, to look at both feelings and consequences.

All children have such stresses, changing in impact as they grow older and more able to cope. Nona, at three, had recently gotten lost in a store, and was for a time fearful about leaving the house. As if to further communicate this anxiety to me, her mother, she showed me her drawing and explained: "It's a man crying for his mommy 'cause he got lost in the dark. He can't find his way home, 'cause it's too dark, and he's afraid."

Fig. 16-1. A boy crying because he lost his bike. Tempera. Age 10.

Viola tells about a mother whose boy was having nightmares: "The mother with her right instinct asked her boy if he would not like to draw the bogey man and the other unpleasant things he dreamt of. After a time the dreams ceased." (1944, p. 59) Like Nona's nightmare picture (Fig. 0-1), the creation of forms that are symbolic of the feared object can often help, as when Ruth Shaw's students fingerpainted "awful things" (Shaw, 1938, ch. 4) or when Natalie Robinson Cole's pupils were encouraged to draw and write about "secret crimes" and other such loaded subjects (1966, ch. 10).

There is a widespread belief, reflective I think of a wish that childhood be pure and protected, that normal children don't really have such awful fears or violent wishes, and that to encourage them to express these through art is to initiate and foster an unnecessary evil. It is interesting in this regard to note the following spontaneous comments about an exhibit of art work by children from all over the world, presumably selected for its technical and aesthetic quality: "One could not help spotting in their work a great pre-occupation with annihilation, war, bloodshed, mutilation, hospitals and doctors. This seemed to hold true regardless of the country from which the painting came, and regardless of whether the country of the child artist was directly involved in a war or in riots. Children also showed their fear of shots and preventive medicine in drawings of doctors, hospitals, ambulances and the like. . . . One could see the therapeutic value of working out the child's fears through art. In discussing the art exhibit, the importance of giving children enough time and materials to communicate their pre-occupation with fears in a non-verbal way was emphasized." (Gitter, 1968, p. 33)

Separation. An event with which all children must deal is separating from dependency on their mothers, especially when going off to school and coping with new people and a new place. Nona, about to enter a new school at twelve, did a drawing about a girl who was doing the same (Fig. 16-2) and described it: "The father is bringing the daughter to school, and she's kind of frightened by it, because she's never been to school before . . . and she doesn't know anybody, and she's frightened of a big school." I, her mother, asked her why the girl was frightened, and she explained: "Because she's afraid of what the teachers will be like, and if they will be mean or nice. And she wants her dad to stay in school." Then, reflecting

Fig. 16-2. A girl going to a new school with her dad. Pencil. Age 12.

Fig. 16-3. A bird knocking another bird off the nest. Marker. Age 5.

upon her own early experience, she added, "I remember I wanted you to stay, but I knew you couldn't, and I was embarrassed, so I told you to go away." In her drawing she was letting me know how this new school revived some of the same anxieties she had felt when she was little.

Sibling Rivalry. Having frequent times and places and materials available for expression enables children to use art to deal with urgent feelings. Perhaps equally important is an ongoing analysis of what children are concerned about and an occasional explicit effort to help them deal with currently burning issues. Almost all children have to cope at one time or another, for example, with the birth of a sibling, the separation from mother, and the advent of a new rival which such an event entails. During the pregnancy, they may be preoccupied with curiosity about what is growing in mother's tummy, sometimes imagining it to be food or an animal which moves about inside. Many of the children in one kindergarten class had mothers who were pregnant, and were buzzing with fantasies and questions, so the teacher suggested that they draw pictures of babies inside, and then discuss both fact and fancy (Fig. 3-6).

Sammy's drawing, on the other hand, was done spontaneously in his kindergarten, and reflected to his understanding teacher his anger at the new baby (Fig. 16-3). His mother had just brought home a little girl, the first one in the family, and everyone was making a big fuss over her. Sammy made a fuss too. He helped with the diapers, kissed the baby, and told all his friends and relatives about how much he loved his new sister. But he was jealous too. His mother used to have more time for him, and now she was always busy or tired, and seemed less interested in him than before. So one day at school he drew a picture of a bird diving down toward a nest, and told his teacher: "That big boy bird's gonna knock that other one off the nest. There ain't no room for two!" Sammy could not get rid of his sister in reality, nor would he want to all the time; but he could safely express that wish in symbolic disguise in his drawing.

Tommy was a little farther along than Sammy in accepting his new baby, when he drew a picture at home(Fig. 16-4). He told his mom, "It's a mother pushing a baby in a carriage. It's a *new* baby, and it's crying—wha! wha! It's raining, and they want to go home." Tommy seems to have accepted in his picture not only the presence of his new sibling, but even the fact that his mother must give the infant a lot of attention. The only sign of any hostile feelings is that the baby is crying, and getting soaked by Tommy's rain. When baby brothers get bigger, they can be a real problem for the older child, who both likes and resents the presence of another in his play space. Nona at five drew a picture of a crying girl (Fig. 16-5), and explained: "She's sad, because her baby brother broke the head off her teddy bear." Nona's teddy bear had indeed been damaged by her infant brother, and was a highly-prized "transitional object" which comforted her at bed time. (Winnicott, 1971a) Her ability to use crayons and paper to express her sadness helped her to avoid more destructive ways of dealing with her feelings. She could easily have withdrawn to her room to cry or refused to eat supper, might have felt guilty over her anger and provoked punishment from others, might have expressed her anger physically at her brother, his toys, or displaced it into someone else. And she could easily have denied her sad and angry feelings to herself, repressing them, so that they might then or later have emerged in distorted or confusing behavior.

Five-year-old Vince's dad was a minister, who encouraged his children to articulate their wishes and fears in both words and images. One day he brought me some drawings done by Vince, one expressing destructive wishes toward a sibling, the other reflecting anxiety about punishment. The first was a drawing of "a Bad Scissors," about to cut off the very long nose of a brother(Fig. 16-6). Vince assured his dad that the big brother on the right was not going to let the scissors hurt his sibling, but instead was going to save the one who was being attacked. Worries about punishment for such angry wishes are also common for young children. In his other picture, entitled "I Hope This Didn't Happen" (Fig. 16-7), he worried aloud about what might happen to someone who got thrown off a mountain because he was bad. He also worried about the rescue party, and added men and a net to his drawing.

Getting older does not necessarily reduce the rivalry and competition between siblings. Nona, at eight, followed a fight with her older sister by making an "ugly" drawing of Jenny(Fig. 16-8). Four years later, Jon, her own younger sibling, made a similarly nasty drawing of her, distorted with a beard and elongated nose, following an argument (Fig. 16-9). Meanwhile, Jenny, the oldest, had herself attacked by not only siblings but parents too, following the birth of Jonathan. She had drawn at the

Fig. 16-4. A mother pushing a new baby in a carriage. Line drawing of a pencil original. Age 6.

Fig. 16-5. A girl crying because her brother broke her doll. Crayon. Age 5.

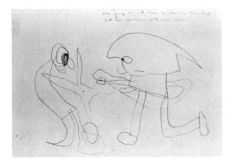

Fig. 16-6. A "bad scissors" about to cut off a brother's nose. Pencil. Age 5.

Fig. 16-7. "I hope this didn't happen." Pencil. Age 5.

Fig. 16-8.   Ugly drawing of older sister Jenny by Nona. Pen. Age 8.

Fig. 16-10. Ugly drawing of parents by Jenny. Crayon. Age 5.

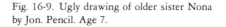

Fig. 16-9. Ugly drawing of older sister Nona by Jon. Pencil. Age 7.

time an "Ugly Mommy" and an "Ugly Daddy," missing eyes, hair, limbs, etc., along with a "Beautiful Jenny" (Fig. 16-10). The parents, she explained at age five, had gotten "ugly" by making "too many children."

Anger toward Adults. Angry feelings are the hardest for most children to deal with, especially when felt toward those they also love, as is usually the case. It is interesting that "violence" and "vitality" have the same Latin root (vis), and can be conceptualized as related but different: "Violence is the life force turned in a negative and destructive direction; vitality is the life force channeled into constructive and creative forms." (Barron, 1970) Angry feelings toward adult authority figures, parents and teachers, must be acceptable to those adults in order for children to feel comfortable expressing them. The workshop leader must have been at ease with such thoughts, or the eleven-year-old boy could not have drawn and shown him his humorous attack on adult authority, "Jerky Teacher" (Fig. 16-11). Jon could not have left an angry pictorial "message" on my chair—a picture of a "Killer Shark" devouring me—had he not been secure that I could both accept and understand it without retaliation (Fig. 16-12).

Expressions of anger are often mingled with and caused by feelings of affection, especially during the time when a child is struggling with the "oedipal" conflict, wishing to have one parent all to himself, yet loving and fearing his rival. Asked to make a funny family drawing, Jon created a picture of three clowns in a circus (Fig. 16-13). "The big one is the father. The little one in the middle, the son, is very curious. He likes to see if it hurts when he sticks his arrow point into his mother's butt. The mother is yelling because she's being stuck, and the father is

Fig. 16-11. Sticking a nail into a "jerky teacher." Pencil. Age 10.

Fig. 16-13. A funny clown family. Pencil. Age 8.

Fig. 16-12. Killer shark devouring bad mother. Pencil. Boy, age 8.

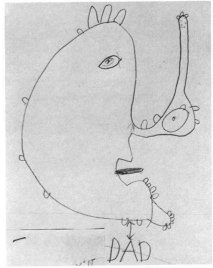

Fig. 16-14. Ugly drawing of father. Pen. Age 9.

kicking and yelling at the boy for sticking the arrow point into his wife." When asked about the ambiguous extensions on the mother's body, Jon giggled and said. "I started to make boobs, but decided on arms instead." His thinly-disguised oedipal wish fused with anger, along with the expected punishment from father, is as common for young boys as the anal-aggressive nature of his humor.

Jon's ugly portrait of his Dad, on the other hand (Fig. 16-14), stemmed from an argument about privileges which the nine-year-old boy had lost. Images of little creatures winning out over larger ones are often created, like superheroes, representing the child's wished-for strength in the face of his realistic relative weakness (Fig. 16-15). The same kind of wish is probably represented in the images of phallically potent cars, tanks, ships, planes, and rockets so common for young boys, often bristling with weapons for both aggression and protection (Fig. 16-16).

Losses. Michael was five when his parents separated. He became very involved with drawing superheroes, full of action, like a flying Superman or Spiderman. Often, the superhero would have a smaller figure attached to it (Fig. 16-17). Maybe he was representing not only his own need for power, but also his wish to hang on to his dad, who had indeed moved out of their home and saw him only on weekends at that time and after the divorce.

Lori was also five when her parents got divorced. She had seen little of her father since he left the home. He was first omitted from her family drawing, but later added as the largest figure, wishfully reinstated in a fantasized intact family picnic. Sadly she said, "I love my daddy. He is beautiful. But he is not a live-at-home daddy." Several months later she drew a sad girl and said, "that girl is crying . . . because

Fig. 16-15. A small creature wins over a larger one. Pencil. Age 9.

Fig. 16-17. A flying superhero with a little boy hanging onto him. Marker. Age 5.

Fig. 16-16. An aggressive-looking ship, fully armed. Pencil. Age 8.

her house falled apart . . . 'cause there was a big, big storm, and lightning cut it in half." Perhaps this was Lori's way of saying how her own house had been split, how torn she felt, and how the divorce had seemed to her like a painful bolt from the blue, unexpected and shattering in its impact.

Sometimes children have to deal with losses, often of pets, at times of people. When a teacher asked some second graders to draw pictures of feelings, one boy defined "Sadness" as "when my grandfather died." When asked by her teacher to draw the very worst thing she could think of, a ten-year-old girl drew a picture of herself in her grave and her mother mourning at the tombstone. A second-grader worried openly about the possible danger of his aggression, defining sadness in his picture as "Fighting with your Friend who then Falls and Hurts Himself."

As a psychologist said four decades ago, art "appears to be a good method of mental hygiene in emergency programs . . . It could give release to children who suffer from shock or other traumas." (Brick, 1944, p. 146) Such was the case with Christopher, whose mother had committed suicide, and whose dad was concerned about how the seven-year-old boy was dealing with the loss, about which he had spoken very little. Indeed, the child himself had asked me after the funeral if he could please come and paint with me some time. He came within a few weeks of the event for one session and a year later for a follow-up hour.

In his first session he worried about getting messy with chalk and fingerpaint because "my Mommy would yell at me." He tried hard to "keep in the lines," but eventually enjoyed the regressive tactile pleasure of the fingerpaint, saying it was "good and smudgy." He projected an image of a dog onto his first abstraction, telling me that it must have been the dog he had wanted so badly, but could not have because of his mother's illness. He then made a much messier darker finger-painting, and commented anxiously on how angry his mother would be if she could see him. He wondered aloud, as he painted, whether she was angry at him, and if his being bad and naughty or wanting the wrong things (e.g., dog) had anything to do with her leaving him. His story about the fingerpainting, as he drew lines in it with a stick, was that it was a road, but "You'll never find your way out. . . . No one can stop me . . . They'll never find their way out. They'll feel so sad. . . . They'll be stuck there forever." I asked what "they" would do, and he placed his hand in the black paint, lifted it up to show me, and then smashed it aggressively down onto the paper, expressing nonverbally his rage at his mother for leaving him.

In his second session he symbolically represented his mother's suicide in a drawing: a pink person falls off a road, as she had fallen off a bridge. Later, he dramatized with clay and tools a crash, an emergency, and an operation in which he, as the doctor, magically but unsuccessfully tried to restore the injured patient. He was very productive in this hour, one year after his loss. His art work represented not only an opportunity to release his anger and frustration, but also to clarify and to cope in fantasy with the painful reality with which he had to live. While not all children suffer such devastating losses as Christopher, most have some traumas to deal with at some point, for which art can be a way of both understanding how they perceive an event and helping them to deal with it.

Finding Meaningful Themes and Activities. Sometimes feelingful art emerges spontaneously; at other times it is deliberately evoked by a sensitive teacher. Art activities can "allow them to communicate about what really matters . . . a teacher who listens can learn what really matters to his/her students." (Armstrong 1970, p. 21) Certainly, themes which relate to the children's current interests are one way of creating a relevant art curriculum. Tasks which are attuned to present needs are equally appropriate, as when a teacher of four-year-olds struggling with problems in impulse control, helped them to master progressively smaller pieces of paper for fingerpainting, making a game out of their increasing ability to control their movements and their strong impulse to smear beyond the boundaries.

Although one might think that ten-year-olds have mastered reality-testing, perhaps because television perpetuates the confusion, many (like many adults) still fear ghosts and monsters. One day, a group of nine- and ten-year-olds in a school were discussing scary things, and the topic that really grabbed their interest was ghosts. I therefore suggested that they draw them, in order to help them to both see and discuss their fantasied fears. On another day, the same group was having a hard time talking about the angry feelings that were very evident in their disruptive behavior. Again, it seemed helpful to suggest they draw about those feelings, in order to gain both control and some distance.

Attempts have been made to develop art curricula or approaches specifically attuned to the needs of such groups as delinquent adolescents (Cohen, 1969), disadvantaged youth (Silverman and Hoepfner, 1969), and the learning disabled (Knill and McNiff, 1975). In situations of extreme stress, teachers and others have encouraged children to draw and write about their experiences, like the drawings and poems from a Nazi concentration camp in *I Never Saw Another Butterfly* (Volavkova, 1962); the stories, poems, and drawings by Israeli children during the six days war in *Childhood Under Fire* (Kovner, 1969); or the stories, poems, and pictures of black children living in ghettos racked by violence in the riots following Martin Luther King's death in *Children of Cardozo . . . Tell It Like It Is.* (1968)

In a project carried out by an undergraduate education student in a black neighborhood, activities were specifically selected that might foster self-esteem in the children—things like having each child make his own book about himself (his history, interests, wishes, and goals), or learning to make jewelry which could be worn by himself or given to a loved one.

In work with two groups of black twelve-year-old girls for six weeks one summer, I tried to think of projects that would enhance both self-awareness and self-esteem, like using African sculptures as stimuli for discussion and art work, or "soul music" to paint by. One activity involved first choosing finger puppets from a set with different skin colors, dramatizing spontaneously with them, then selecting from leather scraps the one closest to the child's skin tone and the color the child most wished to be (sometimes lighter, sometimes darker). This was followed by suggesting that each girl mix the skin colors of everyone in the group, and then paint a picture with them.

Melissa had been inspired by the African sculpture to sculpt the head of a man in clay, and in her last-session interview chose that one as her favorite. I interviewed her about it:

JR: Of all the things you've done, what do you like the best?
Melissa: The head of the man.
JR: Okay. Why do you think that means so much to you?
Melissa: Because it's black.
JR: Do you mean because the color of the paint is black, or because it's a black man?
Melissa: Because it's a black man.
JR: Being black means a lot to you, doesn't it?
Melissa: Yeah.
JR: How do you feel about it, when you think about being black?
Melissa: I like it. . . . I wouldn't like any *other*.
JR: You wouldn't want to be a different color?
Melissa: UnHuh, I *would*.
JR: Is it hard because your skin is light?
Melissa: Yep!
JR: What color skin would you want if you could have any color you wanted?
Melissa: Black.
JR: Like what shade?
Melissa: Brown.
JR: Like the shade you are, or darker, or lighter?
Melissa: Darker.
JR: Show me on your picture.
Melissa: Denise's (pointing to the color she had mixed of Denise's skin, one of the darkest girls in the group).

I told Melissa that there was a time, not very long ago, that many black people had wished to be as light as she was, and had even used skin creams in an attempt to lighten their skins. She said she guessed it was " 'cause they want to be white" but said that for her to be so light, "it's *hard*!" When I asked how it was hard, she replied in a louder voice than usual, "People don't believe how much you *care* about being black!" I wondered if they made fun of her lightness, and she said, "Like whenever I get in an argument with them, they call me halfbreed, or white, or yellow." I asked how that made her feel, and she replied softly, "Not too good." I asked what she thought about that, and she answered with feeling: " 'Cause I feel *more* black about myself than like if somebody, like she [pointing to a very dark worker]—she's dark, but I feel more black about being black than *she* does!" And about the other kids, she went on, "Well, they say, 'Well, how can you be *black* and you're half white?' or something like that." I commented that not being dark really could cause problems, and she said, "Yeah. If you feel not sure about it. If you're not too sure whether you believe that you're black or not, or well—you're still that color."

In this group we had spent some time looking at African sculpture and using it as a stimulus for the girls' own clay modelling. Art by others can be used to stimulate feelingful kinds of responses, the format depending on the age level and context.

When fourth graders were asked to look at Van Gogh's painting "The Potato Eaters" and to say how it made them feel, Patty wrote the following: "When I look at the picture or think about it it gives me a scarie and sad feeling. The people look like they're very poor. It gives me a feeling that they never had anything nice or enough food to eat, and that they had to work hard and grow there own food, and they did not have enough room in there house or they didn't have enough food. . . . It gives me a feeling that they were very sad too, because they did not have the nice things that we have. Maybe they are happy sometimes."

Her classmate, Deena, also got "a gloomy and sad feeling," from which she concluded that "the artist must have been sad at the time that he drew this painting." Sandy, a third grade boy, was reminded by a painting of "The Goldfish" of his own pets: "I like the goldfish because they remind me of my goldfish. And I like goldfish very much. These goldfish are very happy and so are my goldfish." Debby, a fourth grade girl, projected a story onto a Toulouse-Lautrec lithograph that might have reflected some tension in her environment: "It is about a man and a lady that is in a bar having a drink. The lady is very mad at the man. The man does not like his drink. The lady would not talk to the man." John, looking at the same painting, said "It makes me think of my grandmother and grandfather at the breakfast table."

Conclusion

Almost twenty years ago, an art teacher writing conclusions to a study of the use of art with emotionally disturbed children said: "I should like to close this paper with what is possibly the biggest question raised by this study: If involvement in creative activity can play a vital therapeutic role in an individual's emotional rehabilitation, what role could the arts play in preventing the need for such therapeutic treatment if everyone could partake of them generously from early childhood on?" (Orzehowski, 1959, p. 173) As if to validate the implicit response to that question, I once found the following statement on the term paper of an art education student who had been hospitalized for mental illness: "I can't help wondering if I would be a better adjusted person if I had had a more flexible art background—or for that matter, an art background at all—where I could have had an avenue for self-expression. It is strange that three other emotionally ill people, who also had very little art instruction, of any kind, also agreed that maybe this might have made a difference in our lives. I will probably never know about this; but one thing I do know is that if I do teach, my children are going to have as many opportunities for self-expression as I am able to give them."

It does make sense to me that if art can be helpful to troubled and to handicapped children, it can also be helpful to "normal" children in school and at home, as a way of expressing and clarifying, and perhaps coping with some of the complicated feelings like jealousy, anger, and fear that every child has when growing up. These are not always easy to talk about, and some feelings are really difficult—if not impossible—to put into words, no matter how articulate a child may be. Moreover, you can hurt somebody in make-believe, as did Vince in the "Big Scissors" drawing

(Fig. 16-7) without anything really bad happening. Because art is symbolic, no one actually gets hurt, and the wish has been expressed in a safe and manageable way. Maybe if more children had a chance to express their feelings in and through art, there would not be so many who would need specialized help for their emotional problems. Art is a very natural form of "primary prevention."

Perhaps as important as expressing feelings, is the fact that a child can feel very good about himself as a competent person, through mastering the skills involved in using art materials. He has not only experienced the pride and pleasure of mastering a medium, he has also learned that he himself can do something and can do it well. If there is a finished product, he may have an additional pride in his creation, along with the admiration of those who view it. And much of what goes on, even in art, helps a child to become sensitive to others, to their styles and ways of working. If children experience sharing, working together, and interacting supportively, as on a mural, then interpersonal growth is possible too.

So whether you think of art as helping children to master skills or feelings, or as a way of developing respect for self and others, the broadly therapeutic values and educational goals for children in art do not seem so far apart. It seems to me that the most therapeutic thing one can do in a classroom, is to provide a setting in which each child can become himself. First it is necessary to watch and listen, to understand just who each child is, and where he is, and where he seems to want to go. Then one can try to help him get there, by helping him to overcome inner and outer roadblocks, and by honestly valuing his own creative definition of himself. Through understanding, through provision of appropriate conditions, through permitting and focusing on areas of concern and conflict, a teacher can make art in the classroom a powerful tool in preventing problems, as well as in helping each child to grow as well and as beautifully as he can.

CHAPTER 17.

Helping the Handicapped Child through Art

Desmond Morris, an anthropologist, once published a volume about man's closest relatives and their picture-making activities called *The Biology of Art* (1962). It is fascinating to learn therein that apes and chimpanzees can be genuinely interested in drawing or painting. In fact, when deeply involved in their work, they are at times oblivious to other normally prepotent needs, including hunger and sex. Their surprising investment led Morris to suggest that picture-making is for apes a "self-activating activity" which satisfies an innate "exploratory urge." Visually clear in the book, and equally interesting, is the stylistic individuality in the art of different animals: Alexander the Orang-utang has a way of painting distinct from that of Congo the Chimpanzee! And, based upon some experiments with their apparently deliberate use of picture space, Morris concluded that the apes seem to have an intuitive sense of compositional order.

While one might object to the use of the word "art" to describe their creations, it is significant that critics were fooled at several staged openings in fashionable galleries, actually praising the unknown painters' work. The purpose of this illustration is not to suggest a parallel between handicapped children and apes, but rather to emphasize the universality of that "exploratory" or "making" urge, and to underline the biological roots of stylistic individuality and a sense of order.

It took some imagination on Morris's part to find ways of making painting and drawing possible for apes and chimpanzees. Once the mechanics had been solved, however, the art activity itself seemed to come quite naturally, with little training or teaching necessary. The similar challenge in work in art with the handicapped is often one of needing to stretch one's own creativity and imagination in order to make it possible for what will still come naturally to happen (cf. Anderson, 1978). "Wherever there is a spark of human spirit—no matter how dim it may be—it is our sacred responsibility as humans, teachers, and educators to fan it into whatever flame it conceivably may develop. . . . We are all by nature more or less endowed with intrinsic qualities, and no one has the right to draw a demarcation line which divides human beings into those who should receive all possible attention in their development and those who are not worth all our efforts. One of these intrinsic qualities is that every human being is endowed with a creative spirit." (Lowenfeld, 1957, p. 430) For myself, it is now a firm belief "that every human being is endowed with a creative spirit," for at many times and in many places I have been told that children with a certain diagnostic label would be unable to do anything productive, creative, or even nondestructive with art materials. And time after time, the children have proven the prophets to be wrong, and have surprised even their most hopeful advocates.

The first such group I met were hospitalized and suffered from one of the most severe forms of psychotic illness possible for youngsters, childhood schizophrenia. They were all performing at a level below their chronological age, though the degree of real or functional retardation varied. It was thought in advance by some professionals who knew them, that they would eat or smear the art materials, become disorganized and destructive, or get further lost in a world of autistic fantasy. Nevertheless, the chairman of the Department of Child Development, Guinevere Chambers, Ph.D., and I were allowed to try out a plan of art sessions on a voluntary individual basis. Thus, once a week for eight months, I went to a small room on the sixth floor of the psychiatric hospital where these ten schizophrenic children were being treated. The youngsters would come to the room one at a time. Once there, they were free to choose what art materials they would use, where they would use them, and what they would make.

As with the apes, it was soon clear that each child had a style and a way of working that was all his own. Dan, for example, would pull his chair up to the easel, put a brush in each color of paint in the tray, and, holding his brush with a relaxed grip like a Japanese Sumi painter, would move it up and down, up and down, rhythmically and visibly relaxing. Selma also painted often at the easel, with a similar motor-kinesthetic rhythm. Yet her work was unique in her preference for repetitive circular motions involving the whole body. Karen, too, preferred easel painting, and engaged in an active rhythmic and vocal dialogue, with and through her bright splotches of color. She really danced as she worked, moving away, coming back, intently tuned into her picture and its dabs and swirls of bold, rich color.

They each grew, each in his own way. Dan learned to "know" and to indicate when he was done swabbing paint on one piece of paper, and was ready for the next. Selma enlarged her repertoire to include not only monochromatic circular sweeps, but also linear splashes and bouncy dabs of varied hue. Four-year-old Jonny's easel paintings changed over time from tense, small blobs above each jar in the tray to free sweeping movements of the brush, in which colors, at first separated, often mingled and blended later in lovely tones.

Teddy concentrated on linear drawings of objects, animals, and above all, people. For months, he worked on human-figure possibilities, exploring a wide range of graphic body-image statements, finally settling on a stable symbol of a boy (Fig. 1-7). Bobby loved to talk while he worked, telling imaginative stories about his drawings and paintings. One favorite theme was a scene of his uncle's farm with many details, of which there were several versions. Another was the creation of pictorial "charts" on such topics as Holidays of the Year, How to Stay Healthy, and How a Pumpkin Grows from a Seed. As described earlier, both Dorothy and Randy used their art time in equally unique and varied ways. (See Chapter 7)

It is important to remember that all of these children had been diagnosed as suffering from the same disease, childhood schizophrenia. Yet, while they shared the same descriptive label, what stood out most strongly in their art work was their individuality, despite a literature which implies a greater uniformity. Certainly, they used the opportunity with art media in different ways—some primarily for manipulative play and relaxation, some for clarification of realistic and fantastic concepts, and some for organizing and "mapping out" their worlds. And because they were individualistic and varied, their products often displayed a normality, perhaps reflecting capacities rather than deficits.

There is much to be learned from this experience, and from a study which grew out of it, where judges were unable to discriminate randomly-selected products by the schizophrenic children from those by a matched group of "normals" (Rubin and Schachter, 1972). One implication is that a diagnostic category like childhood schizophrenia, while useful and valid for some purposes, cannot adequately describe an individual's wholeness, richness, or creative language. Neither in comparison with the control subjects nor with each other, can the art work of these children be described with any meaningful generalization. The only one which makes any sense is that, like all children, they demonstrated through art the essential uniqueness of their individual selves—in spite of the degree of alienation from self and world from which they all suffered.

While extremely rich as a source of information about him, a child's art cannot be translated through some neat process, form, or symbol guidebook into a diagnostic label. The above experience serves as a reminder that, as with any other group of people, children who have been judged to belong in the same diagnostic category may still be, think, feel, paint, and draw in ways that are radically different from one another. It is well to remember that "every person, from the moment of birth, is a unique individual, unlike any other being that ever existed." (Moustakas, 1969, p. 66)

There are yet others who have taught me a great deal about human capacity and growth potential. Four years after the experience with the schizophrenic children, I was asked to help start an art program at an institution for orthopedically and multiply-handicapped children. I shall never forget the first meeting with the dozen or so staff members involved with the children who had cerebral palsy. They presented myself and the new art teacher, to whom I was the consultant, with a list of about ten names. When I discovered that there were perhaps four times as many who had already been ruled out for a variety of sensible-sounding reasons, I suggested we try evaluating everyone, just to see what might be possible. As a result of these individual assessments, it was found unnecessary to exclude anyone from the art program.

Some of the brain-damaged, hyperactive children who were expected to be destructive in the art room were so very constructive there that, when a token-reward behavior-modification program was introduced for them, the most popular reinforcement was a period in the art room (although it cost the highest number of tokens). Equally amazing, those with severe orthopedic and muscular handicaps, such as extensive spasticity or athetosis, seemed able to mobilize unimagined resources, so that they could function both independently and creatively(Fig. 17-1).

Fig. 17-1. A boy in a wheelchair paints his ceramic slab pot.

We all learned a great deal from children like Claire, a deaf-mute of ten, whose drawings were so articulate that they helped the staff to change her label from profoundly to mildly retarded (Fig. 17-2). Because she could not talk and could make few gestures, picture-making became a vital expressive tool for her. One day she came into the art room, propelling her wheelchair, screaming inside with the agony of a visit to the dentist. She wheeled herself in, up to the table, grabbed a marker and paper, and drew a picture which, more eloquently than any words, told what it feels like to be "attacked" by a dentist—to be all teeth and mouth, stretched wide open, helpless as the intrusive tools of the doctor enter your body (Fig. 17-3). Her drawings also helped her in the classroom with learning concepts, and in speech therapy, where they became a bridge to spoken language through her "talking book."

Fig. 17-2. A drawing of the art therapist by Claire. Crayon. Age 10.

Fig. 17-3. Claire's drawing done immediately after a visit to the dentist. Marker.

In a recent experience at a school for the deaf, I was again reminded of the communicative value of art for those with language handicaps. Asked to explore the possibility of an art therapy program by working for a term with individual students, I found myself debating among a developmental approach (Williams and Woods, 1977), a cognitive one (Silver, 1978), and a psychodynamic one. I had already learned from Claire and others like her the special need for art as an alternative form of speech, but I was genuinely uncertain about just what kind of visual communication would be most helpful.

The sixteen children referred for diagnostic interviews quickly told me, by saying quite eloquently that what they needed—even more than an opportunity to organize their thinking—was a chance to express and cope with powerful feelings through expressive art therapy. Since an art education program was already available for more cognitive and creative goals, the best approach seemed to be a psychotherapeutic one, in which the individuals who came used art and dramatic play to express and then deal with confused and conflicted feelings and fantasies. The intensity of their need for this kind of help was reflected in their ability to relate to me, despite my complete lack of signing skills. Though I could understand some of the speech of the few who talked, and though I could use writing with some others, our communications were largely nonverbal—through art, gestures, facial expressions, and pantomime.

As an illustration of the intensity of their response to the opportunity to express themselves in art, I shall share a middle session with Eleanor, the adolescent whose initial art interview was described in Chapter 8 (when I suggested that she draw "a feeling"). Eleanor, whose suicidal impulses had been known to the staff for some time, had tried to cut her wrist the night before our fourth art therapy session. Realizing, after describing to me what had occurred, that she had hurt herself rather than the real target of her rage, she drew—with much excitement—a picture of what she would like to do to the grownup who had angered her.

In the drawing (Fig. 17-4), a many-toothed, monstrous creature is holding a huge knife over a small, fearful person. She first said that she was the big one and the adult was the small one; then she reversed herself, explaining that in reality she felt helpless to deal with the power of those in charge of her. I suggested that she might also feel frightened of the extent of her own rage, of what she would really like to do to the grownup in the picture. I wondered if she had turned the anger on herself as a punishment, as well as a way to protect the adult, who she then said cared a lot about her. She spent the remaining time in the session drawing a volleyball net, as if to screen out the fearful imagery of her first picture, and then used colorful fingerpaint to make four balloons tied together. Eleanor was thus able to use the art therapy session first to express the feared impulse and then to defend against it; both were helpful to her in the ongoing task of self-awareness and self-control.

On the basis of the pilot study which involved Eleanor and several others seen weekly for a term, a part-time art therapist was hired and has worked at the school for the past few years, seeing both individuals and groups. I have had the pleasure of remaining involved as a consultant, and of helping the therapist to design and evaluate an outcome study, which indicated some positive behavioral changes in those children involved in the art program (Kunkle-Miller, 1983).

Another positive experience was working for several years with a group of retarded preschoolers and their teachers. Much to our delight and (I confess) surprise, these tiny tots of gravely limited intellect were able to choose and initiate independent art work in a variety of media, with gradually reduced support and assistance from adults. Some revealed unknown abilities to concentrate and to organize themselves, and all responded with joy and vigor, albeit on a primarily manipulative level. The range of capacities, even within this young, fairly homogeneous group, was impressive. Asked to draw a picture of a person, for example, one child produced a labelled scribble of "A Kid," while another created a well-organized face called "A Monster." Both children were four, both were retarded, and yet one was obviously functioning at a rather age-appropriate level, and even the labelled scribble was within the norm for young children's drawings.

In their imaginative play with the art materials, many of the children helped us to see their capacities for expression in other forms. Thus, although the program began with an emphasis on the visual arts, it later expanded to include various kinds of creative play—with sand, water, blocks, musical instruments, dolls, puppets, dress-up clothes, props, and housekeeping equipment. This expansion

Fig. 17-4.   Eleanor's drawing of "what she would like to do." Marker.

came as a natural development, as the children revealed their interests, needs, and propensities for expression in other modalities.

The largest group of such children from whom I learned were blind and partially-sighted. They were also mildly or greatly retarded (average I.Q., 65), and suffered from other disabilities, such as cerebral palsy, speech and language disorders, deafness, brain damage, and emotional disturbance. As in the instances described above, the prior expectations of those who knew them were far from hopeful. An experienced teacher of art to blind youngsters, for example, predicted chaos; saying that these multiply-handicapped children would have clay on the ceiling and a mess on the floor without step-by-step instructions. Once more, the experience with art was a pleasant surprise, and is documented in visual and auditory detail in a film, "We'll Show You What We're Gonna Do!" (Rubin, 1972)

Since the children had not had art before, I began with individual assessments, evaluating each child's responses to different media, and to various sensory stimuli. On the basis of each child's degree of vision, intellectual level, and behavior in these interviews, the program director, Janet Klineman, Ph.D., and I arranged small homogeneous groups of two to five children, who met weekly for a half hour, for a seven-week period. We hoped to explore the children's potential for creative growth, given a free choice of materials within a planned learning environment.

Indeed, the exploratory art program truly opened the eyes of the sighted adults involved, while it broadened the children's worlds. It made us acutely aware of their creative potential and of their unexpected capacity for growth. Not only did they not mess as feared, they responded enthusiastically and constructively. We saw children, some in their first contact with new materials, creating art work of sometimes surprising beauty. While at first uncomfortable with freedom of choice, the children soon understood that we really expected them to make their own decisions about medium, theme, and place of work. They then exercised the newly acquired privilege (or is it a right?) with gusto. These experiences contradicted the "frequent arguments . . . that handicapped persons need the security and confidence which result from mere imitative occupation, such as copying or tracing." (Lowenfeld, 1957, p. 431)

Often the children opened our eyes to previously hidden capacities. Jimmy's meaningful response to color, for example, initiated his individualized visual stimulation program. Carl's skill and interest in wood scrap constructions resulted in a successful after-school woodworking club (Fig. 17-5). All of them revealed a surprising ability to function independently in a setting which involved freedom of choice, leading to open classrooms the following school year.

In yet another way, the art program revealed to us the values, the uniqueness, the beauty in their different ways of perceiving and knowing. Although in our society, "handicaps are not recognized as differences or unique aspects of self, but [are] seen as inadequacies" (Moustakas, 1959, p. 247), the children with whom we worked enabled us to revise our perception of "handicap" as primarily "defect" to primarily

Fig. 17-5. Carl, who has no useful vision, making one of his many wood-scrap compositions.

"difference." It was impossible to deny the existence of their disabilities, or the many painful feelings they caused. One could not, in candor, say that their perceiving and creating in art were the same as the sighted as has been suggested (Freund, 1969). What we did find, however, was "that blindness may become the basis of a specific and unique creativeness," (Lowenfeld, 1957, p. 446) and that "sighted individuals may be missing great riches by the lack of kinesthetic awareness." (Haupt, 1969, p. 42)

As we opened ourselves to their unique ways of being, we learned to value their otherness, to treasure the ways in which they sensitized us. The children expanded our sensory awareness, by referring to "clay that smells like candy," "ether markers," or "soft paper." They tuned us in to sounds, like Billy, who took intense pleasure in "a marker that squeaks a whole lot . . . that makes a whole lotta noise." Although one would not have chosen a felt-tip marker as the most appropriate tool for a boy with no vision, Billy taught us not to allow our own preconceptions to interfere with what media we might offer a handicapped child. Indeed, rather than finding a "best" medium for these blind children, we discovered that almost every one selected his own preferred material from those available (clay, wood, wire, paint, chalk, markers, crayons, etc.)

Through their sensitive use of their hands, those who could see nothing taught us about a kind of free-floating tactile attention, in their approach to shape, form and texture. They seemed to know where to position their wood scraps, suggesting a tactile aesthetic different from a visual one, later explored in a pilot study (Rubin, 1976). Indeed, when we put blindfolds on our eyes, we found that their sculptures felt quite different to us than they looked. We wondered if there could be a kind of "tactile thinking," analogous perhaps to "visual thinking" (Arnheim, 1969). Similarly, those with limited vision sensitized us to the excitement and impact for them of new visual experiences. Peter, for example, responded with a kind of "color shock" to the intense tempera paint hues. And deaf-blind Terry literally jumped for joy, after accidently discovering that wet clay pressed on white paper made a visible mark, and that *she* had made it happen.

Their use of materials was often quite free and inventive, perhaps in part because of a genuine naiveté and openness. David made, with foam tubes and pipe cleaners, a delightful sweeper, and then zoomed around the room with it, making sweeper noises. Greg used wood scraps and glue for his sculpture, "The Office of Peace and Quiet," with bright lights made of pipe cleaners. There was poetry in Peter's painting titles, like "A Mountain Hilltop Way out West and a Coyote Howling in the Night, with a Full Moon." And there was charm in his animistic description of his wood scrap sculpture, "The Memorial Toll Bridge," which "lets the people walk across it, and it lets cars through it." Perhaps because of their developmental immaturity, they were less self-critical than most children their age. Thus, Peter could say of his creation with unself-conscious pride, "It's a pretty good sculpture!"

The children also opened our eyes to the intensity of their feelings about being blind, and their needs for expression. One day, four youngsters with no useful vision sat around a table, each working on a different project of his choice, and shared an intense discussion of disabilities—of people who are out of shape, who are deaf, crippled, or retarded. They recalled when people close to them had been injured, or had been seriously ill. They talked of themselves, and the danger of other losses. Barry, for example, said, "This is very, very important. Everybody listen! This could happen to you guys, too. When you get sick, you know, you could lose your hearing—and see—the time I got my earache, I almost got deaf. . . . And something else—if you don't sleep and wake up, you'll feel sickly too! You'll get sick—Yeah! I don't think you'll *lose* anything." Barry's eyes had been removed when he was five, and when he later spoke of his dad's kidney stone operation he said, "*He* still has everything."

The group continued to work on their projects, and shared scary experiences, worrying aloud about what would happen to themselves. As Barry put it, "like if I got hit by a car—see, say like if I *die*—say like now, if I *die*." Finally, Tammy told of a person she knew who "couldn't hear and couldn't *see* either." I asked the children how they felt about that, and Barry said, "That's one thing I got right now! I can't see. . . . And I'm sad about it." I asked Bob how he felt about it, and, with much blocking and stammering, he explained his attempt at denial: "I don't care. Even if I can't see, I'm—I just don't—I just pretend that—I just pretend—you know." [You just pretend that you really *can* see?] "Yeah, I don't even—I don't like—I don't even let—I don't even *talk* about it. I just pretend it's not even there!" Barry quickly empathized, saying, "That's what I do too. . . . You know what I do at night? Every night when I sleep, I just pretend it's not even there! That's all." The group was relieved, and went on to talk about how sad and angry it made them to be blind, and how badly they wished to see.

It seemed that the children in this art program grew perceptibly in the formal quality of their work, in the controlled freedom of their working process, and in their good feelings about themselves. It was as if, in the process of creating their increasingly complex and personalized products, the children were also discovering and defining (and perhaps actualizing) themselves as unique individuals. And, paradoxically, they were in the process teaching us—in spite of their blindness, they opened our eyes. We learned that "eventual levels of attainment may be curtailed not only by whatever inherent limitations may be present in the children themselves, but also by the restrictions imposed upon them by adults." (Weiner, 1967, p. 7) We learned, too, that "the only meaningful readiness . . . is a flexibility and a willingness to meet the child as he is, and a belief in him as a whole person of immeasurable potential." (Moustakas, 1959, pp. 217–218)

Unfortunately, negative expectations are not at all uncommon, as can be seen with a quick glance at the literature on art for the handicapped. That on art for the retarded, for example, reveals "a definite attitude that the retarded child [is] not capable of developing creative and imaginative concepts." (Saunders, 1967, p. 4) Despite the positive and successful free approaches of a few (Baumgartner and Schultz, 1969; Crawford, 1962; Gaitskell, 1953; Lindsay, 1968; Lowenfeld, 1957;

Saunders, 1967; Site, 1964; Uhlin, 1972); the more common assumption has been that retarded children require "highly organized . . . step-by-step procedures" (McNeice and Benson, 1964, p. 14), that "only one activity at a time is desirable," that they "have to be constantly supervised to see that they do not misuse materials and supplies," and that "retarded children generally lack imagination." (Schmidt, 1968, pp. 3, 4)

Similarly condescending attitudes are frequent in the limited literature on art for the blind: "negative sentiment exists concerning the creative aspects of the blind child and feasible art activities . . . with the result that the child's handwork time has been consistently devoted to learning repetitious movements which evolve a craft skill." (Decker, 1960, p. 105) Again, despite many reports of successful creative art teaching experiences (Fukurai, 1974; Haupt, 1966, 1969; Kewell, 1955; Kramer, 1971; Lisenco, 1971; Lowenfeld, 1952, 1957), there remains a strong feeling that "repetitive skill work . . . should not be underestimated or discredited." (Coombs, 1967, p. 81)

Even those who often seem to have greater faith in the potential of an exceptional child to succeed in art, point out the need of "keeping to rules" such as: "no painting should be attempted without some preliminary drawing in blackboard chalk or charcoal." Although this same educator recognizes that "keeping to rules may at first appear to be the antithesis of freedom for self-expression," she asserts that such procedures "enable many backward children to state clearly in paint what they have to portray, which they would otherwise not do if left to their own resources." (Lindsay, 1968, pp. 22, 23) At times, the condescension is difficult to bear: "Even in the more freely expressive experiences provided for exceptional children, there is little evidence of any kind of growth. A characteristic of the work of these children is the unvarying repetition of the visual forms they are able to produce. Their products compare with developed art expressiveness approximately as their speech patterns compare with poetry or dramatic speech. . . . When well-meaning teachers believe that the severely handicapped child is experiencing "art," they are misinformed, or are deluding themselves." (Schwartz, 1970, p. 40) That statement characterizes some pervasive attitudes which one must disprove and overcome, in order to bring the pleasures of creative art to the handicapped. Certainly, it helps to develop a healthy skepticism for at least some of what one reads in this area. It may also help to be aware of some of the conditions which make it possible for even the most disabled to create.

Facilitating Conditions

The first, and perhaps most essential condition, is to believe sincerely what Lowenfeld was able to say with such conviction, "that every human being is endowed with a creative spirit." (1957, p. 430) It is not something which can be learned, but if felt honestly and conveyed to the child, can have immensely positive effects.

It seems equally important to believe that all human beings, given the proper facilitating conditions, have an inherent and natural tendency toward growth, order, and integration. In order to permit any kind of freedom within a facilitating framework, one must have confidence in the child's ability to become himself, to make choices and decisions about his own work.

It may also be necessary to expand one's notion of art, so that it can encompass the manipulation of collage materials with feet by an armless child, or the rhythmic repetitive swabbing of paint by a psychotic child. In a way, such manipulative and making activities are to art, as babbling and jargon are to speech. They are a preparation for formal expression, and constitute as legitimate a part of art with the handicapped, as reading readiness for the average learner. There may be some severely disabled children, for whom formless sensory play with art materials is the most they will ever be able to achieve developmentally. Why deny them these pleasures, and why impose upon them our need for them to produce more "legible" work? Such an imposition is found in the many prepared outlines within which the children are asked to color, meaningless for a child at a prefigurative level of graphic development. It seems ironic that such filling-in of others' boundaries should be considered more legitimate as art than the independent manipulation of media by a child. Art with the handicapped can and should include the whole possible range of manipulative and making activities, with any media or tools controllable by the child, not necessarily the traditional ones.

While true for work with all children, it seems especially important to clarify the goals and values of art for the handicapped child, for whom a good thing like art is often provided for the wrong reasons. This is not to say that such activities are not useful for filling leisure time, developing manual dexterity, learning to share, etc., but perhaps there are even more important values in art for a handicapped child.

Pleasure and joy, for example, are luxuries often denied the handicapped, who need sensory-manipulative and motor-kinesthetic pleasures for tension-release, as well as for permissible regression. The blind children, who at first seemed lifeless and depressed, who were characterized by an observer in the first session as "compliant and docile," came alive as they became involved in art. They began to smile, to move and laugh and speak more freely, and to show real pleasure in both process and product. Some have suggested that the need to play may be as fundamental as the need to love (Curry, 1971), that "the opposite of interplay is deadness" (Erikson, 1972), and that "playfulness makes life worth living" (Sutton-Smith, 1971, p. 21).

The intensity of the blind children's sensory-motor pleasure in the art experience was inescapable. The paintings of David, for example, who often pretended that his brush strokes represented cars careening down roads and around curves, were "muscular equivalents of total experiencing" (Pasto, 1964, p. 67). The notion of expressive art activities as a tension-release is often found in the literature on art for the handicapped, and the vigorous pounding of clay, or rhythmic zooming of arms and hands with brush or paint, was eloquent testimony to that need. Because they must often inhibit and control their motoric responses in order to be safe, it seems especially important for blind children to have opportunities for free movement. As Burlingham has noted, "As soon as conditions of absolute safety are provided, the blind child too will hop and jump eagerly." (1972, p. 239)

Art provides a handicapped child with important opportunities to function as independently as possible, while he must so often be dependent on others. Through independent choice and decision-making, the child is helped to define himself in symbolic-productive terms, developing his personal tastes and style. While some avenues of learning or expression may be blocked, experiences with materials can help a child further develop those sensory and productive avenues open to him— like touch for the blind, vision for the deaf, and manual dexterity for those whose legs are immobilized.

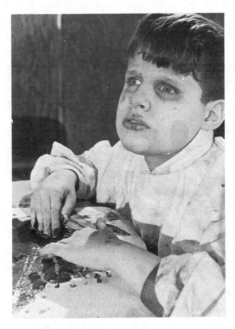

Fig. 17-6. A blind child experiencing finger paint.

Through practice, a handicapped child can develop mastery of tools, materials, and processes. He thus learns the joy and pleasure and pride of skill development, and the pride in a product made completely by himself. Since the handicapped child so often feels out of control both physically and psychologically, it seems especially important for him to have materials and a modality in which he can indeed be in charge (where he can be the "boss").

One major value of art for exceptional children is that they can be the active ones who do something to and with materials, since so often they are passively led, dressed, doctored, etc. In another way, they are able to achieve mastery through dramatic play with art media. In reliving traumatic situations, the blind children often assumed the stronger and more controlling role, rather than the original and often helpless one. Thus Kay, a victim of child abuse, played the role of an angry, punitive, withholding mother to her clay babies, screaming, "You go to bed! You don't get no more food. You don't get nothin' to eat today!" Handicapped children certainly have greater stresses, more traumas, and many fewer ways of coping with them than others.

In art, a handicapped child can safely "let go" and regress, especially when anxiety about fluid media is allayed through the use of physical boundaries, like bowls or trays. He can also symbolically "let go" and express strong feelings of anger or fear that are hard to express directly, especially when one feels vulnerable and dependent on others. Feelings may be released and evoked through media contacts, as well as through symbolic representation. Barry, for example, smelled "ether markers," which stimulated much of his doctor play; and with clay he created symbols of free movement, his many rockets (Fig. 9-4). Thus, it is possible for a handicapped child to express many feelings in and through art, safely relieving inner tensions while creating aesthetic forms.

The ensuing task, then, in providing art for the handicapped, becomes one of stretching the imagination in order to adapt the art-learning situation to the needs of that particular person. This may mean a physical adaptation, like chocolate-pudding fingerpaint for those who cannot always inhibit the putting of hands in mouths, or the taping of paper on a table, so that an athetoid child can concentrate his energy on controlling the drawing tool. It may mean thinking anew about time, and the span of attention of which a retarded preschooler is initially capable, measured in seconds, or at best, minutes. It may mean arranging space and groupings, so that a very needy or extremely hyperactive child will have the lack of distraction and competition he requires for involvement in his work. It means, in other words, being open to and making any and all necessary adaptations so that the individual can be as much in control as possible.

In order to find his preferred medium or modality, even a disabled individual must have the opportunity to explore and to choose. Only then can any child discover his personally congenial way of making things. Thus, a broad choice of media, and an openness to the use of other related expressive modalities, is essential for these children as for others.

If self-definition and independent functioning are two of the main goals of art for the handicapped, the structure within which these occur is critical. One aspect of such a facilitating structure is consistency and predictability in the availability of art materials, and the arrangement of these materials in such a way that even a handicapped child may be maximally independent in procuring and using them.

Several who have taught art to the visually and orthopedically handicapped have noted the helpfulness of providing physical outlines or boundaries within which the children could work comfortably (Lindsay, 1972). Bowls and trays indeed seem to be helpful containers, not only because they reduce chance of mishap, but because they enable the regressive and potentially "naughty" or disorganizing behavior to remain "contained" psychologically as well (Fig. 17-7). Messy media, like clay or fingerpaint, initially stimulated anxiety in many of the blind children, but such physical boundaries eventually helped them to master the discomfort (Fig. 1-1).

Fig. 17-7. A hydrocephalic girl drawing in her crib on a raised tray.

Perhaps an equally important facilitating condition is a psychological framework which permits true freedom and exploration. By this I mean primarily an acceptance, an attempt at understanding the meaning of the experience to the child; not what it means to the adult who observes, but cannot ever fully enter the child's frame of reference. This is not easy, because it requires a kind of openness and empathy which are extremely difficult even with normal children, and especially hard with the handicapped. It means accepting any honest response on the part of the child, no matter how unexpected, bizarre, regressive, or messy, so long as it does no realistic harm.

A child may, for example, first need to explore a new medium; this may mean smelling, tasting, banging, squeezing, smearing, playing, and possibly never making a finished product. It means accepting the unexpected, like Billy's love for squeaky markers. With a handicapped child, it means accepting even the most agonizingly slow progress, the painstaking efforts to put things together.

There may be a greater need with these children, especially at first, for adult intervention, sometimes to "simplify the learning situation for each individual child" (Lindsay, 1972, p. 139), sometimes to help him get started, as in Lowenfeld's "closure" technique (1957, p. 435). It may be necessary more often to join into the play as with disadvantaged children who do not know how to play spontaneously. Often it means doing what Wills recommended to mothers of blind children, functioning "as the child's auxiliary ego, helping him to . . . organize his world without the aid of sight." (1965, p. 363)

Most important, perhaps, it is essential to value the child's own work above any product made even in part by another. While the crude creations of the handicapped may seem inartistic or ugly to some, one cannot improve on Lowenfeld's assertion that "the most primitive creative work born in the mind of a blind person and produced with his own hands, is of greater value than the most effective imitation." (1957, p. 446)

Just as it is essential to accept and value what the individual himself can produce as independently as possible, so one must be able to accept all of the feelings and fantasies that are expressed symbolically or verbally. In the process of helping children to freely create their own work, and to express their honest feelings, ideas may emerge for which an adult's calm acceptance can be a truly therapeutic experience. It is vital to remember that there can be no right or wrong in art, or in inner thought.

But it can be difficult to accept the vitality and the violence of the feelings hidden inside these often quiet and submissive youngsters. Perhaps because they dare not oppose those on whom they are truly dependent, feelings of anger at adults seem even more common among the handicapped, and more often hidden. As if bursting for release, they often emerge quickly and spontaneously in symbolic play and work with art media. The child may wish, for example, to smash his product, in fantasied destruction of another person. He may need to tell a gory or scary story about what he is doing or has made. Terry, for example, reacted with intense anger during her first art interview at the School for the Blind. First she squeezed, then pounded the clay, while speaking resentfully of "my sister . . . she just sits there and she laughs at me. That ain't funny! It's not! She laughed at me, and I squashed her half to death. I squashed her half to death! I just spanked her!" Pounding the clay with vigor, it was safe for Terry to imagine her make-believe revenge. Thus, the framework of fantasy, inherent in the symbolic nature of art, helped provide a safe release for such otherwise frightening impulses.

Despite their greater needs, there are real problems for an adult wishing to play a supportive, empathic, accepting role with exceptional children, due to the fact that handicapped individuals stir up such strong, irrational feelings in others. It seems especially vital here to be aware of one's own feelings, impulses, wishes, etc. so they do not get in the way. One can unwittingly keep a child too dependent, for example, through a need to give or to compensate for the injury, yet conversely may deny a necessary degree of dependency, through anxiety about too great an attachment. One must be watchful that expectations are neither too high nor too low, and must avoid interfering with the children's progress through premature interventions or excessive restrictions. Similarly, one must be careful not to pressure or seduce the children to work in a way that one knows would impress other adults, such as parents or colleagues.

One must be careful not to join the child in an attempt to deny the reality of the handicap, like Bob who said "I like to pretend it's not even there." Of course, one must also be sensitive to the child's wishes, and his need at times to pretend, as part of the process of coming to grips with reality. The ultimate, painful, but necessary challenge is to help him to come to an acceptance of the reality of his handicap, and of all his feelings and fantasies about it. Only then will he be free to grow, and to develop fully the healthy parts of himself.

Handicapped youngsters are rarely easy to work with in art, but the rewards are immense. They do need more help from the adult—not in being told what to do or how to do it—but in being understood, and being helped to articulate their unique creative strivings. It may require more energy to empathize, to understand a child who is so different from oneself. It may require more imagination, to find a way for that child to have independence and personal definition in and through art. It may require much patience, and much time for the learning to begin to show. But to help a child to become himself is a much more beautiful experience than nudging, leading, or seducing him into some prearranged mold, no matter how attractive. It is also much more exciting, because it is totally unpredictable.

Art cannot give a blind child sight, a retarded child clear comprehension, or a crippled child free mobility; but it can and does give a child an exciting, stimulating, and pleasurable way to enjoy and explore the sensory world. It gives him a way to be in charge, even in a limited sphere, of a medium or tool which he controls as he wishes. It gives him an opportunity to master whatever tools or processes are appealing and within his reach, and to savor the pleasure of skills achieved with practice. It gives him a way to safely let loose, to regress and smear and pound and release body tensions, or to let loose and express symbolically or verbally powerful scary feelings.

It gives him a way to control, to order, to "map out" a confused sense of his body or of his environment, of time or space—to make sense out of things through organizing them, or to organize himself in the productive activity. It gives him a way to discover and define himself through genuine choices and decisions, and creations which are uniquely his. It gives him a way to create products of which he can be proud, which he can give to others, through which he may at times add true beauty to the world (cf. Selfe, 1977). More important, in the productive-creative experience, he can add true meaning to his life—to his reality as well as to his fantasy.

Art for the handicapped can and must be more than a way of filling time, or a means of improving manipulative skills. For all human beings, and especially for the disabled, "art experiences can also be a way of performing mentally a desired activity which it is impossible to do physically." (Alkema, 1971, p. 3) If it is true that "man creates, as it were, out of his mortal wounds" (Meerloo, 1968, p. 22), then the handicapped child has a need for creative experience which is much greater than that of the youngster who has not suffered irreversible wounds. Since he must ultimately learn "to live in a world that is made by and for the fully functioning," art is especially important as "one area where a symbolic world can be indeed adapted to the handicapped's needs, and where he is not only at liberty to tell of his world and experiences, but where he is *expected* to do so." Moreover, by so doing, "he contributes to our general understanding by giving form to his own [unique] experiences" (Kramer, 1983), something Lowenfeld must have known when he titled a book about his work with the blind, *The Nature of Creative Activity*.

CHAPTER 18.

Helping Parents through Art and Play

Family Art Groups

Since it is my firm belief that art is good for all people—children and their parents—I derive great satisfaction from making art activities available to families. One such example is the Family Creative Arts Center, which was initiated over a decade ago and is now an integral part of a local annual week-long arts festival. There, parents and children are invited to work with clay, paint, wood scraps, and other art materials, sometimes expanding into the surrounding environment, such as the sailing of styrofoam boats that they made on a small pond near the working area. Thousands of children and parents are thus enabled to have pleasure and productivity together in the setting of a community arts event (Fig. 18-1).

While some may feel concerned about the risks of adult pressures on children, I would agree with Lowenfeld that "just as children of different age levels can work happily, respecting each other's way of expression, so can parents participate without influencing their children's concepts." (1954, p. 44) Going a step further, the same author hypothesized two decades ago: "I dare say that our world would be quite different if parents would set aside weekly 'creative afternoons' for themselves and their children. . . . Above all, parents would learn more about themselves, their children, and their relationships to them." (1954, p. 46)

Parent education groups have used art activities in many different settings as a way of expressing and reflecting on common as well as individual concerns. There are many possible formats, depending entirely on the purpose and nature of the particular group. In a single-parent education group in a local community center, mothers were asked to do life-space pictures. One young widow explained that her picture (Fig. 18-2) showed schematically her feelings of concern and confusion about the burdens of homemaking, bill-paying, and child-rearing on her own. Although she saw her hobbies and the church as sources of recreation and renewal, her view of the future was dominated by thoughts of deterioration (air pollution) which she felt powerless to halt. Other single parents in the group empathized with her feelings of being overwhelmed by responsibilities; and many were helpful, as they shared with her their own ways of coping and managing.

Fig. 18-1. Children and parents working on the "endless easel" at a community arts festival.

Fig. 18-2. A young widow's "life-space" drawing of her many concerns.

One morning, toward the end of a parent-run summer recreation program at a local elementary school, there was a family art workshop for twenty mothers and thirty children, ages four through twelve. The joint art activity took place in a comfortably large kindergarten room, where paint, crayons, and clay were available in separate areas. As each family group entered, it was suggested that they might like to do something together, though this was not required. The groups ranged in size from dyads to one mother and three children, and included a triad of three generations. The art activity lasted a scant forty-five minutes, but was busy and productive, with a surprisingly relaxed atmosphere, considering the number of people involved. The most striking thing about it was the obvious enjoyment on the part of almost all participants. With the exception of one mother who looked anxiously around the room for most of the time, the parents seemed to be having as much fun as the children. In most cases, at least one joint project was undertaken, though there was also a good deal of observing and parallel play (Fig. 18-3).

Hour-long discussion groups of ten mothers each led by psychiatric social workers followed the art activity. The mothers shared with each other feelings and thoughts aroused by the joint art session. One emphasized the pleasure for herself and her son to be alone without the new baby: "For me, I think, the important thing was this: the very fact that it was *just* David and me going to a *special* place at a *special* time was very important and very exciting. And we do it very rarely—once in a while, but generally with the new baby tagging along." Another mother expressed rather eloquently the personal impact of the experience of working with her nine-year-old daughter: "She and I both grew. Things I wanted *from* her and

a   b

Fig. 18-3a,b. Mothers and children at a "family art workshop" in a school.

with her I couldn't get really in any other way. It was a pleasure to see her loosen up and to let herself flow. As we went from one project to another, I felt we were moving together. It was a very important moment for me."

In addition to sharing a special activity with the child in a place away from home, several mothers referred to the increase in understanding which the joint experience had provided. "First, I was able to share my daughter's thoughts about the creative process. That is, she explained to me why she painted in a particular way, or why she would use specific colors."

The following fall the same parents requested another family art workshop to include husbands and older children. Then they changed their minds and asked for an evening workshop for parents only, saying they wanted something "just for us, without the kids around." A large number came and worked in a big classroom set up with supplies, for a full hour and a half one evening. Though they enjoyed themselves, those who had participated in the summer workshop were surprised by how much harder it was to get started and how much more self-conscious and inadequate they felt, compared to the session with their children. The momentous discovery of the evening, in fact, was that the children had indeed helped and given support to their parents—who felt unexpectedly ill at ease without them.

Once a month a group of women gather for a Mothers' Morning Out at a local church, bringing their toddlers and preschoolers, who are cared for away from their mothers. The mothers usually spend their time listening to a speaker, drinking coffee, and having a discussion following the presentation of the morning. I had visited these women twice before, and one woman, having heard of the program at the school described above, asked if such a session would be possible at the church. A joint art session was therefore held one morning with twenty-five mothers and twenty-two children attending (Fig. 18-4). The children ranged in age from nineteen months to five years. After an hour spent working together, the children went back to their rooms, and the mothers had a large group discussion, sitting in a circle surrounded by art work on the walls. These mothers focused on feelings about themselves and their children in terms of competency, creativity, and artistry.

Fig. 18-4. Mothers and preschoolers at a parent-child workshop.

Many spoke of the jealousy they had felt while watching their children work with ease and freedom, and some worried aloud about their own lack of creative ability. As one mother stated, "I could find this myself, that my rigid upbringing showed, because I was making Christmas trees and Santa Clauses that looked like those things, and my daughter made a psychedelic tree, and changed the season. She's certainly uninhibited about expressing herself, and I envy her freedom, really, especially here." Another mother recalled how painful her own art experiences in school had been, and how no one ever said a word about her pictures: "I can remember shedding tears over it! . . . And anything that I ever made always was uglier, or graded down, and this tended to go through somehow. When I try to sit with my children and do things with them, I have a bit of an inferiority complex, which is sad, I think—it doesn't have to be that way." Another expressed feelings of inadequacy, saying she was "inhibited. I find myself, when I pick up a piece of clay, totally inhibited. I just have no idea what to do with it! I'd like to just sit there and squeeze it, but to make anything!" The fear of exposure was well-articulated by one mother who said, "The feeling I got was—I didn't really want to do anything. Because, as I said to my neighbor, after these papers are all put together and she holds them up, she'll say, 'Oh, look at this. This looks like about a five-year-old did it,' and it'll be my paper!"

Some were genuinely concerned that their own felt lack of artistic ability might hurt their children, either genetically or through learning. "I know myself that I'm not a very creative person. But I noticed it also in my son, at least I did this morning, and those around me seemed to be quite creative. But I felt like my lack of creativity showed up in what he did." Or, as another woman said of her son, "I don't want him to have the same feelings about art that I have." Toward the end of the hour, a previously silent woman tried to settle the issue for the group: "It always bothers me when a parent talks about a child, in that they put their child into themselves, and then they throw off this thing, that 'I'm not creative.' And I have heard it so much in my life, that parents come to you and say, 'I'm not creative. I don't know how Johnny can be creative.' And the hairs on my back just bristle, sort of, because it's not fair. You haven't had the opportunity and the experience and the marvelous thoughts that have been started, just recently really, in art for little people." Or perhaps it was sentiments like these that "settled" the issue for those many concerned parents. "Well, I was excited by the materials, and I—I hate art! But I really had fun with those oil things [paintstiks], and they made such great colors, and I couldn't really make anything, but the colors were exciting and I enjoyed myself! I was really surprised. I found that my daughter stayed with the magic markers, and really liked that, and wasn't very interested in what I was doing, but that we both really enjoyed it."

The mothers also dealt with some interactional issues, like how dependent or independent their child had been, or how his behavior that morning compared with his behavior at home—"My little three-year-old goes to nursery school and smears colors, but at home she draws things." They talked of how sometimes their wish for their children to achieve had prompted behavior they knew was not best for them: "I found this myself today, because I walked up to him and I said, 'Don't scribble—make something! . . . And I realized that if he wants to draw a house or a man, he can very easily, but if he wants to scribble, he can too. He was up there having a ball with a paint brush, but I couldn't resist asking him to make something!" Another mother spoke warmly, telling a tale that brought forth laughter: "So often—we always go up to a child and say, 'What're you making? What does it look like?' And at one point, a little boy over at the easel—I don't even know who he was—He looked at me. I hadn't even said anything. He looked up and he said, 'I don't know!' "

On a more practical level, the mothers found themselves sharing ideas about how to provide art activities at home. They told of cooperative arrangements with mothers of same-age children taking turns, of a basement workshop set-up where there is no concern about mess, of crayons and shelf paper on the refrigerator door for the active toddler during dinner hour, etc. They also shared realistic concerns about household maintenance, when making art media available to young children: "I think our lives, and mine included, are so ordered and so orderly in our home, that it's very difficult to do this kind of thing that we were doing here in our homes, unless you have a room for it. And yet you don't, and you think, besides the paper that's on the wall, they're gonna go on through the hall and the bedroom! But we're hung up on this, and I think it's just a tragic thing in our lives."

Some expressed annoyance at the presence of the children, at being "too busy supervising, just supervising. If they hadn't been here, then of course I could've done more of my work." The majority, however, seemed to find, as did the elementary school mothers described earlier, that their children helped them to feel more comfortable. "I think it was Steichen who said, 'Happily, growth is not for children only.'. . . We're all lucky, really, and we really needed our own children to kind of let us do it legally, to slop in the paint, and paint with them, and color, etc. Really, it's part of the fun." Or, from another point of view: "You know, I think it's important that they can see their mother do these things. You know, so many times we just do things mothers do, and I think it's great if we can just sit down with paint and clay in their world—on their level. It's kind of like, when you make a mistake, it's good for them to see that we're not always up here and they're just the little people."

The art activity took place in mid-December, and one mother stated: "I found this particularly valuable this week. Everything's so tense, with Christmas coming and getting things for four children and all that stuff, and I really found that we relaxed together this morning." Stressful seasons aside, many felt that spending time together was not easy. "I think it was of value for me to do something with them. As they get older and can do more on their own, you're more apt to say, You go color. And you need to make an effort to do things together, you need to set a time aside." The majority echoed these sentiments, with a final decision to repeat the experience at some future date. "It would be fun to have a longer session, mothers and children again. I thought it was valuable for the kids and mothers just to do something together. At home, you're so busy, you don't sit down together, even if you know you should!"

Clearly the use of joint or separate art experiences followed by some discussion or reflection, can be useful in parent education. The nature and goals of the particular group should determine in large part the precise format. Such an experience might well be related to more or less structured instruction in normative stages of child development, a discussion of how one feels about one's child, or any of a number of other possible topics. It is my feeling that in most cases, allowing the content of the discussion to come from the group, provides the opportunity for most participants to use the experience to the fullest.

In a special summer program at a school for the blind, a group of eight mothers had weekly art-discussion groups (while their children had art and drama). One week they had a joint session with their children. The art activities which initiated each of the mothers' discussion group meetings included modelling with blindfolds or closed eyes, family drawings, life-space pictures, scribble drawings, and free drawing or modelling. Looking at her family drawing in which her blind son and her husband were given shaky outlines and looked weaker than the others, Barry's mother began to talk about how frustrated she was in trying to help her assertive son: "I want to be his right arm, that's what I want. I want to be his buddy. I want to be his mother and his very good friend, and I don't have it!"

During the joint art session three weeks later, she and Barry successfully completed a joint drawing they had planned at home—a pizza, a subject of deep significance for both. It was one of the few things she made for him that he trusted as a communication of her love. After that, however, they were unable to work together on a joint project to their mutual satisfaction. She next took him to an easel, where she attempted to paint a picture with him, with much attendant frustration and resistance on Barry's part. His mother's wish to deny the reality of his two plastic eyes was poignantly evident in a similarly inappropriate request for him to hand her a red crayon during the pizza drawing. In the mothers' group discussion following the joint session, her choice of visual media stimulated an intense and frank discussion of the difficulty of accepting the reality of a blind child. The following week in the mother's group, Barry's mother stated with relief, "It's all over now. He's a new kid. You said tell him about his handicap? Well, we told him. I think he's realizing it. He even talks about it. He told the bus driver this morning, 'I can't see.' He never said that before!"

In the joint session, however, Mrs. N. had persisted in trying to get Barry to make further joint products with her to no avail. They finally ended up, still side by side, at a table near another mother-child pair, with each "doing his own thing." Barry was happy, but his mother was sad. In the discussion following that experience, she said with much feeling, "He was just agitating me! He wouldn't take any suggestions. He has a mind of his own, a definite mind of his own . . . I was just frustrated. I tried real hard to get him to work with me, but he had a mind of his own, and I was just agitating him trying to. But after the pizza, forget it! That was it! He will *not* let me help him. He won't let me *see* for him, in other words. He can do it himself, and I thought I could show him about it. But he don't want no part of it. And I think that's why I loused it up. He just didn't want me to do anything with it!" Her need to help, to keep him dependent on her in an overprotective way, as if to compensate for his loss, was shared and empathized with by many other mothers.

Some mothers, however, while sympathizing with her frustration, were able to show Mrs. N. how she could enjoy a blind child's growing independence. One mother told proudly about how her usually timid boy had played a teacher role with her. "He told me to draw like he was drawing, but I tried it, and I didn't like it so much. So I used clay and that was okay too." (Fig. 18-5) Another woman spoke of her gradually worsening retarded girl, with a warm appreciation of the child's assets: "She has so many ideas. She does her thing, and I do mine. She's under so much pressure at school, why pressure her any more?" Mrs. N. thus began to see her own possible motives for trying to pressure her son into doing only joint projects: "I think I feel guilty, like I'm somehow to blame for him losing his eyes. I know it's crazy, but I hit him hard, and the next day the doctor told us the news. I feel like I just have to make it up to him."

Some mothers were able, through the joint art session, to see their handicapped children in a new light. One totally blind boy surprised his mother and others by being interested in art at all, and especially by being willing to use and even enjoy fluid media like fingerpaint. Another woman, herself an artist, spoke of her cerebral palsied, partially sighted son with genuine astonishment: "He seemed very much at ease. He likes to paint! And I'm surprised because he didn't used to like to do anything that would make his hands dirty, and I notice now that he doesn't seem to mind a lot of the materials. You know, I was kind of surprised." Her remarks about his rapid painting technique revealed less approval, and even a deprecating attitude: "When he was finished with it, I thought I'd die! I didn't know, you know. . . . Those paintings, he just knocks them off, one a second! . . . Quantity not quality! I think his talent lies more with the verbal than with something like this." This mother also made a poignant nonverbal statement about her perception of her son's artistic ability, laying her hand on his and guiding it during the making of a joint mural (Fig. 18-6).

While all of these mothers found the joint art session to be rather embarrassing and uncomfortable, half of them referred to it spontaneously in their post-program evaluations, suggesting more such activities. One woman wrote with candor: "Having to work with my son was the hardest. I know it was the best and most important for both of us, but it wasn't easy. . . . But we should do more things together like this." Another mother, also self-conscious about being on display, stated: "More involvement with the children and the parents together, I think would make for a better relationship, say, even for just a half hour. . . . I think when the parents are happy, the kids are happier and more adjusted to their handicap."

Fig. 18-5. A mother and her partially sighted son each do their own thing.

Fig. 18-6. An artist-mother "helps" her blind child to paint better.

Parent Play Groups

Whether attention is drawn to process or product, whether art work is done in groups of mothers, couples, or families, art activities can be a useful tool in parent education. One of the most imaginative approaches was developed by a psychoanalyst, Tobias Brocher, in the 1950s in Ulm, Germany (Time, 1971). In this approach, parents are asked to participate in play activities, many involving art media, as a way of "understanding children by repeating childhood behavior." (Smart, 1970, p. 14) The emphasis is on the experiential or process aspects of the adults' play with art media and other modalities. The activities are conceived of "as a bridge to the essential re-experiencing. It was important that the parents should experience again the way they themselves felt as children, and in this manner discover an easier, more direct access to their own children." (Brocher, 1971, p. 1)

With the conviction that "the peer group of parents is other parents," (Smart, 1970, p. 15) Brocher and his colleagues devised a curriculum centered around play, in which a series of carefully selected activities were designed to stimulate feelings and fantasies from infancy, childhood, and adolescence, based on current psychoanalytic theory (Erikson, 1959). Following participation in the play activities, parents share feelings and memories in group discussions, relating the here-and-now experience of the play to the there-and-then feelings of their own childhood, and then to the current rearing of their own children. Through the direct experience of the play, and in "giving expression to the thoughts that arise along with the play," (Brocher, 1971, p. 4) parents are led to contribute to their own and each other's experience, to consider the past and its connections to the present.

Inspired by Dr. Brocher, who worked in Pittsburgh for several years, a movement and drama therapist and I developed our own activities for each developmental level, and worked with both parents and group leaders in a training context, using the parent play model (Rubin, Irwin, and Bernstein, 1975). The following are sample activities we developed for successive developmental phases.

Examples of Activities for Successive Developmental Phases

I. *Infant: Core Issues*

Trust vs. Mistrust, Sensori-motor Exploration, Differentiation of Self and Non-Self, Primacy of Oral Zone.

A. *BODY AWARENESS.* With participants on the floor, eyes closed in a darkened room, the leader speaks softly. At first, verbal suggestions may encourage relaxation of body boundaries, symbolically simulating the primary nondifferentiated relationship with the environment. Eventually, attention is called successively to different body parts and their relationships, and to environmental stimuli (sound, temperature, shadows, etc.)

B. *SENSORY AWARENESS.* Seated in a circle, the lights still dimmed with soft flowing music and no verbalization, the participants are given by the leaders a series of items of different shapes and textures (cloth, sponge, fur, paper, steel wool) and encouraged to explore these thoroughly. As with tactile awareness, other senses are stimulated in a similar way, with participants being given items of different smells (cotton saturated with various odors), and of different tastes and colors (fruit, candies, cheeses, drinks). These are all passively received by the participants, "fed" by the leaders.

C. *ORAL SENSATIONS. 1. SUCKING.* Activities involving oral-incor-porative sensations, such as sucking a lifesaver, drinking sweet liquids through straws of various widths (necessitating more or less effort), holding sweet objects in the mouth; and holding on to soft, warm cuddly objects like pillows or blankets. *2. BITING.* Activities involving oral-sadistic or aggressive actions, such as biting, chewing, spitting (gum, chewy candy, licorice), and bobbing for apples; blowing bubbles of gum or soap, and blowing thin paint, using a straw or the mouth to direct the liquid on smooth, glossy paper (Fig. 18-7).

Fig. 18-7. An adult blowing soap bubbles in a parent play group.

D. *INTERACTION WITH ANOTHER.* Participants are guided in dyadic movement activities with both individuals seated back to back, mirroring each other's patterns, so that there is no leader or follower, and the movement is felt as originating from a symbiotic fusion. Similarly, one person may gently rock another, trying to get into that other's rhythm. Individuals are asked to feed each other toward the end of the sensory-awareness activities, and typically become involved in playful interactions around various stimuli, especially tactile ones. Bobbing for apples may become competitive. Another useful biting game is to have two participants chew from either end of a licorice string to see who can get to the lifesaver in the middle first.

II. *Toddler: Core Issues*
Impulse Control, Autonomy, Ambivalent Power Struggle with Mother, Indepen-dence/Dependence, Control of Locomotion.

A. *UNSTRUCTURED MEDIA-PLAY.* Participants are encouraged to play with such fluid media as fingerpaint (on trays, paper, and walls, often used spontaneously as makeup on faces). They also play with sand (with and without water), and various plastic modelling materials: homemade play dough, water-base clay, plasticene, etc. In addition, wearing plastic smocks they are encouraged to play with water, filling, emptying, mixing, pouring, sailing toys—and more aggressively with water pistols, balloons, and targets.

B. *LETTING GO vs. HOLDING ON.* Participants are directed to engage in activities involving seizing and releasing, such as a tug of war with a rope or a piece of elastic cloth; or the towel game, in which one partner has the towel, teases the other with it, and the objective is to try and get it away from the other.

C. *ASSERTION-OF-SELF GAMES.* One participant is the child, the other the parent; the parent tries to get the child to do something (go to bed, put toys away, eat) while the toddler stubbornly says a foot-stamping, loud-shouting "NO!"

III. *Preschooler: Core Issues*
Curiosity, Inclusion/Exclusion, Rivalry and Competition, Intense Fantasy Play, Concern about Retaliation and Punishment, Sex-Role Identification.

A. *INCLUSION/EXCLUSION.* This element is present in a game where one member "fights," pushing and shoving to get into a circle of the others, who cling together and try to keep him out. A triad may also be emphasized, in a role play where two people are engaged in doing something together, while the third tries to join the activity.

B. *CONSTRUCTIVE PLAY.* Building or constructing with wood scraps and glue (three-dimensional) or collage (two-dimensional); and using construction toys like blocks, Tinkertoys, Lincoln Logs, etc. They also may use tools with wood and nails, engaging in sawing, hammering, etc.

C. *FANTASY PLAY.* Individually, participants may construct miniature worlds or microcosmic symbolizations of reality, which they then play on and in using miniature life toys. In pairs or small groups they may use or make puppets, or engage in dramatic play, using "dressups" and props to act out a spontaneous drama.

D. *ACTIVE COORDINATED MOVEMENT PLAY.* Participants are encouraged to play movement games, involving leaping or jumping (as in jump rope), or invoking ballistic patterns of a masculine nature (any competitive sport), or more feminine undulating, ballet-like movements.

IV. *School-age Child: Core Issues*
Competence, Mastery and Learning, Peer Group Interaction and Acceptance, Same-Sex Groups, Development of Rules and Standards.

A. *CREATIVE ACTIVITIES INVOLVING SKILLS.* Participants are asked to practice with a new tool, medium, or process, to experience mastery; emphasis is on doing it well (e.g., drawing, painting, or sculpting) or making something useful (e.g., weaving, printing, large-scale building, sewing, etc.)

B. *PEER GROUP INTERACTION.*   Males and females can work separately in same-sex groups at any of the above tasks, or can use found materials to build clubhouse or hideway environments. Males and females can each prepare for and stage a "birthday party," deciding on the games, refreshments, favors, etc.

C. *GAMES WITH RULES.*   Participants may engage individually or in groups in games of skill (darts, jacks, marbles, hopscotch), chance (board games, card games, dice games), and competition (games with teams, and choosing sides like tag, red rover). It may stimulate participants to be asked to use structured pieces of paper, plastic, etc. to make up a game with rules in small groups, to play it, then to write a description of it so others can try it out.

V. *Adolescent: Core Issues*

Revival of Oedipal Wishes, Dependence/Independence, Autonomy and Control, Concern for Privacy, Future and Work Choice, Sex-Role Orientation Established, Interest in Identity in General: Self-Consciousness, Self-Definition, Self-Esteem.

A. *PRIVACY & CONTROL.*   In a Discovery Game two people role-play a situation in which the "parent" makes a symbol (or pretends to have one) for something found in the young person's room which causes concern; both then play out the discovery and confrontation. Participants take both roles in turn and discuss the transaction.

B. *TRIADIC POWER GAME.*   In a Boss-Slave game, one parent of a mother-father-teenager triad "bosses" the teenager in a task (usually making or doing something) while the other parent observes and intervenes or not as he wishes. Roles are changed so that all can experience bossing and being bossed. A similar role-play can occur around planning a floor model of a new house together with the same triad, focusing on the adolescent's room and planning for it.

C. *IDENTITY ISSUES.*   Participants may be asked to draw, write, or role-play around such themes as "Who I Am Now," "What I Like and Dislike in Me," "How I Want to be Five Years from Now," "The Ideal Mate for Me," etc. Poetry may be a useful medium here, and the issue of "finding one's preferred modality" may be used as an example of discovering and defining individuality.

Parent play groups, like art therapy groups, can be conducted in many ways, for differing time periods, with different numbers of participants, and various configurations of leaders and meeting times. In our work, we most often combined play and discussion in one session of two hours, though they can also occur at alternate meetings. One can follow a normal developmental sequence (most appropriate if training leaders or teaching child development). One can begin where the group seems most comfortable, or at the age level of most of their children, and move in either direction depending on what occurs over time. As with any other group, it is vital to maximize comfort and minimize stress. Sometimes a brief discussion and explanation of the meaning and purpose of the activity, helps those who need "permission" to regress and to play. It also seems to help to suggest that people "let go" and become as involved as they can, but keep an "observing ego" watching what goes on in themselves as they play, so they can discuss it later.

As with other groups, leaders may play multiple roles, as observers, coplayers, protagonists, and role-models, teaching others how to play. At times, there may be a need for reassurance and support, and at others, a leader may need to serve as a teacher or as a symbolic "good parent." On occasion, the group may request the leader to act as an authoritative parent and to "control" the bad children, especially if play with regressive media (like fingerpaint or water) gets out of hand. Such wishes become "grist for the mill" in the group discussion which follows the play. Karen, for example, became frightened during water play and said to the leader, "Don't you think you ought to stop them?" In the discussion afterward, she acknowledged that she was angry with the leader for "not stopping the play, because someone might have gotten hurt." Such thoughts led to her childhood, where her mother, an anxious woman, did not allow the children to play or jump because they might get hurt. With some awareness, she then spoke of her own overprotectiveness toward her two latency-age children.

During the discussion phase, as with any activity-discussion art group, leaders act as facilitators, trying to help all participants to be involved. It is important to keep the discussion centered on the shared group themes, and to clarify if necessary the comments of the participants. It is often essential to help people to make sense of the experience, in that way to gain control over it, and to perceive and use it as an opportunity for learning through play.

The emphasis in the parent school approach is on the recall of childhood memories and feelings stimulated by the creative experience. While the qualitative and symbolic aspects of the art activities still exist, the focus in both doing and discussing is on process rather than product. Instead, one looks at the totality of the experience, especially its connection to the childhood past and parental present of the adult group member. Even in more orthodox approaches to art therapy or parent mental health education through art, one may always choose whether to focus on process or product, form or content, conscious or unconscious dynamics.

In these groups, participants learn about child development, and they learn about themselves—their impulses, fantasies, feelings, ideas, and wishes. They also learn something about media and the use of materials with children, the facilitation of play, and the pleasures of creative experiences. Often a parent discovers the fun of participation in one or more art forms, as a work-weary adult who does not care to become an expert, but who can still have an awfully good time, and feel much better, after "playing around" with clay, paint, on a drum, or in a drama. Many times a parent has spoken of the renewal felt following a creative play experience. Such renewal is one source of the strength of art in therapy and "growth" in all places— that it comes from a deep sense of being in touch with one's self, of exploring one's full potential for becoming a creative person, as well as a better parent. Perhaps the poet was right, after all, when he said "Man is human only when he plays." (Schiller, 1875)

PART V:

GENERAL ISSUES

CHAPTER 19.

Why and How the Art Therapist Helps

Central to understanding and helping children and their families through art is an assumption, a conviction, that "every person is, by nature, a potentially creative being." (Moustakas, 1969, p. 1) Though not yet actualized, such a spark is assumed to be present, and able to blossom if nurtured, even if long dormant. I believe too that all human beings have within them a natural tendency toward growth, toward actualizing that creative potential at increasingly mature levels. And I feel equally certain that each individual is likely to have some preferred media, modalities, and themes, which must be discovered or even invented, in order for that person to fulfill his promise.

I assume that all humans have an inner desire to create form in some way. The impulse to touch, to make contact, to manipulate, and to make marks is evident in the sand play of the toddler. It is also present when a child is irresistibly drawn by the seductive power of moist clay, glowing tempera paints, or a brand new box of crayons. Even apes and chimpanzees take naturally to art media; and when a hungry ape prefers finishing a painting to eating his dinner, one must wonder whether such an activity could not be a fairly basic, perhaps universal, impulse or need (Morris, 1962). The philosopher, Martin Buber, feels that there is "an autonomous instinct, which cannot be derived from others, whose appropriate name seems to . . . be the 'originator instinct.' Man, the child of man, wants to make things. He does not merely find pleasure in seeing a form arise from material that presented itself as formless. What a child desires is its own share in this becoming of things. . . . What is important is that by one's own intensively experienced action something arises that was not there before." (1965, p. 85) Freud said that a healthy man is able to love and to work; Erikson has suggested that he also needs to be able to play. If play and art can include each other, and I think they do, then the creation of one's self through art is not only a right and a possibility for all children—it may

267

even represent a need which, if unfulfilled, leaves a kind of deprivation all the more insidious, as its effects are not easily visible.

Perhaps the need to make one's mark through creative endeavor stems from a simple sensory response to attractive materials, from a primitive desire to give form to that which is formless, or to interact with a manipulable environment. Perhaps, too, it comes from a more complex psychic need to reconcile, to integrate, to give order and balance to one's experience. Man is uneasy when things do not fit, make sense, or rest comfortably. In the effort to re-establish an optimal level of comfort, it is necessary to reduce cognitive and affective "dissonance" and conflict. There appear to be strong inner pressures toward both constructive and destructive acts, seen in responses to art media, as well as elsewhere. In order for progressive and integrative tendencies to gain ascendance, internal conflict must be reduced. Energy can then be free, both to express and to control that expression aesthetically.

The stimulus for unrest may come from inside, outside, or some combination of the two. The child may feel a need to make sense out of feelings, fantasies, and thoughts from within, as well as to sort and map out the confusing reality without. And it is then still necessary to both integrate and separate the two, in order to be free to grow, in touch with both. Here is where art can be so helpful, for as Ulman so eloquently says, it is "the meeting ground of the inner and outer world." (1971, p. 93) "Its motive power comes from within the personality; it is a way of bringing order out of chaos—chaotic feelings and impulses within, the bewildering mass of impressions from without. It is a means to discover both the self and the world, and to establish a relation between the two. In the complete creative process, inner and outer realities are fused into a new entity." (Ulman, 1961, p. 20)

The Creative Process as a Learning Experience

In art, even a child may have what Maslow calls a "peak experience" (1959), or may feel a sense of heightened awareness and aliveness, what Ulman calls "a momentary sample of living at its best." (1971, p. 93) Through art, a youngster may experience not only the momentary release of tension through a discharge of surplus energy, but the release of unconflicted energy, newly available for constructive use, through the sublimation and resolution of conflicts once draining his resources. Through art, a process in which one is in touch with all levels of consciousness (Kubie, 1958), and with external stimuli, one's level of awareness may be enlarged, expanded, deepened, and sharpened. "This openness to experience may itself be experienced: first, as a mood; secondly, as understanding; and thirdly, as expression." (Kaelin, 1966, p. 8)

During a creative activity there are times to stop and look, in the middle as well as at the end, and times to reflect upon and think about the experience of the process as well as the product. This reflective mode is as much a part of a total creative process as immersion in doing, and a good art experience—at home, in school, or at a clinic—partakes of both. In learning to be involved as well as to step back, to do as well as to think, a child learns to make use of his energies in a way that enables him to create formed aesthetic statements.

A child can, in art, develop autonomy and independence, taking responsibility for both process and product. He can learn to choose, to make, to act, to revise decisions, to appraise and evaluate, and to learn from past experiences. In art a child can experiment symbolically, may try out in both process and product feelings and ideas which may eventually become possible in reality. He can manipulate media which do not talk back, enabling him to experience a kind of power and mastery at no risk. He can master tools and processes, and can feel competent. He can learn to accept his regressive/aggressive symbolic self, and can come to value his creative/productive self, leading to a deep feeling of self-worth. He can discover, develop, and define his uniqueness, creating in and through his art a sense of himself as special. He can experience the pleasure of an aesthetically fine product, the joy of sharing it with a loved one, the pride in the affirmation of another.

Gendlin has said that "Feeling without symbolization is blind; symbolization without feeling is empty." (1962, p. 5)* The artistic symbol is a way for a child to communicate to himself and others about vague, nonverbal, essentially ineffable feeling experiences. It is important to remember that "It makes no basic difference whether a child, or an adult artist paints circles and triangles or animals and trees. Both methods represent the inner world and the outer world, and neither psychology nor art separates the two." (Arnheim, 1967, p. 341) The awareness of what has been expressed may not and need not be translated into words, often remaining at the level of perceptual-emotional impact; and there are times when it seems that "knowing for one's self on the perceptual level is the most valid kind of knowing." (Rhyne, 1971, p. 274)

In a nonlinguistic fashion, it is the peculiar power of art to be able to symbolize not only intrapsychic events, but interpersonal ones as well, and to collapse multileveled or sequential happenings into a single visual statement. The artistic symbol is a condensation, a carrier of many meanings, and by its very nature able to integrate apparent polarities—like reality and fantasy, conscious and unconscious, order and chaos, ideation and affect. There is much experiential evidence in art therapy that the giving of form to complex feeling is in itself helpful. Perhaps this is true because it enables the creator to feel some control over the confusion, as Frankl suggests: "Emotion, which is suffering, ceases to be suffering as soon as we form a clear and precise picture of it." (1959, p. 117)

Throughout these values in the art experience runs a thread called "person," the individual whose energy, potential, exploration, expression, mastery, autonomy, release, awareness, acceptance, liking, pleasure, and growth are both cause and outcome of all the rest. I believe there is a false dilemma in the dichotomy of process vs. product. For me, it is always "person" that matters most, without whom there

---

*Based on Kant, who said, "Ideas without facts are empty; facts without ideas are blind." (Kramer, 1983)

could be neither process nor product, nor art itself. Thus, the values in art for me are human values, which is probably why I went from art history and the impersonal iconography of the museum to art education and the life of the classroom, to art therapy and the challenge of unblocking people stuck, detoured, or constricted in their growing. Thus, it is not "art for art's sake" nor "art for the sake of therapy," but "art for the sake of the person" which makes the only human(e) sense to me, whatever the context.

The Art Therapist as a Real Person and a Symbolic Other

Perhaps one of the ways in which art therapy differs from art in other contexts is the importance of the relationship between the therapist and client(s). For creating art within a therapeutic relationship is different from drawing by yourself or working in a class. It is a kind of special protected situation, where one person creates an environment, physical and psychological, in which one or more others can fully explore, expand, and understand themselves through art. In this relationship, the child voluntarily exposes himself to another, and learns to look with that other person at his creative statements and at himself. Often there are few or no words, yet the being together and sharing of both process and product offer protection, validity, even permanence, to the event, which could otherwise be so vulnerable, so fragile.

While the art therapist in his encounter with a child is in many ways a very real person, there are symbolic aspects of the role which are important, especially in clinical settings. In one sense, these refer to the distorted symbolic ways—the transference—in which the relationship is experienced by the client(s). In another sense, they refer to the particular activities of the art therapist, which themselves carry symbolic meanings. The two are related, for the behaviors of the art therapist inevitably influence the kind of transference which develops, as well as its understanding and use as a vehicle for change.

The concept of transference is a useful one for an art therapist to know, and is quite congenial, for it is simply an extension to the human sphere of what is already suspected about the meaning of artistic symbols. That a color or theme can stand for something to an individual in terms of his past experience, is not so different from the notion that people project similar meaning and feeling ideas onto other people. In general, human beings always have a need to make sense out of the stimuli with which they are presented, and the unknown of a new person must be "filled in" mentally, like a visual gestalt. We all tend to perceive new people on the basis of past experience with similar others, and to color that perception affectively, in terms of unresolved wishes and conflicts.

In therapy, we can make good use of that human tendency to distort what is perceived in terms of what is inside. In many ways, the conditions which facilitate transference perceptions, are not unlike those which foster the emergence of meaningful material in art. In the latter, we present primarily unstructured media in a free situation, allowing the individual to find and express his own images. Similarly, the therapist can present himself in a relatively neutral fashion, so that the individual can project upon him feelings and ideas related to still-active inner conflicts. The neutrality and nonjudgmental attitude of the therapist thus allow the child to project onto the adult feelings and fantasies, in the same way that he projects onto the material his inner world.

Such distortions in perception become evident over time, as the child responds in a way that is out of proportion or in some way inappropriate to the stimulus, suggesting that he has colored his view of the therapist on the basis of inner issues. While the particular meaning of a particular distorted perception may not be immediately clear, any more that one can at first be sure of the meanings of a symbol, one can first identify, and then explore such apparently unreasonable reactions. Sometimes they are in relation to the art process or product, such as concern over the therapist's anger because of the messiness of a fingerpainting, or an expectation that the therapist will be critical of a drawing. At other times they relate primarily to the relationship, as when Barry asked after two months of therapy "Do you think about me all the time when I'm not here?" or assumed that when he didn't come to the clinic, I didn't either. Such thoughts as these conveyed his wish to be the therapist's "only child," not surprising in a boy from a family with five children and much sibling rivalry.

But the art therapist is not and cannot be totally neutral. The role demands certain behaviors on his part which themselves carry symbolic meaning, and tend to influence the transference. For example, in giving the child materials and supplies, the art therapist is a "feeder," the food sometimes being experienced as good and sometimes as "not enough" or "not quite right." On the other hand, in offering messy materials in a permissive setting, the art therapist may be felt as a "seducer," inviting the child to engage in potentially "bad" forbidden experiences. In expecting the child to think for himself, the art therapist may be seen as "asking too much," while in limiting destructive uses of media, he may be felt as mean and restrictive. In his expectation that the child use the materials, and in the implicit request for a product, the art therapist may be felt as "too demanding." In his looking-at function, he may be experienced as "exposing" the child, or perhaps encouraging excessive "voyeurism." In asking questions, the art therapist is often felt as an intrusive "prober," and is sometimes seen as a "judge" of what is produced. When the art therapist teaches a child about a medium or process, he may be experienced as "giving," or, conversely, as "getting in the way." In all of these functions, the art therapist is responded to by the child in ways reflective both of the roles and of the child's reactions to them.

Children often reflect transference reactions in art therapy through their behavior with the materials. Sometimes they refuse to use them at all, as when angry in a withholding way; and sometimes they will show their anger at the adult by using media in a destructive, aggressive, or regressive manner. At other times, that same anger may be reflected more directly by making a parent or authority figure in clay and chopping him up. With even less disguise and more control, it may be revealed in a funny or ugly picture of the therapist (Fig. 19-1). Conversely, the therapist may be represented directly or symbolically as omniscient, omnipotent, or all-giving; and the treatment itself may be represented—perhaps as a prison when the child is feeling "caught" or as a game when the child is feeling "free." What is important is to be alert to the symbolic meanings of the therapist, the relationship, and the treatment as these evolve over time, using them as a way of understanding how the child perceives and copes with his feelings (cf. Rubin, 1982b).

Because the art therapist is also an artist, there are some peculiar risks for him in the symbolic aspects of the transaction. He must be careful, for example, not to overvalue the production of multiple or skilled products for their own sake, always trying to tune in to what they mean to his client. He must be careful, too, that his own

Fig. 19-1. An ugly picture of the art therapist during a period of angry feelings.

media, content or style preferences do not subtly interfere with his appreciation and facilitation of an individual's mode of expression. If he has needs to control, he may unwittingly influence what a child uses, or may find reasons to impose tasks or methods more often than is really necessary. If he has needs to give, he may do more "feeding" or "teaching" or even "doing for" a child than is helpful to that child's developing autonomy. If he is especially curious, he may inadvertantly pressure a child with more direct questions than the child can handle, perhaps precipitating withdrawal. What matters here, is to be as tuned in to one's own inner life as to the child's, so that the therapist's conflicts do not get in the way of the child's treatment.

In order to be maximally helpful, the art therapist should combine in one person the virtues of both artist and therapist, of creator and facilitator. These two roles and perspectives are not so opposed or different as they may seem. Both artists and psychologists, for example, are concerned with making sense out of the human experience (diagnosis), as well as with uplifting the souls of men (therapy). Both reach for contact with unseen forces, and seek an understanding and articulation of them. Sandor Lorand, a psychoanalyst, wrote of the artist: "He seems to combine psychoanalytic knowledge with artistic intuition of the way in which the human emotions work. . . . He seems to have been led by an insight of his own, and the results are an inspired accomplishment." (1967, p. 24) The artist, like the psychologist, affirms "the validity of the inner view," (Shahn, 1960, p. 50), but differentiates their perspectives, as did Ben Shahn, the painter: "So while I accept the vast inner landscape that extends off the boundaries of consciousness to be almost infinitely fruitful of images and symbols, I know that such images mean one thing to the psychologist and quite another to the artist." (1960, p. 51) The art therapist—artist, educator, and clinician (Kramer, 1971)—hopefully has made peace with those differences, indeed finds them complementary.

In that sense, the art therapist combines both an intuitive, inspired approach with a rational analytic one, alternating and integrating them in tune with the needs of the situation. An art therapist's comfort with both words and images, enhances the possibility of helping people to use both for expression (and translation, where possible). I think an art therapist's comfort with both free association and discipline, with passive and active modes, and with looking as well as making serves to broaden the range of possible communication for those with whom he works. Thus, he can be most creative, free to use his resources most imaginatively, because he has access to different modes of thinking, including different ways of thinking about art. There are moments when words can get in the way, and there are moments when words can create relief, order, or calm. The important thing is to be able to sense and to choose.

Whether diagnostician or therapist, teacher or group leader, collaborator or supervisor, consultant or public educator, artist or researcher, the art therapist tries to use what he understands and feels about people and art to help others to grow. Whether the goal is growth in an individual, a family, a group, a classroom, an institution, or a community, there are certain general steps in the process of being a change-agent which seem to me common to all. In the challenge of finding ways to utilize the strengths and capacities of the individual, family, or institution for growth, it is first necessary to know how the person or system with which one is dealing functions, in general and in particular. Thus, in work with individuals, developmental and intrapsychic phenomena are part of one's frame of reference; while in work with groups or institutions, group and systems phenomena are necessary for understanding the particular situation.

The history and peculiarities of the particular person, family, or community are also important to know, for only then can one begin to analyze how it is and what it can become. With a child it is essential to first discover who he is, and where he is, and where he seems to want to go, and then to try to understand what is getting in his way and how to help him to get there. So it makes sense to start not only in therapy, but also in teaching and consultation, by observing, listening, and trying to learn as much as one can about the particular person, group, or place at hand.

Then, in collaboration with that person, place, or group, it is possible to begin to formulate goals, to create a "design" for change, using one's perspective of the situation and understanding of the background. Having set general objectives, it is then possible to think about what might be done to reach them, what artistic and human events might be likely to help a child to get better or a school to develop a more therapeutic art program. As the work progresses, it is important to be open, for no curriculum for change can be tightly-planned, or can take into account the organic, uneven, and unexpected nature of growth.

At various points, it may be necessary to step back and assess where one is, perhaps to refine or revise goals, perhaps to test certain assumptions. And when it seems that the individual, family, or institution is ready to go on functioning independently, then it is necessary to start planning and working toward termination of the formal contract, working through the feelings—as well as working out the facts—of that event. At the end, one says goodbye, one lets go; one might even engage in a review and critique, and perhaps a pictorial or printed publication or "display" of what has been accomplished, always with the permission of those involved.

Extending Opportunities in the Community: Art Therapy Consultation

If one is convinced of the therapeutic importance of art for children and families, one may also be able to influence others toward facilitating such experiences. Art therapy is in a peculiarly favorable position as a base for mental health consultation. This is especially true when the agency requesting help is not a clinical one, but is instead educational, recreational, or custodial. A school, a community center, or an institution for retardates will already have or can easily envision activities in art. If an art program doesn't exist full-blown, chances are its seeds are there, if only in the form of an occasional box of crayons, and a stack of old (perish the thought!) coloring books. Many institutions see a therapeutic art program as somehow more in keeping with their goals than a regular one, perhaps because the institution serves a handicapped or deviant population, or a normal population under conditions of exceptional stress. While I believe that the values implicit in a program determine its therapeutic nature, not the population served, it is still true that the two are often confused.

In any case, the art therapist can use art as a *wedge* to open many doors commonly closed to mental health consultants, or open only under narrow and limited conditions. Art can be a *bridge* to minds formerly fearful of and hostile to the "shrink." In this sense, art in consultation may be a *tool* analogous to its sometime-function in therapy; it may be a way of reaching and communicating with a resistant institution in a safe and mutually-meaningful way. In some cases, art serves to sugar-coat the bitter pill of emotional awareness, which may need later to be swallowed and eventually digested. In others, a taste of mental health thinking through art therapy, may help to develop a greater appetite for more information on the part of a previously resistant staff or administration. Through art, it is often possible to meet felt needs for program improvement, while establishing the kind of mutually respectful relationships that permit later ventures into new and potentially fearful territory. At the end of a year of programatically prolific consultation to an institution for handicapped children, for example, the agency was ready to consider a previously rejected proposal for a part-time art therapy effort, in addition to the existing art and craft programs. That institutions, like people, can be led to look at, understand, and cope with previously avoided issues is no great discovery. That art therapists are in a particularly good spot to use art as a wedge, a bridge, and a tool in such cases is now quite apparent to me, and no doubt to others doing similar work.

The peculiar hybrid identity of the art therapist, as artist and mental health worker, is perhaps part of his potential effectiveness. For, just as in therapy or teaching or supervision, in consultation too he can use himself in any number of possible ways. I would submit that he is best-equipped to use himself with maximal flexibility when his understanding of mental health concepts is as deep and rich as his feeling for art. For consultation requires the same interpersonal sensitivities and skills as any helping relationship; from the first contact through the final leave-taking, one must explore in a fashion that is both careful and caring what is asked, wished, and even feared. Then, if one is open to different possibilities, one may use oneself to help the institution, program, or individual to grow in a natural and organic fashion.

An art therapy consultant may serve as a resource for practical information, such as appropriate materials, supplies, and equipment, and where to get them and how to use them once secured. An art therapy consultant may also serve as a resource for other kinds of information, such as relevant readings, similar arts programs, opportunities for training, etc. If the information requested is conceptual, it is vital to find ways of getting it across which are neither beyond nor beneath the learning capacities of the people wanting to know. Sometimes minimal input can achieve maximal results, especially when those asking for help need only a small amount of information, guidance, or permission, in order to build on already existing strengths.

An art therapy consultant may find it useful to show or to demonstrate, modeling behaviors which might be misunderstood or hard to visualize if conveyed only verbally. Conducting preprogram art evaluations at various schools has served not only to help me know the children's potential, but also to expose the observing staff members to a radically new child-centered way of working with youngsters in art. In order to help staff members to function in this different way, it may be necessary not only to meet with them and hear from them about their work, but also on occasion to observe what they do or to work alongside them.

Helping people and places to grow in providing healthy art experiences for children is an exciting and challenging task. The particular form a consultant's activities take may change even in the course of one contact, and will almost certainly vary over time. During a year of consultation to an institution for physically handicapped children, my activities included ordering supplies, arranging equipment, organizing schedules, training staff members, meeting and negotiating with administrators, and, even over that brief period of time, seeing the organic development of a therapeutic art program. What began with one art classroom grew into an additional full-time craft program, a part-time roving art teacher for bed-ridden children, and an elaborate series of bulletin boards and display cases for the children's products. Less visible developments were the changed attitudes of the staff towards the children's creative capacities, and the therapeutic values of art.

Sometimes I have had the pleasure of remaining in contact with an agency over a long period of time, as with The Western Pennsylvania School for Blind Children, where I have participated in its struggles to grow, seeing many spinoffs and developments from an initial input. A twelve-week after-school exploratory art program led to a six-week summer art-and-drama program for children and parents, and ongoing mothers' groups. Eventually I trained mothers to lead the groups; and then there was a part-time, and later a full-time arts specialist, who worked with both children and staff in ongoing program development. My consulting role varied over the years, and included work with the children, the parents, the staff, and the administration. What has developed in the school is a bigger and more secure place for the arts, as well as a deeper unerstanding of the children's needs to express and to deal with their feelings in creative ways. What has also developed is a wiser me, enriched as much by contacts with institutions as by those with individuals or groups.

CHAPTER 20.

How the Art Therapist
Learns through Research

In all of the experiences described in this book, the patients and the institutions are not the only ones who grow and change. Such work is infinitely complex, and I find quite consistently that the more I do and learn, the more I become aware of how much I do not know. Then I develop a further motivation to learn some more, which sometimes leads to the kind of systematic assessment known as "research." Earlier chapters have dealt with assessment through art for individuals and families. The precise form taken by the evaluative procedure and analysis of the data depends on many variables, primarily the particular questions being asked. A worker must therefore be clear about goals, before it is possible to decide intelligently how to reach them. This reasoning applies to helping as well as to understanding, to treatment as well as to diagnosis, to service as well as to research.

For many years, those who worked in the arts were hostile to research, in large part because they knew that some things important to them were not easily quantifiable, measurable, or even visible. A leader in art education research recently turned from an approach emphasizing quantification and statistical analysis, to one valuing subjective, introspective reports of internal processes (Beittel, 1973). The question, however, is not an either/or one, any more than it is ever an issue of process vs. product or affect vs. cognition. All are false dichotomies. What matters is to formulate one's questions and to explore ways of asking and answering them, settling finally on an approach which seems best fitted to the problem in an authentic and practical way.

It is possible to create a situation for purposes of assessment with varying degrees of structure, utilizing all of the options at hand—space, time, media, theme, and manner of work. For example, one might offer a child a choice from among two or more alternatives, suggest a selection from among a class of materials, or specify use of a particular medium. The theme may be left open, as in the individual art interview, or may be more or less specific, like representing the family in the family art evaluation. The manner in which the task is to be performed may be left open or specified, so that the drawing may be timed (as in a one-minute gesture drawing), or the person may be required to work with someone else, possibly in a specific way (as in a nonverbal dyadic drawing).

How one then looks at the behaviors and/or products which emerge, also depends on the purpose of the assessment. For example, with a family mural, one might focus either on the family's decision-making behavior, the cohesion of the finished product, or the underlying themes therein. I think of research, assessment, evaluation, and diagnosis quite broadly, as slightly different semantic ways of expressing systematic attempts to understand. Sometimes we are most interested in comprehending a child and his developmental level, sometimes a child and his problems, and sometimes a child within his family. It is not only useful to think of alternative ways of eliciting particular behaviors about which one is concerned, but also to explore different means of noting and assessing them as objectively as possible.

It is important to remember that research can be more or less formal. It is fascinating, once one has decided just what it is one wishes to investigate, to create situations or to look at available data in terms of a particular question. Sometimes an informal examination lessens the motivation for systematic study; at other times, hypotheses get refined for more formal investigations. Because some degree of objectivity in describing behaviors or products is central to all assessment and research, I shall begin by describing ways of helping people to become more accurate and more empathic observers.

Objective Observation

In order to help teachers and therapists-in-training to sharpen their art process observation skills, so vital to accurate assessment, I have found it useful to print up an *Observation Guide*, adapted from specific suggestions in the literature (Hartley et. al., 1952, pp. 346–350). The value of such a Guide, I think, is that it serves to alert the neophyte to behaviors involved in the art-making process, and to the kinds of things about each behavior which may be noted through careful observation. It serves both to define and focus what might otherwise be a kind of confused, chaotic looking, determined as much by the observer's past and present experiences as by what is being observed. The items on the Guide include: the child's approach to the material, degree of absorption, energy expended, manipulative action, attitude toward the material, tempo of work, body movements, verbalization, and development or change apparent over time. There are also some additional suggestions for observing specific activities, examples of the kind of detailed, in-depth observation possible with particular media.

It is also useful to involve learners in workshop experiences which help to sensitize them to watching others. I recently led a workshop for a dozen teachers and aides in a special school with such a goal. First, people paired up and used art materials for an active watching "mirroring" exercise, like that described in Chapter 13. Next, they took turns "playing" with their partners and observing other teams at play with a variety of available materials. The observers and players then compared notes on what they had seen or felt, and were surprised to discover that they were having difficulty separating what was seen from what was inferred. The opportunity to look with others at differing perceptions and interpretations of the same observed event, was one of the many useful outcomes of this shared learning experience.

Subjective Clinical Assessments

While guides help one to focus one's viewing, there are many times when observations meant for assessment must, given the conditions under which they may be obtained, be quite global and subjective. In a follow-up study at the Center of a group of toddlers with schizophrenic mothers, we decided to observe and to keep samples of art work produced spontaneously in a play group situation. There was no attempt to systematically control what was presented or how, since the activity was going on in the context of an essentially free, unstructured play environment. Nevertheless, it was possible for me to attend the first and last of six group meetings, to make detailed observations of each child (usually by sitting next to him when he was involved with art media), and to look at the first and last week's art behaviors of the children. It was possible, for example, to note in the final session "a large and observable difference" in one girl's behavior, "in general being more expansive and freer than she had been during the first session," an impression gleaned from her art work, her behavior with materials, and her way of relating to me. Another child on the other hand, was observably "more focused" in her art work and behavior than had been true at the first session. While frankly impressionistic, such clinical observations at different points in time by the same individual can be useful adjuncts to other more quantifiable measures.

Grouping and Goal-Setting

Quite often the purpose of assessment is very pragmatic and practical, as with a recent project at a preschool for retarded children. A new "creative art and play room" was being set up, so it was necessary to decide how to group the children, and to set goals for work with individuals. The teacher and I therefore devised an evaluation interview, which consisted of a series of tasks in each of the creative play modalities available in the room (drawing, painting, modelling, block construction, sand play, miniature life toys, dramatic play). Though one task was specified ("draw a person"), the rest were simply presentations to the child of the equipment, along with a request that he play with it. If a child was unable to begin independently or with verbal stimulation, he was briefly shown by the teacher how the materials might be used, after which most of the children were able to proceed.

The teacher who conducted these individual interviews, began to get a sense of the range of behaviors among the thirty children at the school, and by noting them briefly on a recording form, learned how to observe each activity. The products or play in each area were then ranked according to rough developmental norms (Fig. 20-1), and the quality of the child's play was also assessed in terms of issues like independence and spontaneity. From these evaluations it was then possible not only to group the children, but also to map out preliminary goals for each child, which would be met not by prescription, but by selectively reinforcing those more advanced and more healthy behaviors desired.

In an exploratory art program, blind children were also first interviewed individually, in order to be able to group them most effectively. Because of their disability, they were presented with a wide range of sensory stimuli, such as foods (taste, smell), musical instruments (hearing), and objects of different sizes, textures, and consistencies (touch). When giving them a choice of art media, it was necessary to verbalize the options available, which included wood scraps and glue, clay, fingerpaint, and drawing tools.

Two observers were given a twenty-four-item nine-point rating scale, in order to note where each child was on each of the behavioral dimensions which seemed most relevant for grouping. These included items descriptive of their overall behavior, such as passive/active, tense/relaxed, distractible/involved, and de-pressed/alert. Other items referred to the nature of their interaction with the adult, such as dependent/independent, suspicious/trusting, and withdrawn/outgoing. Still others related to their use of the materials, such as awkward/coordinated, impulsive/deliberate, stereotyped/original; and to their attitude toward their work, such as critical/pleased. Yet others related to the creativity of their thinking, such as barren/fluent, rigid/flexible. An average of the two observers' ratings on each dimension was used, though they agreed surprisingly often (close to ninety-percent of the time).

Following seven weeks of group art sessions, we were interested in seeing how and where individuals had changed, if at all, on these same dimensions. We therefore repeated the individual interviews with each child, and again used the mean of two observers' ratings on each dimension. Differences between pre- and post-program ratings were all in the desired direction, and were significant for the group of thirteen present both times on the following dimensions: independence, flexibility, relaxation, involvement, and originality. These more objective assessments were seen as supplementing our subjective sense of individual and group gains, and were especially meaningful since they supported each other. (Rubin and Klineman, 1974)

In the developmental scales used at the preschool for retarded children, the interest was primarily in *what* (descriptively) the child could do in each play area. In the behavioral scales used at the school for the blind the interest was primarily in *how* (qualitatively) the child reacted to the art media and the invitation to create. In a more recent study at the same school, described below, both existing and home-

Name _____   Date _____

	1.0–1.5	1.5–2.0	2.0–2.5	2.5–3.0	3.0–3.5	3.5–4.0	4.0–4.5	4.5–5.0	COMMENTS
Age In Years	1.0–1.5	1.5–2.0	2.0–2.5	2.5–3.0	3.0–3.5	3.5–4.0	4.0–4.5	4.5–5.0	
Age In Months	12–18	18–24	24–30	30–36	36–42	42–48	48–54	54–60	
DRAWING	Disordered Scribble	Swing Scribble	Circular Scribble	Figure-Ground and Vertical Line	Suggested Shaping	Definite Shapes	Primitive Figurative Representational	More Detailed Figures	
CLAY	Pinch Pound	Roll (Coils)	Making a Ball	Naming	Decorate Surface	Definite Labeled Shapes	Primitive Figures	Detailed Figures	
BLOCK PLAY	Carrying and Dumping	Rows	Towers	Bridging	Enclosures	Simple Labeled Constructions	Elaborate Labeled Constructions	Drama Around Block Play	
DRAMATIC PLAY	No Evidence of Dramatic Play	Solitary Dramatic Play	Elaborate Solitary Dramatic Play	Parallel Dramatic Play With Others	Dramatic Play With Others (Interaction)	Cooperative Dramatic Play With Others	Sustains Role Through the Play	Creates Roles and Stories in Dramatic Play Cooperatively	

Fig. 20-1. Chart for Assessment of Developmental Levels in Art and Play: Preschoolers.

made instruments were used to assess both developmental and affective issues, with particular focus on the areas thought to be most relevant and likely to change through the arts program.

Assessing Change in Blind Children

In a recent study done with Susan Aach, Creative Arts Specialist, at the same school for the blind, pre- and post-art program assessments of individuals were developed in order to evaluate possible changes during the school year in areas of particular interest, e.g., creativity, body-image representation, independence, and awareness of feelings. Since an existing instrument had already been used successfully with blind children (Halpin, Halpin and Torrance, 1973), three items from the *Torrance Creativity Tests* (Torrance, 1966) were administered, and scores of fluency, flexibility, and originality were used as a measure of verbal creative thinking. Since Witkin had reported successful use with the blind, a five-point body concept scale was also used, as a measure of articulation in the clay representation of the human figure (Witkin et. al., 1968).

It was necessary to create measures of both independence and feeling awareness, however, since none were known to exist or to be applicable to this population. Independence was measured inversely, in terms of the number of times during the making of the clay figure that the child asked the adult for assurance, ideas, or assistance. The number of "dependent" statements, so defined, became the child's score on this measure. In order to get at awareness of feelings, each child was asked to make up a story about the clay figure he had created, and his score was the number of "feeling words," like "happy," "angry," "sad," spontaneously utilized therein.

When the dozen children were tested at the end of the year, after having weekly group sessions in art, drama, movement, and music, changes on all measures were in the predicted direction. Only a few, however, reached a statistically significant level, among them one of the creativity measures (fluency on unusual uses of cardboard boxes, $p < .01$); and the independence measure ($p < .01$), with the change in the feeling awareness scores approaching significance ($p < .10$). While the body image scores improved, the five-point scale devised by Witkin proved not to be sufficiently sensitive to the fine differences apparent in the relatively primitive products of these young, multiply-handicapped blind children, and a more differentiated scale is therefore being developed.

Several years later, even less success was had using an existing instrument, the teacher's rating scale of a widely-used Self-Esteem Inventory (Coopersmith, 1967). In this attempt to assess change, teachers referring children for individual art therapy filled out the questionnaires before and after the intervention, most often at the beginning and end of the school year. Although their informal reports of growth in the youngsters had been rich, especially in the area of self-esteem, the items on the scale failed to reflect such change clearly or consistently. Indeed, the inherent difficulties of measuring such complex areas as creativity or self-esteem are formidable, and are further magnified by the associated problems of using instruments designed for the normal child on the handicapped youngster.

What is clear from this example is the need first, to define what it is one wants to assess, then to explore available instruments in terms of the particular situation or population involved, then to modify these or develop new ones if necessary, then to administer them under controlled conditions in order to be able to use such data as an index of the behaviors being studied. In the case of the blind populations described above, it was not possible to have a matched control group, since there were not enough of such multiply-handicapped children to make up such a sample, and because it was important that all such children have access to the arts program. In order to assess change at the end of the school year, therefore, the same children were retested, becoming their own "controls."

A Phenomenological Investigation

Many questions regarding children and art must be approached not only with an open mind, but also with an open kind of design which does not preclude valuable information. A recent study on the aesthetic responses of blind children was first conceptualized in terms of a series of choices among paired comparisons. After consultation with psychologist, Jack Matthews, Ph.D., familiar with work in experimental aesthetics, it was decided to include only two such tasks. First, I presented the blind, partially-sighted, and sighted judges with comparable three-dimensional art work created by all three populations, asking each child judge to select what he most liked and most disliked and to tell why. This procedure elicited a wealth of information, not only in terms of the specific choices made, but also in regard to all items noticed (touched and/or commented upon) by all of the judges. There was, in fact, quantitative support for the hypothesis that children would prefer art work done by someone like themselves, in regard to useful vision ($p < .05$).

What may have been a more important outcome, however, were the qualitative similarities and differences in the responses of the three groups of judges, useful clues to the basis for an equal but different aesthetic for the blind. Most of the children preferred sculptures with some degree of variety, as well as those with a sense of order. The visually-impaired were different from the sighted, however, in their need to label the objects as representational, as well as their lack of response to abstract elements in general. They also reacted more strongly to certain structural features, particularly projections (which they disliked), holes, and enclosures (which they usually liked). While the sighted judges tended to be fairly objective in their responses, the visually-impaired were more subjective, often relating things to themselves, and reacting with some anxiety to anything which might be perceived as dangerous or unstable. A blind girl preferred one sculpture to another, for example, "because it won't get knocked over as easy as this one. Things make me nervous that can fall over easily." What thus became apparent was not only that the blind have a different aesthetic, but that it is in some ways related to their experience of their handicap. (Rubin, 1976)

Self-Assessments of Art Products

Some questions, however, are fundamentally subjective ones, and can only be answered in that way. Such was the case with another sort of evaluative art interview, held with each of fifty children following a summer program in which every child had six weekly one-hour sessions of group art therapy. The format of these individual review sessions, was to lay out before the child all of the products he had made over the six-week period. He was then asked to react to his creations, at first in an open-ended fashion, then with more directed questions concerning most- and least-liked products, experiences, etc. This provided an opportunity not only for the child to assess himself, but also for the worker to judge what was recalled, repressed, valued, rejected, etc. from the short but intensive program.

Don reviewed the sequence of his art work, from its first compulsive beginnings in a design redone because at first it did not meet his standards (Fig. 13-3(a)). This ten-year-old boy looked at this as well as at all his other products, and finally chose as the favorite, his clay sculpture of "somebody" dead in a pool of blood (Fig. 13-3(b)). His production of this sculpture during the fourth session had represented a breakthrough and made possible insight into his intense rivalry with his younger brother (the symbolic victim). This insight enabled this previously tense and constricted child who had spoken in a whisper to begin to move freely, to speak loudly, and even to smear and mess without fear of loss of control or overwhelming guilt. Although some rather smeary paintings were his last products of the summer, his choice of a balanced, free painting (Fig. 13-3(c)) as a gift for his therapist months later reflects the integration he was by then able to achieve.

Objective Measurement of Media Popularity

In order to investigate the subjective aspects of work with different art media, one would need to record and observe all facets of expressive behavior; while to simply gauge which is most popular, all one needs to do is to count. Thus, it was possible to review the records of fifty individual art interviews conducted in the Center with children of different ages, all of whom had been offered the same choice of materials, to get a picture of which media were used most frequently. It was found that the most popular material was clay (24.1%), closely followed by tempera paint (22.4%), then dry drawing materials—crayons, chalk, and pencil (20.5%), watercolor markers (16.1%), fingerpaint (8.9%), and finally wood scraps and glue (8.0%).

Clearly, how one organizes such data influences the results, for it would also be reasonable to group clay and fingerpaint as contact media, clay and wood scraps as sculpture, tempera and fingerpaint as fluid media, or to group watercolor markers with the other drawing tools. Any of these changes would modify the resultant sequence of choices. It would similarly be possible to analyze the data according to age, sex, or diagnostic category. One could look also at sequences of choices within the hour, in order to see if there were any repeated patterns. All of these questions, however, can be answered by looking at the recorded facts, while many other kinds of questions about why and how people use different media are less simple to answer in such a numerical fashion.

Connecting Group Drawings with Group Dynamics

In another kind of attempt to understand just what can be inferred from products, a psychologist colleague, Neil Rosenblum, Ph.D., and myself recently looked at the relationship between certain judged aspects of group murals and the group members' perception of their interaction while creating them. A preservice training session for staff members of a children's residential treatment unit provided the opportunity to collect the necessary data. Three small groups (five or six members) were asked first to silently create a chalk drawing standing around a table, each person using a different color of chalk. Each group then did a wall mural with markers, following discussion of a theme. Finally, each member represented his group with pieces of cellophane, using a different color for each individual. A month later, each person answered a questionnaire on which he indicated the most and least dominant people in his group on each task. He also rated the group's degree of cohesion, order, freedom, and disorganization on each joint activity.

Judges in an expressive therapy course rated the two murals by each group on the same dimensions: degree of cohesion, order, freedom, and disorganization. The judges also assessed the most and least dominant colors on each chalk mural, as well as on the cellophane representations of the groups. The data analysis focused on the question of how the judges' ratings of color dominance and of the nature of the group product, related to the members' assessments of individual dominance and the nature of the group interaction. Results indicate widely different degrees of correlation, varying noticeably both by group and by task. Some are significantly high, but some are low or negative, suggesting that what one "sees" in a picture may or may not reflect what members felt went on in the group. (Rubin and Rosenblum, 1977)

Diagnostic Questions about Child Art

Some of my earliest work with disturbed children was with a group of schizophrenic youngsters, who were on a special inpatient unit at a psychiatric hospital. The chairman of the department for which I worked, asked if and how their art was more "disturbed" than that of normal children, whom I also saw weekly in an after-school recreation program. I had difficulty delineating significant differences in the art work itself, though there was no question that their behaviors in regard to materials and in relation to me were radically different, and generally quite bizarre. In order to look more systematically at the question of whether and how their art work differed, a study was designed in which a group of normal youngsters matched for age and sex were seen for a series of individual art interviews, identical in format to those of the hospitalized children. Products were then randomly selected from work by both populations, and presented as slides to judges varying in experience with children, art, and pathology.

The judges were asked if they thought they could discriminate the work of schizophrenic from that of normal youngsters, and most of them replied in the affirmative. They were then asked to identify each of forty items (half from each population, presented in random order) as schizophrenic or nonschizophrenic, and to note their degree of certainty (unsure, fairly sure, sure) as well as the reasons for their decision. Thinking that they might be able to be more accurate with a larger sample of art work, groups of products from a single session were also presented in the order in which they had been done, and the same judgments requested. Having begun with a skeptical hypothesis born of my own difficulty in answering the department chairman's question, it was still surprising that only three of forty judges were able to judge correctly beyond chance expectation on both single items and groups of products. Two of these three individuals were in the group of ten judges with no experience in child art or psychopathology! Even when given information on chronological age and sex, their accuracy was no greater. What did emerge, however, was a significant correlation between judged normality and judgments of aesthetic value (which were made at the end on the forty single products), suggesting that what looks "good" also looks "normal" to most judges. (Rubin and Schachter, 1972)

What also emerges from the brief description of this study is the necessity of first formulating the question, then devising a way to answer it, and of then formulating subsidiary questions regarding important variables (such as groups of items vs. individual products, information on age and sex, or the experience of the judges) in order to find some answers from a controlled investigation.

A recent study, part of a large series on schizophrenic mothers and their children done at our center, has enabled us to look briefly at the possible relationship between some measurable aspects of drawings and pathology (Rubin, Ragins, Schachter, and Wimberly, 1979). In this study, we were interested in seeing whether or not art work would discriminate between a group of schizophrenic and matched nonschizophrenic mothers and their two groups of school-age children. In order to maximize the likelihood of finding some significantly discriminating measures, we used a variety of drawing tasks and treatments of the data. The children's tasks included specific topics for which standardized measures are available (person, self), or which have been thought significant by clinicians (family, kinetic family), as well as free drawings and a free media choice. The mothers did person, self, and family drawings, as well as one free drawing each.

Developmental scores were assessed on all person and self drawings (Harris, 1963), "Emotional Indicator" scores (Koppitz, 1968) on the first two person drawings, and Self-Concept scores (Porter, 1971; Bodwin and Bruck, 1960) on the self drawings. Heights of person and self drawings were measured, as well as the distance between the self and mother figures in each child's family drawing. Some attempts were made to analyze content, using such quantifiable aspects as: sex of figure drawn, frequency in person drawings of children vs. adults, frequency in free drawings and paintings of figurative vs. nonfigurative work, etc. Finally, blind judgments of pathology were made by graduate art therapy students on some of the art work, as in the earlier study. The family drawings were rated globally for such things as degree of anger and of organization.

The two groups of children and the two groups of mothers were then compared, and were found not to be differentiated significantly on any of the measurements employed. The two groups of children differed significantly, however, on some of the content analyses, such as the frequency of fantasy figures or inclusion of family members in person drawings, and the frequency of nonfigurative work in free paintings. As in the earlier study, even with the drawings of the (diagnosed) schizophrenic and control mothers, the judges were unable to discriminate pathology significantly often. None of the qualities of the family drawings were significantly different as judged. In general, the implications for the use of art work as an "early warning signal" of incipient pathology in the children of schizophrenics are far from hopeful, at least in regard to formal drawing characteristics.

Variability in Children's Art

Based in part on the judges' difficulties in these two studies, my colleagues and I decided to look at what might have contributed to some of their inability to give children's art work accurate diagnostic "labels"—the variability which seemed so often to be present in groups of products by the same child. This phenomenon was one I had often noted in my clinical work, though I was not sure whether it occurred more often with any age level or type of disability. In order to study "variability" as a developmental phenomenon, it was finally decided to utilize human figure drawings—since the scoring system for them was most reliable—and to collect art work from children ages 4 to 12, 20 subjects (10 boys and 10 girls) at each level. Teachers of art and elementary school in the public schools in a course with me at the time were willing to collect the data in their classrooms, omitting the work of any child suspected to have any emotional disturbance or intellectual handicap (Rubin, Schachter, and Ragins, 1983).

The children each did four drawings of "a person" with pencil on 9-by-12-inch paper ("the best you can"), at the same time of day on a Monday, a Tuesday, and the following Monday and Tuesday. The coded drawings were scored by trained judges using the Goodenough scale (Harris, 1963); and variability was assessed by determining the standard deviation among the four drawing scores. In addition to *score variability,* we also developed a code for *content variability* (man, woman, boy, girl), and one for *visual variability* (how alike or different the four pictures looked). The correlations between each pair of variabilities were significant, suggesting that they were all aspects of the same phenomenon. The developmental "line" that emerged, however, was a surprise, since it was not a straight line of gradually decreasing variability with advanced age as I expected, but rather an up and down picture with lows at 5 and 10, peaks at 4 and 8, and an upswing at 12.

One obvious implication of these findings is that drawing scores based on one or even two figure drawings, whether used to determine developmental level (Harris, 1963) or emotional problems (Koppitz, 1968), are more reliable at some ages than at others. In addition to developmental factors, one must also wonder about other possible correlates—creativity (if variability is seen as flexibility), or emotional disturbance (if variability is seen as instability). I believe that this study is a good example of the kinds of research questions which can emerge from the practice of art therapy, but which have implications for the work and decision-making processes of many professionals. Perhaps even more exciting, such studies open the door to a better understanding of how the mind works when it expresses itself pictorially, something which is just beginning to be investigated systematically.

Free Association in Imagery

Such a motivation to understand the mind's imagery processes lay behind yet another recent study. Fascinated by the experience of free association in words and mental imagery in psychoanalysis, both as patient and as analyst, I decided to see what would happen if people were invited to follow one picture or sculpture with another, allowing images to emerge in as free and non-deliberate a fashion as they could achieve. A class in "imaging" was offered through a psychoanalytic center, in which ten people with art or mental health backgrounds came for five weeks and, in two-hour meetings, experimented with "free association" in: drawing, clay modeling, painting, and collage—in the final session choosing one image to develop in a more finished fashion.

Six participants responded to my invitation to come in for individual interviews reviewing both products and process, from which I got a deeper understanding of the nature of their experiences. In addition to my pleasant surprise at how relatively easy the process seemed to be, I was even more surprised to discover during these interviews that a large number of individuals had found the class to be personally therapeutic, often in a dramatic way (as in overcoming long-standing creative work blocks), though that was neither promised nor expected.

The process itself turned out to be a complex one, not having a consistent pattern from one person to another or from one medium to another. Patterns emerged, but they varied from those with a climax at the end (a culminating image to which all else seemed to lead in a straight line), to those with a rhythmic up-and-down or back-and-forth flow (one kind of imagery or direction alternating with another), to those where the peak seemed to be somewhere in the middle (with a feeling of dénouement following a central pictorial statement). Existentially, participants reported a high level of emotional involvement, sometimes a feeling of being "swept along" by the flow of images which seemed to "come" from somewhere other than themselves, often in rapid succession.

Recent work in the rapidly-burgeoning field of mental imagery indicates a much greater presence of visual images in the mind at all times than has been supposed. Not only are they utilized consciously for organized problem-solving, but they are constantly available for other, non-conscious modes of mentation, including creative thinking. This investigation opens further windows on the inner world upon which art therapy draws, with exciting possibilities for future study as well as for eventual clinical applications (Rubin, 1981a).

Assessing Relationships between Creativity and Mental Health

In an early study of teachers-in-training, I attempted to look at the relationship between creativity and mental health, a critical one for the field of art therapy. Although it was difficult to find reliable and valid measures of either variable, a standardized instrument for measuring dimensions of personality was finally chosen (EPPS—Edwards, 1959), and creativity tests were developed, based on the work of Wallach and Kogan (1965).

Eight students chose to take a ten-week "Self-Designed Learning Process" (SDLP), a kind of "sensitivity group" in which trust, expressiveness, caring, separateness, and empathy were taught via exercises and discussions. Ten randomly-selected students participated in a ten-week "Creativity Workshop," which I led; here, the weekly two-hour sessions involved an experiential exploration of creative approaches to all elementary school curriculum areas, via the arts. The ten "control" subjects took the same required block of methods courses as the others throughout the term, and all took the EPPS and the creativity tests before and after the ten weeks, during which some had special experiences.

The hypothesis was that students exposed to either the Creativity Workshop or the SDLP group would demonstrate changes on both creativity and personality measures. All subjects tested comparably on both pre-program measures, as well as on a test of perceptual rigidity (Breskin, 1968) and faculty ratings of creativity.

Although the interventions were brief, there were some statistically significant differences in post-program scores on both the creativity tests and the EPPS. All were in the predicted direction, indicating limited support for the hypothesis, with significant increases in the creativity test scores and changes in the direction of greater personal freedom on the EPPS for members of both experimental groups, and with no change in either category for members of the "control" group. Given the brevity of the interventions, it is perhaps surprising that any changes at all were visible, and we speculated optimistically that the hints of movement in the test results would have shown themselves more strongly had there been more time for the special experiences (Rubin, 1982a).

Reviewing the literature in writing up the study, I was reminded that the area of creativity and its relation to mental health is still full of speculation, with few relevant empirical studies, and those with conflicting results. The finding, however, that experiences in the Creativity Group led to some growth in mental health suggests that experiences in the arts are also therapeutic, perhaps measurably so. Since there was both doing and talking in the Creativity Workshop, it is not known how much of the growth may have been due to the creative experiences themselves, and how much to their possible integration through discussion and reflection. This question relates to one of the central debates in art therapy: the relative value of art *as* therapy vs. art *in* therapy. The issue is one which has yet to be addressed experimentally.

Comparing Products from Art and Drama Interviews

This particular study grew out of an earlier investigation. A colleague, Eleanor C. Irwin, Ph.D., and I had asked five experienced clinicians to read the protocols of ten boys seen in art and drama interviews on the same day, and to try to match them (cf. Rubin and Irwin, 1975). We were stunned that they were able to do so only one-fourth of the time. This unexpected outcome stimulated a later study during which we spent several years re-reading, reviewing, and finally evolving a meaningful analysis of the material.

It was possible to make comparisons, because we had been able to see the same children for both kinds of interviews on the same day (half in each sequence), could keep the conditions constant, and had sufficient subjects (twenty-four) to be able to generalize about conclusions. The collection of data occurred in the course of interviews held prior to placement in treatment groups. The analysis of the data required a long period of examining and discussing the material, in order to find appropriate dimensions on which to compare the two art modalities. We eventually looked at those elements of form and content in both areas which were genuinely comparable. We considered productivity, specific form elements, and different aspects of the content: primary themes, developmental level, and the nature and degree of disguise, including the treatment of time and space. We also included the child's attitude toward his product, because this was quite different in the two modalities. We discovered that what was most apparent in art was form, while in drama it was content, and that anxiety in the art sessions almost always related to some regression in form, while in drama it was usually associated with the content of the story.

Conclusion

There are special problems with doing research in and through art therapy, since all the elements we want to study are so complex and hard to measure. As is evident from the studies in this chapter, finding really appropriate, valid, and reliable ways to assess psychopathology or progress through art *products* is extremely difficult. Observing the art *process* in a truly objective and at the same time empathic way is very hard, even with normal children (Brittain, 1979; Gardner, 1980). How much more difficult it is to do so when the child is different, especially since observers wish to find commonalities between themselves and others. Although distortions in perceptions of the handicapped tend to be unfairly negative, there is an equal danger in not seeing and accepting the very real differences in their life-experience, including their creative work with art (Rubin, 1981(c)).

The most difficult and yet most important area for study is that of *progress*—the outcome or effect of art therapy on the children we serve. Again, the problem is considerable, since we so often work with populations for whom "normal" assessment instruments are invalid, and because so many of the kinds of changes we expect from art therapy are so hard to see externalized in measurable indices. In addition, when dealing with children, we often find that the developmental variables are so hard to disentangle from those whose effects we hope to measure that they present yet another complication in an already confusing situation.

However, despite all these difficulties and complexities—and they are very real—doing research in and through art therapy can be enormous fun. While identifying the questions to be asked and ways to ask them are the formal steps necessary for any kind of assessment or research, most studies derive their motive power from multiple sources. It is probably not accidental that most of the studies described in this chapter were stimulated less by the needs of the institution, than by those of the investigator(s).

Such wishes to comprehend an observed phenomenon, to explore territory as yet uncharted, or to question widely-held assumptions are based on inner strivings as much as are making and looking at art. As with art activities, the fact that research derives from unconsciously-determined motives makes it possible to understand why it is so deeply satisfying. Like looking at art, research is an acceptable way to indulge one's curiosity; like making art, it is a valid way to try to bring order into one's view of the world and to explore new areas within controlled boundaries. What is important here as elsewhere, is to be aware of one's private motives for systematic question-asking, so that they do not in any way impede or distort the research undertaken. For myself, the process of formulating questions and discovering answers through research is as deeply satisfying for the mind, as helping people through art is pleasurable for the heart.

CHAPTER 21.

What Child Art Therapy Is and Who Can Do It

Since a good deal of space and energy in this book is devoted to describing the "therapeutic" aspects of art for normal and handicapped children and their parents in the community, I think it necessary to clarify the distinctions between art in therapy and art in other contexts. One common misconception is that "art therapy" means working in art with those who are different from the norm. But the definition of art therapy does not depend on the population with which one works, any more than it is a function of the setting in which the work occurs. When art activities are made available to handicapped or disturbed children, they may be educational or recreational. When one is teaching or providing art for the purpose of constructively filling leisure time, one is *not* engaged in art therapy. Even when the setting is a psychiatric one, if the primary purpose of the art activity is learning and/or fun, then it is *not* art therapy (cf. Rubin, 1981b).

The essence of art therapy is that it must partake of both parts of its name—it must involve art *and* therapy. The goal of the art activity, therefore, must be primarily therapeutic. This might, of course, include diagnosis as well as treatment; for in order to be an effective therapist, you must understand who and what you are treating. In order to be an effective *art* therapist, you must know a great deal about both components of this hybrid discipline. You must know *art*—the media and processes, their nature and potential. You must know the creative process—the language of art, the nature of symbolism, form, and content. You must also know *therapy*. You need to know about yourself and about others in terms of development, psychodynamics, and interpersonal relations. Finally, you must know about the nature of the treatment relationship, and the mechanisms that underlie helping others to change.

Because the work includes helping others to create, there is also an element of education involved; but the teaching in art therapy is secondary to the primary aim, which is diagnostic or therapeutic. In other words, if an art therapist teaches techniques, it is not for the sake of the skill itself, but rather in order to help the person to achieve, for example, a higher level of sublimation or an increased sense of self-esteem.

Conversely, there are therapeutic aspects of art education. Indeed, I think that the very best art teachers are growth-enhancing personalities, who nurture the student's sense of self and of competence in a broadly therapeutic way. There is no question that art activities, even in a classroom for "normal" children, may be conducted in a way that promotes social and emotional development. Art itself is in many ways "therapeutic," for it permits the discharge of tension and the representation of "forbidden" thoughts and feelings in socially acceptable forms (cf. Chapter 16).

I believe, however, that we must distinguish between art in *therapy* and art activities which happen to have some therapeutic components. The field of psychotherapy is itself a complex one, encompassing many different ways of understanding human beings and of helping them to overcome difficulties in development and adjustment. In order to offer art as *therapy*, it is essential to know what one is doing as a therapist. Even the most sensitive artist or art teacher is not automatically a therapist, no matter who the student happens to be. Just as it takes years of training and discipline to master the visual arts, so it takes time and learning to master what is understood about psychodynamics and psychological change. It also takes special training, involving hundreds of hours of supervised work with patients, to be able to integrate what one knows about art with what one knows about therapy. Indeed, that task is a lifelong one, and it is not one which can be mastered without experienced clinical guidance. This is as true for the art therapist working in a school for exceptional children as for the art therapist working in an outpatient clinic or a psychiatric hospital.

One reason why it is so important to distinguish between art for primarily educational purposes and art for mainly therapeutic goals is that the activities themselves may not appear different to the untrained observer. An individual art interview with a child or adult may look and sound like an art lesson, and an art therapy group with members of any age level or with a family may look much like an art class. The difference is not necessarily visible on the surface, for the materials are the same and the approaches in both can range from open-ended to highly structured. Even the verbalization of the therapist, depending on the setting and age level, may be indistinguishable from what a friendly teacher might say. The primary distinctions are invisible—inside the head of the worker and, eventually, of the patient(s).

When I am doing a diagnostic art interview, for example, I am looking with a clinically-trained eye and listening with a psychologically-sophisticated ear to what is happening. I am tuned in to all aspects of behavior, hoping to understand not simply what the person can do with art materials, but where he is developmentally, what his primary conflicts are, and how he is coping with them. His messages to me are received in terms of assessing him as a complex being, to be understood in as many dimensions as possible in order to be helped with whatever problem has brought him to me.

Similarly, when I am working with a family, I am interested in what they make and how they create; I am also interested in their individual and interpersonal dynamics, in how they relate to one another as a group, and in how that interaction may help me understand the specific problems of the identified patient. Anyone watching a "family art evaluation" would see an interesting exercise in which family members make things individually and jointly and then talk about them to one another. If they are relaxed about it, it might look like a pleasant recreational activity for the family. And yet, while they may have fun or learn new skills, the therapist's primary goal is understanding family dynamics through the symbolic medium of their art, in the context of their behavior.

Eventually, the individuals involved in art therapy themselves become aware that this is a "different" kind of art experience, even when the goals have not been made explicit. While it is customary to explain the diagnostic or therapeutic purpose of the art activity to those who can understand, that is not always possible. The very young and those with communication problems, however, soon grasp at some level the special nature of art therapy.

I was impressed with such a response in some children I was seeing individually at a school for the deaf. When two of the teachers asked to observe what went on in an art session, both youngsters declined, apparently sensing a need for privacy which had never been stated. Given the powerful nature of the feelings and fantasies they were already expressing in their art after only three meetings, it was not surprising that they were uncomfortable with the idea of letting others view their violent images or their sometimes messy play with media. They were probably right in assuming that their teachers would have had difficulty understanding or accepting either the aggression or the regression, despite the fact that both were contained in the art itself. Another youngster, a teenager, "signed" out the window to his friend that he was with "an art lady who helped him with his problems," though we had never discussed the purpose of his visits to me. These events impressed upon me once again the unique quality of art in a therapeutic situation, even when the word "therapy" has never been spoken.

There is a difference, then, but it is not always visible or easy to explain. Of course, there are times when what goes on in art therapy becomes primarily educational or recreational, when learning or pleasure is focal for the moment. Similarly, there are times in art classes when what is occurring is mainly therapeutic, whether at the level of release or of reflection; but the differences in the primary goals remain, and it is these to which we must look when trying to comprehend the distinction between art therapy and art education.

There is a similar lack of clarity for many people about the differences between play therapy and art therapy with children. As with art therapy vs. art education, the differences are not always visible to the unsophisticated observer. A session of art therapy with an individual child or group might look very much like play therapy, especially if there is sensory play with media or if there is any kind of dramatization. Of course, there is a close relationship between art and play: playfulness is often part of a creative process, and, there is much artistry in good play therapy. These overlappings are, however, analogous to the educational aspects of art therapy and the therapeutic aspects of art education; here, too, there are important distinctions (cf. Schaefer & O'Connor, 1983).

In thinking about the differences between art therapy and art education, it became clear to me that the modality (art) was the same, but the goals (therapy vs. education) were different. Similarly, in the two kinds of child therapy, the goal (therapy) is the same, but the modalities (art vs. play) are different. Theoretical orientation is not the key to distinguishing the two, since both art therapy and play therapy include a wide variety of approaches, orientations, and attitudes toward the activity itself.

There are those, for example, who feel that a child, given a supportive environment and a reflective therapist, can "play out" his or her problems (Axline, 1947; Moustakas, 1953). Similarly, there are those who feel that the creative process itself is the main healing element in art therapy with children (Kramer, 1958; Lowenfeld, 1957). Conversely, there are clinicians for whom the child's play is seen mainly as a communication of unconscious conflicts, which must then be interpreted and understood in order for change to occur (Freud, 1946; Klein, 1932). There are also child therapists who view the child's art as "symbolic speech," to be explained and grasped as an essential part of the therapeutic process (Naumburg, 1947, 1966; Ude-Pestel, 1977).

Despite my advocacy of other expressive modalities in child art therapy, I do believe that there are real differences between art therapy and play therapy, and that they lie both in the expertise of the worker and in what is presented to the child. Although most play therapists provide some art materials, they are usually rather limited in scope and variety and are offered along with a wide variety of other play equipment, including games. An art therapist, on the other hand, usually makes available a much greater range of art media and tools, and is able to teach and to facilitate the use of materials—something the average play therapist is not equipped to do. Since the creative process itself is so often central to the art therapeutic encounter, the clinician's ability to facilitate that process is as important a component of successful art therapy as his equally refined understanding of the symbolic meanings of the child's visual communications.

As for the other expressive modalities advocated elsewhere in this book, I do not see them as "play" any more than I see art as equivalent to play, though the two are clearly related. The drama, movement, music, or creative writing which can also be facilitated for a child by an art therapist are other art forms, available like the visual arts for both sublimation and communication. However, if no expert in another expressive therapy is part of the work, as in the groups I ran with Dr. Irwin, there are limits to how far an art therapist can help a youngster to express himself in music, drama, writing, or movement, just as there are limits to the play therapist's expertise in art. In addition, the age limits for play therapy are narrower than those for art therapy, which is appropriate for all young people.

Both play therapists and art therapists who work with *children* need to possess some special qualities which, while still desirable, may be less critical in work with adults. Perhaps most vital is a liking for—indeed, a loving of—children. Child patients can create severe strains and stresses, and in order to endure these with good humor, a sincere enjoyment of the young is essential. Not only does a liking of children ease those difficult moments, it also enables one to respond with honest delight to the creative and progressive steps they take, even when these are tiny. If one does not warmly regard children in general, it is highly unlikely that one could enjoy being with many of those in need of therapy, who can easily stimulate negative reactions in others.

In order to like children enough to want work with them in art therapy, a clinician must also like the child inside himself. The therapist must be comfortable with childish thoughts, feelings, and impulses. Only when peace has been made with one's youthful/primitive self is it possible to help a child to accept what an adolescent once called "the green creature within." It is those green, primitive impulses of love and hate, merger and destruction, which are evoked so powerfully through art and which are often hard for the therapist to handle.

Since moments of strong feeling often involve impulses to action as well, they call on another essential element in the child therapist's repertoire: it is as important to be able to limit as to be able to permit, and the child who feels like destroying the art supplies or the room or the worker requires a calm, firm, adult hand to contain such chaotic feelings. Only a clinician who feels the inner capacity to "contain" affect and impulse can provide the kind of "framework for freedom" described earlier.

In order to sustain a containing role at times of urgent pressure, it helps if one has sincere confidence in the ultimate efficacy of the therapeutic process, as well as in the child's ability to grow therein. Such an optimistic attitude is best built not on blind faith, but on a coherent frame of reference for understanding what goes on within the child, within oneself, and between the two parties in the therapeutic transaction. Such a theoretical underpinning is best if it includes not only developmental considerations, but psychodynamic ones as well. My own bias is for a psychoanalytic framework, which I find most useful in understanding what is going on, and in deciding how best to intervene. Any clear and consistent theory of personality and psychotherapy helps the child art therapist to know where to go, and to do so consistently. Consistency is especially vital in work with children, who require the security inherent in dependability.

Because their verbal skills are not as highly developed as those of adults, children need therapists who can communicate and receive messages in all non-verbal modalities. Movement, gesture, imagery, and sound are the basic vocabulary of the arts as well as of play. Anyone working creatively with children does well to nurture an ability to "swing" with the child in different expressive dimensions. This capacity to "flow" with all forms of communication used by the young requires, in addition to ease in non-verbal modes, a fluency and flexibility in the therapist, an ability to "shift gears" as well as to follow, permitting the child to move naturally and with comfort.

Both fluency and flexibility are hallmarks of the creative process and suggest that the effective child art therapist is also a creative person. One ought to be able not only to promote freedom in the child, but also to regress in the service of one's own ego. In addition to facilitating one's ability to empathize with the child, it also enables one to fully experience the role in which one is placed by the child, whether in the transference or in a drama. The judicious use of the self as a facilitator in the expression and working through of conflict can be a powerful tool in child art therapy. Like all direct involvements, however, it is fraught with hazards, and should be undertaken only with a full awareness of the meaning of the event to the child and to the treatment process.

In fact, all of the elements noted so far as critical to effective child art therapy may be thought of as two-edged swords: they are powerful if used thoughtfully, dangerous if used naively or under the pressure of countertransference reactions. But how can that be? you may ask. Is it possible to like young people too much or to be too supportive with them? Yes, in a sense; for while there are times when a warm holding in lap or rocker is the most appropriate action, there are others at which touching is too threatening or seductive. In addition, while genuine appreciation of the child's art is often just the "gleam in the eye" that will be most useful to his shaky valuation of himself (cf. Lachman-Chapin, 1980), there are times when too much applause for his creative products would promote an unhealthy narcissism and dependency on the responses of others.

While it is essential to be able to like even the most unlovable and provocative child patient, it is not helpful for a youngster to be rewarded for destructive behavior, or to engage in a sado-masochistic relationship with the therapist. Although a good child art therapist should like and accept his own childish impulses, to give into them freely in work with children would be self-indulgent and potentially frightening to the youngster. Even a spirit of playfulness, while often liberating, can be threatening to a withdrawn child, overstimulating to an impulsive one, and quite insensitive when the issues demand an earnest and respectful response.

It is important to accept even the most primitive art and fantasy, but it is not good to exult in or to glorify unmodulated impulse. Promoting aggression is just as detrimental as suppressing it. On the other hand, too many limits can be as harmful as too few, especially if the therapist's own anxieties lead to premature or harsh limit-setting, presumably intended to be in the child's best interests. What better way is there to confirm the youngster's conviction about the malignant power of his impulses? And how sad it is when the limit-setting is not on behavior but on symbolic fantasy, which knows no boundaries.

Even therapeutic optimism can be dangerous, if the desire to rescue or to cure blinds the worker to problems within the child, the self or the process. Even a consistent theoretical framework can be detrimental, if it is understood and held too rigidly, perhaps obscuring the therapist's vision of events which do not seem to "fit." The best clinicians I know, including the most orthodox, are also the most open-minded and modest about their uncertainties. A similar kind of flexibility is needed in behavior as well as in perception. In other words, the notion of consistency and predictability is not to be wrongly understood as rigidity.

Too much flexibility is not best, either, for "flowing" with the material is not always the optimal stance in art therapy with children. There are many times when stopping, stepping back, looking, and organizing what has occurred are the most helpful clinical behaviors; and, while it is generally good to be creative in areas like interviewing, such creativity in the therapist must always be used in the service of the child's treatment rather than of his own exhibitionistic or narcissistic needs.

Further, it would seem evident that characteristics such as those noted above are by themselves not sufficient for good child art therapy. Although they may indeed be essential conditions, without which the worker could not be effective, they alone—like love or art—are not enough. Being able to communicate non-verbally or symbolically, for example, is of little use without an understanding of the meanings of such transactions. Similarly, a tolerance for ambiguity or a love of children has only limited value in the absence of a clear sense of overall direction in the treatment process. While confidence in oneself, as well as in the child or process, is essential, a grandiose disregard for the scientific aspects of treatment is hardly helpful. Rather, a modesty about one's magical powers is an essential condition of a continuing search for understanding.

I believe that any kind of therapy is neither a scientific nor an artistic endeavor alone, but in its highest form is a synthesis of the two modes. Creative thinking in science is the wellspring of new discoveries, while any art form involves a large element of skill and technique. I believe that it is possible for a child art therapist to be quite thoughtful and scientific in orientation, while at the same time valuing artistry and spontaneity in the refinements of method. Since children, like all humans, are creatures of both thought and feeling, it makes sense that, in order to reach and help them as whole people, one would need to engage both cognition and affect. It also makes sense that, in order to communicate both thought and feeling, one would need to be equally open to either.

I think that an ability to be at home with both feeling and thinking is related to the art therapist's comfort with images and words, with primary process and secondary process, with mentation dominated by either right or left hemisphere. To be able to synthesize these apparently distinct aspects of the self in a constructive way may be the essence of mental health. To be in charge of one's capacities, rather than being at the mercy of one's passions or ruminations, is a reasonable therapeutic goal for children as well as for adults. For a therapist to be able to help a youngster achieve such an end, he must have access to all that lies within. When an art therapist is able to use both heart and mind, both thought and feeling in the service of another's growth, and to do so with creativity and enthusiasm, then the child he treats is indeed a fortunate person.

A Cautionary Note

The procedures described in this book may seem simple, perhaps deceptively so. Art is a powerful tool—one which, like the surgeon's, must be used with care and skill if it is to penetrate safely beneath the surface. Using media with those who are significantly handicapped or disturbed (even without analysis of process or product), requires an understanding not only of art, but also of the world of those with whom one is working. The use of art with all kinds of children or families as a symbolic communicative medium is a clinically-demanding task, which carries with it both a tremendous potential and an equally great responsibility.

A parent or teacher without clinical training can indeed provide children with genuinely helpful—and in many ways "therapeutic"—art experiences. Caution is required, however, in the use of such experiences for a deeper understanding or remediation of internal psychological problems. There, in both diagnosis and treatment, close clinical supervision in the learning phases and early work stages of art therapy seems to me to be not only desirable, but essential.

Dealing with those who are already vulnerable, or "opening up" others in a way that creates a certain vulnerability, can be either helpful or harmful. One need not be afraid to do many wonderful and meaningful things with children in art, but one must always respect the importance and the uniqueness of a child's emotional life. One also grows to respect, with some awe and humility, the potency of art, especially in the context of those special human relationships promoted in art therapy.

Finally, one must always respect, when working with children, the primary relationship with the family. It may appear, from some of the highly condensed vignettes in this book, that art therapy with a troubled child consists simply of helping the youngster to express his repressed hostility toward significant others. One must always maintain a delicate balance, however, in order to protect the child from either excessive guilt feelings or possible retaliation from the environment. This is one reason why someone should work with the parents when a youngster is involved in a change process like therapy, which can unleash overt behaviors that may be threatening if the family is not prepared. Even with parental support for the treatment, one must always respect the child's need for sufficient defenses, as much as his need for tolerance of forbidden impulses.

The message of this note, therefore, is this: be neither fearful nor fearless, but proceed with open eyes, and with respect for the value of the child as well as the power of art. If you are just beginning, be sure you have someone who understands diagnosis and therapy much better than you do to guide you. If that person also understands art, so much the better. Even "natural clinicians" can add depth of understanding to their intuition. All who undertake the awesome task of helping others, I think, have a responsibility to carry out their work with as much sensitivity and skill as they can possibly develop. The book ends, therefore, with the hope that those who have read it will indeed carry on, but that they will do so with care.

References

*Alschuler, R. and Hattwick, L. W. *Painting and Personality*, Vols. 1 and 2. Chicago: University of Chicago Press, 1947 (Rev. Ed., 1969).

Alkema, C. J. *Art for the Exceptional.* Boulder, Colorado: Pruett Publishing Co., 1971.

Anderson, F. *Art for All the Children.* Springfield, Illinois: Charles C. Thomas, 1978.

Anderson, J. P. "Humanism, Art Educational Philosophy in Transition." *Art Education*, 1972, 25 (7): 18-19.

Armstrong, C. "Black Inner City Child Art: A Phantom Concept?" *Art Education*, 1970, 23 (5): 16-21, 34-35.

*Arnheim, R. *Art and Visual Perception.* Berkeley: University of California Press, 1954.

_____. *Toward a Psychology of Art.* Berkeley: University of California Press, 1967.

_____. *Visual Thinking.* Berkeley: University of California Press, 1969.

Axline, V. M. *Play Therapy.* New York: Ballantine Books, 1947.

_____. *Dibs: In Search of Self.* New York: Ballantine Books, 1964.

Bach, G. R. *Intensive Group Therapy.* New York: Ronald Press, 1954, pp. 136-151.

Barclay, D. L. "Art Education for the Culturally Different." *School Arts*, 1970, 69 (7): 14-17.

Barron, F. "Creativity in Children." In *Child Art: The Beginnings of Self-Affirmation*, edited by H. P. Lewis, Berkeley: Diablo Press, 1966, pp. 75-91.

_____. Commentary for *No War Toys.* Los Angeles, California, 1970.

_____. *Artists in the Making.* New York: Seminar Press, 1972.

Baruch, D. W., and Miller, H. "The Use of Spontaneous Drawings in Group Therapy." *American Journal of Psychotherapy*, 1951, 5 (1): 45-58.

_____. "Developmental Needs and Conflicts Revealed in Children's Art." *American Journal of Orthopsychiatry*, 1952, 22: 186-203.

Baumgartner, B., and Schultz, J. B. *Reaching the Retarded through Art.* Johnstown, Pennsylvania: Mafex Associates, 1969.

Beittel, K. E. *Alternatives for Art Education Research.* Dubuque, Iowa: William C. Brown, 1973.

_____. "Formative Hermeneutics in the Arting Processes of an Other: The Philetics of Art Education." *Art Education*, 1974, 27 (9): 2-7.

Bender, L. (Editor). *Child Psychiatric Techniques.* Springfield, Illinois: Charles C. Thomas, 1952.

Bessell, H., and Palomares, U. *The Human Development Program.* El Cajon, California: Human Development Training Institute, 1970.

*Betensky, M. *Self-Discovery through Self-Expression.* Springfield, Illinois: Charles C. Thomas, 1973.

_____. "The Phenomenological Approach to Art Expression and Art Therapy." *Art Psychotherapy*, 1977, 4: 173-179.

Bettelheim, B. *Love Is Not Enough.* Glencoe, Illinois: The Free Press, 1950.

_____. "Art: A Personal Vision." In *Art: The Measure of Man.* New York: The Museum of Modern Art, 1964, 41-64.

*Bion, W. R. *Experiences in Groups.* New York: Basic Books, 1959.

Bodwin, R. F., and Bruck, M. "The Adaptation and Validation of the Draw-A-Person Test as a Measure of Self-Concept." *Journal of Clinical Psychology*, 1960, 16: 414-416.

Boenheim, C., and Stone, B. "Pictorial Dialogues: Notes on a Technique." *Bulletin of Art Therapy*, 1969, 8 (2): 67-69.

*Asterisked items are those books which I have found especially helpful.

Breskin, S. "Measurement of Rigidity: A Non-Verbal Test." *Perceptual and Motor Skills,* 1968, *27:* 1203–1206.

Brick, M. "Mental Hygiene Value of Children's Art Work." *American Journal of Orthopsychiatry,* 1944, *14:* 136-147.

Brittain, W. L. *Creativity, Art, and the Young Child.* New York: Macmillan, 1979.

Brocher, T. "Parents' Schools." *Psychiatric Communication (WPIC),* 1971, *13* (2): 1-9.

Brown, E. V. "Developmental Characteristics of Clay Figures Made by Children from Age Three through Age Eleven." *Studies in Art Education,* 1975, *16:* 45-53.

Buber, M. *Between Man and Man.* New York: Macmillan, 1965.

Buck, J. N. "The H-T-P Test." *Journal of Clinical Psychology,* 1948, 4: 151-159.

*Burlingham, D. *Psychoanalytic Studies of the Sighted and the Blind.* New York: International Universities Press, 1972.

Burns, R. C. *Self-Growth in Families. K-F-D: Research and Application.* New York: Brunner/Mazel, 1982.

Burns, R. C., and Kaufman, S. H. *Kinetic Family Drawings.* New York: Brunner/Mazel, 1970.

————. *Actions, Styles and Symbols in Kinetic Family Drawings.* New York: Brunner/Mazel, 1972.

Buxbaum, E. *Your Child Makes Sense.* New York: International Universities Press, 1949.

*Cane, F. *The Artist in Each of Us.* 1951. Reprint. Craftsbury Common, Vermont: Art Therapy Publications, 1983.

Cartwright, D., and Zander, A. (Editors). *Group Dynamics: Research and Theory.* 3d ed. New York: Harper & Row, 1981.

Children of Cardozo . . . Tell It Like It Is. Cambridge, Massachusetts: Education Development Center, 1968.

Cohen, F. "Introducing Art Therapy into a School System: Some Problems." *Art Psychotherapy,* 1974, *2 (2):* 121-136.

Cohen, H. "Learning Stimulation." In *Art Education for the Disadvantaged Child,* edited by D. L. Barclay. Washington, D.C.: National Art Education Association, 1969, 20-25.

Cohn, R. C. "The Theme-Centered Interactional Method: Group Therapists as Group Educators." *Journal of Group Psychoanalysis and Process,* 1969-70, 2 (2): 19-36.

Cole, N. R. *The Arts in the Classroom.* New York: John Day, 1940.

————. *Children's Arts from Deep Down Inside.* New York: John Day, 1966.

Comins, J. "Art Motivation for Ghetto Children." *School Arts,* 1969, *69* (2): 6-7.

Coombs, V. H. "Guidelines for Teaching Arts and Crafts to Blind Children in the Elementary Grades." *International Journal for the Education of the Blind,* March, 1967: 79-83.

Coopersmith, S. *The Antecedents of Self-Esteem.* San Francisco: W. H. Freeman, 1967.

Corcoran, A. L. "Color Usage in Nursery School Painting." *Child Development,* 1954, *25:* 107-113.

Crawford, J. W. "Art for the Mentally Retarded." *Bulletin of Art Therapy,* 1962, *2* (2): 67-72.

Culbert, S. A., and Fisher, G. "The Medium of Art as an Adjunct to Learning in Sensitivity Training." *Journal of Creative Behavior,* 1969, *3* (1): 26-40.

Curry, N. E. "Consideration of Current Basic Issues in Play." In *Play: The Child Strives Toward Self-Realization,* edited by N. E. Curry. Washington, D.C.: National Association for the Education of Young Children, 1971: 51-61.

Davidson, A., and Fay, J. "Fantasy in Middle Childhood." In *Child Psychotherapy,* edited by M. R. Haworth. New York: Basic Books, 401-406.

Davis, R. M. "Teaching Art in a Therapeutic Milieu." *American Journal of Art Therapy,* 1969, 9 (1): 17-23.

Decker, R. J. "Creative Art Experience for Blind Children." *International Journal for the Education of the Blind,* 1960, 9 (4): 104-106.

DeMille, R. *Put Your Mother on the Ceiling: Children's Imagination Games.* New York: Walker and Company, 1967.

Denny, J. M. "Techniques for Individual and Group Art Therapy." *American Journal of Art Therapy,* 1972, *11* (3): 117-134.

Despert, J. L. "Technical Approaches Used in the Study and Treatment of Emotional Problems in Children II." *The Psychiatric Quarterly*, 1938, *12:* 176-194.

Dewdney, S., Dewdney, I. M., and Metcalfe, E. V. "The Art-Oriented Interview as a Tool in Psychotherapy." *Bulletin of Art Therapy*, 1967, 7: 4-19.

*Dewey, J. *Art as Experience*. New York: Capricorn Books, 1934.

Diamond, F. R. "The Effectiveness of a Children's Workshop in the Creative Arts in Forwarding Personal and Intellectual Development." *Studies in Art Education*, 1969, *11* (1): 52-60.

Di Leo, J. H. *Young Children and Their Drawings*. New York: Brunner/Mazel, 1970.

――――. *Children's Drawings as Diagnostic Aids*. New York: Brunner/Mazel, 1974.

Dougherty, C. A. "Group Art Therapy: A Jungian Approach." *American Journal of Art Therapy*, 1974, *13* (3): 229-236.

Dunn, M. D., and Semple, R. A. *"But Still It Grows": A Use of Spontaneous Art in a Group Situation*. Devon, Pennsylvania: Devereux Foundation, 1956.

Dunnett, R. M. *Art and Child Personality*. London, England: Methuen, 1948.

Edwards, A. L. *Edwards Personal Preference Schedule*. New York: The Psychological Corporation, 1959.

Ehrenzweig, A. *The Psycho-Analysis of Artistic Vision and Hearing*. New York: George Braziller, 1965.

――――. *The Hidden Order of Art*. London: Weidenfeld and Nicholson, 1967.

Elkisch, P. "Children's Drawings in a Projective Technique." *Psychological Monographs*, 1945, 58, No. 1.

――――. "The 'Scribbling Game'—a Projective Method." *Nervous Child*, 1948, 7: 247-256.

England, A. O. "A Psychological Study of Children's Drawings: Comparison of Public School, Retarded, Institutionalized, and Delinquent Children's Drawings." *American Journal of Orthopsychiatry*, 1943, *13:* 525-531.

*Erikson, E. H. *Childhood and Society*. New York: W. W. Norton, 1950.

――――. "Growth and Crises of the Healthy Personality." In *Identity and the Life Cycle, Psychological Issues*, 1959, *1* (1): 50-100.

――――. "Play and Vision." *Harvard Today*, May, 1972: 13.

Erikson, J. M. *Activity, Recovery, and Growth: The Communal Role of Planned Activities*. New York: W. W. Norton, 1976.

Finley, P. "Dialogue Drawing: An Image-Evoking Communication Between Analyst and Analysand." *Art Psychotherapy*, 1975, *2* (1): 87-99.

Flannery, M. "Aesthetic Education." *Art Education*, 1973, *26* (5): 10-14.

Frankl, V. E. *Man's Search for Meaning*. New York: Pocket Books, 1959.

*Freud, A. *The Ego and the Mechanisms of Defense*. New York: International Universities Press, 1936.

――――. *The Psychoanalytical Treatment of Children*. New York: Schocken Books, 1946.

*――――. *Normality and Pathology in Childhood: Assessments of Development*. New York: International Universities Press, 1965.

Freud, S. "Creative Writers and Day-Dreaming." *Standard Edition*, Vol. 9, 1908: 141-156.

――――. "Leonardo da Vinci and a Memory of his Childhood." *Standard Edition*, Vol. 2, 1910: 63-138.

*――――. "Group Psychology and the Analysis of the Ego." *Standard Edition*, Vol. 18, 1921: 67-145.

Freund, C. "Teaching Art to the Blind Child Integrated with Sighted Children." *New Outlook for the Blind*, 1969, *63* (7): 205-210.

Fried, E. *Artistic Productivity and Mental Health*. Springfield, Illinois: Charles C. Thomas, 1969.

*Fukurai, S. *How Can I Make What I Cannot See?* New York: Van Nostrand Reinhold, 1974.

Furman, E. "Treatment via the Mother." In *The Therapeutic Nursery School*, edited by R. A. Furman and A. Katan. New York: International Universities Press, 1969: pp. 64-123.

Gaitskell, C. D., and Gaitskell, M. R. *Art Education for Slow Learners*. Peoria, Illinois: Charles A. Bennett Company, 1953.

Gantt, L. and Schmal, M. (Editors). *Art Therapy: A Bibliography*. Rockville, Maryland: National Institutes of Mental Health, 1974.

Garai, J. "New Horizons in the Humanistic Approach to Expressive Therapies and Creativity Development." *Art Psychotherapy*, 1979, 6: 177–183.

Gardner, H. *The Arts and Human Development*. New York: John Wiley, 1973.

_____. *Artful Scribbles: The Significance of Children's Drawings*. New York: Basic Books, 1980.

Gendlin, E. T. *Experiencing and the Creation of Meaning*. New York: Free Press, 1962.

Gezari, T. *Art in Our Classrooms*. New York: Jewish Education Committee Press, 1967.

*Ginott, H. G. *Group Psychotherapy with Children*. New York: McGraw-Hill, 1961.

_____. *Between Parent and Child*. New York: Macmillan Company, 1965.

Gitter, L. "World Organization for Education of Preschoolers Holds Biennial Meeting." *Children's House*, 1968, 3 (1): 32-33.

Goldstein, S. B., Deeton, K. D., and Barasch, J "The Family Joint Mural: Family Evaluation Technique." Paper presented at the California State Psychological Association Convention, Anaheim, California, March 7, 1975.

*Golomb, C. *Young Children's Sculpture and Drawing*. Cambridge, Massachusetts: Harvard University Press, 1974.

Gondor, E. I. *Art and Play Therapy*. New York: Doubleday, 1954.

Gonick-Barris, S. E. "Art for Children with Minimal Brain Dysfunction." *American Journal of Art Therapy*, 1976, 15: 67-73.

Goodnow, J. *Children Drawing*. Cambridge, Massachusetts: Harvard University Press, 1977.

Grözinger, W. *Scribbling, Drawing, Painting: The Early Forms of the Child's Pictorial Creativeness*. New York: Humanities Press, 1955.

Halpin, G., Halpin, E. and Torrance, E. P. "Effects of Blindness on Creative Thinking Abilities of Children." *Developmental Psychology*, 1973, 9 (2): 268-274.

*Hammer, E. F. (Editor). *The Clinical Application of Projective Drawings*. Springfield, Illinois: Charles C. Thomas, 1958.

Hammer, M., and Kaplan, A. M. *The Practice of Psychotherapy with Children*. Homewood, Illinois: Dorsey Press, 1967.

*Hanes, K. M. *Art Therapy and Group Work: An Annotated Bibliography*. Westport, Connecticut: Greenwood Press, 1982.

Hare, A. P., and Hare, R. P. "The Draw-A-Group Test." *Journal of Genetic Psychology*, 1956, 89: 51-59.

Harms, E. "Play Diagnosis." *Nervous Child*, 1948, 7: 233-246.

*Harris, D. B. *Children's Drawings as Measures of Intellectual Maturity*. New York: Harcourt, Brace, and World, 1963.

*Harris, J. and Joseph, C. *Murals of the Mind: Image of a Psychiatric Community*. New York: International Universities Press, 1973.

*Hartley, R., Frank, L., and Goldenson, R. *Understanding Children's Play*. New York: Columbia University Press, 1952.

Hartman, G., and Shumaker, A. (Editors). *Creative Expression*. New York: John Day, 1932.

Hatterer, L. J. *The Artist in Society*. New York: Grove Press, 1965.

Haupt, C. "Self-Realization—But Not through Painting." *New Outlook for the Blind*, 1966, 60 (2): 43-46.

_____. "Creative Expression through Art." *Education of the Visually Handicapped*, 1969, 1: 41-43.

Havelka, J. *The Nature of the Creative Process in Art*. The Hague: Martinus Nijhoff, 1968.

*Haworth, M. R. (Editor). *Child Psychotherapy*. New York: Basic Books, 1964.

Henderson, P. and Lowe, K. "Reducing Focus on the Patient Via Family Videotape Playback." Paper presented at the annual meeting of the American Association of Psychiatric Services for Children, Washington, D.C., November, 1972.

Hill, A. *Art Versus Illness*. London: George Allen and Unwin, 1945.

_____. *Painting Out Illness*. London: George Allen and Unwin, 1951.

*Horowitz, M. J. *Image Formation and Cognition*. 2d ed. New York: Appleton-Century Crofts, 1978.

Howard, M. "An Art Therapist Looks at Her Professional History." *Bulletin of Art Therapy*. 1964, 4: 153–156.

Hulse, W. C. "Childhood Conflict Expressed through Family Drawings." *Journal of Projective Techniques*, 1952, *16:* 66–79.

Hurwitz, A. "Group Art: The Neglected Dimension." *Art Education*, 1975, *28* (1): 5–7.

Irwin, E. C. and Malloy, E. S. "Family Puppet Interview." *Family Process*, 1975, *14:* 179–191.

Irwin, E. C., and Rubin, J. A. "Art and Drama Interviews: Decoding Symbolic Messages." *Art Psychotherapy*, 1976, *3:* 169–175.

Irwin, E. C., Rubin, J. A., and Shapiro, M. I. "Art and Drama: Partners in Therapy." Paper presented at the meeting of the American Society of Psychopathology of Expression, Staten Island, New York, 1971.

————. "Art and Drama: Partners in Therapy." *American Journal of Psychotherapy*, 1975, *29:* 107–116.

Irwin, E. C. and Shapiro, M. I. "Puppetry as a Diagnostic and Therapeutic Technique." In *Psychiatry and Art*, Vol. 4, edited by I. Jakab. New York: S. Karger, 1975, pp. 86–94.

Jackson, V., and Radcliffe, W. "Stylized Birds in Stitchery." *School Arts*, 1969, *68* (9): 20–21.

*Jakab, I. (Editor). *Psychiatry and Art.* New York: S. Karger, Volume I (1968), Volume II (1970), Volume III (1971), Volume IV (1975).

Jersild, A. *When Teachers Face Themselves.* New York: Teachers College Press, 1955.

*Jung, C. G. *Man and His Symbols.* New York: Doubleday, 1964.

Kaelin, E. F. "The Existential Ground for Aesthetic Education." *Studies in Art Education*, 1966, *8* (1): 3–12.

Kantor, G. V. "Art in Everyday Life Uncoils Springs of Tension." *School Arts*, 1971, *70* (8): 22–23.

Kauffman, Irving. Statements Made at Eastern Regional Meeting, National Art Education Association. New York City, 1969.

Kaye, G. "Color Education in Art. *Color Engineering*, 1968, 15–20.

Kellogg, R. *Analyzing Children's Art.* Palo Alto, California: National Press Books, 1969.

Kerr, M. "Children's Drawings of Houses." *British Journal of Medical Psychology*, 1936, *16:* 206–218.

Kewell, J. *Sculpture by Blind Children.* New York: American Foundation for the Blind, 1955.

Keyes, M. F. *The Inward Journey: Art as Psychotherapy for You.* Millbrae, California: Celestial Arts, 1974.

Kiell, N. (Editor). *Psychiatry and Psychology in the Visual Arts and Aesthetics: A Bibliography.* Madison, Wisconsin: University of Wisconsin Press, 1965.

Kinget, G. M. *The Drawing Completion Test: A Projective Technique for the Investigation of Personality.* New York: Grune and Stratton, 1952.

Klein, M. *The Psycho-Analysis of Children.* London: Hogarth, 1932.

Klepsch, M., and Logie, L. *Children Draw and Tell: An Introduction to the Projective Uses of Children's Human Figure Drawings.* New York: Brunner/Mazel, 1982.

Knill, P., and McNiff, S. "Art and Music Therapy for the Learning Disabled." *New Ways*, 1975, *1* (2): 5, 21.

Konopka, G. *Social Group Work: A Helping Process.* Englewood Cliffs, New Jersey: Prentice-Hall, 1963.

*Koppitz, E. M. *Psychological Evaluation of Children's Human Figure Drawings.* New York: Grune and Stratton, 1968.

Kovner, A. (Editor). *Childhood Under Fire: Stories, Poems and Drawings by Children During the Six Days War.* Israel: Sifriat Poalim, 1968.

Kraft, I. A. and Austin, V. "Art Therapy in the Educational Use of Multiple Impact Therapy." In *Psychiatry and Art*, Vol. 1, edited by I. Jakab. New York: S. Karger, 1968, pp. 106–115.

*Kramer, E. *Art Therapy in a Children's Community.* Springfield, Illinois: Charles C. Thomas, 1958.

————. "Art and Emptiness: New Problems in Art Education and Art Therapy." *Bulletin of Art Therapy*, 1961, *1* (1): 7–16.

*_____. *Art as Therapy with Children*. New York: Schocken Books, 1971.

_____. *Childhood and Art Therapy*. New York: Schocken Books, 1979.

_____. *Personal Communication*, 1983.

*Kris, E. *Psychoanalytic Explorations in Art*. New York: Schocken Books, 1952.

*Kubie, L. *Neurotic Distortion of the Creative Process*. New York: Noonday Press, 1958.

Kunkle-Miller, C. "Research Study: The Effects of Individual Art Therapy on Emotionally Disturbed Deaf Children and Adolescents." *Proceedings, 13th Annual AATA Conference* [1982], In Press, 1983.

Kwiatkowska, H. Y. "Family Art Therapy: Experiments with a New Technique." *Bulletin of Art Therapy*, 1962, *1:* 3-15.

_____. "The Use of Families' Art Productions for Psychiatric Evaluation." *Bulletin of Art Therapy*, 1967, *6:* 52-69.

_____. *Family Therapy and Evaluation through Art*. Springfield, Illinois: Charles C. Thomas, 1978.

Lachman-Chapin, M. "Kohut's Theories on Narcissism: Implications for Art Therapy." *American Journal of Art Therapy*, 1980, *19* (1): 3-9.

*Landgarten, H. *Clinical Art Therapy*. New York: Brunner/Mazel, 1981.

Landsman, M.; and Dillard, H. *Evanston Early Identification Scale*. Chicago: Follett Publishing Company, 1967.

*Langer, S. K. *Philosophy in a New Key*. Cambridge, Massachusetts: Harvard University Press, 1942.

_____. *Feeling and Form*. New York: Charles Scribner's Sons, 1953.

_____. "Deceptive Analogies: Specious and Real Relationships Among the Arts." In *Problems of Art*. New York: Charles Scribner's Sons, 1957.

_____. "The Cultural Importance of the Arts." In *Aesthetic Form and Education*, edited by M. E. Andrews. Syracuse: Syracuse University Press, 1958, pp. 1-8.

Lantz, B. *Easel Age Scale*. Los Angeles, California: Test Bureau, 1955.

Lehman, L. "Let There be Art!" *School Arts*, 1969, 68 (8): 46.

Lettis, D. R., and Summers, L. D. "Learning Is its own Reward." *Art Education*, 1970, *33* (1): 8-11, 38-39.

Levick, M. F. *They Could Not Talk and so They Drew: Children's Styles of Coping and Thinking*. Springfield, Illinois: Charles C. Thomas, 1983.

Levy, S., and Levy, R. A. "Symbolism in Animal Drawings." In *The Clinical Application of Projective Drawings*, edited by E. F. Hammer. Springfield, Illinois: Charles C. Thomas, 1958, pp. 311-343.

Lindsay, Z. *Art Is for All: Arts and Crafts for Less Able Children*. New York: Taplinger Publishing Company, 1968.

_____. *Art and the Handicapped Child*. New York: Van Nostrand Reinhold, 1972.

Lisenco, Y. *Art Not by Eye*. New York: American Foundation for the Blind, 1972.

Lorand, S. "Preface." In *The Emotional Self*, Rev. Ed. by A. Zaidenberg. New York: Bell Publishing Company, Inc., 1967, p. 24.

*Lowenfeld, M. *Play in Childhood*, 2nd Ed., New York: John Wiley and Sons, Inc., 1971.

*Lowenfeld, V. *The Nature of Creative Activity*, 2nd Ed. London: Routledge and Kegan Paul, 1952.

_____. *Your Child and His Art*. New York: Macmillan, 1954.

*_____. *Creative and Mental Growth*, 3rd Ed. New York: Macmillan, 1957.

_____. *The Lowenfeld Lectures* (Ed. J. A. Michael.) University Park, Pennsylvania: Pennsylvania State University Press, 1982.

Lowenfeld, V., and Brittain, W. L. *Creative and Mental Growth*, 6th Ed. New York: Macmillan, 1975.

Luscher, M. *The Lüscher Color Test*. New York: Random House, 1969.

*Lyddiatt, E. M. *Spontaneous Painting and Modelling*. London: Constable and Company, 1971.

Machover, K. *Personality Projection in the Drawing of the Human Figure*. Springfield, Illinois: Charles C. Thomas, 1949.

Maslow, A. "Creativity in Self-Actualizing People." In *Creativity and its Cultivation*, edited by H. H. Anderson. New York: Harper and Row, 1959, pp. 83-95.

Marril, E. L. *The Self in Art Education.* Research Monograph No. 5, Washington, D.C.: National Art Education Association, 1972.

McFarland, M. B. "Reality as a Source of Creativity." In *Perspectives on Art Therapy,* edited by E. A. Roth and J. A. Rubin. Pittsburgh, Pennsylvania: Pittsburgh Child Guidance Center, 1978, pp. 5–6.

McKim, R. H. *Experiences in Visual Thinking.* Belmont, California: Wadsworth Publishing Company, 1972.

McNeice, W. C., and Benson, K. R. *Crafts for Retarded.* Bloomington, Illinois: McKnight and McKnight Publishing Company, 1964.

McNiff, S. *The Arts and Psychotherapy.* Springfield, Illinois: Charles C. Thomas, 1981.

McVickar, P. "The Creative Process in Young Children." *Journal of Nursery Education,* 1959, *14* (3): 11-16.

*Meares, A. *Hypnography.* Springfield, Illinois: Charles C. Thomas, 1957.

_____. *The Door of Serenity.* London: Faber and Faber, 1958.

_____. *Shapes of Sanity.* Springfield, Illinois: Charles C. Thomas, 1960.

Meerloo, J. A. M. *Creativity and Eternization.* New York: Humanities Press, 1968.

*Milner, M. *On Not Being Able to Paint.* New York: International Universities Press, 1957.

_____. *The Hands of the Living God.* New York: International Universities Press, 1969.

Montague, J. A. "Spontaneous Drawings of the Human Form in Childhood Schizophrenia." In *An Introduction to Projective Techniques,* edited by H. H. and G. L. Anderson. Englewood Cliffs, New Jersey: Prentice-Hall, 1951, pp. 370-385.

Moore, R. W. *Art Therapy in Mental Health.* Washington, D.C.: NIMH, 1981.

Morris, D. *The Biology of Art.* New York: Alfred A. Knopf, 1962.

Moustakas, C. E. *Children in Play Therapy.* New York: Ballantine Books, 1953.

*_____. *Psychotherapy with Children.* New York: Ballantine Books, 1959.

_____. *Personal Growth.* Cambridge, Massachusetts: Howard A. Doyle Publishing Company, 1969.

Murray, H. R. "Vicissitudes of Creativity " In *Creativity and its Cultivation,* edited by H. H. Anderson. New York: Harper and Row, 1959, pp. 96-118.

Namer, A., and Martinez, Y. "The Use of Painting in Group Psychotherapy with Children." *Bulletin of Art Therapy,* 1967, 6 (2): 73-78.

Napoli, P J. "Finger Painting." In *An Introduction to Projective Techniques,* edited by H. H. and G. L. Anderson. Englewood Cliffs, New Jersey: Prentice-Hall, 1951, pp. 386-415.

*Naumburg, M. "Studies of the 'Free' Art Expression of Behavior Problem Children and Adolescents as a Means of Diagnosis and Therapy." *Nervous and Mental Disease Monograph,* No. 71, 1947. (2nd edition, *An Introduction to Art Therapy.* New York: Teachers College Press, 1973)

_____. *Schizophrenic Art: Its Meaning in Psychotherapy.* New York: Grune and Stratton, 1950.

_____. *Psychoneurotic Art: Its Function in Psychotherapy.* New York: Grune and Stratton, 1953.

_____. *Dynamically Oriented Art Therapy: Its Principles and Practices.* New York: Grune and Stratton, 1966.

Neumann, E. *Art and the Creative Unconscious.* Princeton, New Jersey: Princeton University Press, 1971.

Nixon, A. "A Child's Right to the Expressive Arts." *Childhood Education,* 1969, 299-310.

Orzehowski, J. J. "A Pilot Study Involving Art Education for Emotionally Disturbed Youth. *NAEA Yearbook No. 9,* 1959: 168-173.

Pasto, T. A. "Art Therapy and Art Instruction." *Confinia Psychiatrica,* 1962, *5:* 243-250.

_____. *The Space-Frame Experience in Art.* New York: A. S. Barnes, 1964.

Pasto, T., and Runkle , P. R. "A Tentative and General Guide to the Procedure for Administering the Diagnostic Graphic-Expression Technique to Children." *Ars Gratia Hominis,* 1955, 2 (5): 30-31.

Peckham, M. *Man's Rage for Chaos: Biology, Behavior and the Arts.* New York: Schocken Books, 1965.

Peller, L. E. "Libidinal Development as Reflected in Play." *Psychoanalysis*, 1955, *3* (3): 3–11.
Petrie, M. *Art and Regeneration*. London: Paul Elek, 1946.
Piaget, J. (1936) *The Origins of Intelligence in Children*. New York: International Universities Press, 1952.
*Pickford, R. W. *Studies in Psychiatric Art*. Springfield, Illinois: Charles C. Thomas, 1967.
Plokker, J. H. *Art From the Mentally Disturbed*. Boston: Little, Brown and Company, 1965.
Pluckrose, H. *Let's Make Pictures*. New York: Taplinger, 1967.
Porter, J. D. R. *Black Child, White Child*. Cambridge, Massachusetts: Harvard University Press, 1971, Appendix 4.
Potts, L. R. "The Use of Art in Group Psychotherapy." *International Journal of Group Psychotherapy*, 1956, *6* (2): 115–135.
*Prinzhorn, H. *Artistry of the Mentally Ill*. New York: Springer-Verlag, 1972 (Reissue).

*Rabin, A. I., and Haworth, M. R. (Editors). *Projective Techniques with Children*. New York: Grune and Stratton, 1960.
*Read, H. *Education through Art*. New York: Pantheon Books, 3rd Ed., 1958.
Rhyne, J. "The Gestalt Art Experience." In *Gestalt Therapy Now*, edited by J. Fagan and I. L. Shepherd. New York: Harper Colophon Books, 1971, pp. 274–284.
*————. *The Gestalt Art Experience*. Monterey, California: Brooks/Cole Publishing Company, 1973.
Robbins, A., and Sibley, L. B. *Creative Art Therapy*. New York: Brunner/Mazel, 1976.
Robbins, A. et al. *Expressive Therapy: A Creative Arts Approach to Depth-Oriented Therapy*. New York: Human Sciences Press, 1980.
*Robertson, S. *Rosegarden and Labyrinth*. London: Routledge and Kegan Paul, 1963.
Rosenthal, R. and Jacobson, L. *Pygmalion in the Classroom*. New York: Holt, Rinehart and Winston, 1968.
Roth, E. A., and Barrett, R. P. "Parallels in Art and Play Therapy with a Disturbed Retarded Child." *Arts in Psychotherapy*, 1980, *7:* 19–26.
Rubin, J. A. *"We'll Show You What We're Gonna Do!" (Art for Multiply-Handicapped Blind Children)*, 16mm. sound film in black-and-white and color. New York: ACI Media, Inc., 1972.
————. *Children and the Arts: A Film About Growing*. 16mm. sound film in color and black-and-white. Pittsburgh Model Cities, 1973.
————. "The Exploration of a 'Tactile Aesthetic'." *New Outlook for the Blind*, 1976, *70:* 369–375.
————. "Art and Imagery: Free Association with Media." In *Proceedings of the Twelfth Annual Conference of the American Art Therapy Association*, Baltimore, Maryland: AATA, 1981.(a)
————. "Art for the Special Person: Roles and Responsibilities of Art Therapists." In *Art in the Lives of Persons with Special Needs*. Washington, D.C.: National Committee, Arts for the Handicapped, 1981, pp. 15–19. (b)
————. "Research in Art with the Handicapped: Problems and Promises." *Studies in Art Education*, 1981, *23* (1): 7–13. (c)
————. "Creating Creative Teachers: An Experimental Study." *The Arts in Psychotherapy*, 1982, *9:* 101–111. (a)
————. "Transference and Countertransference in Art Therapy." *American Journal of Art Therapy*, 1982, *21* (1): 10–12. (b)
Rubin, J. A., and Irwin, E. C. "Art and Drama: Parts of a Puzzle." In *Psychiatry and Art*, Vol. 4, edited by I. Jakab. New York: S. Karger, 1975, pp. 193–200.
Rubin, J. A., Irwin, E. C., and Bernstein, P. "Play, Parenting and the Arts: A Therapeutic Approach to Primary Prevention." *Proceedings of the American Dance Therapy Association*, 1975, pp. 60–78.
Rubin, J. A., and Klineman, J. "They Opened Our Eyes: An Exploratory Art Program for Visually-Impaired Multiply-Handicapped Children." *Education of the Visually Handicapped*, 1974, *6:* 106–113.
Rubin, J. A. and Levy, P. "Art-Awareness: A Method for Working with Groups." *Group Psychotherapy and Psychodrama*, 1975, *28:* 108–117.
Rubin, J. A., and Magnussen, M. G. "A Family Art Evaluation." *Family Process*, 1974, *13:* 185–200.

Rubin, J. A., Magnussen, M. G., and Bar, A. "Stuttering: Symptom System Symbol (Art Therapy in the Treatment of a Case of Disfluency)." In *Psychiatry and Art*, Vol. 4, edited by I. Jakab. New York: S Karger, 1975, pp. 201-215.

Rubin, J. A., Ragins, N., Schachter, J., and Wimberly, F. "Drawings by Schizophrenic and Non-Schizophrenic Mothers and Their Children." *Art Psychotherapy*, 1979, 6: 163–175.

Rubin, J. A., and Rosenblum, N. "Group Art and Group Dynamics: An Experimental Study." *Art Psychotherapy*, 1977, 4: 185–193.

Rubin, J. A., and Schachter, J. "Judgements of Psychopathology from Art Productions of Children." *Confinia Psychiatrica*, 1972, 15: 237-252.

Rubin, J. A., Schachter, J., and Ragins, N. "Intra-Individual Variability in Human Figure Drawings: A Developmental Study." *American Journal of Orthopsychiatry*, 1983, 53: 654–667.

Salant, E. G. "Preventive Art Therapy with a Preschool Child." *American Journal of Art Therapy*, 1975, 14 (3): 67-74.

Sanders, B. "Art as an Approach to Children's Emotional Problems." *Art Education Today*. New York: Teachers' College Press, 1938, pp. 119-125.

Saunders, R. J. *Art for the Mentally Retarded in Connecticut*. Hartford: Connecticut State Department of Education, 1967.

Schaefer, C. E., and O'Connor, K. J. *Handbook of Play Therapy*. New York: Wiley, 1983.

Schaeffer-Simmern, H. *The Unfolding of Artistic Activity*. Berkeley: University of California Press, 1961.

Schiffer, M. *The Therapeutic Play Group*. New York: Grune and Stratton, 1969.

Schildkrout, M. S., Shenker, I. R., and Sonnenblick, M. *Human Figure Drawings in Adolescence*. New York: Brunner/Mazel, 1972.

Schiller, F. *Essays, Aesthetical and Philosophical*. London: George Bell, 1875.

Schmidl-Waehner, R. "Formal Criteria for the Analysis of Children's Drawings and Paintings." *American Journal of Orthopsychiatry*, 1942, 17: 95-104.

————. "Interpretation of Spontaneous Drawings and Paintings." *Genetic Psychology Monographs*, 1946, 33: 3-70.

Schmidt, A. C. *Craft Projects for Slow Learners*. New York: John Day Company, 1968.

Schwartz, F. *Structure and Potential in Art Education*. Waltham, Massachusetts: Ginn-Blaisdell, 1970.

Scott, E. "Relieving Anxiety through Art Activity in an Inner City School." *School Arts*, 1971, 70 (7): 44-46.

*Sechehaye, M. *Symbolic Realization*. New York: International Universities Press, 1951.

Selfe, L. *Nadia: A Case Study of Extraordinary Drawing Ability in an Autistic Child*. New York: Academic Press, 1977.

Shahn, B. *The Shape of Content*. New York: Vintage Books, Inc., 1960.

Shaw, R. F. *Finger Painting*. Boston: Little, Brown and Company, 1938.

*Silver, R. A. *Developing Cognitive and Creative Skills in Art*. Baltimore, Maryland: University Park Press, 1978.

Silverman, R. H. and Hoepfner, R. *Developing and Evaluating Art Curricula Specifically Designed for Disadvantaged Youth*. Final Report, Project No. 6-1657, U.S. Department of Health, Education, and Welfare. March, 1969.

Sinrod, H. "Communication through Paintings in a Therapy Group." *Bulletin of Art Therapy*, 1964, 3 (4): 133-147.

Site, M. "Art and the Slow Learner." *Bulletin of Art Therapy*, 1964, 4: 3-19.

Slavson, S. R. and Schiffer, M. *Group Psychotherapies for Children*. New York: International Universities Press, 1975.

Smart, A. "Play Therapy Schools for Parents." *Menninger Perspective*, Aug.-Sept., 1970, 12-15.

Smith, N. "Developmental Origins of Graphic Symbolization in the Paintings of Children Three to Five." *Review of Research in Visual Arts Education*, No. 13, Winter, 1981.

Sutton-Smith, B. "The Playful Modes of Knowing." In *Play: The Child Strives Toward Self-Realization*, edited by N. E. Curry. Washington, D.C.: National Association for Education of Young Children, 1971, pp. 13–25.

Swenson, C. H. "Empirical Evaluations of Human Figure Drawings: 1957–1966." *Psychological Bulletin*, 1968, 70: 20–44.

Time Magazine. "Play Schools for Parents." January 11, 1971, p. 55.

Themal, J. H. "Children's Work as Art." *Bulletin of Art Therapy*, 1962, 2 (1): 12–22.

―――. "Reflections on Art and Art Education." *Bulletin of Art Therapy*, 1965, 4 (4): 149–152.

Torrance, E. P. *Torrance Tests of Creative Thinking.* Princeton, New Jersey: Personnel Press, 1966.

Ude-Pestel, A. *Betty: History and Art of a Child in Therapy.* Palo Alto, California: Science & Behavior Books, 1977.

Uhlin, D. M. *Art for Exceptional Children.* Dubuque, Iowa: William C. Brown Company, 1972.

Ulman, E. "Art Therapy: Problems of Definition." *Bulletin of Art Therapy*, 1961, 1 (2): 10–20.

―――. "A New Use of Art in Psychiatric Diagnosis." *Bulletin of Art Therapy*, 1965, 4: 91–116.

―――. "The Power of Art in Therapy." In *Psychiatry and Art*, Vol. 3, edited by I. Jakab. New York: S. Karger, 1971, pp. 93–102.

*Ulman, E., and Dachinger, P. (Editors). *Art Therapy in Theory and Practice.* New York: Schocken Books, 1975.

*Ulman, E., and Levy, C., eds. *Art Therapy Viewpoints.* New York: Schocken Books, 1980.

Vich, M. A., and Rhyne, J. "Psychological Growth and the Use of Art Materials: Small Group Experiments with Adults." *Journal of Humanistic Psychology*, Fall, 1967.

Viola, W. *Child Art*, 2nd Ed. London: University of London Press, 1944.

Volavkova, H. (Editor). *I Never Saw Another Butterfly . . . Children's Drawings and Poems from Terezin Concentration Camp, 1942-1944.* New York: McGraw-Hill, 1962.

Wadeson, H. S. "Art Techniques Used in Conjoint Marital Therapy." *American Journal of Art Therapy*, 1973, 12 (3): 147–164.

―――. *Art Psychotherapy.* New York: Wiley, 1980.

*Waelder, R. *Psychoanalytic Avenues to Art.* New York: International Universities Press, 1965.

Walker, D. F. "Toward More Effective Curriculum Development Projects in Art." *Studies in Art Education*, 1970, 11 (2): 3–13.

Wallach, M. A., and Kogan, N. *Modes of Thinking in Young Children.* New York: Holt, Rinehart & Winston, 1965.

Weiner, B. B. "Arts and Crafts for the Mentally Retarded: Some Hypotheses." In *Expressive Arts for the Mentally Retarded*, edited by D. Ginglend. New York: National Association for Retarded Children, 1967, pp. 5–8.

Wiggin, R. G. "Teaching Mentally Handicapped Children through Art." *Art Education Bulletin*, 1962, 19 (5): 20–24.

Williams, G. H., and Wood, M. M. *Developmental Art Therapy.* Baltimore, Maryland: University Park Press, 1977.

Wills, D. M. "Some Observations on Blind Nursery School Children's Understanding of Their World." *Psychoanalytic Study of the Child*, 1965, pp. 344–364.

Wilson, L. "Theory and Practice of Art Therapy with the Mentally Retarded." *American Journal of Art Therapy*, 1977, 16 (3): 87–97.

Wilson, B. and Wilson, M. "Recycling Symbols: A Basic Cognitive Process in the Arts." In *The Arts, Cognition and Basic Skills*, edited by S. Madeja. St. Louis, Missouri: Cemrel, 1978, 89–109.

*Winnicott, D. W. *Playing and Reality*. New York: Basic Books, 1971, pp. 1-25. (a)

*———. *Therapeutic Consultations in Child Psychiatry*. New York: Basic Books, 1971. (b)

Witkin, H. A., Bimbaum, J., Lomonaco, S., Lehr, S., and Herman, J. L. "Cognitive Patterning in Congenitally Totally Blind Children." *Child Development,* 1968, *39* (3): 767–786.

Wolf, R. "'Art Therapy in a Public School." *American Journal of Art Therapy*, 1973, *12* (2): 119-127.

Wolff, W. *The Personality of the Preschool Child*. New York: Grune and Stratton, 1946.

Woltmann, A. G. "Diagnostic and Therapeutic Considerations of Non-Verbal Projective Activities with Children." In *Child Psychotherapy*, edited by M. Haworth. New York: Basic Books, 1964, pp. 322-337. (a)

———. "Mud and Clay, Their Functions and Developmental Aids and as Media of Projection." In *Child Psychotherapy*, edited by M. Haworth, New York: Basic Books, 1964, pp. 349-371. (b)

Yalom, I. D. *The Theory and Practice of Group Psychotherapy*. 2d ed. New York: Basic Books, 1975.

Zierer, E. Sternberg, D., and Finn, R. "The Role of Family Creative Analysis in Family Treatment." *Bulletin of Art Therapy*, 1966, *5:* 47-63; 87-104.

Zinker, J. "Art in Gestalt Therapy." In *Creative Process in Gestalt Therapy*. New York: Vintage Books, 1978, Ch. 9.

Index